MW01505214

Asian and Feminist Philosophies in Dialogue

Asian and Feminist Philosophies in Dialogue

LIBERATING TRADITIONS

Edited by Jennifer McWeeny and Ashby Butnor

Columbia University Press
New York

Columbia University Press
Publishers Since 1893
New York   Chichester, West Sussex
cup.columbia.edu
Copyright © 2014 Columbia University Press
All rights reserved
Library of Congress Cataloging-in-Publication Data
Asian and feminist philosophies in dialogue: liberating traditions /
edited by Jennifer McWeeny and Ashby Butnor.
p. cm.
Includes bibliographical references and index.
ISBN 978-0-231-16624-9 (cloth: alk. paper) — ISBN 978-0-231-16625-6 (pbk.: alk. paper) —
ISBN 978-0-231-53721-6 (e-book)
1. Feminist theory.   2. Feminist theory—Asia.   3. Philosophy, Asian.
I. McWeeny, Jennifer.   II. Butnor, Ashby.
HQ1190.A85 2014
305.4201095—dc23
2013033033
∞
Columbia University Press books are printed on permanent and durable acid-free paper.
This book is printed on paper with recycled content.
Printed in the United States of America
c 10 9 8 7 6 5 4 3 2 1
p 10 9 8 7 6 5 4 3 2 1

COVER ART: Album/Art Resource, NY
COVER DESIGN: Milenda Nan Ok Lee

References to Web sites (URLs) were accurate at the time of writing. Neither the authors nor
Columbia University Press is responsible for URLs that may have expired or changed since the
manuscript was prepared.

To all our teachers, beginning with our parents

Contents

Foreword   *Eliot Deutsch*   xi

Acknowledgments   xiii

Feminist Comparative Philosophy: Performing Philosophy Differently
Ashby Butnor and Jennifer McWeeny   1

PART ONE   Gender and Potentiality

CHAPTER ONE   *Kamma*, No-Self, and Social Construction:
The Middle Way Between Determinism and Free Will
Hsiao-Lan Hu   37

CHAPTER TWO   On the Transformative Potential of the
"Dark Female Animal" in *Daodejing*
Kyoo Lee   57

CHAPTER THREE   Confucian Family-State and Women:
A Proposal for Confucian Feminism
Ranjoo Seodu Herr   78

PART TWO   Raising Consciousness

CHAPTER FOUR   Mindfulness, *Anātman*, and the Possibility
of a Feminist Self-consciousness
Keya Maitra   101

CHAPTER FIVE   Liberating Anger, Embodying Knowledge:
A Comparative Study of María Lugones and Zen Master Hakuin
Jennifer McWeeny   123

PART THREE   Places of Knowing

CHAPTER SIX   What Would Zhuangzi Say to Harding?
A Daoist Critique of Feminist Standpoint Epistemology
Xinyan Jiang   147

CHAPTER SEVEN   "Epistemic Multiculturalism" and Objectivity:
Rethinking Vandana Shiva's Ecospirituality
Vrinda Dalmiya   167

PART FOUR   Cultivating Ethical Selves

CHAPTER EIGHT   Confucian Care: A Hybrid Feminist Ethics
Li-Hsiang Lisa Rosenlee   187

CHAPTER NINE   The Embodied Ethical Self:
A Japanese and Feminist Account of Nondual Subjectivity
Erin McCarthy   203

CHAPTER TEN   Dōgen, Feminism, and the
Embodied Practice of Care
Ashby Butnor   223

PART FIVE   Transforming Discourse

CHAPTER ELEVEN   De-liberating Traditions:
The Female Bodies of *Sati* and Slavery
Namita Goswami   247

Philosophy Uprising: The Feminist Afterword
Chela Sandoval   271

Feminist Comparative Philosophy and Associated Methodologies:
A Bibliography   279

Contributors   301

Index   305

Foreword

ELIOT DEUTSCH

Asian and Feminist Philosophies in Dialogue is a work that is much needed today in light of the growing interest in comparative (some among us favoring the term *cross-cultural* or *global*) philosophy in colleges and universities throughout the world. This is attested to by the large number of conferences held each year, books and new journals published, invited lectures given, academic positions offered, and so on. However, it is clearly the case that one thing, for the most part, has been missing, and that is the contribution that feminist philosophers may make when extending dialogues and critical engagements with non-Western philosophical practices in a way that could deepen and enhance all parties to the conversation.

This volume is a carefully crafted collection of essays covering selectively a wide range of issues in epistemology, metaphysics, philosophy of mind, ethics, social and environmental philosophy, and the like. It displays a rather unique comparative methodology—one that works within a pluralistic context involving many styles of philosophical inquiry (analytic, deconstructionist, phenomenological together with distinctive non-Western ways of thinking) and that emphasizes in many cases a welcome uniting of the theoretical and practical. In this regard, the editors clearly announce their belief that feminist comparative philosophy, in addition to rigorous philosophical thinking, bears a social responsibility to work for the liberation of persons in many cultures from needless suffering and oppression or other impediments to full personhood. The essays as a whole thus point to and embody a notion of comparative philosophy as a creative practical undertaking and not simply as an academic exercise.

The essays also exhibit a subtle hermeneutical awareness that we inevitably bring our own predispositions to interpret and judge what is initially alien to us, as these are informed by our cultural and personal experience. It demonstrates how, accordingly, we need to develop a negotiating process, as it were, between our prejudgmental forms and patterns and the conceptual content and structures of another tradition. In this way, that "other" tradition can speak to us in its own terms. One is enabled thereby to alter one's presuppositions in the light of that negotiation or encounter and attain an openness to develop new and richer forms of philosophical understanding. This is especially the case when feminist philosophy, in its many forms, enters the picture in the highly sophisticated manner exhibited by this groundbreaking work.

Acknowledgments

We first envisioned a book that combined feminist and comparative approaches to philosophy in 1998, when we were both pursing graduate degrees in comparative philosophy at the University of Hawaii, Manoa. Our earliest interactions with each other took place in Vrinda Dalmiya's feminist philosophy course, where our shared intellectual interests and common position as some of the few women in our program fueled an immediate and lasting friendship. The following semester we both enrolled in Eliot Deutsch's seminar in comparative methodologies. It was in this context that we realized the intersection of feminist and Asian philosophies was incredibly ripe with possibility and yet seemingly undeveloped. We therefore set out to inspire dialogue between these two fields and to find a way to show our discipline how exciting this kind of feminist comparative thinking could be. More than a decade later, our vision has come to fruition in this book.

With such a long gestation period, there are numerous people who helped us along the way. We would first like to thank Vrinda Dalmiya and Eliot Deutsch who originally provided us with the intellectual space to pursue this new avenue of inquiry and who have continued to foster our project by each making contributions to this collection. In addition, the other faculty members and graduate students of the Philosophy Department at the University of Hawaii, Manoa stimulated our thinking on this subject and, through discussion and conversation, helped us formulate our present articulation of feminist comparative philosophy. We are particularly grateful for the encouragement of Tamara Albertini, Roger Ames, James Behuniak Jr., Steve Bein, Ron Bontekoe, Garth Bregman, Arindam Chakrabarti, S. Charusheela, Chung-ying Cheng, Steven Coutinho, Kathy Ferguson, Thomas Jackson, Kenneth Kipnis, Renee Kojma-Itagaki, Matthew LoPresti, Benjamin Lukey, Matthew MacKenzie, Amy Olberding, Bradley Park, Graham Parkes, Rodney Roberts, Li-Hsiang Lisa Rosenlee, Cindy Scheopner, Geir Sigurdsson, Zachary Smith, Virginia Suddath, Sor-hoon Tan, James Tiles, Mary Tiles, Karma Lekshe Tsomo, and many others.

Similar to the University of Hawaii's department in regard to its investment in philosophical pluralism and diversity, the Philosophy Department at the University of Oregon also helped to nurture the early stages of this project. Faculty members Mark Johnson, Don Levi, John Lysaker, Bonnie Mann, Scott Pratt, Cheyney Ryan, and Naomi Zack as well as the department's graduate students encouraged the pursuit of feminist philosophy, cross-cultural philosophy, and other alternative philosophical traditions in rigorous ways. We are especially grateful to the Feminist Working Group Initiative, who created a collaborative, yet challenging forum in which to develop feminist ideas. In this capacity, the Feminist Working Group Initiative read, commented on, discussed, and refined multiple versions of the introduction that appears in this book. The organization's members include Celia Bardwell-Jones, Dana Berthold, Kimberly Garchar, Rochelle Green, Chaone Mallory, Amy Story, Lisa Yount, as well as Jennifer McWeeny.

Many of our colleagues offered advice and guidance during the creation of this book. In addition to those already mentioned, we would like to thank Linda Martín Alcoff, Daniel A. Arnold, Robert E. Carter, Pedro Di Pietro, Thomas Kasulis, María Lugones, Shireen Roshanvaran, Nancy Tuana, and Michiko Yusa. We'd also like to thank our close friends who could always be counted on to boost morale and provide motivation to forge ahead during this book's development, notably David Allamon, Malia Curran, Julie Lindsay, Julie Meiser Rioux, Lynna Scranton, and Emily Stowe.

We would also like to acknowledge the academic societies that first sponsored panels on the essays that would eventually become this book and thus provided the editors and authors of this collection with invaluable opportunities to receive informed feedback on our ideas. These events include a plenary session at the annual meeting of the Society for Asian and Comparative Philosophy (2007), a Society for Asian and Comparative Philosophy panel at the Eastern division meeting of the American Philosophical Association (2008), a special session of the Society for the Advancement of Asian Philosophy and Asian-American Philosophers at the Central Division meeting of the American Philosophical Association (2009), and a feminist comparative panel at the annual meeting of the Association of Feminist Ethics and Social Theory (2009).

Several institutions generously provided us with assistance that was instrumental in bringing this project to completion. Appreciation is due to our respective universities, Worcester Polytechnic Institute and Metropolitan State University of Denver, both of which played a vital role in supporting us intellectually and financially in the final stages of our book's development. Colleagues Kristin Boudreau, Bethel Eddy, Michelle Ephraim, Roger Gottlieb, Peter Hansen, John Sanbonmatsu, and Ruth Smith at Worcester Polytechnic Institute and Cynthia Baron, Daniel Considine, Joan Foster, Vicki Golich, Adam Graves, Brian Hutchinson, Randy Hyman, Heather Lindsay-Carpenter, Sandra Posey, Ian Smith, and David Sullivan at Metropolitan State University of Denver offered their interest and encouragement. John Carroll University also supported this project in its earlier stages. Members of the Philosophy Department and East Asian Studies program, notably Michael Eng, Susan Long, Pam Mason, Patrick Mooney, Keiko Nakano, Paul Nietupski, Mariana Ortega, Roger Purdy, Dianna Taylor, and Brenda Wirkus, tirelessly promote alternative modes of thinking. Thanks as well to Rick Kaufman at Ithaca College and Laura Purdy of Wells College for their early enthusiasm for this project.

Additionally, we are grateful for the editorial staff at Columbia University Press, most notably Wendy Lochner, philosophy and religion publisher, and Christine Dunbar. We are reassured to be in such knowledgeable and conscientious hands. We also owe thanks to Susan Pensak, who copyedited our book and to Robert Swanson, who created the book's index. Both of these tasks were extensive, considering the vast number of traditions, cultures, texts, and vocabularies discussed herein. Importantly, John Wiley gave us permission to reprint a major portion of Jennifer McWeeny's article "Liberating Anger, Embodying

Knowledge: A Comparative Study of María Lugones and Zen Master Hakuin," which first appeared in *Hypatia* 25 (2) in 2011. We appreciate the publisher's willingness to have this work included here.

This vision of feminist comparative philosophy could not have been realized without the expertise, creativity, and careful scholarship of each of our contributors. We are especially appreciative of their goodwill and endurance through what was undoubtedly a demanding editorial process. We are inspired by their enthusiastic pursuit of feminist comparative philosophy and awed by the range of their defining contributions to this emerging field of inquiry. Sadly, one of our contributors, Lucinda Joy Peach, passed away in the early stages of this project. She and her contributions to philosophy, especially in the areas of feminism, Buddhism, and moral philosophy, are greatly missed by all of us.

Finally, we would like to thank our families and close friends for their ongoing encouragement as we work to cultivate new philosophies and our best selves. Jennifer is deeply grateful for the care of all of her parents: Cameron DeMarche and Thomas DeMarche, William McWeeny and Amy Knowlton, and Caren Plank. Ashby also acknowledges her indebtedness to her parents, John and Edith Butnor, as well as her siblings, John and Courtney, for a lifetime of support, and especially her husband, Matt MacKenzie, for his endless love, patience, and proofreading, and son, Quinn, for his joyous good nature.

Asian and Feminist Philosophies in Dialogue

Feminist Comparative Methodology

Performing Philosophy Differently

ASHBY BUTNOR AND JENNIFER MCWEENY

THE SUBTITLE and guiding theme of this collection—*Liberating Traditions*—refers to those philosophical traditions that are deeply concerned with the liberation of persons, whether from suffering, oppression, illusion, harmful conventions and desires, or other impediments to full personhood. We believe that when the liberatory aspects of these diverse traditions are considered collectively and engaged in dialogue, fresh possibilities for transforming selves and societies become visible. This book therefore places classical Asian traditions such as Hinduism, Buddhism, Daoism, and Confucianism in conversation with one or more contemporary feminist traditions. Examples of the kinds of dialogic investigation found here include an examination of the fluidity of self-identity through analyses of the Buddha and Judith Butler, the improvement of care ethics by integrating the Confucian virtue of *ren*, a reinterpretation of the role of objectivity and the epistemic value of trust in contemporary Hindu-influenced ecofeminist politics, and a consideration of differential attitudes toward Indian and African women's bodies within the feminist tradition itself, as well as many other similarly innovative juxtapositions. Our express goal in fostering such comparative, coalitional thinking is to cultivate liberation at the philosophical level by examining, recovering, and reweaving the very conceptual fabrics and patterns of thought that are operative in our cultures and traditions of origin.

According to its philosophical usage, *tradition* signifies distinct groupings of theories and thinkers such as the "analytic tradition," the "feminist tradition," or the "Daoist tradition." Nancy Tuana has described this understanding of *tradition* as "a way of doing philosophy that has similar aims and concerns, and emerges from a common history, but where there will be welcome and productive disagreements and differences between practitioners" (Tuana 2001, 2).[1] However, *tradition* can also refer to a habitual practice or set of practices that gets passed down from one philosophical generation to its progeny *implicitly,* without being articulated formally in writing and thus without exposing itself to criticism and questioning. Ben-Ami Scharfstein's definition is fitting in this regard: "a chain of persons who relate their thought to that of their predecessors and in this way form a continuous transmission from one generation to the next, from teacher to disciple to disciple's disciple" (Scharfstein 1998, 1). We are just as concerned with the need to liberate exclusionary or otherwise pernicious philosophical traditions in this sense of the term as we are with the need to form intellectual companions and coalitions across traditionally separate intellectual domains.

In addition to the unique content of each chapter, the value of this collection lies in its ability to demonstrate and articulate a new mode of philosophical practice—one that could well serve as an exemplary methodology for any twenty-first-century philosophy. In order to navigate a plurality of different traditions, experiences, ideas, contexts, and histories with disciplinary and interdisciplinary rigor, we have developed a particular approach to our subject matter that we have aptly labeled feminist comparative philosophy.[2] An essential principle of feminist comparative methodology is that philosophical works should be assessed both in terms of their explicit content and in terms of the claims that they *perform* within the wider social-political contexts in which they are situated. Readers are likely familiar with various notions of performativity and speech act theory that have been put forth by thinkers as diverse as J. L. Austin, John Searle, Judith Butler, Karen Barad, and others.[3] Such ideas share in their attention to the ways that words and discourses "do things" above and beyond the mere expression of their conceptual content. Barad writes, "Discursive practices are specific material (re)configurings of the world through which local determinations of boundaries, properties, and meanings are differentially enacted" (Barad 2008, 138). Butler's monumental claim that gender is "performative" also emphasizes the mutually constitutive relationship between concepts and practices. Butler thus explains, "gender is instituted through the stylization of the body and, hence, must be understood as the mundane way in which bodily gestures, movements, and enactments of various kinds constitute the illusion of an abiding gendered self" (Butler 1988, 519). We believe that just as our beliefs about the essence of gender are dependent on the ways that we experience that phenomena practiced, instantiated, and performed within a given society, so too with our concepts of philosophy. As we will argue, performing philosophy differently with a feminist comparative approach not only enhances the philosophical content and rigor of our discipline, but, more importantly, helps us to craft a world with less suffering and oppression.

In this introduction, we provide an initial articulation of the scope, methods, content, and aims of feminist comparative philosophy with reference to three guiding questions: 1. What is the relationship between feminist comparative philosophy and each of its namesakes—feminist philosophy and comparative philosophy? 2. How can this new methodology overcome those patterns of exclusionary vision that have frustrated its predecessors' capacities for consistently recognizing privilege and difference? and 3. Why does it makes sense to think of feminist comparative philosophy as a *liberatory* practice, that is, as an activity that helps people politically and spiritually? After addressing these defining questions in the following three sections, we go on to provide summaries of the book's themes and chapters. We conclude by considering the future of feminist comparative philosophy in terms of its potential for development and transformation.

The Emergence of Feminist Comparative Philosophy

In its most basic formulation, feminist comparative philosophy is the practice of integrating feminist and non-Western philosophical traditions in innovative ways, while still being mindful of the unique particularity of each, in order to envision and enact a more liberatory world. As such, feminist comparative philosophy explores the intersections of multiple, diverse traditions and acknowledges that the insights generated in these spaces may not only be greater than the sum of their parts but also transformative of these traditions themselves. Although we recognize that non-Western is a category that encompasses many more traditions than we cover here, all the essays in this collection have in common the engagement of at least one Asian philosophical tradition through one or more of its defining texts, rather than through data, facts, or prevalent ideas about that tradition. With a few notable exceptions, there has been little scholarly work produced that would warrant the label *feminist comparative philosophy* in this sense.[4] Indeed, the bibliography that readers will find at the end of this volume is our best attempt at a comprehensive list of publications in this field. However, none of these sources uses the phrase *feminist comparative philosophy* to describe their projects and none argue that their guiding methodology constitutes a distinct kind of philosophical practice. This omission is partly due to the fact that each of these sources puts one kind of feminism into conversation with one Asian tradition, whereas the present collection takes a broader stance and, in addition to exploring specific philosophical questions, asks what it means to employ feminist comparative methodology in general.

In establishing feminist comparative philosophy as a field, we are not claiming total originality in our approach. As its name implies, feminist comparative philosophy is a natural outgrowth of the guiding principles of feminist philosophy, on the one hand, and those of comparative philosophy, on the other. Each of these respective fields is both diverse and complex in their histories, thereby inviting multiple and competing descriptions of their identities. Bearing this complexity in mind, we might say, nonetheless, that a given work of philosophy is appropriately labeled *feminist* insofar as it regards the voices and experiences of women as philosophically significant in a manner that is not sexist or discriminatory, but instead promotes the expression and flourishing of those who have been oppressed due to this social location.[5] Likewise, we could deem a given work of philosophy *comparative* insofar as it regards the ideas of more than one disparate tradition of thought as philosophically significant in a manner that respects each tradition's individual integrity and promotes its expression.[6] Though limiting in a variety of ways, these content-based definitions are useful insofar as they prompt explorations and juxtapositions across historical periods and geographic regions, connecting seemingly disparate thinkers and ideas by a common theme or attitude. And yet we can also understand feminist philosophy and comparative philosophy in narrower senses as indicating particular fields of study with their own formalized methodologies that have emerged within academic institutions in the twentieth century. Under this view, the two fields signify separate networks of thinkers who are connected to each other by shared interests and training, similar ways of framing problems, and the histories of influence and disagreement among them.

However one wishes to conceptualize the originating sources of feminist comparative philosophy, we can readily see commonalities across the concrete works and practices that make up their respective corpuses. Most obviously, feminist philosophy and comparative philosophy both treat diversity as a philosophical resource, although frequently the former has focused on gender diversity whereas the latter has attended to cultural diversity. Both traditions also recognize that a hermeneutic of openness and respect for difference are necessary for engaging this diversity. In addition, feminists and comparativists have traditionally been critical of assumptions of objectivity, neutrality, and universalism within the wider discipline. For example, Lorraine Code, Sandra Harding, and other feminist epistemologists have long challenged the way that mainstream epistemology downplays the subjectivity of knowers and instead champions a universal knower who is neither culturally nor socially situated.[7] Such hasty assumptions of universality invite precisely the kind of philosophical confusions that Indian philosopher Raimundo Panikkar warns against: "speak[ing] of a universal reason and of the unity of human nature, though we mean, obviously, our own conception of universality, reason, and human nature" (Panikkar 1988, 131). When we enact this confusion, we establish what feminist Chandra Talpade Mohanty identifies as a discourse that "sets up its own authorial subjects as the implicit referent, that is, the yardstick by which to encode and represent cultural others" (Mohanty 2003, 21).

Moreover, feminists and comparativists have not only questioned the content of many of Western philosophy's foundational claims, but they have also worked to transform philosophy for the better by reexamining our disciplinary habits and practices. Janice Moulton's critique of "the adversary method" as a paradigm for philosophy is a key example of this kind of study (Moulton 1989), as is Susan Sherwin's attention to the cooperative nature of feminist work (Sherwin 1988) and Arindam Chakrabarti's condemnation of the "bogus" yet present dichotomy between analytic philosophy and comparative philosophy (Chakrabarti 2002). This attention to transformation is related to a shared orientation toward humanistic goals that extend beyond the aims of a particular philosophical inquiry or argument. Through the pursuit of alternative ways of instantiating our discipline and attention to marginalized perspectives, feminists and comparativists engage philosophical projects that have the potential to effect concrete, positive changes in our cultures, societies, institutions, and manners of relation on local and global scales.

Despite their shared aspirations to openness, diversity, and self-reflective critique, the feminist and comparative philosophical traditions have been limited by their own frames and histories. That both fields are subject to the same insularity as the wider discipline is evidenced by the fact that each rarely engages work from the other, even though there is significant overlap in their aims and methods. In some respects these traditions have also repeated the very oppressive and homogenizing structures that their methodologies were established to counter. For instance, when feminist philosophy recognizes the category of gender as the primary site of theoretical interest, it is likely to overlook real differences between women in favor of a homogeneous theory that posits white, Western, middle-class, heterosexual, able-bodied women as the implicit subjects of feminist discourse. As Chela Sandoval puts it, many feminists "insisted on organizing along the binary gender division male/female alone" (Sandoval 2000, 45). This criticism is well known in feminist philosophy, albeit not adequately addressed by that tradition as a whole. Feminist comparative philosophy is therefore particularly inspired by those feminist methodologies that acknowledge the dangers of homogenization and attempt to account for the cultural complexity of women's lives and experiences. Such feminisms include Anzaldúa's "mestiza consciousness," Mohanty's "feminism without borders," Sandoval's "U.S. third world feminism," Lugones's "pluralist and decolonial feminism," Maxine Baca Zinn and Bonnie Thornton Dill's "multiracial feminism," and Kimberlé Williams Crenshaw's "intersectional feminism," among others.[8] Nonetheless, as Namita Goswami emphasizes in chapter 11, contemporary feminism would benefit from greater use of comparative methods to help expose the ways that oppressive histories structure the creation and production of theory.

In light of their common aim to give voice to difference, it is un-surprising that the history of comparative philosophy suggests a methodological problem similar to that of the feminist tradition. The field's emphasis on culture, language, and geography as the primary markers of philosophical difference directs its attention away from the manner in which gender, class, and other social identities con-tribute to philosophical diversity. As Yoko Arisaka notes, rarely do comparativists take up Asian or Asian American identities in the ways that black or Latino identities are discussed in philosophy; compara-tivists are more likely to be interested in the hermeneutics of read-ing classical Asian texts than in showing how the categories Asian or Asian American foster the oppression of individuals belonging to these groups (Arisaka 2000, 209). Furthermore, we can see that the means by which comparative philosophy has been instantiated over time repeat wider, oppressive disciplinary attitudes with regard to its lack of sustained attention to women's lives, experiences, and voices.[9] This tendency is evidenced by the fact that it is rare to see a text writ-ten by a woman referenced or interpreted in the comparative canon. The most common comparisons pursued instead involve prominent Asian male philosophers, such as Nāgārjuna, Dharmakīrti, Confucius, Zhuangzi, the Buddha, and Dōgen, with prominent Western male phi-losophers, such as Aristotle, Descartes, Hegel, Kant, Heidegger, and Dewey. When viewed from a feminist perspective, comparing the texts of privileged Western males with those of privileged Asian males is not necessarily an exercise in open-mindedness and sensitivity to difference; after all, some differences are much more comfortable to explore than others. Few comparativists would deny that gender and race are aspects of culture, but acknowledging this connection does not necessarily entail that those who attend to culture will also at-tend to social categories. Whereas a long list of feminist philosophers has taken up the question of cultural difference over the past two de-cades, far fewer comparativists have reflected on the roles of women and gender difference in comparative thought.[10]

Feminist comparative methodology guards against the limitations of its namesakes by providing a framework that intentionally attends to gender and culture *at the same time*. Our methodology is a response to the idea that the exclusions currently present in the feminist and comparative philosophical traditions are themselves indications of structural and methodological inadequacies. We are thus led to ask along with Sandoval, "How did this systematic repression occur within an academic system that is aimed at recognizing new forms of knowledge?" (Sandoval 2000, 47). Even liberatory philosophical traditions can work against their goals by succumbing to prevailing social habits and narrow structures of approbation at play in the wider discipline. Born from a keen awareness of these internal limitations, feminist comparative methodology works to adapt, attune, repattern, and recover many of the disciplinary conventions developed by each of its two namesakes for the sake of increased philosophical rigor, insight, and liberation.

World-Traveling as Methodology

Our methodology begins in the idea that philosophical content is inseparable from its context; which truths are revealed depends on how the picture is framed. As Kathy E. Ferguson observes, "The questions we can ask about the world are enabled, and others disabled, by the frame that orders the questioning" (Ferguson 1993, 7). To better expose this relation of content and context, the feminist comparative philosopher creates her insights by "traveling" between the texts of distinct traditions and among multiple philosophical framings. Her movements, however, are not haphazard, nor do they compromise her ability to take up the specialized perception she has achieved through her disciplinary training. Instead, such travel expands her range of knowledge and cultivates skills that can enhance her disciplinary repertoire. Through this very activity, the feminist comparativist performs philosophy differently and helps to transform the defining features of its landscape for the better. In this sense, we can view her as an agent of liberation insofar as she seeks to liberate our revered philosophical traditions, disciplinary boundaries, and areas of study from their implicit assumptions and self-imposed limitations.

Conceiving of philosophical methodology in terms of "travel" is a strategy that feminist comparative philosophy inherits from its namesakes. Feminist philosophers and comparative philosophers alike have frequently used the metaphor to emphasize the distinguishing features of their respective methodologies, albeit it in different ways. In his 1986 Presidential Address to the Society for Asian and Comparative Philosophy, Gerald James Larson employs the idea as follows:

> When philosophies or modes of philosophical analysis "travel" from one culture to another, how much "luggage" is necessary, or perhaps better, how much "luggage" is permitted? Related to this, who grants the "passport" and who confers the "visa"? What restrictions are there on "passports" and "visas" and for how long are they valid? Should philosophy only apply for a "tourist visa" or can there also be a "study visa"? Can philosophy from one country take up "permanent residence" in another? Is an application for "citizenship" a realistic possibility, or are there philosophical laws of "immigration and naturalization" that make "citizenship" highly unlikely?
>
> (LARSON 1986, 132–33)

With this series of questions, Larson asks how it is possible, if at all, to explore and inhabit philosophical traditions that are different from one's tradition(s) of origin without compromising their integrity. For Larson, this possibility hinges on attending to the relationship between a philosopher's own cultural subjectivity and the traditions that he or she studies—a relationship that changes and deepens in the course of the comparative project. The ideal of achieving "permanent residence" or "citizenship" is an epistemological one that is reached when the philosopher finally learns enough of another tradition's language, culture, and history such that it becomes "second nature." Larson's recognition that this ideal may be difficult, if not impossible, to realize is an indication of his belief that we philosophers are tightly bound to our own subjectivities and the cultural landscapes that give rise to them. Our traditions of origin may have generated the kind of luggage that, no matter how many trips we take, will never be lost or forgotten.

Around the same time as Larson's address, Latina, Chicana, and U.S. third world feminist thinkers were using metaphors of travel to describe the complex relationships between sexist, racist, and colonialist structures of oppression and women's strategies for resistance. In her famous essay, "Playfulness, 'World'-Traveling, and Loving Perception" first published in 1987, María Lugones identifies the practice of traveling between oppressive and liberatory structures as essential to any pluralistic feminist methodology. In other words, some form of traveling must occur if feminism is to affirm "the plurality in each of us and among us" (Lugones 2003b, 77).[11] Contrary to Larson's imagery, however, Lugones does not speak of traveling in terms of national boundaries, but in terms of "'worlds' of sense"—hierarchical social arrangements that render certain subjectivities visible and others invisible.[12] When a woman travels from an oppressive "'world' of sense" where she is perceived only in virtue of her capacity to be an object for another to a resistant "'world' of sense" where her subjectivity is recognized, she becomes a different kind of self. Correspondingly, the oppressed/resistant woman experiences a kind of epistemic shift that opens upon a different way of organizing and perceiving reality. Although such "'world'-traveling" is a matter of survival rather than choice for most oppressed people, Lugones encourages feminist theorists to willfully employ this strategy for the sake of a feminism that genuinely advocates for all women across diverse races, ethnicities, sexualities, and nationalities.

Despite the obvious benefits of utilizing travel metaphors to illustrate certain aspects of feminist and comparative methodologies, such analogies are not without their difficulties. For example, in her influential essay on the subject, Janet Wolff points out that the practice and concept of travel is not gender neutral, but rather there is an "intrinsic relationship between masculinity and travel" (Wolff 1992, 230). She emphasizes that, in many societies, the difference between men and women is marked by the increased mobility of the former, including men's ability to "leave home" at regular intervals (229). This observation that a person's access to travel is dependent on her social, historical, geographical, and economic location leads Wolff to challenge those appropriations of the metaphor that gloss over this fact.[13] While the suggestion of "unbounded and ungrounded movement" does much to destabilize and resist the fixity of modern categories of identity (235), it also encourages us to deemphasize our own original points of departure and discount the power relations at play whenever two theoretical perspectives come into contact. The importance of cultivating an awareness of our own philosophical locations and taking into account relevant relationships of power is especially pronounced in regard to comparative philosophy, where there are devastating histories of colonization and domination that background intellectual encounters between East and West, South and North. Within such contexts the motives for intellectual travel are suspect, since the habits and perceptions of its practitioners are likely wrought with these colonialist legacies. Panikkar thus notes the dangers of comparative travel: "The West not being able any longer to dominate other peoples politically, it tries to maintain—most of the time unconsciously—a certain control by striving toward a global picture of the world by means of comparative studies" (Panikkar 1988, 116).[14] In order to avert the problems that Wolff and Panikkar discuss, feminist comparative methodology must be tied to a specific kind of traveling—one that does not lose sight of the philosopher's evolving location and the wider social, political, economic contexts that facilitate her theory construction.

What unites feminist and comparative approaches to travel metaphors is the idea that bringing different traditions and perspectives into contact with one another in a philosophically fruitful way requires a robust, practical knowledge of different worlds and ontological landscapes. Genuine travel is not tourism, sightseeing, imperialism, colonization, assimilation, or exoticization. As J. Kwee Swan Liat writes, "excessive reverence for ancient Oriental revelations is just as great an obstacle to the adequate understanding of Eastern philosophy as is prejudice of one's own superiority" (Liat 1951, 11). A methodology of world-traveling requires more than just reading a text from the tradition in question or imagining what it would be like to be Chinese, Indian, a woman, or a lesbian. The point of feminist comparative travel is not to discover new concepts, ideas, and problems that we can fit into our own frames of reference or worlds of sense, but to shift our frames altogether so that we see things differently from another perspective, a unique angle, and the standpoint of a new location. Mariana Ortega's description of world-traveling is especially consistent with this aspect of feminist comparative methodology: "World-traveling has to do with actual experience; it requires a tremendous commitment to practice: to actually engage in activities where one will experience what others experience; to deal with flesh and blood people not just their theoretical constructions; to learn people's language in order to understand them better not to use it against them; to really listen to people's interpretations however different they are from one's own; and to see people as worthy of respect rather than helpless beings that require help" (Ortega 2006, 69). Loosening the cognitive patterns of our original subjectivities in this manner so that we may learn anew is no easy task. It takes perseverance, discipline, and spontaneity. World-traveling involves "a knowing-how-to-function in situations that are ambiguous, dangerous, or hostile, and, more than that, a knowing-how-to-function in situations that are unique, unpredictable, ad hoc, or unrepeatable" (Larson 1986, 136).

In considering what genuine world-traveling entails, we should not forget Lugones's point that world-traveling is a familiar mode of survival for some and a choice for others. For a philosopher who already inhabits multiple traditions—an Indian woman trained in the Western academy, for example—world-traveling may be less about learning another's language and engaging in unfamiliar activities than it is about learning how to give expression to her own contradictory, mobile subject-position within a discourse that erases such multiplicity. In other words, the challenges and comforts that one encounters when employing feminist comparative methodology are thoroughly dependent on the philosopher's own social location at the time of departure.

Drawing on what elsewhere has been labeled the "paradoxical theory of change" (Beisser 1970), we could characterize feminist comparative methodology in terms of the idea that philosophical insight and the personal, intellectual transformations that it entails occur when a philosopher 1. endeavors to acknowledge and embody, rather than ignore and transcend, her own subjectivity and 2. makes genuine, authentic contact with another philosophical perspective. This guiding principle of feminist comparative philosophy may seem paradoxical because it is precisely in cultivating awareness of one's own subjective location that the philosopher is best able to access and articulate a fuller, less partial view of reality. Feminist comparativists must develop a "negotiating process, as it were, between our prejudgmental forms and patterns and the conceptual content and structures of that tradition that get disclosed to us as we enable that tradition to speak to us in its own terms" (Deutsch 2002, 24). By having a rich picture of who she is that includes her habits of disciplined and specialized perception, the feminist comparative philosopher is able to self-consciously position herself in ways that will allow her to learn new habits and animate new selves. Cultivating this kind of self-awareness—what Keya Maitra calls feminist self-consciousness in chapter 4—involves cultivating relationships with other people and other perspectives. As Lugones writes, a pluralist methodology entails that each of its practitioners knows that "self-knowledge is inter-active, that self-change is interactive" (Lugones 2003b, 74).

We must expect, however, that the selves that we discover in re-lation with others, especially in postcolonial and patriarchal con-texts, may not align with our self-image because these relationships could reveal ways that we ourselves perpetuate logics of racism, sex-ism, and imperialism. As is the case with any embodied practice, the first time a person world-travels to another philosophical perspec-tive, the encounter may be uncomfortable and perhaps unsuccessful. Feminist comparative philosophy is thus a risky scholarly endeavor that involves considerable amounts of uncertainty and openness to criticism. However, with repeated practice, continual self-revision, negotiation between worlds, due attention to criticism, and coopera-tion, such traveling is indeed possible, as the essays in this collec-tion attest. What the feminist comparative philosopher endeavors to do through the activity of world-traveling is view reality from as many angles as possible, foster the expression of perspectives that are rarely considered essential, and avoid confusing what is visible from her own partial perspective with the whole of reality and the truth. By reorienting her very self (mind and body) along multiple lines of travel, the feminist comparativist breaks with her disciplined training and reconfigures what is possible—philosophically, person-ally, *and* politically.

Feminist Comparative Philosophy as Liberatory Praxis

Praxis can be defined as the action that is created by theory—the pur-posive and performative movement that is entailed by a given out-look, intellectual method, or stance. Feminist comparative philoso-phy is not only a methodology but also a distinctive kind of political praxis that actively resists oppressions within its content and styles of expression.

We believe feminist comparative philosophy is first and foremost a liberatory praxis because it reconfigures trends of inclusion and ex-clusion within the discipline and our wider social and cultural prac-tices. Given the conceptions of "philosophy" and "philosopher" most frequently performed by the discipline itself through its syllabi, text-books, and faculty, it is probably not coincidental that philosophy has some of the least diverse demographics of any discipline.[15] Furthermore, it is probably not coincidental that philosophy departments that claim specializations in (or otherwise indicate strong respect for) feminist philosophy and comparative philosophy have both significantly more women and people of color as faculty and students than disciplinary averages.[16] Although many professional philosophers would disagree with the claim that women and non-Westerners do not produce philosophy, they nonetheless instantiate their work in ways that demonstrate that they do possess such a belief. Rada Iveković writes, "Women and the Orient are the two principal figures of the Other in the Occidental tradition. They are traveling companions with regards to a variety of practices of exclusion, as much in the real as the symbolic. But their paths do not entirely coincide" (Iveković 2000a, 223). All feminist comparative projects ask us to reconsider our notions of philosophy insofar as they engage sources, genres, and thinkers that are not automatically accorded philosophical status in the academy. Recognizing these philosophies is not a charitable act, but a means of casting a wider net of intellectual responsibility and exposing our work to more critical perspectives than has traditionally been done in our discipline. By engaging different, unfamiliar perspectives in genuinely receptive ways and repatterning the embodied habits of its practitioners away from the status quo of accepting unjustified privileges and dismissals, feminist comparative methodology helps us to envision alternative, more liberatory ways of being.

The political work of feminist comparative philosophy also lies in a philosopher's performing her theorizing in such a way so as to minimize or eradicate harm to persons. To apply one of Lugones's distinctions, this methodology is less concerned about the harm that not recognizing different philosophical traditions does to theorizing than it is about the harm that theorizing does and has done to women and people of color (Lugones 2003b, 72). Performative alterations as seemingly minor as self-consciously including works by women and non-Westerners in our syllabi; referencing one or more of these sources in genuine ways in our books and articles; or expressing interest rather than condemnation or skepticism when feminism, critical race theory, queer theory, or comparative philosophy are mentioned can have profound liberatory effects on the experiences of actual people who participate in the discipline.

Feminist comparative philosophy is, additionally, a liberatory praxis because it provides a framework designed to support the development and articulation of feminisms that are compatible with a variety of cultural grounds. Women who live in and originate from non-Western cultures often feel at odds with the tenets and techniques of Western feminisms while also struggling with the patriarchal structures of their own cultures. For example, Arisaka discusses this "double-alienation" with reference to Asian women by emphasizing the inconsistencies between Confucian cultures and Western feminisms. She observes that "traditional feminist consciousness has focused predominantly on notions of oppression, subversion, and revolutionary change. . . . The idea of oppositional 'agency' (to patriarchy, capitalism, male-domination, injustice, disempowerment) is an essential component of the [Western] feminist movement" (Arisaka 2000, 225). However, women who come from Confucian cultures where passivity, service, and harmony are considered virtues are likely to find these confrontational feminist methods to be alienating because they are often antithetical to Confucian women's "cultural selves."[17] All the essays in this collection employ feminist comparative methodology to establish philosophical places where a woman can be *both* feminist *and* part of non-Western cultures or traditions at the same time. In honoring the contextual and situated character of liberation, feminist comparative methodology does the necessary feminist work of crafting a politics that is relevant not simply to one group of women but to a diversity of persons from a variety of national, cultural, and social backgrounds.

The political nature of feminist comparative philosophy is also evidenced in its practice of forming effective coalitions amidst genuine differences without ignoring, exaggerating, or homogenizing those differences. If Western frames of reference and Western philosophers are to remain in the center of academic discourses, then non-Western philosophies and philosophers must be kept separate from each other so their voices do not find strength in numbers. According to Sandoval, this "apartheid logic" molds the landscape of "cultural studies" and their associated academic disciplines in the U.S. academy (Sandoval 2000, 67–79). While the general trend in academia over the past several decades seems to be one of recognizing and cultivating diversity, those theoretical domains at the forefront of this movement including feminist, poststructural, postcolonial, queer, postmodern, disability, critical race, globalization, and comparative studies have each developed separate terminologies and practices for achieving this aim. Sandoval believes that "differential consciousness" is an effective political antidote to this segregation and inefficacy: "the differential occurs when the affinities inside of difference attract, combine, and relate new constituencies into coalitions of resistance" (63). She imagines an "agreed-upon interdisciplinary approach for bringing these languages together in the shared project that underlies their many articulations" (78). Feminist comparative methodology is intended to be one such approach that welcomes the insight and technicality of specialized discourses at the same time that it rejects their insularity and narrow applicability. The wide range of philosophical traditions and the unconventional juxtapositions explored in this book encourage us to see lines of similarity and difference that we may not have noticed before. The political nature of feminist comparative philosophy lies not only in its ability to raise an individual's consciousness but also in its ability to cultivate a "coalitional consciousness" (79) that collectively resists multiple forms of oppression at the same time.

How much uptake a new mode of seeing receives within the discipline of philosophy is dependent upon the networks and structures of approbation that are currently operative in our profession. For example, the claims and ideas put forth from "marginal" philosophical positions like feminist philosophy, comparative philosophy, and the other theoretical domains already mentioned are often ignored out of hand by the mainstream, not because they are shown through argumentation to be ill-founded, but because those individuals at the "center" of the discipline incur no professional penalties by readily ignoring them. The authors we read, the audiences we write for, the other philosophers with whom we interact, the graduate courses that we are required to take, the type of dissertation that we are supposed to write, the ways that jobs are advertised, and the kinds of recognition that we seek all structure the practical habits that enable our disciplined modes of perception. When we evaluate a given work of philosophy, we often focus on its content and argument without attending to those practical aspects of our disciplinary training that beckon us to admire one content or argument rather than another. But our disciplinary frames and patterns are not inconsequential to recognizing the truth of what we encounter. Iveković remarks, "Cultural continuity and identity are sustained by a style and a manner of proceeding more than by content. They are *choices of civilization . . .* more than choices of belief" (Iveković 2000b, 231).[18] In the case of philosophy, we should be mindful of the ways that our habitual professional practices and familiar cultural grounds can bestow undeserved legitimacy to certain topics and methods over others. Arisaka's insight is relevant here: "The real power of colonization is the ability to achieve this willing participation by transforming the colonized subjects' own point of reference from the native culture to the western one" (Arisaka 2000, 219).[19] Decolonization therefore involves an openness to decentering Western frames and narratives as well as patriarchal ones. Although few philosophers have either the courage or interest to denounce the importance of feminist theory or cultural studies publicly—and this silence itself is quite telling—the professional practices of the wider discipline, such as what areas of specialization are in highest demand, what is rewarded for being good philosophy, who gets through the tenure process *without question*, and the unbalanced demographics of the discipline in general and of its highest ranks in particular, get the message across clearly.[20] In the case of such unexamined but perpetuated exclusions, the method of following what has always been done—what is traditional—prevails over the method of considering what is true, right, defensible in the face of critique, and best supported by exploration and argumentation. Due to such disciplinary tendencies to defer to tradition, the feminist comparative philosopher will often find herself going against the grain whenever she attempts to reconfigure these conventions.

Finally, feminist comparative philosophy is a political praxis because all philosophy is a political practice whether it intends to be or not. Feminist comparative methodology thus proceeds in line with Mohanty's claim that "there can of course be no apolitical scholarship" (Mohanty 2003, 19). Larson makes this point as follows: "The forces of power, domination, resentment, racism, inferiority, prejudice, and a host of other human characteristics are very much a part of our world view, ideologies, philosophies, and conceptual frameworks, but they receive almost no attention whatsoever" (Larson 1986, 16). If we agree with Mohanty and Larson, then the task of philosophy is not to aspire to be apolitical and objective, but to be informed by politics that actually foster liberation and to present ideas and methodologies that are capable of disrupting, rather than affirming, systems of oppression. Feminist comparative methodology assumes this charge in an explicit way and, in so doing, invites reflection, criticism, and dialogue as to how well the tasks of philosophy and liberation are performed.

Chapter Themes and Summaries

Readers will find that several of the chapters in this collection present arguments for one or more of the defining features of feminist comparative methodology already mentioned, such as the necessity of taking into account multiple perspectives when constructing interpretations, the situated nature of knowledge, the cultivation of practices designed to repattern embodied habits, the primacy of relational selves and nonindividualistic subjectivities, and the promise of liberatory transformation at political and personal levels. This fact does not mean that the thematic *content* of feminist comparative philosophy is merely a meta-reflection on the wider discipline or a descriptive accounting of philosophy's justified and unjustified boundaries. All of the chapters in this book focus on specific philosophical problems and explore perennial topics such as free will, consciousness, knowledge, objectivity, sexual difference, emotion, morality, selfhood, hermeneutics, embodiment, language, and the relationship between the individual and society. The congruence between content and method throughout this work speaks rather to the integrity of feminist comparative philosophy as a theory *and* a practice—as a system of thought *and* an embodied performance. It is also a natural consequence of emphasizing intersecting themes between Asian and feminist philosophies, since both traditions take seriously a person's situation, embodiment, relationality, and liberation. In what follows we discuss the themes of each of the five parts of the book and give summaries of each chapter in order to help the reader decide how best to move through the volume.

Gender and Potentiality

The chapters in part 1 employ gender as a vehicle through which we can rethink the potentiality of selves by means of philosophical reconstruction. In this sense, *potentiality* contains multiple meanings, each of which alludes to the variety of ways in which selves can be transformed—spiritually, politically, and philosophically. To think the potentiality of gender and the gender of potentiality is to think the very structures of reality: the sediment of *kamma*, the primal valley (谷神) in chapter 6 of the *Daodejing*, or the *yin* and *yang* of all that is. However, we must also rethink the ways that these underlying metaphysical structures have been interpreted to the disadvantage of women as well as others. The authors of this section, while acknowledging the role of patriarchal systems and worldviews to justify female subjugation, reread classical Asian traditions for metaphysical insights into and solutions to such oppression.

In chapter 1, "*Kamma*, No-Self, and Social Construction: The Middle Way Between Determinism and Free Will," Hsiao-Lan Hu highlights our individual and shared responsibilities to rethink the potential of our actions and our exercised free will. In so doing, Hu provides an interpretation of the classical Buddhist notion of *kamma* (Sanskrit: *karma*) that is compatible with Judith Butler's postmodern feminism and specifically with her descriptions of performativity and social transformation. In both traditions one central task is to recognize and address our unconscious, sedimented behaviors that promote harm, suffering, and oppressive norms and customs. Hu argues that both *kamma* and socially constructed selves are neither overly determined nor incapable of free will and moral agency. Rather, it is precisely because of the fluidity and codependence of these respective constructions of the self that we can account for will and agency at all. Hu's theory thus offers us a "middle way" between free will and determinism that can satisfy Buddhists and feminists alike. In both traditions our moral responsibility to recognize and then reconfigure our norms, conventions, and karmic patterns is paramount.

Whereas Hu's focus is Buddhism, the author of chapter 2, Kyoo Lee, turns her attention to Daoism. In "On the Transformative Potential of the 'Dark Female Animal' in *Daodejing*," Lee performs a deconstructive analysis of various interpretations and standardized understandings of *xuanpin* 玄牝 (dark female animal) as well as a reconstructive rendering of the latent potentials of this concept. Lee notes the inconsistencies, tensions, and confusions in various attempts to describe the female by scholars and translators who are predominantly male. These contradictions include 1. the female's dual and simultaneous state of transcendence (described as mysterious, profound, subtle, and mystical) and immanence (as dark, animal, and bestial); 2. the Daoist female (and feminine) understood as both complementary to the Daoist male (and masculine) as in the relationship of *yin-yang*, and as always already source, originator, and cosmic universal of all things; and 3. the utilization and appropriation of the female in Daoist interpretations while at the same time continuing to downplay its importance. By acknowledging rather than suppressing these contradictions, Lee gives a fascinating account of how the sexed nature of *Dao* challenges heteronormativity and spurs feminists to a more creative account of gender.

Chapter 3, "Confucian Family-State and Women: A Proposal for Confucian Feminism," emphasizes our potential to rediscover, reclaim, and rewrite traditional frameworks to serve our contemporary ideals. Ranjoo Seodu Herr's study of Confucianism details how this tradition has become historically linked to a cultural and ideological support of women's subjugation. As an example, Herr considers gender oppression in the formation of the Chosŏn Dynasty—a Korean society founded explicitly on Confucian values and traditions. In her account, Herr uncovers how the rigid gender restrictions of Chosŏn are not, in fact, Confucian in nature. Rather, they are the result of a distorted interpretation of the virtue of *li* 禮 (ritual propriety) within families and a mistaken association of the Chinese doctrine of *yin-yang* with metaphysical gender differences. By revisiting these core ideas, Herr argues that Confucian virtues demand equal gendered participation in the private and public spheres. In order to achieve this, Herr recommends a renewed look at the role of nation-states and their support of individual and social flourishing.

Raising Consciousness

In part 2, we see how consciousness can be heightened through clearer insight into one's particular location in the world. Both authors employ Buddhist notions of mindfulness, bare attention, and spontaneous responsiveness to show how an enlightened consciousness can be useful for furthering our feminist awareness. Specifically, Keya Maitra argues that feminist awareness is dependent on the cultivation of feminist *self*-consciousness and Jennifer McWeeny describes how liberatory awareness can emerge in the context of turbulent and angry emotional experiences. In both chapters we see how Buddhist philosophy and embodied practice can help extend our feminist analyses of ontology and philosophy of mind as well as enable feminist activism.

In "Mindfulness, *Anātman*, and the Possibility of a Feminist Self-consciousness," Maitra discusses the importance of mindfulness (as developed in the Buddhist tradition) to the formation and development of a specifically feminist *self*-consciousness. Maitra finds problems with the notions of a generalized feminist consciousness as theorized by Sandra Bartky and others in terms of consciousness-raising movements. She observes that such theories focus on "women's experience" without due attention to the individualized nature of particular women's experiences and identities—which is precisely what tends to spark a woman's own feminist activism. Maitra argues that the purpose of feminist self-consciousness is a thoroughgoing reflective analysis of one's particular positioning in the social-political matrix so as to be well informed and prepared to effect liberatory change for oneself and others. With the assistance of mindfulness, we can attain a sensitivity to our own subjectivity as well as a clearer insight into the constitutive factors of our specific social positionalities. Such insight is necessary if we are to locate personal and social obstacles and identify various pathways to shared flourishing.

Expanding on a call for heightened awareness, McWeeny discusses the possibilities for political awakening through an ontological and epistemological investigation into the mechanisms of anger in chapter 5, "Liberating Anger, Embodying Knowledge: A Comparative Study of María Lugones and Zen Master Hakuin." Employing María Lugones's and Hakuin Ekaku's respective accounts of anger along with Maurice Merleau-Ponty's conception of operative intentionality, McWeeny explains how angers are perceptions that are created by the negotiation between bodies and worlds. She shows how profound anger emerges out of the various disconnects between selves and official, or conventional, "worlds of sense" as well as out of a person's inability to locate a suitable framework for the expression of this incommensurability. Rather than obstacles to knowing, she argues that these angers, though difficult, are epistemological because they awaken us to fundamental truths of our situation as well as to the possibilities of alternative meanings and solutions to our common suffering.

Places of Knowing

Both essays in part 3 challenge universalist claims to knowledge. The Daoist, feminist, Hindu, and postcolonial criticisms that fuel these challenges, however, are not aimed at the idea of objectivity per se, but rather at claims to objectivity that come from partial and/or distorted locations without acknowledging such shortcomings. Contrary to epistemological relativism, these essays argue for a renewed sense of objectivity that incorporates marginalized perspectives, including voices and lives that have hitherto been ignored or dismissed such as those of rural women. By including more voices in our epistemic programs and supporting participatory political projects, objectivity is something we can strive to achieve without reducing the value of alternative ways of knowing. As such, these chapters construct much-needed bridges between various places of knowing: the metaphysical and mystical, on the one hand, and the social, economic, political, and material, on the other.

In "What Would Zhuangzi Say to Harding? A Daoist Critique of Feminist Standpoint Epistemology," Xinyan Jiang compares the epistemological claims of ancient Daoists and contemporary feminist standpoint theorists. These two groups share in 1. their criticisms of universal and objective knowledge claims that are purportedly achieved by neutral, disembodied, and autonomous knowers and 2. their advocacy of situational and perspectival knowledge. However, feminists and Daoists disagree as to the epistemological meaning of differences in perspective. While Zhuangzi maintains a kind of egalitarianism in regard to situated knowledge, standpoint theorists such as Sandra Harding argue that some locations are better than others for producing less distorted knowledge claims, especially in terms of inquiries that investigate the causes and maintenance of inequality within a given society. By contrast, Zhuangzi advocates an overall rejection of conventional values and ways of life—including those values and practices that resist oppression—and a return to the simplicity of nature. Jiang's overall argument is to show that both theories of situated knowing ultimately must maintain some objective claims to support their own positions. Jiang sees this not as an inherent contradiction, but as a necessary move for all viable epistemological projects.

While Jiang looks to Daoism for resources to address feminist concerns about objectivity and universality, Vrinda Dalmiya turns to Hindu concepts to foster the democratization of epistemic projects in chapter 7, "'Epistemic Multiculturalism' and Objectivity: Rethinking Vandana Shiva's Ecospirituality." Specifically, Dalmiya examines the employment of religious symbols and practice in modern political activism in India—particularly around cultural, economic, and environmental issues. Such invocations of the mystical have drawn criticism because of their common connection to ultraconservative politics and values. This chapter takes up an analysis of Vandana Shiva's use of *prakriti*, a feminine creative principle represented by the Goddess who bears its name, in her progressive politics and in her strident criticisms of the mingling of capitalist ideologies and modern scientific practice. Dalmiya argues that prakriti-spirituality is an epistemological tool that locates the rural poor in an indispensable epistemological standpoint that is capable of providing creative, holistic, and sustainable alternatives to the reductionisms of modern science and global capitalism. Following this logic, if modern scientific movements want to gain traction with rural populations, such local knowledges and knowers must be recognized and brought into the conversation.

Cultivating Ethical Selves

The focus of part 4 is moral cultivation and the ways that our conceptions of ethical personhood can be enhanced through attention to diverse philosophical traditions. Chapter 8 begins with an argument for a cross-cultural dialogue regarding ethics and how attention to Asian philosophies, particularly Confucianism, can help improve feminist theories, particularly care ethics. Chapter 9 continues the trajectory of looking to Asian traditions—in this case, contemporary Japanese philosophy—for alternative models of ethical subjectivity. The author is particularly interested in nondual models of subjectivity, especially those that give equal consideration to neglected aspects of personhood, such as the body, emotion, the feminine, and relationality. Picking up on this call for embodied morality, chapter 10 looks at the role of the body in ethical action, especially the practice of caregiving. In all three, we see how comparative dialogue helps us think more carefully and thoroughly regarding our ethical lives and see how ethics is not only a theory, but also a set of actions, behaviors, and a way of life that must be cultivated and refined over time.

In "Confucian Care: A Hybrid Feminist Ethics," Li-Hsiang Lisa Rosenlee discusses an essential component of the feminist comparative project—the need for true openness to alternative perspectives and traditions in order to expand our theoretical resources and enrich our philosophical thinking. Using Virginia Held's recent dismissal of the compatibility of Confucianism and feminism as a springboard, Rosenlee sets out to establish a form of Confucian care ethics grounded in the virtue of *ren* 仁 (benevolence, humanity). To counter claims that Confucianism is inherently sexist and patriarchal, Rosenlee argues that Confucian care can actually address and correct many of the shortcomings of a traditional care ethics—such as the confinement of care to the domestic sphere, the inability to address violent relationships, and the lack of focus on women's own self-cultivation. Rosenlee is not arguing for the opposite of Held's position, that is, a rejection of feminist care ethics in favor of Confucianism. Rather, she is beginning the necessary feminist project of building a cross-cultural "hybrid" ethics for the benefit and flourishing of all.

Erin McCarthy's "The Embodied Ethical Self: A Japanese and Feminist Account of Nondual Subjectivity" can be likened to Rosenlee's essay insofar as McCarthy sees the insights of Asian philosophies as a significant supplement to feminist theory. McCarthy argues that Western feminist theorists (specifically, Elizabeth Grosz and Luce Irigaray) have a difficult time eluding dualistic, either/or constructions given the limited resources of their own traditions. McCarthy offers contemporary Japanese philosophical concepts, such as *ningen* 人間 (ethical selfhood) and bodymind (*shinjin* 身心), as one answer to the problems of Western dualistic subjectivity that have been the object of repeated feminist criticism. By appealing to the Japanese tradition, McCarthy uncovers alternatives that did not coevolve with dualistic constructions in the first place. Philosophers Watsuji Tetsuro and Yuasa Yasuo, while never intentionally feminist, provide models for embodied, nondualistic, and nonhierarchical ethical selfhood that meet feminist demands for holistic conceptions of subjectivity. Again, we see how cross-cultural exchange can provide fruitful solutions to our shared practical and philosophical problems.

In chapter 10, "Dōgen, Feminism, and the Embodied Practice of Care," Ashby Butnor continues McCarthy's discussion of embodied ethical selfhood by analyzing the ethical significance of embodied know-how. In addition to highlighting the significance of the body in even our most common intersubjective experiences, the author examines how mindful attention and care can be cultivated through attention to the body. Butnor claims that care is often stunted through our sedimented bodily habits—whether these habits are those of perception, attention, and responsiveness or those that reflect social disvalues and prejudices. In order to make transparent embodied habits that limit our ability to care well, Butnor offers strategies found in both Buddhism and feminism. By attuning ourselves to our own moral psychology (as highlighted in the Buddhist tradition) and the social context in which embodied habits take shape (as emphasized in feminist discourse), we will be more capable of refining caring skills and, therefore, becoming more cultivated ethical selves.

Transforming Discourse

Chapter 11, "De-liberating Traditions: The Female Bodies of *Sati* and Slavery," serves as the book's concluding essay because it provides the first meta-analysis of the feminist comparative project. Namita Goswami is critical of the ways in which cross-cultural feminist theorizing has been constructed and the ways in which power undoubtedly, though perhaps often unconsciously, affects the manner in which theory emerges. This chapter fulfills an important function insofar as it warns us of our systemic shortcomings when trying to represent the voices of others and pushes us to be cognizant of our colonizing tendencies. If we heed these warnings, we can indeed transform discourse, and these fresh, liberatory discourses can in turn transform our selves, our societies, and our world.

Through an analysis of the differential historical treatment (both materially and symbolically) of the black female body and the Hindu female body, Goswami makes an argument regarding both the legacy of colonial sexism that permeates our conceptions of these bodies and the associated hierarchical status of contemporary feminist theories, specifically in relation to postcolonial and African American feminisms. Goswami criticizes feminist theorizing for repeating the colonialist practices that it seeks to undermine when it comes to understanding the material, historical, and gendered lives of real women. We engage this hypocrisy by approaching female bodies as representations and texts (thereby denying and overwriting their real lives), which in turn replicates the colonialist notion that a body is a signifier of agency at the very moment when we undermine this agency by treating it as an object of discourse. A comparative philosophical methodology can remedy these failures within feminisms by helping us to recognize and therefore subvert this hierarchy. Ultimately, a feminist comparative approach can help us to forge solidarity between women of color and, more generally, between all theorists and the real lives they seek to understand.

The Future of Feminist Comparative Philosophy

As the discipline of philosophy evolves over time, we frequently find ourselves in positions where the cognitive and practical habits that have served us well in the past are found to be neither useful nor suited to our current purposes. Though, like other habits, our conventional, predictable, and "disciplined" patterns of thought can be changed through the repeated engagement of different philosophies and participation in alternative ways of seeing. Feminist comparative methodology involves knowing when to perform the skills one has developed in the course of one's training and knowing when to cultivate fresh modes of interpretation and perception. This kind of flexibility enhances philosophical rigor through the inclusion of more critical perspectives, the widening of the subject matter that a philosopher is expected to engage, and the invitation to play imaginatively and concretely with new frames and perspectives on classic problems.

Feminist comparative philosophy is a liberatory methodology for philosophical inquiry and a liberatory praxis designed to effect social change. However, as more and more people begin to participate in this fresh philosophical practice, it risks becoming "disciplined" and narrowly traditional like its predecessors. With this consideration, it is our hope that the practice of feminist comparative philosophy itself will broaden and expand as more voices are included in our everyday conceptions of philosophy. When attending to how the essays in this collection perform the categories of feminist and non-Western, one cannot help but notice that the category of non-Western is represented almost exclusively by Asian philosophical sources. Likewise, our choice of feminism as a central point of comparison and departure seemingly excludes other liberatory methodologies. These decisions were deliberate on our part for several reasons. Since a primary goal of this collection is to provide the first explicit articulation of feminist comparative philosophy as field of study, we wanted to emphasize its distinctive features as much as possible. One of these features is its historical and methodological connections to its namesakes, wherein comparisons between East and West have been taken as a primary subject matter. Another is the feminist comparativist's focus on *philosophical* traditions and locations. Working with classical texts that have served as the respective touchstones for major systems of thought is an obvious way to hold the philosopher hermeneutically accountable for her own point of view on different cultures and the conception of philosophy that informs her work.

Though there are a significant number of places throughout this work where we question our performed concepts of feminist and non-Western, it is still the case that our constructions of both categories could easily be expanded to include many more voices. The future of feminist comparative philosophy portends more dialogues than are represented in this collection, including those that involve African, Eastern European, Western Asian, and Islamic philosophies, as well as North-South comparisons and multiple types of social identities. As Panikkar writes of comparative philosophy, "It is a creative encounter. And there is no blueprint for creativity" (Panikkar 1988, 133). This claim is certainly within the spirit of our methodology, and we welcome all expansions to include more politically focused methodologies as well as more global philosophies.

As globalization progresses and national and social borders become even more permeable in the twenty-first century, philosophers inevitably find themselves faced with Iveković's pressing question: "Will we allow ourselves those cross-fertilizations, connections, contiguities, chances, those encounters which arise in the midstream of the problems that philosophers pose here and there?" (Iveković 2000b,

232). Feminist comparative methodology shows us a way to answer in the affirmative and to participate in the transformation of philosophy in the process. We see the future of feminist comparative philosophy as the ongoing inclusion of diverse voices in the philosophical dialogue, the performance of new cognitive and practical habits that will enable us to self-reflectively and explicitly measure up to our intellectual ideals, and the promotion of liberatory effects that can only come about through deliberate political awareness and action. Although reinvigorating the entire practice of philosophy may seem like an overwhelming project, the alternative—an insular, oppressive, and irrelevant discipline—is surely not an alternative for most of us.

Notes

1. For a definition of *tradition* that is perhaps more suited to comparative philosophy than Tuana's because it attends to cultural difference in an explicit way, see Joseph Kaipayil: "A philosophical tradition is . . . the accumulated philosophical beliefs of a culture crystallized into a definite set of concepts and categories" (Kaipayil 1995, 20).

2. See Butnor and McWeeny (2009).

3. Austin (1962), Searle (1975), Butler (1988, 1990), and Barad (2008).

4. These exceptions include Anne C. Klein's *Meeting the Great Bliss Queen: Buddhists, Feminists, and the Art of the Self* (1995), Chengyang Li's edited collection *The Sage and the Second Sex: Confucianism, Ethics, and Gender* (2000), Joanne D. Birdwhistell's *Mencius and Masculinities: Dynamics of Power, Morality, and Maternal Thinking* (2007), and a handful of chapters and articles that consider the status of women in the context of Confucianism, Buddhism, Daoism, or Hinduism. See "Feminist Comparative Philosophy and Associated Methodologies: A Bibliography," this volume, for a more complete listing.

5. Nancy Holland provides a content-based definition of this sort: "By women's philosophy I mean philosophical work (i.e., discussion of traditional philosophical issues) that arises from, explicitly refers to, and attempts to account for the experience of women . . . women's philosophy seems to entail a healthy skepticism about easy generalizations" (1990, 1). For a general discussion of feminist philosophy, see Tuana's article on the subject in the *Stanford Encyclopedia of Philosophy* (2011). For further reflections on the development of feminist philosophy in the U.S. academy since the 1970s see Thompson (2002), Sandoval (2000, 41–64), Ferguson (1994), and McAlister (1994).

6. Similarly broad definitions of comparative philosophy are offered in Smid (2009) and Kaipayil (1995). Smid, for example, writes, "Comparative philosophy

can be defined by its attempt to move across the boundaries of otherwise distinct traditions—especially insofar as these traditions are divided by significant historical and cultural distance—thus enabling a comparison of what lies on either side of the boundary" (2009, 2).

7. See Harding (1992, 1998), Code (1993), Lloyd (1984), and Haraway (1991) for feminist challenges to the purported neutrality of knowledge.

8. Anzaldúa (1999), Mohanty (2003), Sandoval (1991, 1995, 2000), Lugones (2003b, 2010), Zinn and Dill (1996), and Crenshaw (1989, 1994).

9. On this point, see Butnor and McWeeny (2009), where we discuss our experiences as graduate students pursuing feminist philosophy in the leading comparative program.

10. See "Feminist Comparative Philosophy and Associated Methodologies: A Bibliography," this volume. It is noteworthy that much of the work at the intersections of feminist and comparative philosophy has been authored by women, and few of the most famous thinkers in the field of comparative philosophy have written on feminist topics. We are hopeful, however, that this pattern is beginning to change.

11. See also Anzaldúa (1999) and Sandoval (1991).

12. See chapter 5 in this book for a thorough description of Lugones's ontology.

13. See also Kaplan (1996) on these points.

14. See also Daya Krishna, who writes, "The anthropological studies from which most comparative studies have arisen were, by and large, an appendage of the extension of some western European countries' political and economic power over the globe during the past three hundred years or so. . . . Comparative studies, thus, meant in effect the comparison of all other societies and cultures in terms of the standards provided by western societies and cultures, both in cognitive and noncognitive domains" (1988, 72).

15. The most recent statistics cite that women constitute approximately 21 percent of professionally employed philosophers in the United States (Solomon and Clarke 2009, 191–92). It is also estimated that approximately 1 percent of professionally employed philosophers are black and that there are less than 30 black women philosophers employed in a philosophy department in the United States, although no formal studies of the percentages of people of color who are professional philosophers have been undertaken (Gines 2011, 429, 435). Gender Divides in Philosophy and Other Disciplines cites philosophy as producing a lower percentage of female PhDs (less than 30 percent) than twenty other disciplines in 2009, with only engineering, computer science, and physics showing a smaller percentage of women (Healy 2011).

16. For example, in 2012, 42 percent of the permanent faculty and 26 percent of the graduate students in the philosophy department at the University of Hawaii, Manoa, which offers advanced degrees in comparative philosophy, are people of color. Similarly, 36 percent of the permanent faculty and 58 percent of the graduate students in the philosophy department at the University of Oregon,

which boasts the only philosophy Ph.D. program requiring courses in feminist philosophy, are women. See the American Philosophical Association's *Summary of Doctoral Degree Programs in Philosophy: Faculty and Student Demographics* (2012).

17. See also Narayan (1988) for a discussion of how the voices and locations of women of color are often ignored within feminist movement.

18. Iveković is here referencing Haijime Nakamura's phrase as he expresses it in *Ways of Thinking of Eastern Peoples: India-China-Tibet-Japan* (1964).

19. See also Krishna (1988, 72).

20. See note 16, this chapter.

References

Addelson, Kathryn Pyne. 1994. Feminist philosophy and the women's movement. *Hypatia* 9 (3): 216–24.

American Philosophical Association. 2012. *Summary of Doctoral Degree Programs in Philosophy: Faculty and Student Demographics.* http://www.apaonline.org/APA Online/Web_Resources/2012_APA_Graduate_Guide/APAOnline/2012_Graduate _Guide/2012_Guide_to_Graduate_Programs_in_Philosophy.aspx.

Anzaldúa, Gloria. 1999. *Borderlands/La Frontera: The new mestiza.* 2d ed. San Francisco: Aunt Lute.

Arisaka, Yoko. 2000. Asian women: Invisibility, locations, and claims to philosophy. In *Women of color and philosophy*, ed. Naomi Zack, 209–34. Malden, MA: Blackwell.

Austin, J. L. 1962. *How to do things with words.* Cambridge: Harvard University Press.

Barad, Karen. 2008. Posthumanist performativity: Toward an understanding of how matter comes to matter. In *Material feminisms*, ed. Stacy Alaimo and Susan Hekman, 120–54. Bloomington: Indiana University Press.

Beisser, Arnold. 1970. The paradoxical theory of change. In *Gestalt therapy now*, ed. Joen Fagan and Irma L. Shepherd, 77–80. New York: Harper Colophon.

Birdwhistell, Joanne D. 2007. *Mencius and masculinities: Dynamics of power, morality, and maternal thinking.* Albany: State University of New York Press.

Butler, Judith. 1988. Performative acts and gender constitution: An essay in phenomenology and feminist theory. *Theatre Journal* 40 (4): 519–31.

——. 1990. *Gender trouble: Feminism and the subversion of identity.* New York: Routledge.

Butnor, Ashby, and Jen McWeeny. 2009. Why feminist comparative philosophy? *American Philosophical Association Newsletter on Asian and Asian American Philosophers and Philosophies* 9 (1): 4–5.

Chakrabarti, Arindam. 2002. Analytic versus comparative: A bogus dichotomy in philosophy. *American Philosophical Association Newsletter on Asian and Asian American Philosophers and Philosophies* 2 (1): 39–42.

Code, Lorraine. 1993. Taking subjectivity into account. In *Feminist epistemologies*, ed. Linda Alcoff and Elizabeth Potter, 15–48. New York: Routledge.

Crenshaw, Kimberlé Williams. 1989. Demarginalizing the intersection of race and sex: A black feminist critique of antidiscrimination doctrine, feminist theory, and antiracist politics. *University of Chicago Legal Forum* 140:139–67.

——. 1994. Mapping the margins: Intersectionality, identity politics, and violence against women of color. In *The public nature of private violence: The discovery of domestic abuse*, ed. Martha Albertson and Roxanne Mykitiuk Fineman, 93–118. New York: Routledge.

Deutsch, Eliot. 2002. Comparative philosophy as creative philosophy. *APA Newsletter on Asian and Asian-American Philosophers and Philosophies* 2 (1): 23–26.

Ferguson, Ann. 1994. Twenty years of feminist philosophy. *Hypatia* 9 (3): 197–215.

Ferguson, Kathy E. 1993. *The man question: Visions of subjectivity in feminist theory*. Berkeley: University of California Press.

Gines, Kathryn T. 2011. Being a black woman philosopher: Reflections on founding the collegium of black women philosophers. *Hypatia* 26 (2): 429–37.

Haraway, Donna J. 1991. Situated knowledges: The science question in feminism and the privilege of partial perspective. In *Simians, cyborgs, and women: The reinvention of nature*, 183–202. New York: Routledge.

Harding, Sandra. 1992. After the neutrality ideal: Science, politics, and "strong objectivity." *Social Research* 59 (3): 567–87.

——. 1998. *Is science multi-cultural? Postcolonialisms, feminisms, and epistemologies*. Bloomington: Indiana University Press.

Healy, Kieran. 2011. Gender divides in philosophy and other disciplines. http:// crookedtimber.org/2011/02/04/gender-divides-in-philosophy-and-other -disciplines/.

Holland, Nancy. 1990. *Is women's philosophy possible?* Savage, MD: Rowman and Littlefield.

Iveković, Rada. 2000a. Introduction. Trans. Penelope Deutscher. *Hypatia* 15 (4): 221–23.

——. 2000b. Coincidences of comparison. Trans. Penelope Deutscher. *Hypatia* 15(4): 224–35.

Kaipayil, Joseph. 1995. *The epistemology of comparative philosophy: A critique with reference to P. T. Raju's views*. Rome: Centre for Indian and Inter-religious Studies.

Kaplan, Caren. 1996. *Questions of travel: Postmodern discourses of displacement*. Durham, NC: Duke University Press.

Klein, Anne C. 1995. *Meeting the great bliss queen: Buddhists, feminists, and the art of the self*. Boston: Beacon.

Krishna, Daya. 1988. Comparative philosophy: What it is and what it ought to be. In *Interpreting across boundaries: New essays in comparative philosophy*, ed. Gerald James Larson and Eliot Deutsch, 71–83. Princeton: Princeton University Press.

Larson, Gerald. 1986. Interpreting across boundaries: Some preliminary reflections. Society for Asian and comparative philosophy presidential address. *Philosophy East and West* 36 (2): 131–42.

Li, Chengyang. 2000. *The sage and the second sex: Confucianism, ethics, and gender*. Chicago: Open Court.

Liat, J. Kwee Swan. 1951. Methods of comparative philosophy. *Philosophy East and West* 1 (1): 10–15.

Lloyd, Genevieve. 1984. *Man of reason: 'Male' and 'female' in Western philosophy*. Minneapolis: University of Minnesota Press.

Lugones, María. 2003a. On the logic of pluralist feminism. In *Pilgrimages/peregrinajes: Theorizing coalition against multiple oppressions*, 65–76. Lanham, MD: Rowman and Littlefield.

——. 2003b. Playfulness, "world"-traveling, and loving perception. In *Pilgrimages/Peregrinajes: Theorizing coalition against multiple oppressions*, 77–102. Lanham, MD: Rowman and Littlefield.

——. 2010. Toward a decolonial feminism. *Hypatia* 25 (4): 742–59.

McAlister, Linda Lopez. 1994. On the possibility of feminist philosophy. *Hypatia* 9 (3): 188–96.

Mohanty, Chandra. 2003. *Feminism without borders: Decolonizing theory, practicing solidarity*. Durham, NC: Duke University Press.

Moulton, Janice. 1989. A paradigm of philosophy: The adversary method. In *Women, knowledge, and reality: Explorations in feminist philosophy*, ed. Ann Garry and Marilyn Pearsall, 5–20. Boston: Unwin Hyman.

Nakamura, Hajime. 1964. *Ways of thinking of Eastern peoples: India-China-Tibet-Japan*. Trans. Philip P. Wiener. Honolulu: University of Hawaii Press.

Narayan, Uma. 1988. Working together across difference: Some considerations on emotions and political practice. *Hypatia* 3 (2): 31–48.

Ortega, Mariana. 2006. Being lovingly, knowingly ignorant: White feminism and women of color. *Hypatia* 21 (3): 56–74.

Panikkar, Raimundo. 1988. What is comparative philosophy comparing? In *Interpreting across boundaries: New essays in comparative philosophy*, ed. Gerald James Larson and Eliot Deutsch, 116–36. Princeton: Princeton University Press.

Sandoval, Chela. 1991. U.S. third world feminism: The theory and method of oppositional consciousness in the postmodern world. *Genders* 10: 1–23.

——. 1995. Feminist forms of agency and oppositional consciousness: U.S. third world feminist criticism. In *Provoking agents: Gender and agency in theory and practice*, ed. Judith Kegan Gardiner, 208–26. Urbana: University of Illinois Press.

——. 2000. *Methodology of the oppressed*. Minneapolis: University of Minnesota Press.

Scharfstein, Ben-Ami. 1998. *A comparative history of world philosophy: From the Upanishads to Kant*. Albany: State University of New York Press.

Searle, John R. 1975. A taxonomy of illocutionary acts. In *Language, mind, and knowledge*, ed. Keith Gunderson, 344–69. Minneapolis: University of Minneapolis Press.

Sherwin, Susan. 1988. Philosophical methodology and feminist methodology: Are they compatible? In *Feminist perspectives: Philosophical essays on method and morals*, ed. Lorraine Code, Sheila Mullett, and Christine Overall, 13–28. Toronto: University of Toronto Press.

Smid, Robert W. 2009. *Methodologies of comparative philosophy: The pragmatist and process traditions*. Albany: State University of New York Press.

Solomon, Miriam, and John Clarke. 2009. Committee on the Status of Women *Jobs for Philosophers* Employment Study. *Proceedings and Addresses of the American Philosophical Association* 82 (5): 189–95.

Thompson, Becky. 2002. Multiracial feminism: Recasting the chronology of second wave feminism. *Feminist Studies* 28 (2): 337–55.

Tuana, Nancy. 2001. Introduction. In *Engendering rationalities*, ed. Nancy Tuana and Sandra Morgen, 1–22. Albany: State University of New York Press.

——. 2011. Approaches to feminism. In *The Stanford encyclopedia of philosophy*, ed. Edward N. Zalta. http://plato.stanford.edu/archives/spr2011/entries/feminism approaches/.

Wolff, Janet. 1992. On the road again: Metaphors of travel in cultural criticism. *Cultural Studies* 7 (2): 224–39.

Zinn, Maxine Baca, and Bonnie Thornton Dill. 1996. Theorizing difference from multiracial feminism. *Feminist Studies* 22 (2): 321–31.

PART ONE

GENDER AND POTENTIALITY

CHAPTER ONE

Kamma, No-Self, and Social Construction

The Middle Way Between Determinism and Free Will

HSIAO-LAN HU

THE TERM *kamma* (Sanskrit: *karma*) had been used in various ways before the time of the historical Buddha, Siddhāttha Gotama (Sanskrit: Siddhārtha; sixth to fifth centuries BCE).[1] Even within the tradition of Buddhism, the term has been multivalent. Buddhists and non-Buddhists alike have taken it to be a deterministic doctrine that says every experience a person has in this life has already been decided by previous events. In particular, this deterministic misunderstanding of kamma has been used to justify male dominance: a female rebirth and the mistreatments a woman endures in this life are understood to be the result of negative kamma from past lives (Khuankaew 2007, 174–91). The Buddha's teaching regarding kamma as recorded in the Pāli canon, however, is by no means deterministic, especially if it is considered together with another central teaching of Buddhism: no-Self (Pāli: *anattā*; Sanskrit: *anātman*).

At a glance, it may seem that the concept of kamma contradicts the concept of no-Self: if there is no "Self," who is making and receiving kamma? The relation between no-Self and kamma may become clear in the light of, unexpectedly, poststructuralist feminist theory regarding subjectivity and agency, especially Judith Butler's work, which is strikingly similar to the classical Buddhist understandings of no-Self and kamma.[2] In the same way that people might ask, "if there is no 'Self,' who is making and receiving *kamma*?" critics of Butler have questioned, "if the subject is socially constructed and not autonomous, how can the nonautonomous subject have the agency to make any social change?" This chapter explores this paradox by examining the meaning of kamma in the context of other basic teachings of the Buddha, such as no-Self and the five aggregates. Butler's theory regarding gender construction and subject formation, the lack of complete autonomy, and the sedimentation of performatives will be referenced to expound the social dimension of the Buddha's teachings on kamma and no-Self. At the same time, a feminist analysis of gender construction is a much-needed corrective to the traditional androcentric interpretation of the Buddhist *dhamma*.[3]

Kamma in Early Buddhist Discourses

Before the time of the historical Buddha, the word *karma* had been used in the ancient Brahmanic texts as well as in Jainism. In the earlier layers of the Vedas,[4] *karma* referred to ritual actions only (Obeyesekere 2002, 2–3; Harvey 1990, 11), and the main focus of discussion was the negative leftovers (*karmaphalasesa*) of imprecise performances of sacrificial rituals. In the *Śatapatha* and *Jaiminiya Brāhmaṇas*, for instance, those who were in hell were said to be those who had killed and eaten animals, and even herbs, without performing the correct rituals (Obeyesekere 2002, 100). In the pre-Buddhist Upaniṣads,[5] such as the *Bṛhadāraṇyaka Upaniṣad* and the *Chāndogya Upaniṣad*, the meaning of karma was broadened from the effects of ritual actions to the effects of all kinds of actions (4–5), and the effects of actions were linked to the destination of one's rebirth: the effect of pleasant behavior was rebirth in a pleasant womb, and the effect of foul behavior was rebirth as a dog, a pig, or an outcaste woman (11–12). In Jainism, karma was conceived as fine material particles that would accumulate on one's originally luminous soul (Sanskrit: *jīva*) with every bodily, verbal, and mental action, regardless of intention (Smith and Green 1995, 545).[6] In the hope of exhausting all karmic particles and eventually releasing one's soul from the encasement of karmic dusts, severe austerities were practiced. That is, Jainas considered karma to be the material results of actions, rather than actions themselves. In short, in all these pre-Buddhist usages, karma was understood to be the effects of actions, focusing on the actions already taken instead of those about to be taken.

James R. Egge's analysis of the early Buddhist discourses on kamma points out that the Buddha completely dispensed with the term's original reference to sacrifices; instead, he used it to refer to ethically accountable acts (Egge 2002, 41–67), thereby shifting people's attention from ritual actions to the actions that affect others and have impacts on the ways in which all beings coexist. More important, the Buddha talked about kamma in the present sense; that is, he focused on the actions to be taken here and now. Regarding the actions supposedly taken in past lives, the Buddha's attitude was consistent with his attitude toward metaphysical speculations. For the Buddha, "any conception of truth not relevant to making human life wholesome and good would simply be metaphysical and therefore unedifying" (Kalupahana 1995, 35). Devoting one's energy to metaphysical speculations is "unbeneficial," because "it does not belong to the fundamentals of the holy life" and "it does not lead to disenchantment, to dispassion, to cessation, to peace, to direct knowledge, to enlightenment, to Nibbāna" (MN i.431, i.485–86).[7] Metaphysical questions are therefore "unfit for attention" (MN i.8). What is "fit for attention" is conducting oneself in wholesome ways.

In the same vein, in a conversation with some Jainas who believed that they had to practice extreme austerities in order to burn off the kammic dusts accrued to their souls due to actions in past lives, the Buddha asked: "But, friends, do you know that you existed in the past . . . that you did evil actions in the past . . . that you did such and such evil actions . . . that so much suffering has already been exhausted, or that so much suffering has still to be exhausted, or that when so much suffering has been exhausted all suffering will have been exhausted?" (MN i.93, ii.214). Those Jainas answered "No" to all of the above questions. The Buddha then asked, "Do you know what the abandoning of unwholesome states is and what the cultivation of wholesome states is here and now?" (MN ii.215). Instead of discussing the actions already taken in past lives, which remained unknowable to most people and could not be undone anyway, the Buddha focused on cultivating wholesome states and abandoning unwholesome ones. He urged his followers to contemplate their responsibilities for the actions yet to be taken (AN III.72–73) and to contemplate the "ten wholesome courses of kamma" (AN V.57).[8] What is "fit for attention" is the undertaking of ethical actions at every present moment, rather than the consequences of past actions.

Moreover, the Buddha was recorded to have specifically rejected *pubbekatahetuvāda*, the deterministic theory that "whatever a person experiences . . . is caused by what was done in the past" (SN IV.230–31; MN ii.214).[9] Not every experience can be attributed to past actions; some experiences could be caused by "change of climate . . . careless behaviour . . . assault," in addition to physical disorders and imbalance (SN IV.230–31). Attributing every experience to past kamma would be blaming the victims of illness and natural disaster. It would also allow careless and aggressive people not to take responsibility for their actions. Likewise, attributing mistreatments of women to women's negative past kamma not only blames the victims but also allows the aggressors to continue treating others in an inhumane way.[10]

To refute the determinist understanding of kamma is not the same as to assert that past actions do not affect present experience. In the Nikāya texts one's bodily features and embodied existence in the current life were taken to be the *consequences* of past actions, and as such they were on occasion referred to as "old kamma"; the actions about to be taken, by contrast, were referred to as "new kamma" (SN IV.132–33, II.64–65). Due to "old kamma," a person's current body-mind may be particularly gifted or impeded or prone to carrying out a certain kind of behavior. However, given that one cannot be certain of what exactly others have done in past lives, one cannot justify mistreating them in the name of kammic retribution. Nor does the concept of "old kamma" provide a justification for the continuation of misconduct in this life. "Old kamma" might have resulted in some problematic habits, but the way to overcome a certain problematic behavioral pattern is simply to stop the problematic conduct itself:

A person given to cruelty has non-cruelty by which to avoid it.
    One given to killing living beings has abstention from killing living beings by which to avoid it.

    . . .

    One given to avarice has non-avarice by which to avoid it.
    One given to fraud has non-fraud by which to avoid it.
(MN I.44)

One may be prone to a certain type of misconduct due to the habits formed through repeated actions in the past, but that by no means justifies repeating those actions now. To overcome a problematic habit, one simply has to consciously stop the problematic action in question at every turn.

However, the Buddha did not teach people to cease all actions. The Jainas at the time of the Buddha upheld the ideal of refraining from all kinds of actions for the fear of further encasing the soul with kammic dusts, though it probably remained an ideal rather than a reality for most Jainas, for living necessarily involves taking actions. The Buddha, by contrast, differentiated between wholesome conduct and unwholesome conduct on the issue of doing and nondoing: "I assert the non-doing of bodily, verbal, and mental misconduct; I assert the non-doing of the numerous kinds of bad unwholesome deeds. . . . I assert good bodily, verbal, and mental conduct; I assert the doing of the numerous kinds of wholesome deeds" (AN IV.183).

Reformulating kamma as ethically accountable behaviors in every present moment, the Buddha urged his followers to be watchful of what they were about to do, to avoid the slightest misconduct, and to cultivate wholesome qualities (SN V.187; MN i.36, i.415; AN III.6, III.138, IV.152–54, IV.357). In the Buddha's practice-oriented teachings, what is important is what one does here and now, not what one might have done in the past. In contrast to other pre-Buddhist usages, the Buddha's usage of kamma emphasized the possibility of making positive changes even though one may be under the influences of negative actions taken in the past.

Actions in the Process of Individual Construction

With the focus shifted from the results of past actions to the actions to be taken, kamma denotes the possibility of volitionally changing one's current "self," no matter what might have been done in the past. A person is made through intentional actions. Past actions, performed both by others and oneself, certainly influenced the current mode of existence. With every action one chooses to take at every present moment, however, one can remake oneself. The Buddha's usage of kamma thus hinges well with his refutation of the concept of a permanent unchanging Self. It indicates that the making of one's being is an ongoing process and is not completely determined by preceding events. On the other hand, considering that one is influenced by "old kamma," one does not have complete, unadulterated freedom in molding oneself either.

To refocus the meaning of kamma on the actions that one intends to take at the present moment is also to highlight the importance of volition (Pāli/Sanskrit: *cetanā*). Therefore, scholars of Buddhism generally understand that Buddhist kamma refers to volitional actions only (Gier and Kjellberg 2004, 287; Gómez 1975, 82; Robinson Johnson, and Thanissaro 2005, 11–12; Williams 2000, 73–74; Harvey 1990, 40). Volition is a part of *saṅkhāra* (Sanskrit: *saṃskāra*), one of the five aggregates in Buddhist teachings. *Saṅkhāra* has been translated as "mental formations," "mental proliferations," "dispositions," "volitions," and "volitional constructions." Etymologically, the word means "to put together." According to Bhikkhu Bodhi, "*saṅkhāras* are both things which put together, construct, and compound other things, *and* the things that are put together, constructed, and compounded" (Bodhi 2000b, 45). On account of the "things that are put together, constructed, and compounded," *saṅkhāra* is rendered "mental formations" or "mental proliferations;" on account of the "things which put together, construct, and compound other things," *saṅkhāra* is translated as "dispositions" or "volition." The things that have been put together shape a person's dispositions and actions, and a person's dispositions and volition in turn affect the ways in which new things are put together. In other words, one's dispositions and volition both result from the thoughts that have already been formed and mold the ways in which thoughts are being formed. The aggregate of *saṅkhāra* accounts for the different mental formations and dispositions of different individuals. It also holds individuals accountable for what they volitionally do to themselves and to others at the present moment (Kalupahana 1987, 20–21).

Volition is the most significant mental factor in generating kamma (Ñāṇamoli and Bodhi 2001, 1258n581). "It is volition, bhikkhus, that I call kamma. For having willed, one acts by body, speech, or mind" (*AN* III.415). Even the "old kamma" was understood to have been "generated and fashioned by volition." U Rewata Dhamma and Bhikkhu Bodhi explain that volition determines the ethical quality of an action because it is volition that organizes associated mental factors to act (Bodhi 2000a, 80). The exercise of volition makes it possible for people to do things differently now and in the future, even though they are still under the influences of the actions that have already been taken by others and oneself. Without the exercise of volition, the past would determine the present and the future, and there would be no way out of the existing behavioral patterns that produce and induce *dukkha* (Sanskrit: *duhkha*), the dis-ease and sufferings of conventional modes of existence. What the Buddhist kamma teaches is that, "In each present moment, no matter how strong habitual patterns and familiar ways of reacting may be, Buddhist teachings about karma claim that I have some tiny opening of freedom. . . . Likewise, each person who is implicated in my present matrix has similar freedom" (Gross 2001, 176). Kamma as volitional action at the present moment points to the possibility of choosing to make a change now, both on the individual level and on the sociopolitical level, despite the hold of habits formed in the past. The Buddha's usage of kamma is thus nondeterministic, contrary to popular misunderstanding and misuse.

Kalupahana considers the *Buddhadhamma* the "middle way" between *kriyāvāda* and *akriyāvāda* (Kalupahana 1976, ch. 3). *Kriyāvāda* is the teaching that deeds bear fruits (*karmaphala*), and *akriyāvāda* is the teaching that deeds are fruitless. Early Buddhists referred to the Buddha's teaching as *kriyāvāda* or *karmavāda* because the Buddha taught that actions had consequences. The Jainas, however, classified Buddhism under *akriyāvāda* since the Buddha did not teach one-to-one correspondence between action and consequence. Gómez describes Buddhism as "weak," or modified, *kriyāvāda* (Gómez 1975, 81–84), and Gier and Kjellberg describe it as "qualified determinism" or "soft determinism" (Gier and Kjellberg 2004, 285–87). While "modified *kriyāvāda*" is an appropriate description of the Buddha's teaching, "qualified determinism" or "soft determinism" can be misleading, for in the Buddha's teaching past actions do not *determine* current experiences. The bodily features and abilities with which one was born might have been a result of past actions, but past actions do not predetermine the ways in which a person uses her body and abilities in this lifetime, nor do they predetermine the ways in which others treat her body and abilities. Kamma as volitional actions teaches that, with any given conditions, people can still make conscious choices as to how they act and how they react.

Many people misunderstand the teaching of no-Self in that they believe the teaching necessarily negates agency, but as a matter of fact the teaching of no-Self affirms the efficacy of volitional actions. No-Self teaches that the current mode of existence for any individual "self" is not permanent; what a person is right now can be changed through volitional actions. The following words of Judith Butler are strikingly consonant with the implication of no-Self: "Paradoxically, the reconceptualization of identity as an *effect*, that is, as *produced* or *generated*, opens up possibilities of 'agency' that are insidiously foreclosed by positions that take identity categories as foundational and fixed. For an identity to be an effect means that it is neither fatally determined nor fully artificial and arbitrary. . . . Construction is not opposed to agency; it is the necessary scene of agency" (Butler 1999, 187).

A person's "self" is an effect produced through repetitive performances of certain kinds of actions that have been culturally prescribed, such as the kind of behavior that is supposed to be gender appropriate. Through repetitive performances of the body, the culturally prescribed behavior is inscribed on the body and becomes part of a person's self-identity. When a certain kind of "feminine" behavior has been consistently expected of a girl, she performs it repeatedly, to the point that it becomes part of her bodily existence and defines her understanding of her gender identity—to be a girl, then, is to perform that particular kind of prescribed behavior.

To say that gender identity is constructed through repetitive performances of a certain kind of culturally prescribed behaviors, which Butler calls "performatives," is also to indicate that gender identity can be changed through the repetitive performances of an alternative kind of behavior (Butler 1999, 176, 179). Counterintuitively, it is the assertion of a permanent, unchanging Self that precludes the possibility of change and agency. If there were an unchanging ontological essence that exists prior to, and remains above, the actions one takes and the accompanying experiences, then whatever a person does would have no effect on the preexisting essence. If there were an unchanging femaleness at the core of every woman, then she could not help but embody that essence, and it would not matter if she strove to be a different person and do things differently. The assertion of a permanent, unchanging Self would render agency meaningless since the ontological essence would stay the same no matter what one does. Only when self-identity is understood to be an ongoing process of construction can a person's volitional actions make a difference.

Therefore, Butler asserts that construction is the necessary scene of agency, and the Buddha taught there is no unchanging Self while emphasizing kamma as volitional actions. In both strains of thought, there is no unchanging doer prior to the deeds. Rather, the doer is constructed through the deeds (Butler 1999, 181).

The classical Buddhist teaching of no-Self and poststructuralist theory of subject formation, though temporally and spatially apart, both point to the constructedness of individuals and the role that repeated actions play in the construction. They both recognize that a person constructs her identity through repeated actions. They also both acknowledge social factors in the process of construction—a person is not *just* her own doing. Butler uses the concept of "sedimentation" to expound the role of social factors, and in classical Buddhism the same idea is expressed through the analysis of the five aggregates and the social dimension of kamma.

Social Sedimentation and Individual Construction

In classical Buddhist thought, a person is a socio-psycho-physical compound of five aggregates: *rūpa*, sensations (Pāli/Sanskrit: *vedanā*), perceptions (Pāli: *saññā*; Sanskrit: *samjñā*), *saṇkhāra*, and consciousness (Pāli: *viññāṇa*; Sanskrit: *vijñāṇa*). In the ancient Indian usage (including the "heterodox" teachings of Buddhism and Jainism as well as the orthodox teaching of Brahmanism), the Pāli/Sanskrit word *rūpa* refers to six sense organs and their respective sense-objects. Mind is considered a sense organ alongside eyes, ears, nose, tongue, and skin. In early Buddhist texts the six sense organs are referred to as "internal sense bases," and serving as their objects are the six classes of "external sense bases" (*SN* IV.7–14, V.426).[11] "External sense bases" thus refer to all that can be processed by eyes, ears, nose, tongue, skin, and mind. Virtually all phenomena in the world can be considered the "external sense bases" for the mind, since they can all be processed by the mind in one way or another. For instance, colors are eye-objects, and yet the difference between two colors can be a mind-object. That is to say, the term *rūpa*, as both "internal sense bases" and "external sense bases," designates not only physical objects, but also abstract entities such as languages, philosophies, sociocultural norms, interpersonal relationships, and everything else that can serve as a mind-object. Thus considered, the typical translation of *rūpa* as "material forms" is rather inadequate since the word *material* in quotidian English usage does not include mind or mind-objects. Given that *rūpa* actually encompasses both the abstract and the concrete, the mental and the physical, and the internal and the external, it is better translated as "material and sociocultural forms" or "material and symbolic forces."

In this analysis of the five aggregates, material and symbolic forces play an important role in constructing a person because as the "external sense bases" they are processed by the person's "internal sense bases" and help constitute her sensations, perceptions, *saṅkhāra*, and consciousness. Sociocultural forces thus affect the ways that a person thinks and behaves. This, however, does not mean a person is not responsible for the ways she thinks and behaves. For one thing, just as "old kamma" does not *determine* a person, material and symbolic forces do not, either; they only *condition* that person.[12] For another, just as an individual person is socially constructed and not independently existing, a cultural form is also socially constructed and not independently existing. Rather, cultural forms are "sediments" of people's past actions. In the same way that sediments of earth are formed with sand being brought by water to the same place over time, cultural forms exist, and are maintained, through people repeating the same performatives over time (Butler 1999, 177–79, 184–85). Society is the result of the precipitates of the actions of socially conditioned persons, and persons are the precipitates of sociocultural *rūpa* as well as the persons' own volitional actions (Loy 2003, 7). That is, in Buddhist understanding, "People create the social system, but the system creates people" (87).

Buddhism understands actions to be of three kinds: bodily, verbal, and mental. Kamma, as volitional actions, can take the forms of deeds, words, and thoughts. Speech is one form of action in Buddhism, and it is also a focus of analysis in poststructuralist feminism because the space between social sedimentation and individual construction is particularly discernible in speech acts. Although "the speaking subject makes his or her decision only in the context of an already circumscribed field of linguistic possibilities," Butler maintains, "this repetition does not constitute the decision of the speaking subject as a redundancy. The gap between redundancy and repetition is the space of agency" (Butler 1997, 129). Individual persons speak and think in the language spoken by the people around them, and as such they cannot but be conditioned and constrained by the linguistic conventions such as the vocabulary and grammar of the language. At the same time, however, an individual's use of the language also adds to, or unsettles, the sedimentation of the linguistic conventions. Individual persons can cite the linguistic conventions in the same way that other people have done, or they can exercise their volition to break away from conventional usages and start new usages that may eventually become new conventions. For example, just a few decades ago it was the norm in the English language that masculine nouns and pronouns were used to refer to all of humanity. The use of the masculine generic reflected male dominance in society and the continued use of it further reinforced and naturalized androcentrism. If the word *man* stands for *human,* then *man* also defines *human*—that is, the proper *human* is really *man.* When more and more people volitionally use gender-inclusive nouns and pronouns, the convention gradually changes and the use of the masculine generic is less accepted than it was before. The same holds true with other forms of gender norms. "To the extent that gender norms are *reproduced,* they are invoked and cited by bodily practices that also have the capacity to alter norms in the course of their citation" (Butler 2004, 52). Individuals can reinforce what has been normalized and perpetuate what has been naturalized, or they can exercise their volition to alter the sociocultural conventions. The effect of one alternative action is perhaps not discernible, in the same way that a newly coined word or a new usage of an existing word will not necessarily be adopted by others, but the existing sociocultural conventions will change when more people repeatedly take the alternative action and adopt the new word or the new usage. For example, *text* used to be a noun, but it has become a verb with more and more people using the word to refer to the act of sending a short message on mobile phones.

In the analysis of the five aggregates, volition is part of *saṇkhāra.* Like the rest of the five aggregates, *saṇkhāra* is conditioned and confined by the external sense bases that are the material and sociocultural forms. That is, it does not have an eternal Self that is above life experience, either. *Saṇkhāra* refers to the *constructed* and the *constructing,* but it does not refer to any independently existing *constructor.* As part of *saṇkhāra,* volition is constructed and also constructs. It is the most important factor in generating kamma, but it is still influenced by the surrounding material and symbolic forces. Therefore, even though the Buddha's teaching of kamma was nondeterministic and the Buddha put much emphasis on the exercise of volition, "free will" in Buddhism is still conditioned and thus only relatively "free" (Rāhula 1974, 54).

Kamma is volitional actions, volition is conditioned by the sociocultural *rūpa*, and the sociocultural *rūpa* is sedimented through people's repeated actions. That is to say, a person's kamma, as volitional actions, is influenced by others' actions and not purely one's own. Kamma is thus not a "single-channel, closed circuit course" as some would suggest (for example, King 1994, 35). In the *Samyutta Nikāya*, the Buddha said to his disciple Kassapa,

> Kassapa, [if one thinks,] "The one who acts is the same as the one who experiences [the result,]" [then one asserts] with reference to one existing from the beginning: "Suffering is created by oneself." When one asserts thus, this amounts to eternalism. But, Kassapa, [if one thinks,] "The one who acts is one, the one who experiences [the result] is another," [then one asserts] with reference to one stricken by feeling: "Suffering is created by another." When one asserts thus, this amounts to annihilationism. Without veering towards either of these extremes, the Tathāgata teaches the Dhamma by the middle.
>
> (*SN* II.20)

Suffering is created neither completely by oneself nor completely by others. A person is conditioned by the surrounding *rūpa*, and *rūpa* includes the sociocultural conventions that have been constructed and maintained by the actions of all people up to the present moment. Therefore, a person is not *fully* responsible for her suffering. At the same time, a person's actions can reinforce existing *rūpa* or create new *rūpa*, which will condition all other people embedded in it. Therefore, a person is not *only* responsible for his own suffering, but is to some extent responsible for other people's suffering too. The teachings of no-Self, five aggregates, and kamma as volitional actions, viewed together, point to the social facts that we are influenced by one another and that our actions have impacts on one another. To say that one is *fully* or *only* responsible for one's suffering is to presume complete autonomy, as if we had a Self that could exist above the influence of our sociocultural *rūpa*. Saying that one is neither *fully* nor *only* responsible for one's suffering, however, is not the same as saying that suffering is created completely by others and one is merely a victim and has no responsibility. To say so would be to annihilate the ethical accountability of individuals. The Buddha refuted both eternalism and annihilationism, which are called "pernicious views" in the Nikāya texts (*SN* III.109), since these views deny the validity of ethics (*MN* i.402, i.515–18).

Buddhists generally refer to the *Buddhadhamma* as the "Middle Way," for the Buddha taught the middle way between indulgence and asceticism, and the middle way between eternalism and annihilationism. Kalupahana points out that it is also the middle way between determinism and "free will," for it puts moral responsibility neither entirely on society nor entirely on each individual. Considering that people are conditioned by the sociocultural *rūpa*, which are sedimented through people's repeated actions, society is partially responsible for what may appear to be individual failings and crimes. Buddhist scholar David Loy comments, "there is the uncomfortable possibility that offenders today have become our scapegoats for larger social problems" (Loy 2003, 121). Similarly, Butler considers the culpable subject to be retrospectively "resurrected" in order to meet the legal demand of accountability (Butler 1997, 78–80).

Some scholars attribute the "invention" of the social dimension of kamma to the Mahāyāna philosopher Nāgārjuna (King 1994, 36). Others attribute it to the influence of Protestant Christian values or even to Western Buddhists. However, the historical Buddha himself already specifically refuted the understanding of kamma as a retributive mechanism in which each individual is fully and only responsible for her own suffering. Viewed together with the teaching of no-Self and the analysis of the five aggregates, kamma as volitional actions necessarily has a social dimension. The concept of social kamma is neither a Mahāyāna invention nor a Western import. Rather, it is rooted in early Buddhist teachings. Admittedly, the Buddha taught his disciples to watch, and take responsibility for, their volitional actions, and it is true that the following can be read as suggestive of a retributive mechanism:

> The killer begets a killer,
> One who conquers, a conqueror.

> The abuser begets abuse,
> The reviler, one who reviles.
> Thus by the unfolding of kamma
> The plunderer is plundered.
> (SN I.85)

However, the phrase "The abuser begets abuse" does not necessarily suggest that the abuser himself will be the very next receiver of abuse. Instead, with the aid of Butler's analyses of performatives and sedimentation, the phrase can be understood to mean that, with every abusive behavior, the abuser changes the configuration of the sociocultural *rūpa* a little and makes abusive behavior slightly more acceptable in the sociocultural context. And abusive behavior gets more and more acceptable with every person who initiates abuses or imitates abusers. The same holds true for all other forms of violence, domination, and discrimination. It is "by the *unfolding* of kamma," that is, by the ripple effect of people's actions, that "the plunderer is plundered."

People are connected with one another's feelings and thoughts not just through the suggestive power of sympathy (Boonyoros 1994, 173). Rather, others' feelings and thoughts can be the constituents of the feelings and thoughts of the self in a very real way: others' feelings and thoughts eventually manifest in actions, and actions can get sedimented and become sociocultural norms that function as the "external sense bases" of one's self. The feelings and thoughts of the self, likewise, will manifest in actions and become the constituents of the feelings and thoughts of others. In this line of analysis, people's deeds, words, and thoughts are constitutive of one another and are coconstructing one another at every present moment.

Coconstitution and Coresponsibility
Through Volitional Actions

The Buddha understood any individual "self" to be the composite of the five aggregates, which include the existing material and symbolic forces. There is therefore no eternal, unchanging Self, but only ever-changing "selves" that are socially constructed, conditioned, and constrained, though not predetermined. At the same time, each kamma, each volitional action, has the effect of constructing, conditioning, and constraining all others embedded in the same sociocultural context. People's repeated actions get sedimented and become material and symbolic forms. If most people repeatedly conform to the sociocultural conventions, such as gender roles, then conventions will increasingly seem "normal" and "natural," which will further condition people embedded in the same cultural context. If some people repeatedly take actions that do not quite conform to the sociocultural norms, then those alternative actions will become more and more acceptable. With our actions, we make and remake the world, with ourselves in it. Along this line, Peter D. Hershock comments, "In combination, the teaching of karma and no-self direct us to see ourselves—and so what is happening in our worlds—as an ever-dynamic expression of dramatic interdependence. In such worlds, causation is not a linear process, but a coalescent one. It is not that our intentions literally influence the world, but rather that they are an occasion for revised confluence or 'flowing together' with it" (Hershock 2000, 93–94). The Buddha's teaching on kamma reflected his understanding of the fundamental sociality of human existence—we are under the influence of each other's actions and thus "quite literally, part of each other—free neither from indebtedness to our fellow-beings nor responsibility for them" (Macy 1991, 194). A person only becomes a person in the midst of all the material and symbolic forces that constitute her culture and thus is indebted to all those who have preceded her and contributed to the sedimentation of the culture. And a person helps consolidate or unsettle existing sociocultural sediments with every action and thus is responsible for others embedded in the same culture.

Viewed together, the Buddha's teaching of no-Self and his teaching on kamma as volitional actions can be morally demanding and surprisingly empowering at the same time. They can be morally demanding because, seeing the unavoidable ripple effects of one's actions, a person has to be ever watchful of every bodily, verbal, and mental action that he is about to take. No-Self and kamma can also be surprisingly empowering because no one and no action is completely determined by previous events; there is always possibility of change—one does not have to exist in a certain socially sanctioned way for eternity. A person can always exercise her volition to the effect of taking actions to remake herself as well as to reconfigure the existing sociocultural *rūpa* (provided that many other people can be motivated to repeat those alternative actions for a sustained period of time). Kathleen H. Dockett, a community psychologist, finds that the understanding of kamma as an ongoing process is enough to empower people to find the "locus of control" within themselves and to motivate them to make changes (Dockett 2003, 178–79). No matter what may have been sedimented up to this point, it is always possible for one to break away from sociocultural conventions and start taking an alternative kind of action that, through repetition, will change one's mode of existence and even existing sociocultural norms.

With regard to gender stereotypes and socially prescribed gender roles, the teachings of no-Self and kamma together can enable a woman to see, for example, that it is not her inherent nature or her permanent "Self" to be treated as a mere appendage to men. Neither is it the inherent nature or permanent "Self" of the whole society to demand the subordination of women. Socially prescribed gender roles only seem "natural" because, generation after generation, women and men have been socialized to perform those roles and in turn demand that one another and younger generations conform to the same social expectations. What has been performed collectively and continuously takes the semblance of the permanent "Self" of things, and so it seems "natural" for women to act subservient and for men to seek dominance.

The concept of kamma as volitional actions at every present moment, however, empowers and urges people to examine the *dukkha*-producing sociocultural norms and change them for the well-being of everyone embedded in the sociocultural context instead of passively allowing the past to determine the present and even the future. Women and men can exercise their volition to perform different kinds of actions that are wholesome and beneficial to the holistic development of both sexes. Rather than conforming to and perpetuating the socially prescribed female gender role of pleasing men by yielding to their authority and by beautifying themselves, women can exercise their volition and break away from the gender binary that expects them to be dependent and vain. Likewise, men can exercise their volition so that they do not perform the socially prescribed role of aggressors who constantly seek to dominate over others, even if that means resorting to violence. By exercising their volition in such ways, women and men can liberate themselves from the gender binary that has reduced them to one half of a whole person and limited their possibilities. By taking an alternative kind of volitional action, women and men can also make nonbinary gender expressions more acceptable, thus reconfiguring the meaning of masculinity and femininity. The arising of "Mr. Mom," the father who takes care of children in the same way that a traditional mother would, is an example of the changeability of gender roles and the benefit of breaking away from a gender binary. Mr. Mom connects with his own children better and lightens the burden on the mother who, in today's world, is likely to have a full-time job. By sharing the role of the caretaker in the family, Mr. Mom contributes to the well-being of the whole family and sidesteps the *dukkha* that is likely to be produced under the gender binary, such as the children feeling neglected by the father, the mother feeling burned out by full-time work and full-time caregiving, with he himself feeling disconnected from his wife and children.

Herbert Guenther observes that, in the "interlocking system" of Buddhism, "it is he who as 'causal agent' creates his world which, in turn, is a 'causal agent' creating him" (Guenther 1972, 75–76). The rationale behind the teaching of no-Self, paradoxically, is the very same rationale behind the Buddhist teaching of ethical *self*-discipline. No one lives without taking actions, and the actions one takes will inevitably deposit something to the sociocultural contexts and thus condition all people embedded in them, one's "self" included. As the feminist slogan puts it, the personal is political—people's "personal" feelings, thoughts, and actions will have ramifications on the political level. And given that a person only becomes a person in the midst of material and sociocultural forms, being informed and influenced by them, what exists on the sociopolitical level will eventually become personal, too. We are not completely determined by our past actions, we are not completely determined by others' actions up to the present moment, and yet we are not completely self-determined, either. Through our actions, we can perpetuate the sociocultural conventions that generate *dukkha* or we can change ourselves and our world through exercising our volition to choose the most wholesome actions possible. The ever-changing individual "selves" have moral agency and social responsibilities because, with our volitional actions, we coconstruct our world and cocondition everyone in it. We collectively reap what we sow.

Notes

1. For the dating of the historical Buddha, see Prebish (2008, 1–21).

2. By "classical" Buddhism, I am referring to the Buddha's teachings as recorded in the Nikāya texts, the earliest extant Buddhist literature. Later Buddhist texts may or may not reflect the same understanding.

3. *Dhamma* (Sanskrit: *dharma*) is a multivalent word in both Hindu traditions and Buddhist traditions. Rooted in the verb *dhṛ*, meaning to support or to sustain, the word *dhamma* refers to the universal law or natural order underlying the operation of the cosmos in the physical sense as well as the moral sense. In the Hindu traditions it is popularly translated to mean religious-social duty, but can also mean the customary observance of a caste or sect, usage of law, righteousness, justice, norm, morality, virtue, religious or moral merit, piety, religion, sacrifice, and so on. In the Buddhist contexts, the word *dhamma* can denote the totality of the Buddha's teachings, the Buddhist Path as a whole, any specific Buddhist principle, or any individual element or phenomenon that constitutes the empirical world and existence, such as a physical object, an activity, a condition of life, a mental object, a psychological process, and a character trait. In the Mahāyānist usage, the word also designates the reality of Buddhahood (Keown 2003, 74; Smith and Green 1995, 315–16).

4. The *samhitā* and *brahmaṇas* portions of the Vedas were composed around 1500 to 1000 BCE and 1100 to 700 BCE, respectively (Van Voorst 2007, 24–25).

5. The Upaniṣads date as early as the eighth century BCE and as late as the fifth century BCE (Smith and Green 1995, 1110; Van Voorst 2007, 24–25).

6. Mahāvīra, the twenty-fourth "ford builder" in the Jaina tradition, was an older contemporary of the historical Buddha (Smith and Green 1995, 544).

7. *MN* stands for *Majjhima Nikāya*. All quotes from *MN* in this chapter are taken from Ñāṇamoli and Bodhi (2001).

8. *AN* stands for *Aṅguttara Nikāya*. All quotes from *AN* in this chapter are taken from Bodhi (2012).

9. *SN* stands for *Samyutta Nikāya*. All quotes from *SN* in this chapter are taken from Bodhi (2000b).

10. For Jainas who voluntarily took on extreme ascetic practices, the deterministic understanding of kamma would further cause a difficulty: "If the pleasure and pain that beings feel are caused by what was done in the past, then the Niganthas [i.e. Jainas] surely must have done bad deeds in the past, since they now feel such painful, racking, piercing feelings" (*MN* ii.222; see also i.93).

11. The words *external* and *internal* here obviously do not indicate absolute demarcation, for they are expediently used only to explain the function of senses,

which only occur when the "external sense bases" and the "internal sense bases" are in contact or, in Gier and Kjellberg's words, when "the inner flows into the outer and the outer flows into the inner" (Gier and Kjellberg 2004, 282).

12. See Butler (1997, 139), and also Jakobsen (1998, 3).

References

Bodhi, Bhikkhu, ed. 2000a. *A comprehensive manual of Abhidhamma: Pāli text, translation, and explanatory guide of the Abhidhammattha Sangaha of Ācariya Anuruddha.* Onalaska: Pariyatti.

——, trans. 2000b. *The connected discourses of the Buddha: A translation of the Samyutta Nikāya.* Boston: Wisdom.

——, trans. 2012. *The numerical discourses of the Buddha: A translation of the Aṅguttara Nikāya.* Boston: Wisdom.

Boonyoros, Roongraung. 1994. Householders and the five precepts. In *Buddhist behavioral codes and the modern world: An international symposium*, ed. Charles Wei-hsün Fu and Sandra A. Wawrytko, 171–78. Westport, CT: Greenwood.

Butler, Judith. 1997. *Excitable speech: A politics of the performative.* New York: Routledge.

——. 1999. *Gender trouble: Feminism and the subversion of identity.* 10th anniversary ed. New York: Routledge.

——. 2004. *Undoing gender.* New York: Routledge.

Dockett, Kathleen H. 2003. Buddhist empowerment: Individual, organizational, and societal transformation. In *Psychology and Buddhism: From individual to global community*, ed. Kathleen H. Dockett, G. Rita Dudley-Grant, and C. Peter Bankart, 173–96. New York: Kluwer Academic/Plenum.

Egge, James R. 2002. *Religious giving and the invention of karma in Theravāda Buddhism.* Richmond: Curzon.

Gier, Nicholas F., and Paul Kjellberg. 2004. Buddhism and the freedom of the will: Pali and Mahayanist responses. In *Freedom and determinism*, ed. Joseph Keim Campbell, Michael O'Rourke, and David Shier, 277–304. Cambridge: MIT Press.

Gómez, Luis O. 1975. Some aspects of the free-will question in the Nikāyas. *Philosophy East and West* 25 (1): 81–90.

Gross, Rita M. 2001. What Buddhists could learn from Christians. In *Religious feminism and the future of the planet: A Christian-Buddhist conversation*, by Rita M. Gross and Rosemary Radford Ruether, 163–182. New York: Continuum.

Guenther, Herbert. 1972. *Buddhist philosophy in theory and practice.* Baltimore: Penguin.

Harvey, Peter. 1990. *An introduction to Buddhism: Teachings, history, and practices.* Cambridge: Cambridge University Press.

Hershock, Peter D. 2000. Family matters: Dramatic interdependence and the intimate realization of Buddhist liberation. *Journal of Buddhist Ethics* 7: 86–104.

Jakobsen, Janet R. 1998. *Working alliances and the politics of difference*. Bloomington: Indiana University Press.

Kalupahana, David J. 1976. *Buddhist philosophy: A historical analysis*. Honolulu: University of Hawaii Press.

———. 1987. *The principles of Buddhist psychology*. Albany: State University of New York Press.

———. 1995. *Ethics in early Buddhism*. Honolulu: University of Hawaii Press.

Keown, Damien, ed. 2003. *A dictionary of Buddhism*. New York: Oxford University Press.

Khuankaew, Ouyporn. 2007. Buddhism and violence against women. In *Violence against women in contemporary world religion: Roots and cures*, ed. Daniel C. Maguire and Sa'diyya Shaikh, 174–91. Cleveland: Pilgrim.

King, Winston L. 1994. A Buddhist ethic without karmic rebirth? *Journal of Buddhist Ethics* 1: 33–44.

Loy, David R. 2003. *The great awakening: A Buddhist social theory*. Boston: Wisdom.

Macy, Joanna. 1991. *Mutual causality in Buddhism and general systems theory: The dharma of natural systems*. Albany: State University of New York Press.

Ñāṇamoli, Bhikkhu, and Bhikkhu Bodhi, trans. 2001. *The Middle Length Discourses of the Buddha: A translation of the Majjhima Nikāya*. 2d ed. Boston: Wisdom.

Obeyesekere, Gananath. 2002. *Imagining karma: Ethical transformation in Amerindian, Buddhist, and Greek rebirth*. Berkeley: University of California Press.

Prebish, Charles S. 2008. Cooking the Buddhist books: The implications of the new dating of the Buddha for the history of early Indian Buddhism. *Journal of Buddhist Ethics* 15: 1–21.

Rāhula, Walpola. 1974. *What the Buddha taught*. Rev. ed. New York: Grove.

Robinson, Richard H., Willard L. Johnson, and Thanissaro Bhikkhu. 2005. *Buddhist religions: A historical introduction*. 5th ed. Belmont, CA: Wadsworth/Thomson Learning.

Smith, Jonathan Z., and William Scott Green, eds. 1995. *The HarperCollins dictionary of religion*. New York: HarperCollins.

Van Voorst, Robert E., ed. 2007. *Anthology of world scriptures: Eastern religions*. Belmont, CA: Wadsworth/Thomson Learning.

Williams, Paul. 2000. *Buddhist thought: A complete introduction to the Indian tradition*. New York: Routledge.

CHAPTER TWO

On the Transformative Potential of the "Dark Female Animal" in *Daodejing*

KYOO LEE

谷神不死	The spirit of the valley does not pass away.
是謂玄牝	Called the dark womb,
玄牝之門	the gate of the dark womb,
是謂天地根	called the root of Heaven and Earth,
綿綿若存	continuously flowing, seemingly always there,
用之不勤	it is used but not to be used up.
道德經 6章	CHAPTER 6, *DAODEJING*

"AFTER WRITING about the reproductive system, Leonardo declares sarcastically: 'I expose to men the origin of their first, and perhaps second, reason for existing'" (White 2001, 384). This man has a sense of humor. That much seems surgically clear.

Now, deeper than that, shot through this serialized, modern anatomical vacuum is a sense of loss, distance—of and from the "origin" of beings, including and especially human animals. What follows dwells on that visual echo, that which seems to ultimately *matter* in being—the heart of darkness, *gushen* 谷神 (the spirit of the valley), from which beings are said to unfurl.

Indeed, *gu* 谷 (the valley) enjoys a special ontological status in the Daoist imagination. That is where beings are said to start flowing, flowering; that is where the water is, springs. What generates and animates all the flourishing movements in and of cosmic beings, the autocreative itinerary of *Dao* 道, is the spirit of the valley, part of *ziran* 自然 (nature) that is "self-so" (Moeller 2006, xii). *Gushen* is irreducibly material and materially fluid (*DDJ* 15, 28, 32, 66); it retains its shadowy character, which is instantly transmitted or transferable.[1] It is vast, empty, formless, elusively present, and yet not simply "pure" or "transparent," but rather inscriptively generative. Pitch purple, bloody, velvety, rosy, it is in "murky water" (*DDJ* 15). In an earthworm crawling out, one sees, hears, senses, the *gushen* of cosmos at work, unfolding, drawing itself out.

Enter the Dark Female Animal (*Xuanpin* 玄牝)

Witness a transformative movement in feminist phenomenology. What I am focusing on, in other words, is the sex of Dao rather than "the Dao of sex" (Moeller 2006, 21–32): what Dao sexually is rather than what Dao says about (having [a]) sex. The idea that Dao *itself* is or could be sexuated on some fundamental level, while not foreign to Daoism, has been rather curiously evaded by most of the mainstream Daoist scholars, Eastern and Western, who are mainly interested in the question of alternatively healthy sexual practices or gender norms seemingly promoted in Daoism. They range from the male Daoist acolytes in ancient China (Wagner 2000, 224–30; Raz 2008, 86–120) to subtler new kids on the block such as Hans-Georg Moeller who does "not think one can really understand Daoist philosophy without understanding the verses about the valley and the root" (Moeller 2006, viii; see also Kohn 2001, 16)—which is quite right, if only partly. The key issue I am about to highlight is that "the valley and the root" themselves—their literal values—have been metaphysically hijacked or hermeneutically obscured precisely by this analytical inversion or evasion, "the Dao of sex." The task I have set myself, in turn, is to turn it around, turning "back to the things themselves," to *xuanpin* inscriptively lodged in *gushen*, especially to their philo-poetical, vibrant materialities.

Drawing on the "paradoxical politics" (Moeller 2006, 55–57) of *Daodejing*, I seek to rediscover the powerful materiality (*de* 德, "matrix") of the ancient Daoist discourse of animality-natality-vitality. The immanent areality of this discourse remains something of a philosophical dark continent within not only world philosophy but a Chinese canon still dominated by ideologized "axiological" Confucianism that tends to downplay the Daoist tradition for being at best "apolitical" and at worst anarchistic since they tend to "distrust any man-made rules" (Zhao 2007, 162). But/so, "what Gilles Deleuze and Félix Guattari call a 'minor literature' is there, if only we know how to look" (Battersby 2006, 297). There is indeed something special about Daoist feminist philosophy as a material reserved for "a special issue," as admirably utilized, conceived, and realized by Karyn Lai (2000) just a decade ago, arguably for the first time in any systematic manner in the history of Anglophone academic reception and studies of Daoism.

The manifold, revolutionary potential of *xuanpin* is conceptually refreshing as well as gender-bending. And that is not despite but, as I will also highlight, because of "the law of *yin* and *yang*," which is not fixedly sexed or gendered in itself but functions more dynamically as the cosmological matrix of cogeneration that does appear, in *Daodejing*, primarily in the animal psyche (*qi* 氣) of the female. The maternal subject in *Daodejing*, as a key material embodiment of Dao, on which the following section focuses, is therefore not "the other" but ironically *the* norm, *albeit* hidden and constantly made majorly minor; to that end, I will incorporate into the rest of my account of *xuanpin* a critical analysis of heterosexualism and heterosexism mobilized in the mainstream Daoist scholarship.

And Ask: What, and Where, of *Xuanpin*?

This cobelonging provides, or functions as, a phenomenological access to the ontology of Dao, as chapter 1 of *Daodejing* concludes:

兩者同出異名	The two spring from the same named differently
同謂之玄	that same thing is called darkly obscure
玄之又玄	darkly obscure and more again
衆妙之門	the gate of manifold wonders. (*DDJ* 1)[2]

The idea in summary is as follows: 1. Dao is neither essentially nor basically female/feminine nor essentially male/masculine and 2. likewise, it is neither *yin* nor *yang* "in itself" but that which engenders such a structure of fluid complementarity. That given, a finer line of inquiry could and should be drawn this way: that co, the mysterious, immanently reciprocal networks and autogenerative workings of beings, *is* still sexuated in some specifically material terms, and it is to be found in "the female animal" that is "darkly obscure (*xuan*)." Why?

What is the dark female animal "quality," often metaphorically wholesaled and psycho-meta-physically abused *and yet* seemingly *mien mien*, "ongoing" (Moeller 2007, 17)? What is it that seems to go on existing, naturally or not, biologically or not, seemingly regardlessly? What could be the Chinese *femelle*, reserved for plants and animals, which "women and animal have in common" (Battersby 1998, 35), with which Simone de Beauvoir's *The Second Sex* (1952) opens? It is "the ontological status of the sexed body," and in particular the body sexed as female. "What is its 'stuff,' its matter? What of its form?" (Grosz 1994, 189).

Xuan: the "color of heaven or of the mountains seen from far away . . . the mysterious origin and development of the world," "profound and subtle," "obscure and silent," "absence of anything," "unspeakable," or "wondrous" (*miao* 妙) in the sense of "unfathomable . . . often paired with *xu* 虛 (void, emptiness)," "the mysterious conjunction of two complementary and opposite entities" (Pregadio 2007, 1126–27). Thus this image-concept or compound, *xuanpin*, that encapsulates the spirit and orientation of Dao, points to the source from which *wanwu* 萬物 (ten thousand things, all beings and modes of beings) originates. *Xuanpin* is the womb whose "power or virtue" too, by extension, is dark, *xuan* (*DDJ* 10), as well as intriguingly wonderful, *miao*, which is also graphically noted as female or feminine. *Daodejing* later extrapolates *gu* into the *tianxiagu* 天下谷, "the valley of all that is under the heaven" (*DDJ* 28) and *tianxiazipin* 天下之牝, "the womb of all that is under the heaven" or "the female of the world" (Pine 1996, 61). Then, we could say, *xuan* had been there in some significant sense before "the start" (*yuan* 元). *Yuan* is the origin or the original, in reference to and on the basis of which tradition and conventions are supposed to be formed and established. "Supposed to," I said, keeping this obvious ambiguity in mind. Chapter 1 of *Daodejing* designates Dao as the *wanwuzimu* 萬物之母, the "mother of ten thousand things" (*DDJ* 1, 20, 25, 32, 34), rather than—note the absence of—the father. As clearly noted by Wang Bi, the child prodigy–patriarch of Daoist commentators, Dao is first and foremost that which "engenders, the mother of efficacy" (Jullien and Hawkes 2000, 283, citing Wang Bi).

Such an analytically bifurcated reading that discloses, first, the material-sexual specificity and subjectivity of *xuanpin* and, second, its ontopolitical primacy and zoological productivity, helps one see better, in part, how and why "it," "the real," has been studiously avoided or surreptitiously alluded to by most of the subsequent *junzis* 君子 ("exemplary scholar gentlemen"). The foundational golden boy Wang Bi was, in fact, a scholar of so-called *xuanxue* 玄學 (dark/obscure learning) (Wagner 2000, 1; Pregadio 2007, 1126–27): "As its meaning is close to *yuan* (Origin), it has been substituted by the latter when the character *xuan* was tabooed, as in Wang Bi's commentary to the *Daodejing* and in texts dating from almost the entire span of the Qing dynasty" (Pregadio 2007, 1126–27).

Is it purely accidental that *yuan* is the current Chinese currency? Further along, is it not curious that "tradition" comes from *tradere* (to trade, translate, transmit, etc)? What kind of coincidentality is at stake? What kind of transaction of significations exploits and precludes the flow of blood, and which kind of blood money? The material *and* rhetorical circulation and abjection of *xuan*, the dark blood of the world including the menstrual "wastes," has historically been and is still being metasemantically economized this way, in such a clearly, metaphysically, disguised form. The following analyzes such a move— the cover—a move that "covers" the material.

While Questioning the Genealogized Generalization of *Xuanpin*

Unsurprisingly, and yet furtively still, *xuanpin* has been generating two very different interpretative responses and translations throughout the history of Daoist scholarship, Eastern and Western. *Xuan* has been either loosely elevated to "subtle, profound and mysterious" (Lin 1948, 64; Lau 1963, 10; Wang 1998, 39) or else brought "down to earth" to "dark, obscure and primal" (Feng and English 1972, 8; Pine 1996, 12; Wagner 2000, 230). In parallel, *pin* is rendered relatively simply as "the woman/feminine/mother" or "female/animal." The traditional Chinese line of reading, further taken up by more recent Anglophone Daoist scholars attuned to the intricate and contextual nuances of the text, tends to lean toward the second set of options, which I, too, follow, as must be already clear. From there, however, interpretative directions vary.

Some interpreters, mostly pedestrian readers and translators, genealogize *xuanpin* by anchoring it as "the primal mother" (Feng and

English 1972, 8); the biological ("sex") and/or sociocultural ("gender") senses of the phrase are deployed often con-fusedly. On this reading, *xuan* functions as the primary sign of the natural caregiver, that is, one who "by nature" cares. On this level, *xuan* is regarded as both a biological given and biologically determined gender traits.

On a more advanced level, metaphysically nuanced minds general- ize *xuanpin* into the "dark female" (Ames and Hall 2003, 85) or "dark femininity" (Moeller 2007, 17). These are mostly scholars coming primarily from the hermeneutical tradition of Wang Bi, directly or wirelessly, who tend to turn the perceived generic traits of *xuanpin* into a quasi-divine quality as in "the mystical female" (Chen 1999, 13; Wang 2003, 67) or "mysterious female" (Lynn 1999, 62). For some commentators the materiality of "the female" should be put under erasure as much as possible in favor of the pure pleasures of abstrac- tion. For other extremely subtle interpreters, *xuanpin* is "*never* sup- posed to referentialize female-centrism but rather to deconstruct any attempts at semantic unification or centralization. Asked what the space of female emptiness is, we can give no answer" (H. Kim 1999, 110, emphasis added).

At this point, a question arises: in such an intricate, self-canceling interplay or display of meanings, does one not stress or end up stress- ing the "vagina" *or* "emptiness" one way or the other? That is to ask: if "we *cannot but* draw an analogy between the female/feminine and emptiness" (H. Kim 1999, 10, emphasis added), why not attend to, or what to do with, that very *constitutive* metaphoricity or material rhetoricity of Dao? Why usurp—utilize *and then* downplay—the mate- rial specificity of *xuan* and just (try to) forget about it? Why draw on the figure of the vagina and feel suddenly threatened by it and so drive it away as far and "naturally" as possible? Metaphysics, why throw it away? Mainstream Daoism still has yet to come face to face with its "X," or "ex-," that is, its natural history, including its materiality.

In fact, however, it is this metaphysically abstracted and sophis- ticated Daoism that paves a way for the nonmainstream empower- ment and diversification of Daoism, including the feminist rendering of it. It is the very series or process of transferral transvaluation—the figurative codification, codified neutralization, neutralized play and playful reevaluation including reversal—of Dao as female/maternal/ feminine *and* as watery, flowy, billowy, that enables and allows inner revolutions and metamorphoses. Typically, dual textual or intertextual movements within Daoist discourse take place that way. Robin Wang's succinct account of *xuanpin* represents such a standard move:

> From the perspective of the *Daodejing*, women are not excluded, shunned, frozen out, disadvantaged, rejected, unwanted, abandoned, dislocated, or otherwise marginalized. Instead, their basic identity, as complementary and necessary to men, is recognized as embodying the Secret of Life. *Yin* (female) and *yang* (male) embrace each other and blend into a state of harmonious balance. If any name can be given to the Dao in all things, it is "Mother." The "Door of the Mystic Female" (*Xuanpinzimen*) is "the root of Heaven and Earth." Just as "the softest substance of the world goes through the hardest" and "that-which-is-without-form penetrates that-which-has-no-crevice," so "the Female overcomes the Male by quietude and achieves the lowly position by quietude." Success in human affairs depends upon taking no action (*wuwei*), as in the lowly position.
>
> (WANG 2003, 67)

With Wang above, one would readily recognize why and how women in *Daodejing*, otherwise situated "in the lowly position," receive comparatively better treatments; imagine Aristotle trying to read *Daodejing*!—let alone Confucius. I also agree that *xuanpin* as a figure of Dao can also be mobilized rhetorically, politically, ideologically, ontologico-philo-poetically even, as I am trying to do, with and against the Confucian patriarch. That is, *xuanpin* demonstrates inscriptively and performatively the categorical priority or primordiality, and even, in a sense, superiority, of femaleness and femininity—as *the* norm, albeit invisible and inaudible.

What I would question directly, however, is the very notion of complementarity deployed as such, which is the standard analytic framework for this putatively positive evaluation and extraordinary elevation of the woman in Daoism. I see this interpretative move, almost an axiomatically formulaic rhetorical maneuver in Daoist scholarship, as illusorily compensatory. Let me demonstrate this (as an) issue by using this existing, very useful, historical table of "the five roles or images" of the Daoist female/female/woman:

1. the female as the mother goddess, the life-giver and nurturing power of the universe
2. women as representative of the *cosmic* force of yin, *complementary* to the male or yang, reflecting both the *universal* presence of yin and its expression in sexuality and fertility
3. women as divine teachers and bestowers of esoteric revelations
4. women as possessors of supernatural connections
5. the female body as the seat of essential ingredients and processes of spiritual transformation (Despeux and Kohn 2003, 6–7, emphasis added)

Focus on (2), the most pertinent and interestingly con-fused; the middle part (2–4) points to the post-Laozi construction of the gender values or imaginaries, sandwiched between the first (1) and the last (5) where animality and spirituality intersect, coexisting; in this fluid spectrum of immanence (1) becoming transcendent, and transcendence (5) becoming immanent, what remains relatively fixed are the gender role and attributes of *yin* as "female."

Then, back to (2): the question is how (come) *yin* is both universal and feminine/female: How does it become, at once, both universal and not? Where does the ontological *a*symmetry between universal femaleness-femininity and particular maleness-masculinity originate?—given that *yang* can perhaps never be or become universal either. How can one harmonize it with the narrative imperative of egalitarian and fluid Daoism, where the two are supposed to originate *together*, ontologically—to cooperate, to be com-posed? In other words, Dao, *positionally* figured as the female animal sexual organs that produce living beings, is that which grounds and engenders such gendered worldviews; remaining unresolved is the issue of how to think and live through this seemingly ontological, "well-grounded" contradiction, namely, that the Daoist mother, birthing or nurturing, is pre-meta-sexual *and* sexed F. This mother is "pre-meta-sexual" in the sense in which one says an infant (*ying-er* 嬰兒) precedes or transcends sexuality, not temporally but conceptually.

Daoist tropes too then, when deployed in ways that are *oppositionally* complementary rather than profoundly self-complementary, are not radically different from their "dialectical" or dualistic counterparts. They too illustrate this now widely recognized philosophical thesis that the oppositional mode or mold of thinking—the formal-dialectical symmetry in and of historical logos or Dao, Western and Eastern alike in that regard—is gendered or gender differentiated.

By arbitrarily, mindlessly, and habitually assigning, pairing, fixing, and keeping *yin* and *yang* as female-feminine and male-masculine in the name of *ziran* (self-so), do we not in fact turn a blind eye to this more primordial, dynamic, ontological (dis)order of generation, namely, that *yin* in itself *is* cosmic-universal and rather *becomes* female-feminine? That is to ask: what is this "conceptual ruse,"[3] this prearranged pairing, this compulsive comparing, theoretically deployed and maintained as such throughout intellectual histories and cultural practices? Is it an inversion of the Aristotelian-Freudian male-or-hetero-normativity of the fleshed soul? Is it the femme fatale inverted? Whence and whither is this primary/secondary (dis)order of generation? Then, instead of, or in addition to, continuing to "blend *yin* and *yang* harmoniously," why not try and inject some fresh, universal blood into the very discourse of the Daoist Mother Earth? Why not reregister, reanimate, its creative and generative potentials? Is it not about time that the global Daoist Mother, kissed or not, paired up or not, woke up from her ancient slumber, even if that slumber were reportedly already metaphysical, and the opinions there already mysteriously profound? That is to ask: how else, or differently, can sedimented Daoism be delocalized and relocated from its own traditions and laws of transactions (*tradere*), rhetorical, cultural, practical, worldly, etc.?

In that regard, Moeller on "the Dao of sex"—the formulation mentioned earlier, which I have come to see as a position between the metaphysical reading I have questioned and a more materially oriented deconstructive reading to be explored further on—seems to advance the most astute, up-to-date response (Moeller 2007, 8–11) to the question at stake: what should we do with the sex or sexed signs of the metaphysical Dao? The solution Moeller offers is to accentuate cyclic fertility and fluidity as the prime sign of "dark femininity" within the cosmological metaphysics of Daoism. And it is, still, a (kind of party) line that repeats precisely the kind of problem highlighted above. How so? First, Moeller's casual, repeated use of the concept "femininity" in place of femaleness—except, curiously, in the one-paragraph comment on chapter 6 he himself translated[4] would seem a residual sign of metaphysical avoidance of or confusion over the material, the conceptual matter, something to do with the root or heart of *femelle*,

Chinese or otherwise. Quite simply, how can "femininity" be a condition for the possibility of pregnancy or female fertility? The conceptual muddle there, not his own but our very own, is telling. Besides, again quite simply, we are entering into an epochal phase where male pregnancy is perfectly "conceivable" too; the female sexual organs too are technically detachable, although its materiality and maternal areality (area-l; a-real) is irreducible. Second, also noteworthy is Moeller's privileging of reproductive fertility and heterosexuality as the Daoist norm or telos of sex: must Dao that is "capable of becoming or being the mother" (*DDJ* 25, 28) originate from a sexualized order of beings too? On the contrary, it is almost presexuated, always potential: it is "a thing confusedly formed/born before heaven and earth/ silent and void/ . . . capable of being the mother of the world" (*DDJ* 25). To wit, the Daoist mother of all things is, on Moeller's reading too, to a certain extent, transformatively immanent.

Think Animality: The Fertile Metaphorics of the Sex of Dao

So here I am seeking to *animalize or animate xuan* into a "dark womb" (Pine 1996, 12) instead of mystifying, humanizing, or sexualizing it in bipedal terms. I am trying to bring it further "down to earth" as it were, while elevating the level of ontometaphysical respect it should command among us rational animals. Making such an analytically diminutive and materially reinscriptive move from within metaphysical Daoism constitutes something close to "a counter-path (*contre-allée*)" or a "counterdrift (*contre-dérive*)" (Malabou and Derrida 2004, 40), characterizable in this context as transformatively feminist and phenomenologically feminist. So the very last stream of reading followed, we have reached and now are again facing the "dark female animal" (Chen 1974, 51; Wagner 2000, 209–19) as promised, repeatedly; from the "dark female animal," an interpretative phrase attributed to Wang Bi himself—through a translation, a transformative interpretation.

In brief, *xuanpin* marks the sex of Dao. *Xuanpin* inscriptively shows "it," rather ob-scenely, in-differently, beyond what can (not) be seen, what must (not) be seen. The sex of Dao, marked female, is (pro)creative; reproductive. Note this time, with and against Wang Bi, the genital or organic clarity of *xuanpin* as *wanwuzimu* 萬物之母, the mother of all things. Dao is not characterized as, say, the father-creator of ten thousand things or all things under the heaven or the bright testicles from which all things spring or emanate. In fact, "heaven" itself also appears in the form and color of *xuanhuang* 玄黃 (dark or mysterious yellow). Last but not least, let us recall, *xuanpin*, a root rather than a roof of Dao, appears early in the text, in the sixth out of the eighty-one chapters, and all the chapters just "flow" (Moeller 2007) together in the direction of a *xuanmen* 玄門 (dark gate), "a name of Daoism itself" (Pregadio 2007, 1127) as if fertilizing *and* bypassing the visible Dao. Such multiple (*parenthetical and infinitesimal*) layers and dimensions of fertility, of awesome but also monstrous life-giving-and-taking powers, are not just arboreally biological but areally all-inclusive. Such is the animality of *xuanpin* and by extension Dao.

Think Natality: The Sovereign Triangle of Birthing

Take images of birth: almost nothing becoming something, merely something coming into being.

Dao, which famously "cannot be named but names itself" through "constant" autogenerative "activity" (*DDJ* 1) including inactivity (*wu-wei*), is elementally polymorphous and plural; it is one (like the waters) or even nothing (like air) or else countless (like dust), but not strictly two (as in a couple) or synthetically three (as in the dialecticized nuclear family); it is one and can become many ones, but not composed of just two or three. Daoism does not necessarily view the universal origin of heaven and earth (*tiandi* 天地, inclusive of the sky and the land) as strictly two, dually gendered or heterosexualized as such. To recall, the origin is the door, the mother, the female dark animal. On that level, the usual überpairs of cosmosexological ontology, namely, male/female, masculine/feminine, phallic/vaginal, do not apply here. A *xuanpin* lodged in *gushen*, as a living metaphor of Dao, embodies certain moments in time, where time itself seems to break open, up, or loose ... furtively, however, seamlessly even, without any traces of dialectical progression or sublimation. It is the horizontal or horizonal moment of transition: thresholding, one to zero and zero to one, back and forth: living and dying at once, not life and death nominally consolidated, rigorously demarcated, as such.

Dao is fluidity itself, material fluidity, the "the philosophy of yielding" (Wang 2003, 67) at work; it exemplifies powerful "softness" (*rou* 柔). Yet to readily and banally sexualize such qualities or attributes in anthropodramatic terms would be to prematurely limit or even distort its powers. For instance, the philosophy of yielding is not the same as a philosophy of "moist warmth," as in *xuanpin* being "constantly moist and warm, soft to the touch, hidden between two legs, shy about its looks" (Y. Kim 1999, 261), as one popular and prominent Korean philosopher puts it in his televised public lecture, seemingly forgetting or advertising his own moist warmth. Is he saying that a frigid—dry/cold—or infertile or unused *xuanpin* is not a constant *xuanpin*? On the contrary: *xuanpin* does not seem to care whether it is dry or wet. It simply is and vibrates, materially, like the center of all triangles wherein its powerful softness resides and manifests.

Having demoisturized the heterosexualized and heterosexist readings of the Daoist female or Daoist femininity, I would now like to replenish this section by introducing the case of the triangular sexual code, Δ, primally geometricized as such, which, curiously enough, remains lodged in the figure of the Chinese crown (*di* 帝, Xiao 1994, 11). This ideocryptogram, inscribed in and as the *gushen* of *Daodejing*, reappears "silently (or implicitly)" (11) in the very idea of the sovereign or supreme being (*shangdi* 上帝) neatly "capped" thusly. The triangular image of flow, which, when turned clockwise ninety degrees or one hundred degrees, becomes a universal, "statutory" (34) phallic symbol across cultures and histories, resonates back with what *xuanpin* makes abundantly, genitally, clear: the dark valley, the originary location of the world.

All of that, all this textual esotericism, has been largely unworthy of the perhaps otherwise fetishistic *junzi*, as Bing Xiao slyly points that out in the four-volume *Daoist Cultural Anthropology*, the third of which concerns Daoism and sex/sexuality (11, 466). What Xiao shows richly in this text of "painful imaginations" (8), particularly in the third volume that reads the vaginal, rather than virginal, code of *Daodejing* from quite a kaleidoscopic—aesthetical, anthropological, archaeological, cultural historical, ethnographical, mythological, philosophical, sexological, sociopsychological—lens, is that there *are* intertextual links between images of fertility cults found in various ancient cultures and this timeless, philosophical work of concept cast in the Chinese language. Xiao's thesis regarding the animistic and shamanistic worshipping of female reproductive capacity (*mu* 母) and the mother-earth (*dadimuqin* 大地母親, affinity with the continental mother), further cultivated through the agricultural or horticultural ages of the world, is nothing new in itself. His contribution is rather in seeing and forging the inseparable, materially "conceptual" link between such primitive mortal sentiments and metaphysical concepts arising in Daoist contexts.

As Xiao himself indicates (12), this line of reading, re-dis-covered as such, represents a gyno-oriented-but-not-centric (Lai 2000, 146) turn within Daoism's ongoing journey through its own inner, multiple "gates" (*DDJ* 10, 22, 25). It is not some distant gesture from "mommy earth gender essentialism," "a caricature of ecofeminism and constructivism" (Kearns and Keller 2007, 64) or an East-meets-West philosophical paperback romance. It is a way of thinking the world as a (w)hole, as inclusively *and* exclusively as possible at the same time. By bringing to the semantic fold this cosmic concept, *xuanpinzimen*, "the gate of the dark womb" (Pine 1996, 12), "the door of the mystical female" (Wang 2003, 67), Xiao writes:

> In *Daodejing*, they [*Gushen* and *Xuanpin*], along with "the sovereign or supreme being [*shangdi*]" and "the mother," form a linguistic group bound by and revelatory of the cult of female fertility and femininity. And yet, *Xuanpinzimen* originally refers to the female genital hole and "the root" too comes from "the vessel that becomes fundamental and essential (the male sexual organs, the female sexual organs)" . . . "The hole of *yin* becomes a gate and the vessel for life and death, and in view of its utmost importance it is called a root. The male (or masculine) efficacy too is called a root."
> (XIAO 1994, 31–32)

Gushen, xuanpin, and *xuanpinzimen:* the three key words or image-concepts of chapter 6 of *Daodejing,* constellated as such, form an implicitly referential relationship to the *mu* of Daoism, the *shangdi/tiandi* that precedes itself: "*Gushen* can function as that which unifies the great nature of the female animal and its sexual organs. The 'undying' 'valley spirit' and the 'female dark animal,' both belong to *yin,* and the two are interchangeable" (31). Likewise, *xuanpin* as the "arboreal and chemical root (*gen* 根) of the Heaven and the Earth or the sky and the land (*tiandi*)" (31) is extremely concrete and extremely abstract, at once. It is materially conceived and allegorically dispersed rather than formal or transcendentally projected; it can hardly be unified into the external agency of creation and control typified, for instance, by certain institutionalized versions of the Judeo-Christian God. Held in view here is "a linguistic group" or constellation creating its own existential and spiritual habitats and realities. The *xuanpin* family is then, perhaps we can say, Plato's Cave turned inside out the Chinese style, ancient or global.

When Laozi said, "*Xuanpin* becomes *tiandigen,*" the text seems to speak indeed the "mother" tongue of the world too, the universal language of fertility and creative living forces. Dao denotes the auto-generative spirit (*shen* 神) of cosmic being that *is* and is *in* the cosmic space (*tiandi*); it marks the traces of unifying forces or rather invisible points of connections. Populated and energized this way by the living and the dead including the undead in between that are ancestral remnants and genealogical aspirations, the Dao of Daoism becomes the foundation of biocultured life in the traditional Chinese philosophical imaginary. Here again *xuanpin* as a fertile sign and starting point of Dao functions as an immanent index to natural functions or historical consequences of manifold path making at work that requires the energetic coparticipation of engendered opposites as a key—if not *the*—enabling condition.

The remaining question or task is to work out the critical implications of this cosmic puzzle, this seemingly contradictory, ever-so-powerful textual construction called "darkly obscure female animal." In a sense, *xuanpin* is freely transsexual, gender-bending: female and not female at once, heterosexualized and not at once. As with many image-concepts in *Daodejing*, *xuan* of *xuanpin* and *xuanpinzimen* opens up and clears away a zonal space for threshold experiences of ontologically interfused or fermented thoughts. Inspired and repeatedly invited by that door in the dark, I am seeking to contemporize that natural matrix, *xuanpinzimen,* taking it as a feminist figure of constant change at work. Here, with Xiao, I see in *xuanpin* a living sign of immanent transformation, its forces materializing amply, if not entirely, in the body of the dark female animal, literal and figural.

Think Vitality: Thinking with Multiple Signatures of *Xuanpin*

In this chapter I have been attending to the originary and inaugural significance of *xuanpin* taken as a sign of the fertile creativity of

Dao—at work always already. Instead of a conclusion, let me pause for some further, fringe reflections, while reworking the key points I have made so far into the broader framework of thinking.

One may recall what Luce Irigaray did to and with Plato's cave. In fact, that seems to have been at the back of my mind all along, although I have been more critically vigilant about the textual difference or even sexual indifference between the feminine and the female—perhaps a function of writing in English and moving interstitially, queerly, between or through languages that are supposedly heterogeneous. But indeed, as with Irigaray, here I am neither really thinking of nor trying to dispose of the Socratic-Augustinian-Hegelian-Freudian-Heideggerian-canonical work of death. I am and have been trying to think away from thantological economy or to approach it from the other direction.

What I have in mind is something closer to a work of life that simply en*tails* death, a textualized work of biozoological natality and vitality, wherein the Platonic cave, and, by extension, the frillier Freudian "valley" itself ("*lilies of the valley, violets and pinks or carnations*"), "a common feminine dream-symbol" of "pure, expensive, precious, flowery virginity" (Freud 1953, 373), can be reconceived in less linear and more colorfully cyclical terms. Note again: it is *mu*, the birth mother, not a virgin or the virgin mother, that appears in the first page of *Daodejing*. The textual conflation of nature and nurture, of the biological and the sociological, the two categories that are distinguishable although inseparable, occurs later, for instance, in chapter 25. We are talking about the birth of beings in the valley, deep mountains and a vast field of cosmic eventuation. Dao, as manifest in the dark blood, the pitch purple stream, of *xuanpin*, marks the endless beginnings or the ends that ceaselessly turn into beginnings; the Daoist mother, seemingly short-circuited this way, thereby signals "both the beginning and the culmination" (Jullien and Hawkes 2000, 281), but not the end.

Culmination is the key: intensity, the event. It is different from, although relevant to, the Platonic receptacle (*hypodoche*) in *Timaeus*,[5] "the nurse of all becoming" in which the animal vitality and nonmimetic corporeality of becoming remains half-erased in favor and place of typological mimesis, that is, for the sake of the mimetic intelligibility of phallic genealogy. The Daoist mother seems even more distantly related to the Freudian lady in and out of dream, "arranging the center of a table with flowers for a birthday" to fulfill her wish, whose "center" in that dream, Freud concludes, is the vagina, the lost or inverted phallus. Rather than or in addition to nurses and bourgeois ladies who lunch, we are talking about the blood in birth, the bloodbath of creation, the "bleeding madness" of the other gene, genius, and generation of a "great-great-grandmother," of which Alice Walker, notably along with Battersby (1998), speaks:

> For these grandmothers and mothers of ours were not Saints, but Artists; driven to a numb and bleeding madness by the springs of creativity in them for which there was no release. They were Creators, who lived lives of spiritual waste, because they were so rich in spirituality—which is the basis of Art—that the strain of enduring their unused and unwanted talent drove them insane. Throwing away this spirituality was their pathetic attempt to lighten the soul to a weight their work-worn, sexually abused bodies could bear.
>
> What did it mean for a black woman to be an artist in our grandmother's time? In our great-grandmother's day? It is a question with an answer cruel enough to stop the blood.
>
> Did you have a genius of a great-great-grandmother who . . .
>
> (WALKER 2004, 233)

If the increasingly disillusioned—post-Socratic, Cartesian, Husserlian, Heideggerian, Christian, Colonial, Euro-American, posthuman, global-X, extraterrestrial, etc.—thinkers, especially postphenomenologists, are now found in the metropolitan "desert" (Nancy 1997), "shedding all the tears of their beliefs" (Clément 1994, 212), still mourning the increasingly complicated access to and blockage in Being, why not try opening up Being itself, cracking it open differently and more liberally? Differently and liberally? Too obscure?—the kind of mutually transformative feminist philosophical alliance and dialogue I envisage happens *between* and *across*: the Daoist perspective on the inaugural ontological centrality of *xuanpin,* on the one hand, and the various contemporary debates on the very viability of feminist perspectives, on the other hand, as a creative and progressive alternative to deeply oppressive and often self-destructively normative theories and traditions. Take this obvious candidate: the "phallogocentrism" of the oedipal and/or Confucian family, both supported by the "tree" of life rather than the "valley," *gushen,* a general economy of nature and nurture. Indeed, simply: is not the mystery of life more interesting, more intricate even, than the finality of death?

Let me now close, or rather reroute or recast, the discussion so far by noting Xiao's seemingly tiny scholastic contention (Xiao 1994, 27) that we not separate *gu* and *shen* and similarly *xuan* and *pin*; as we will see shortly, this, in some fascinating ways at least in my view, exposes a crucial issue of conformist translation worth noting here, inseparable from the question of interpretation that has been directly and thematically confronted in this chapter from the start. Let us begin by simply contrasting Xiao's view with Keping Wang's, another notable Daoist scholar with a more respectably standard view, who, while keeping the literal senses and shades of "the female," turns the "dark" part immediately into a metaphysical value, a sign of "subtlety and profundity." Note how he keeps *xuan* and *pin* apart, even while attempting to put himself in the position of the "primitive" folks whose mystical realism one might find laughable:

> The term *xuan pin* (subtle and profound female) indicates in its concrete sense the female sex organ as a metaphor for the *Dao*, which is subtle, deep and mysteriously productive. It is worth noting that people in ancient times used to revere what they thought was the magic power contained inside the female organ. This kind of reverence or worship is clearly reflected and expressed in primitive rock paintings and carvings. Nowadays people would probably laugh or jeer at a primitive painting or sculpture portraying the female sex organ in an exaggerated fashion. But we should put ourselves in the position of our ancestors in terms of their primitive cognitive dimensions, of that kind of exaggerated manifestation in art that denotes some form of natural religious feeling and significance.
>
> (WANG 1998, 39–40)

Writing in English, Wang might have "Westernized," consciously or not, that is to say, "Orientalized," his exposition of Dao by jettisoning that which cannot be transported to the other shore of thinking. Perhaps such a discourse of darkness could not reproduce its inner or other brilliance in the proto-Aristotelian language of metaphysical tautology that says dark is dark and cannot be undark and can only turn otherwise, e.g., obscure, mystical, even profound, etc. So has Wang acted out his own Oriental carpet mysticism, following the unwritten script—doubly, first by mystically feminizing *xuan pin*, following the tradition, and second by obfuscating its femininity, following the cartographical dictates of the Greco-Roman-Anglo-European philosophical imaginary?

Whatever the case, the question now more interesting and pertinent to us is again how to break through such a bamboo ceiling of ideas. How does one in the dark play the specter of the past rather than mimicking its shadows? How can we rework the (re)sources of Daoism, in particular, the philosophy of transformative origination and imagination, in ways that transfigure Daoism itself at the risk of—of course—disfiguring it? Again, such a wild-wild-west or world-wide-web of reading is where I find myself heading, sensing an intestinal, infinitesimal, inroad.

Glossary of Chinese Terms

DADIMUQIN 大地母親	affinity with the mother earth, a vast continent
DAO 道	path, route, way
DE 德	virtue, power
DI 帝	sovereign, supreme
GEN 根	root (arboreal and/or chemical)
GU 谷	valley
GUSHEN 谷神	valley spirit, the spirit of the valley
HUANG 黃	sulfur, yellow
JUNZI 君子	exemplary gentleman, Confucian man scholar
MIAO 妙	clever, intriguing, wonderful
MU 母	mother, female
PIN 牝	womb
QI 氣	energy
ROU 柔	soft
SHANGDI 上帝	the sovereign, emperor, godlike figures
SHEN 神	spiritual, divine, divine entity
TIANDI 天地	heaven and earth, the sky and the land, the world
TIANDIGEN 天地根	root of heaven and earth/the world

TIANXIAGU 天下谷	the valley under heaven
TIANXIAZIPIN 天下之牝	the womb of all that is under heaven
WANWU 萬物	ten thousand things, all (modes of) beings
WANWUZIMU 萬物之母	mother of ten thousand things, all (modes of) beings
XU 虛	devoid of content, void, false, empty, vain
XUAN 玄	dark, obscure, subtle
XUANHUANG 玄黃	heaven
XUANMEN 玄門	dark gate
XUANPIN 玄牝	dark female animal, womb
XUANPINZIMEN 玄牝之門	gate of the dark female animal, womb opening
XUANXUE 玄學	dark learning
YING-ER 嬰兒	infant, baby
YUAN 元	dynasty, dollar, primary, first
ZIRAN 自然	nature, organic, being-thus-automatically, self-so

Notes

Unless otherwise noted, all English translations in this chapter, from Chinese or Korean, are my own. The original text referenced can be found in Ames and Hall (2003).

1. *DDJ* here and following refers to the *Daodejing*.
2. The Chinese original I used here for a translation is the one published by Roger Ames and David L. Hall, who edited the line based on the Mawangdui version (168 BCE) excavated in 1973; some other texts, for instance, break or extend the first line, introduced above, into two by adding more words. See Ames and Hall (2003, 77).
3. I owe this formulation to Mary Beth Mader.
4.

This chapter combines a number of important *Daoist* images; the valley (see chapters 28 and 39), the gate (see chapters 1 and 10), the feminine (see chapters 10, 28, and 61), and the root (see chapters 16, 26, 39, and 59). The valley and the gate are, like the bellows and the wheel, *Daoist* images of the emptiness/fullness (or nonpresence/presence) structure.

The valley, the female, and the root are also images of inexhaustible fertility. This chapter makes it clear that the *Dao* is a way of generation and (re)production. The "spirit of the valley" expresses the *Dao*'s function as a permanent source of life (and death).
(MOELLER 2007, 16).

5. Plato (1975, 49a).

References

Ames, Roger T., and David L. Hall, trans. 2003. *Dao de jing: Making this life significant: A philosophical translation*, by Laozi. New York: Ballantine.

Battersby, Christine. 1998. *The phenomenal woman: Feminist metaphysics and the patterns of identity*. New York: Routledge.

———. 2006. Flesh questions: Representational strategies and the cultures of birth. *Women: A Cultural Review* 17 (3): 290–309.

Beauvoir, Simone de. 1952. *The second sex*. Trans. H. M. Parshley. New York: Vintage.

Chen, Ellen Marie. 1974. Tao as the great mother and the influence of motherly love in the shaping of Chinese philosophy. *History of Religions* 14 (1): 51–64.

Chen, Guying. 1999. *Laozi*. Trans. A. Waley. Hunan: Hunan People's Publishing House and Foreign Language Press.

Clément, Catherine. 1994. *Syncope: The philosophy of rapture*. Minneapolis: University of Minnesota Press.

Despeux, Catherine, and Livia Kohn. 2003. *Women in Daoism*. Cambridge: Three Pines.

Feng, Gia-fu, and Jane English, trans. 1972. *Tao te ching*, by Laozi. New York: Vintage.

Freud, Sigmund. 1953. *The standard edition of the complete psychological works of Sigmund Freud, The interpretation of dreams*, vol. 4: ed. James Strachey, Anna Freud, Carrie Lee Rothgeb, and Angela Richards. London: Hogarth.

Grosz, Elizabeth. 1994. *Volatile bodies: Toward a corporeal feminism*. Bloomington: Indiana University Press.

Jullien, François, and Sophie Hawkes. 2000. *Detour and access: Strategies of meaning in China and Greece*. New York: Zone.

Kearns, Laurel, and Catherine Keller, ed. 2007. *Ecospirit: Religions and philosophies for the earth*. New York: Fordham University Press.

Kim, Hyung-Hyo. 1999. *Deconstructive reading of Daoism*. Seungnam: Chungkye (in Korean).

Kim, Ha Poong, trans. 2003. *Reading Lao Tzu: A companion to the Tao Te Ching with a new translation*, by Laozi. Trans. H. P. Kim. Seoul: Moonye (in Korean).

Kim, Yong-Oak. 1999. *Laozi and the twentieth-century*. Seoul: Tongnamoo (in Korean).

Kohn, Livia. 2001. *Daoism and Chinese culture*. Cambridge: Three Pines.

Lai, Karyn. 2000. The *Daodejing*: Resources for contemporary feminist thinking. *Journal of Chinese Philosophy* 27 (2): 131.

Lau, D.C., trans. 1963. *Tao Te Ching*, by Laozi. Baltimore: Penguin.

Lin, Yutang, trans. 1948. *The wisdom of Laotse,* by Zhuangzi and Laozi. New York: Modern Library.

Lynn, Richard John, and Wang Bi, trans. 1999. *The classic of the way and virtue: A new translation of the Tao-te ching of Laozi as interpreted by Wang Bi.* New York: Columbia University Press.

Malabou, Catherine, and Jacques Derrida. 2004. *Counterpath: Traveling with Jacques Derrida.* Stanford: Stanford University Press.

Moeller, Hans-Georg. 2006. *The philosophy of the Daodejing.* New York: Columbia University Press.

———, trans. 2007. *Daodejing Laozi: A complete translation and commentary*, by Laozi. Chicago: Open Court.

Nancy, Jean-Luc. *The sense of the world.* Trans. by Jeffrey Librett. University of Minnesota Press, 1997.

Pine, Red, trans. 1996. *Lao-tzu's Taoteching*, by Laozi. San Francisco: Mercury House.

Plato. 1975. *Timaeus*, vol. 11 of *Plato in twelve volumes.* Trans. Rev. R. G. Bury. Cambridge: Harvard University Press.

Pregadio, Fabrizio. 2007. *The encyclopedia of Taoism.* New York: Routledge.

Raz, Gil. 2008. Way of the yellow and the red: Re-examining the sexual initiation rite of celestial master Daoism. *Men, women and gender in early and imperial China* 10 (1): 86–120.

Wagner, Rudolf G. 2000. *The craft of a Chinese commentator: Wang Bi on the Laozi.* Albany: State University of New York Press.

Walker, Alice. 2004. *In search of our mothers' gardens: Womanist prose.* Orlando: Harcourt.

Wang, Keping, trans. 1998. *The classic of the Dao: A new investigation*, by Laozi. Beijing: Foreign Languages Press.

Wang, Robin. 2003. *Images of women in Chinese thought and culture: Writings from the pre-Qin period through the Song dynasty.* Indianapolis: Hackett.

White, Michael. 2001. *Leonardo: The first scientist.* London: Abacus.

Xiao, Bing 蕭兵. 1994. *Daoist cultural anthropology* 老子的文化解讀 (Daoist cultural decoding or interpretation); 胡北人民出版社, 2000, Korean trans. Seunghyun Noh, *Lao Tzu and sex*, Munhakdongne.

Zhao, Dunhua. 2007. Axiological rules and Chinese political philosophy. *Journal of Chinese Philosophy* 34 (2): 161–78.

CHAPTER THREE

Confucian Family-State and Women

A Proposal for Confucian Feminism

RANJOO SEODU HERR

AS THE dominant cultural and philosophical system of East Asia for over two millennia, Confucianism has played an indisputably central role in subjugating women under one of the most systemic and prolonged patriarchies in human history. Yet Confucianism is not thereby destined to remain an inherently sexist and inveterately reactionary ideology irrelevant to the contemporary world. Confucian patriarchal practices may not be "based on theoretical reasons," but rather on "prejudices or the particular conditions" of traditional Confucian societies (Chan 2008, 164).[1] It is therefore worthwhile and timely for feminists affiliated with Confucian traditions to ask the following questions: Are core tenets of Confucianism compatible with promoting gender equality and protecting women's well-being? If so, what form would Confucian feminism take? In this chapter, I shall advance and defend the position that, with a proper realignment of core Confucian values, an explicitly feminist reading of Confucianism—a conception of Confucian feminism—can be constructed to promote the feminist goals of gender equality and women's well-being in contemporary Confucian societies.[2] I shall argue, in particular, that the Confucian moral goal of embodying the virtue of *ren* 仁 (human-heartedness) applies to both women and men and that the Confucian family-state ought to aid women in achieving this moral goal by actively sharing in the responsibilities of protecting and promoting the well-being of Confucian families.

This chapter proceeds in the following order: first, I shall examine a concrete historical example of Confucian patriarchy in the Chosŏn Dynasty in order to identify sources of the long-standing Confucian subjugation of women. Having identified that women's oppression in Chosŏn was partly predicated on Confucian emphases on *li* 禮 (propriety) and family, I shall then investigate whether Confucianism is inherently antagonistic to feminism by examining these concepts within the comprehensive Confucian philosophical system. It shall be argued that the core precept of Confucianism—what I call the precept of *ren*—is applicable to both women and men and that Confucian emphases on *li* and family, contextualized in relation to this precept, do not necessitate the subjugation of women. Finally, I shall address a practical Confucian concern that promoting the precept of *ren* for both women and men may generate a situation in which the Confucian family would be weakened, as its maintenance in most cases depends on women's wholehearted devotion to the domestic sphere. I shall argue that this problem can be resolved if the Confucian family-state begins to fulfill its primary responsibility to ensure the well-being and flourishing of Confucian families.

Confucianism and Women's Subjugation—the Case of Chosŏn

Confucianism has not served women well, as its ideas were misinterpreted and distorted in its long and tortuous history. The unfair and cruel treatment of women defined normalcy in most, if not all, East Asian states of the past that were more or less Confucian in their state ideology. A paradigm example of the relentless Confucian subjugation of women can be found in the Chosŏn Dynasty 朝鮮 (1392–1910) on the Korean peninsula (Deuchler 1992, ch. 6).[3] Chosŏn was a state founded on explicitly Confucian values, interpreted especially through the lenses of Zhuxi/Chu Hsi's 朱熹 (1130–1200) neo-Confucianism. Consequently, the sexist mistreatment of Chosŏn women was rationalized by the Confucian framework. In order to identify whether Confucianism is necessarily sexist, a first step is to delineate the historical Confucian rationalization of women's subjugation and determine how much is based on Confucianism proper, as was envisioned by Confucius and Mencius, the two founders of the Confucian philosophical and valuational tradition (Herr 2003, 482).

According to Confucius and Mencius, the Confucian family, the essence of which is the father-son relation, is the fundamental wellspring of love and affection and the very basis of *ren*, the most important Confucian virtue (*Mencius* 4A.27, cf. 1A.1, 6B.3, 7A.15; *Analects* 1.2, 2.5).[4] The Confucian founders of Chosŏn, therefore, took seriously the family relations of not only father and son but also husband and wife as constitutive of the Confucian family,[5] and attempted to structure the state of Chosŏn as a distinctly Confucian society by organizing family relations according to their proper norms, or *li* 禮. *Li* refers to intersubjective "norms and standards of proper behavior" (Tu 1979, 6) pertaining to each role in human relations that accord with public expectations. According to Mencius, "between father and son, there should be affection (*qin* 親)," and "between husband and wife, there should be distinction (*pie* 別)" (*Mencius* 3A.4). *Li* pertaining to each relation, as stated by Mencius, is somewhat abstract. Therefore, Zhuxi, the preeminent neo-Confucian of the Song Dynasty 宋 (960–1279), wrote various handbooks with concrete and specific guidelines to elaborate on the *li* of family relations.[6]

Chosŏn Confucians, faced with the urgent task of organizing a new society according to Confucian values and principles, wholeheartedly adopted not only Zhuxi's interpretations of the Confucian classical texts but also his handbooks of *li* as the defining guide for state building (Deuchler 1992, 112). The most significant element in Zhuxi's handbooks of *li* regulating family relations is the "agnatic principle (*jong-beop/zongfa* 宗法)," which takes patrilineal descent groups as basic units of society. Strict adherence to the agnatic principle would result in "a kinship system that rested on highly structured patrilineal descent groups. These patrilineages comprised groups of agnates who derived their common descent from a real or putative apical ancestor (*si-jo* 始祖) and identified themselves with a common surname (*seong* 姓) and a common ancestral seat (*bon-gwan* 本館)" (6). Neo-Confucian theorists, including Zhuxi, took the establishment of the agnatic principle as crucial to guaranteeing "the uninterrupted continuation of the political process" (129), which depended on the continuation of descent groups. Without a clear principle defining the line of descent, they worried that a descent group might disintegrate "at the death of the lineal heir" (130). Elaborate rituals of ancestor worship, mourning, and funerals became vehicles through which the patrilineal social structure was implemented, as performing such rituals necessitated the specification and clarification of the descent line.

The obsession with clarifying the descent line that "would provide the criteria on the basis of which descent group membership and thus social status could be verified," however, clashed with the legally sanctioned custom of "polygyny,"[7] which allowed men, especially of the upper class, to have multiple wives.[8] This generated a sticky problem: how to prioritize the line of descent among multiple sons from multiple wives. Their solution was to "single out one wife and her children as a man's rightful spouse and legitimate heirs" (232). With this aim, it was legally decided in 1413 that a man must have only one legal wife, who is the primary wife (*cheo* 妻), and all other wives were relegated to the status of secondary or minor wives (*cheop* 妾). In this, Chosŏn Confucians followed the "rule of primogeniture operative in China's feudal past," according to which "only the eldest son by the primary wife could succeed his father" (132).

Due to the strict distinction between primary and secondary wives, "lineages (and families) clearly distinguished between main lines formed by the firstborn sons of primary wives, branch lines formed by sons born after the first son by the same mother, and secondary sons, who, as offspring of secondary wives, were of secondary status and therefore not full-fledged lineal members" (7). The distinction between primary and secondary wives functioned to divide the society into "the superior and inferior" and ensured that the power would be confined to a small number of the privileged (232). For the ruling class of Chosŏn, "limiting access to the ranks of the elite" (119) by excluding sons born to secondary wives maintained the political privilege of the elite by restricting political participation of the "inferior." "Descent and political participation therefore came to be inextricably intertwined" (119–20) through the agnatic principle bolstered by the distinction between primary and secondary wives. The agnatic principle, then, served an ideological and political purpose.

The agnatic principle is not only ideological but also inveterately patriarchal, and obsessive adherence to it created an inordinately sexist society. In a social system that was structured to maintain patrilineal descent groups according to the agnatic principle, the *li* of the husband-wife relation (*pie* 別) was taken as a strict physical segregation of the sexes predicated on the inexorable subordination of women to men. A woman's only role was to "bring forth male offspring" in an arranged marriage (237, 240), so that the husband's surname and bloodline would perpetuate into the indefinite future. Women had no identity other than this primary role.[9] From childhood, they were indoctrinated to fulfill this role with complete submission and physically confined to the "inner" sphere to focus solely on their domestic function (257–63).[10] Women who were unable or unwilling to fulfill this role with submissiveness were often severely penalized, both socially and legally, and shunted aside as nonentities. For example, women who were rejected by their husband's family were often refused refuge by their own families. Such women had no option but to return to the husband's family and suffer gross injustice and ignominy for the rest of their lives by the husband and the in-laws (272–76). The legal distinction between primary and secondary wives in a social milieu that sanctioned polygyny pitted even women who were fulfilling their function of giving birth to sons against one another as competitors. Regarding secondary wives, in particular, not only did their well-being and survival depend on the husband's whimsical favors, but their sons were destined to become secondary citizens (269–72).

I shall argue later that such an extreme form of patriarchy is incompatible with the true spirit of Confucianism proper. For the time being, let us examine what made such deviation possible. The first step in this deviation was the misinterpretation of what constitutes the Confucian family and its well-being. For neo-Confucians, the Confucian family *was* the patrilineal descent group and maintaining the well-being of family meant maintaining a clear line of descent in such a group. What made this misinterpretation possible? Aside from the general patriarchal tendencies of traditional societies, a contingent incident in the theorization of Confucianism played a crucial role in turning Confucianism into a patriarchal ideology. This incident was the fateful connection between sex difference and the *yin-yang* 陰陽 principle made by the Han Confucian Dong Zhongshu 董仲舒 (179–104 BCE), who was influenced by the *Book of Changes* (Chan 2008, 147). Subsequently, *pie* was interpreted as implying not just "a separation of functions" but also a metaphysical difference between the sexes that renders women's status inferior to men's in accordance with the cosmological order in which "heaven (*yang*) dominates earth (*yin*)." Hence this rationalized women's confinement to the "inner" (*nei* 內) or domestic sphere, strictly segregated from and completely subordinated to the "outer" (*wai* 外) public sphere of men. As ontologically inferior inhabitants of the subordinate sphere, women's sole virtue was "submissiveness" (*shun* 順; Deuchler 1992, 231; *Mencius* 3B.2; Chan 2008, 156), and their primary obligation was "obey[ing] [their] superiors" who are male: "When unmarried, she had to follow her father's orders; when married, those of her husband; when widowed, those of her son" (Deuchler 1992, 231).

Zhuxi advanced the inherently patriarchal agnatic principle as the ground rule of an ideal Confucian society, predicated on the exaggerated inferiority attributed to women by Dong's alleged metaphysical differences between the sexes. Unfortunately, this proposal was almost universally accepted by Confucian scholars of the time. The agnatic principle rationalized inordinately sexist interpretations of the Confucian family and the *li* of the husband-wife relation. The founders and their descendent ruling class of Chosŏn wholeheartedly accepted this distorted valuational framework and thereby entrenched a severe form of patriarchy in Chosŏn. In a societal system that was inexorably patriarchal, Chosŏn women, especially of the upper class, unwittingly and often unwillingly became the gatekeepers of an unequal and oppressive system and paid the highest price for it. As virtual captives in the inner sphere indoctrinated with the patriarchal ideology from early years, they had no control over their lives whether before, during, or after marriage. Those who challenged the system were severely penalized by the state, their husbands' families, and even their own families, and the only recourse for them was often death.

The Confucian Person

Women's subjugation in the Chosŏn Dynasty and other historical Confucian states was extreme. This was due in large part to widely accepted but distorted interpretations of the Confucian family and the *li* of the husband-wife relation, which were predicated on later Confucian theories of Dong and Zhuxi. Consequently, women's inordinate subordination in Confucian history, as condemnable as it was, need not be taken as the concomitant of Confucianism as originally envisioned by Confucius and Mencius. Some may point out, however, that the Confucian emphases on family and *li*, elements constitutive of the Confucian canon, also played a crucial role in women's subjugation. This line of reasoning suggests that women's subjection, although not as extreme as in historical manifestations, is logically entailed by Confucianism after all. My response to this objection is that the Confucian emphases on family and *li* do *not* necessarily entail women's subjugation when properly understood within the comprehensive philosophical framework of Confucianism. In order to identify this framework, let me elaborate on the Confucian conception of the self at its core.

The Confucian person is a "reflective, and ceaselessly transformative being" conscious of his or her agency (Tu 1989, 45; cf. *Analects* 12.1).[11] The reflection—thinking (*si* 思)—required of this Confucian self (*Mencius* 6A.6, 6A.15), however, is not merely abstract and theoretical (Tu 1979, 67). Rather, it is always connected with the practical and based on the "moral mind" (*xin* 心), which provides not only the "antecedent commitment" to but also the "actual activity" toward moral excellence (Tu 1979, 67; cf. *Mencius* 4A.12, 6A.15). The moral mind, according to Mencius, initially consists of four kinds of feelings that provide the "beginnings" of Confucian virtues: feelings of commiseration (*ceyin* 惻隱), shame and dislike (*xiuwu* 羞惡), modesty and yielding (*cirang* 辭讓), and the sense of right and wrong (*shifei* 是非). If preserved, these feelings would transform into the four "constant" Confucian virtues of *ren* 仁 (human-heartedness), *yi* 義 (righteousness), *li* 禮 (propriety), and *zhi* 智 (wisdom), respectively (*Mencius* 2A.6). The moral mind is "irreducible" (Tu 1979, 65) and *common* to all humanity, sages and ordinary humans alike (cf. *Mencius* 3A.1, 6A.7, 6A.10; *Analects* 17.2). Indeed, the possession of the moral mind is "the defining characteristic of being human" (Tu 1979, 59; cf. *Mencius* 4B.19, 6A.15).

Yet the irreducibility of the moral mind does not guarantee a "spontaneous self-realization" of the Confucian moral self for everyone (Tu 1979, 65). Although all humans have the moral mind, it is often "lost" due to inhospitable external circumstances (see 63; cf. *Mencius* 6A.7, 6A.8, 6A.15). Still, it is "recoverable" (Tu 1979, 64) through the "establishment of the will" (62) to preserve or retrieve these four beginnings. If the original moral mind is preserved or recovered and these emotional germinations are fully actualized, the Confucian person comes closer to the Confucian moral ideal of embodying the four Confucian virtues. The underlying axiom of Confucianism, therefore, is that "*all* human beings are endowed with the authentic possibility to develop themselves as moral persons through the cognitive and affective functions of the mind" (Tu 1989, 46, emphasis added). Women would be included among those capable of "human perfectibility" (Tu 1979, 63), as "there is no clear textual evidence [in the *Analects* and the *Mencius*] that women are thought to be inferior [to men] in their innate intellectual or rational capacities" (Chan 2008, 162).

In achieving the Confucian moral ideal, the most significant Confucian virtue is *ren* and the most important Confucian principle is that we ought to embody *ren*—the precept of *ren*. What, then, is *ren*? Although it is notoriously multifarious and elusive,[12] most Confucians agree that *ren* is not merely a "particular virtue" of human relations, but a "general virtue" in its "inclusiveness" of other Confucian virtues (Chan 1955, 298; Tu 1979, 9; Fung 1948, 72; *Analects* 13.27). Some Confucians even attribute to it a special status as "a principle of inwardness," which is "the self-reviving, self-perfecting, and self-fulfilling process of an individual" toward moral perfection (Tu 1979, 9). Construed thus, the process of actualizing *ren* is "practically identical" to the process of "self-cultivation" (*xiushen* 修身; 6; cf. *Analects* 14.25). Self-cultivation is a very strenuous lifelong process of "self-education" to reach the highest stage of moral perfection, often involving pain and suffering, which stops "only with death" (*Analects* 8.7). The burden, however, is not imposed from without, but is in fact "an internally motivated sense of duty" (Tu 1989, 48), as "the uniqueness of being human is as much a responsibility as a privilege" (45). Self-cultivation is not simply a process to reach an end. Rather, the becoming process is also an "ultimate end in itself" (Tu 1979, 8). Given the arduousness of self-cultivation as a perpetual incremental progress toward moral perfection, however, only a small number of persons persists in self-cultivation to achieve the "authentic self" (9). These persons achieve the status of *junzi* 君子 (noble person; cf. *Mencius* 6A.15, 4B.19).

Confucian *Li* and Family

Ren, however, is inherently linked to human relations. *Ren*'s sociality is due to its inextricable relation to another Confucian virtue, *li*, which is "an externalization of *jen* [*ren*] in a concrete social situation" (Tu 1979, 18). *Li* provides *ren* with concrete content. The relation between *ren* and *li* is suggested in the following pivotal phrase in the *Analects*: *ren* is "to subdue oneself (*keji* 克己) and [to] return to *li* (*fuli* 復禮)" (*Analects* 12.1). Not surprisingly, the first conjunct implies self-cultivation. Deciphering the phrase "return to *li* (*fuli*)," then, is crucial for understanding not only the sociality of *ren* but also the significance of *li* itself. As mentioned, *li* refers to intersubjective "norms and standards of proper behavior" that accord with public expectations pertaining to each role in core human relations. *Fuli*, however, does not imply "uncritical conventionalism" of conforming to accepted conventions of one's society (Tu 1979, 12). When Confucius spoke of *li*, he was referring to the idealized *li* of Zhou 周, which he believed was more in line with *ren* and not the existing conventions of his own time, the chaotic Spring and Autumn period. Further, even though he looked up to the *li* of Zhou, Confucius did not follow it when it seemed "improper" to him. Instead, he showed independence of mind by urging people to follow contemporary customs closer to the spirit of *ren* in such cases (*Analects* 9.3; cf. *Mencius* 4B.6). *Li*, then, represents "enlightened" norms of comportment in the spirit of *ren* (Cua 1996, 162). Consequently, *fuli* implies adhering to standards of proper behavior in human relations that conform to *ren*, as understood by one's self-cultivated and enlightened moral mind (cf. *Analects* 3.3, 15.17; Fung 1948, 66, 70).

What, then, does *ren* imply in concrete human relations? Confucians typically explicate *ren* as "love" (*ai* 愛) for others (Chan 1955, 299; *Analects* 12.22), predicated on the feeling of sympathy. *Ren* as love, however, does not refer to the raw emotion of affection, although affection, especially toward one's family members, does provide its basis. The proper manifestation of *ren* as love is rather, "To be able from one's own self to draw a parallel for the treatment of others" (*Analects* 6.28) and to "put oneself into the position of others" (Fung 1948, 71). This is none other than the Golden Rule, encompassing both of its positive and negative requirements. The positive requirement is expressed in the concept of *zhong* 忠 (conscientiousness),[13] which is to "establish" and "enlarge" others as well as oneself (*Analects* 6.28;

*Zhongyong*中庸13; Fung 1948, 71).[14] The negative requirement is implied in the concept of *shu* 恕 (reciprocity),[15] which prohibits imposing on others what one does not want imposed on oneself (*Analects* 1.4, 4.15, 5.11, 12.12, 15.23; *Daxue* 大學 10).[16] The "one thread that runs through [Confucius's] doctrines" is, therefore, none other than "*zhong* and *shu*" (4.15). I shall refer to the principle of *shu* 忠恕, in particular, as the principle of reciprocity that proscribes imposing on others what one does not want to be imposed on oneself. With the clarification of *ren* as implying the principle of reciprocity in concrete human relations, a clearer meaning now emerges of *li* and *fuli*: *li* represents "enlightened" norms of comportment in the five human relations that accord with the principle of reciprocity and *fuli* implies *restoring* the proper standards and norms of each relational role according to the principle of reciprocity.

Having clarified the meaning of *ren* and *li*, let us return to the concept of Confucian family to determine its proper meaning consistent with the overall Confucian philosophical framework. Recall that among the five core human relations, Confucians, including Confucius and Mencius, have traditionally considered the relation between "father and son" as the most central and essential to the Confucian family. Consonant with our goal, which is to retrieve the true meaning of Confucianism by dissociating it from its patriarchal presumptions, this central Confucian human relation ought to be understood more generally as that between parent and child, which better matches its symbolic status as "the root of *ren*" (*Analects* 1.2). The Confucian emphasis on the parent-child relation as the most significant human relation is well placed, as the parent-child relation is, both symbolically as well as practically, "the natural home for nourishing the self and, specifically, for helping the self to establish fruitful dyadic relationships" (Tu 1986, 183). In other words, the family's central importance for Confucianism is predicated on its function as the wellspring of and practicing ground for the virtue of *ren* for every member of the household, especially children. The Confucian family's raison d'être is to enable its members to become proficient practitioners of *ren*, for whom following the precept of *ren* is second nature.

Once the normative function of the Confucian family has been identified, we can examine its proper form. The typical form of the Confucian family, at the center of which is the parent-child relation, has always been a patrilineal extended family. Yet, if the core function of the family is enabling members to learn and practice *ren*, there is no conceptual necessity that an extended Confucian family must be of patrilineage, as was mandated by the agnatic principle. Indeed, as the primary arena in which children learn and practice *ren*, the Confucian family need not even be an extended family. Indeed, it may even be argued that same sex unions with children may qualify as Confucian families insofar as they enable members to become proficient practitioners of *ren*. Given the prevalence of extended families in Confucian East Asia and the communitarian values they serve to maintain, however, I shall take in this chapter consanguineous extended families, both patrilineal and matrilineal, based on the natural feeling of love and affection, as representative of the Confucian family.

As the most essential Confucian human relation, the obligation to maintain the parent-child relation according to its proper *li*—"affection" (*Analects* 17.21; *Mencius* 7B.24)—is very strict in Confucianism. Traditionally, the obligation rested more heavily on the shoulders of adult children who are required to show absolute devotion and "never disobey" their parents (*Analects* 2.5, 1.7, 13.18; *Mencius* 4A.28, 4B.30). Although Tu argues that the principle of reciprocity applies to this relation (Tu 1986, 181)—children may "remonstrate" (*jian* 諫), albeit "gently" (*yinwei* 隱微), when parents act against *li* (*Xiao Jjing* 孝經 13).[17] Confucians in general believe that children must never overstep what is prescribed by their filial duty even when parents do not mend their ways (cf. *Analects* 4.18). This disproportionate burden on children to fulfill their duty to adhere to the *li* of the parent-child relation is understandable in the context of the Confucian tradition that evolved in small farming villages in which adult children had to stay at their parents' farm for survival. However, in contemporary Confucian societies more emphasis should be placed on the parental correlative duty to maintain the parent-child relation in line with the principle of reciprocity. Coercive social pressure on grown children to obey and stay with unreasonable parents may have worked in small farming villages of yesteryear. In highly mobile and nationwide contemporary Confucian societies, however, only reciprocal efforts to strengthen mutual affection by parents and children alike can maintain the family as the "root of *ren*" and sustain lasting family ties.

The affection that both parents and children ought to and often do express toward each other can be deeper and stronger than in any other human relation. In Confucianism, strong emotional bonds be-tween family members justify our preferential treatment of them, and it is toward them that *ren* as love should be most strongly exhibited. The depth and strength of love in the parent-child relation is aptly reflected in the translation of Mencian *ren* as "love with distinction" (*chadengai* 差等愛; Chan 1955). In the Confucian tradition, love for our parents transcends even death and justifies the Confucian tradition of mourning rites and ancestor worship. As Whalen Lai writes, "Upon the love of kin that even death could not destroy, Confucians would order their society and claim that *xiao* 孝 (filial piety) is the 'one root' or the great principle of Heaven and Earth itself" (Lai 1991, 58).

The notion of "love with distinction," however, does not imply egoism centered on one's family. Despite the Confucian emphasis on the parent-child relation (*Analects* 1.2; *Mencius* 4A.27, 6B.3, 7A.15), the Confucian person must embrace all in his love (*Mencius* 7A.46; Chan 1955, 303). Love with distinction, involving "an order, a grada-tion, or distinction, starting with filial piety," is concerned primarily with "the application of love," which "necessarily varies according to one's relationship" (301). The family is the fundamental wellspring of love and therefore provides an opportunity to practice love. There-fore, "the great exercise of [love] is in showing affection for relatives" (*Zhongyong* 20). However, we must apply the lessons learned within the family to nonfamilial relations, albeit in a diluted fashion. Therefore, Mencius urged, "Treat with respect the elders in my family, and then, by extension, also the elders in other families. Treat with tenderness the young in my own family, and then, by extension, also the young in other families" (*Mencius* 1A.7). Indeed, as implied in Mencius's state-ment that "all the myriad things are there in me" (7A.4), the true Con-fucian self is "an open system" at the center of "a series of concentric circles . . . the outer rim of [which] never closes" (Tu 1986, 183).[18] The precept of *ren*, then, requires "the broadening and deepening 'em-bodiment' of an ever-expanding web of human relationships" (188).

Family, *Li*, and Women

How would women relate to the Confucian emphases on family and *li*, reinterpreted more in line with the Confucian philosophical frame-work? Traditionally, the significance of the husband-wife relation is inextricably connected to the importance of the parent-child relation in Confucianism. In order for the relation between parent and child to be possible, there must first be a heterosexual couple—husband and wife—to form a union in which children would be born. Indeed, getting married and having an heir has been considered the most important filial duty in Confucianism (*Mencius* 4A.26).[19] As mentioned previously, the proper *li* in the husband-wife relation for married heterosexual couples is distinction (*pie* 別). In the Mencian context distinction refers to the separation of spheres between inner and outer (*nei-wai* 內外) "based on functions" (Chan 2008, 150). Accordingly, adherence to *pie* implies that men who occupy the public world ought to focus on affairs pertaining to the outside world and women who occupy the private domestic world ought to focus on affairs pertaining to the household. On the surface, *pie* as functional distinction or the division of labor between husband and wife may seem justifiable for the sake of running family affairs efficiently and thereby maximizing household welfare. Especially in an age when women's public activity was restricted, it is conceivable how women's labor would come to be confined to the domestic sphere.

However, this functional justification of *pie* is unjustifiable according to the Confucian precept of *ren* as reciprocity. Even if one grants that some division of labor may be necessary in the husband-wife relation, the Mencian conception of *pie*, understood as functional distinction that neatly coincides with the sexual divide, contradicts the principle of reciprocity that proscribes imposing on others what one does not want to be imposed on oneself. A husband, especially if he enjoys public participation and dislikes domestic activities himself, ought not to coerce his wife into domestic confinement, but engage in a mutually respectful conversation in order to determine her true preferences and a just division of household labor in accordance with the principle of reciprocity. Given the diversity of human disposition, it is implausible to insist that the household division of labor ought to be predetermined unilaterally for all couples. The principle of reciprocity has to be applied on a case-by-case basis. If a man who enjoys domestic affairs more than public affairs and a woman who has the opposite disposition marry, they may decide to divide their labor according to their preferences. This would still be a division of labor based on functional distinction, but the content of the division would be reversed from what is prescribed by the Mencian *pie*.

The confinement of women in the domestic sphere by emphasizing functional distinction is also fundamentally at odds with the precept of *ren* as entailing "a continuous process of extension" of *li* (Tu 1979, 24). As we have seen, the true Confucian self is "an open system" and the completion of his or her self-cultivation, while starting with the family, must include "the universe as a whole" (29). The precept of *ren*, in other words, requires that Confucian persons, whether women or men, extend their love to others in an ever-wider circle of human relations in the process of self-cultivation by adhering to the principle of reciprocity, while taking family as the center of "concentric circles." Refusing to extend oneself outward "restricts us to a closed circle" (Tu 1986, 188), thereby stunting our moral growth. Confining women in the domestic sphere, then, constitutes an unwarranted restriction of women's moral growth.

Arguing for women's expansion of the "web of human relationships" does not imply that women should abandon their role as mother and/or housewife entirely and become nominal men. Indeed, "taking care of family affairs is itself active participation in politics" (Tu 1986, 189; cf. *Analects* 2.21), as the family itself is intimately connected to the public realm as "the training ground for moral cultivation" (Chan 2008, 150). Yet the role of mothers in educating the next generation to become active participants in the public sphere depends on their understanding the crucial connection between the domestic sphere and the public sphere, which is in turn predicated on their being active participants in the public sphere themselves.[20] In this regard, mothers in traditional Confucian societies were unable to perform this crucial role adequately as a result of their domestic confinement. Therefore, women *must* engage in the public sphere to different degrees, just as men *must* engage in the domestic sphere to different degrees. Variations may exist in the extent to which each person engages in either sphere, depending on their disposition and preferences.

This variation, however, should not pose a problem for Confucianism correctly interpreted, since both spheres enable Confucian persons to practice self-cultivation by adhering to the precept of *ren*, provided that persons maintain a reasonable balance between the two spheres. A woman's decision to cultivate herself by concentrating more on the public sphere would be perfectly acceptable in Confucianism, as would a man's decision to cultivate himself by focusing more on the domestic sphere. Indeed, if a woman decides that she prefers to cultivate herself mainly in the public sphere by opting not to marry, she would still be a respectable Confucian moral person, provided that she fulfills her filial and familial duties to her parents and relatives. In sum, the Confucian emphases on the family and *li* are compatible with the feminist goals of gender equality—understood as women enjoying equal opportunity for moral self-cultivation as men—and women's well-being—understood as women being able to fully actualize their potential to be Confucian *junzis*.

The Confucian Family-State and Feminism

My foregoing argument may be difficult to swallow for many main-stream Confucians. If women are allowed to cultivate themselves by primarily focusing on the public realm to the same extent as men, then who stays home and takes care of the children? As anyone who is or has been a parent knows, children need *constant* attention and guidance from caring adults. In the absence of outside assistance—which is often the case in contemporary East Asia, as most grown children move out of their farming villages and into cities in search of better-paying jobs—at least one parent, whether male or female, must stay home and become the primary parent, especially when children are young.[21] In reality, the primary parent is often the mother, and this has been taken for granted in Confucian societies. In fact, a mother who is not the primary parent is often criticized for reneging on her most important responsibility.

Yet, as we have seen, the Confucian precept of *ren* does not necessitate that the female parent assume the role of primary parent. Women and men are equal in their possession of moral capacity and ought to cultivate themselves to embody the virtue of *ren* and extend the circle of *li* outward. In contemporary Confucian societies, in which more and more families are nuclear, however, the core Confucian precept of *ren* may seem to be in practical conflict with the Confucian emphasis on the family, the well-being of which depends on one parent, often the mother, taking primary responsibility for child care. This practical conflict poses a crucial problem for constructing a feminist conception of Confucianism fit for the contemporary Confucian world.

I believe, however, that a solution to this problem may be found in the idea of the Confucian "family-state" (*guojia* 國家). *Family-state* is a term regularly used for "state" in Confucian East Asia. This suggestion may seem counterintuitive to many Confucians. After all, historical Confucian family-states promoted and maintained extreme forms of patriarchy, as was the case in Chosŏn. Yet, like any other term, this concept can be interpreted in different ways. As indicated earlier, my aim is not to settle with established interpretations but rather to update the parameters of Confucianism by exploring its conceptual and logical implications. The conclusion that I intend to justify is that Confucianism, rightly interpreted, can promote a feminist Confucian family-state.

In order to achieve this aim, we need to restore the true meaning of the Confucian state, which is expressed in Mencius's classical statement that "the people (*min* 民) are the most important [element in a state]" (*Mencius* 7B.14; Fung 1948, 111).[22] A fourteenth-century Korean Confucian, Jeong Do-Jeon (三峰 鄭道傳 1342–1398),[23] accepted and developed this idea further and argued that the people are the foundation (*bon* 本) of the state (Jeong 2006, 63, 236, book 10, book 13). Indeed, the people are "the Heaven of the ruler" (236, book 13), as the Heaven's Will, "unfathomable" in itself, expresses itself through "the will of the people which can be known" (Fung 1948, 117; *Mencius* 5A.5). Therefore "the ruler must love the people wholeheartedly" (Jeong 2006, 236, book 13), and all state policies must aim at promoting the well-being of the people. We may call this the principle of "people-centeredness" (*min-bon/minben* 民本; Han 1999, 139) and take it as the most central political principle of Confucianism.

The principle of people-centeredness is in fact an application of the Confucian precept of *ren*, as politics and morality are one and the same in ideal Confucian politics. The precept of *ren* to cultivate the self and embody *ren*, as we have seen, requires "an ever-extending web of human relationships" (Tu 1986, 188). Practicing politics according to the principle of people-centeredness and loving the people, then, constitutes the consummation of the precept of *ren*. Therefore, when the ruler follows the principle of people-centeredness, which is a manifestation of *ren*, he (or she) practices the politics of *ren* (*renzheng* 仁政; cf. *Mencius* 2A.3), the aim of which is not only cultivating the self (*xiuji* 修己/*zhengji* 正己) but also rectifying others (*zhengren* 正人/*zhiren* 治人; *Analects* 12.7, 13.6, 13.13, 14.44, 15.17, 19.3;

Mencius 2A.4, 5A.5). Rectifying others implies enabling them to cultivate themselves and strive toward moral excellence. The creation of the ideal Confucian polity in which every member is rectified is indeed the Confucian common good, advocated by all self-cultivating members. Rulers who conscientiously strive toward such a goal are not egocentric or power-hungry politicians but *junzis*, who are superior practitioners of morality and moral educators of the people (Jeong 2006, book 11, 81; cf. *Analects* 12.19; *Mencius* 5A.5, 5A.6; Fung 1948, 115–17). When rulers practice *renzheng*, they earn the trust of the people who take them as their symbolic parents who truly care about their moral and economic well-being. The ideal Confucian politics, then, is a kind of trustee politics (*shintak-jeongchi/xintuozhengzhi* 信託政治; Han 1999, 152) in which the people will trust and follow rulers as their caring parents (*Analects* 17.6; cf. *Mencius* 1B.7).[24] This, I believe, is the true meaning of the Confucian family-state.

Some claim that the notion of the Confucian family-state necessarily implies a paternalistic state in which "subjects have no right whatsoever to participate in politics" (Chan 2006). It may act as a benevolent dictator and consider that "the people's consent is automatic" as long as their wants are satisfied (Chan 2006). I disagree. Even if one accepts the hackneyed analogy of the state as "family writ large" literally, a family consists of multiple members who diverge in age and moral maturity. In the traditional extended Confucian family, in particular, grandparents as well as grown but unmarried siblings are included. Therefore the notion of a nuclear family consisting of a pair of adult parents raising preadolescent children, in which parents may sometimes justifiably impose their conception of the family's well-being on children, whose "consent is automatic" as long as their wants are satisfied, is too impoverished to do justice to the negotiations needed to maintain affection among diverse family members. Maintaining affection among diverse family members and thereby enhancing the well-being of the family may require respecting one another as equally valuable members of the family and incorporating feedback in creating harmonious family relations.

If we move beyond this analogy and focus on the ruler-subject, or people-politician, relation, the significance of equal respect for the members of polity cannot be overemphasized in Confucianism. Even in the days of Mencius and Jeong when the majority of the people were illiterate and ignorant peasants, rulers' respect for the people loomed large in Confucianism, as statements such as "the people are the foundation of the state and the Heaven of the ruler" make clear. The people's will as expressive of Heaven's Will could even justify the removal of a hereditary ruler who rules arbitrarily and oppresses the people (Jeong 2006, 214, book 13; *Mencius* 1B.8, 2B.2, 4A.1, 4B.3, 5B.9). Therefore, "whether the people voluntarily consent to the ruler's entitlement to rule is the criterion of his legitimacy" (Han 1999, 143).

Fast forward to the contemporary world. The people of East Asia are some of the most well-educated and well-informed citizens in the world today, providing the pool from which current and future political leaders are selected. It goes without saying, then, that adult members of such polities deserve utmost respect by their politicians and are entitled to full political participation. Such respect deserved by adult members can only be properly materialized in a democracy, and, despite the prevalent view that ideas of equality and democracy are incompatible with Confucianism,[25] a unique form of Confucian democracy *is* compatible with the Confucian philosophical system (Herr 2008, Herr 2009).

One of the most pressing concerns for Confucian persons, who regard family as "the root of *ren*" and consider the parent-child relation as the most significant human relation, would be to maintain the well-being of the family so that the children would grow to be good Confucian persons. Good Confucian persons, however, are not only filial children but also contributing members of the ideal Confucian polity. A democratic Confucian family-state ought to take this concern seriously. Family is indeed the primary arena in which children acquire and practice *ren*, which is necessary for becoming good Confucian persons who in turn constitute the ideal Confucian polity. As we have seen, the creation of the ideal Confucian polity is the Confucian common good, which ought to be the ultimate goal of a democratic Confucian family-state. The democratic Confucian family-state, therefore, must be actively involved in ensuring the well-being of Confucian families and thereby help them raise good Confucian citizens by according priority to policies that support and aid households that raise young and/or adolescent children with institutional and/or financial assistance. Such policies also promote the feminist goal of gender equality by enabling and aiding women to cultivate themselves and embody *ren* by engaging in the public sphere and enlarging the circle of human relations. Raising children to be good

Confucian citizens and enabling women to cultivate themselves and embody *ren* both contribute to the Confucian common good of creating a world in which every member is rectified. The Confucian common good, therefore, requires the democratic Confucian family-state to become a major agent of feminism.

Notes

1. For similar positions, also see Goldin (2000), Wawrytko (2000), Nylan (2000), and Raphals (2000).

2. Although many traditionally Confucian societies, including South Korea, may no longer be explicitly Confucian, the Confucian tradition still operates in South Korea at "the most basic level of the popular consciousness and in the routines of daily life" (Koh 1996, 194).

3. Regarding the romanization of Chinese characters, I follow pinyin for regular Confucian concepts, thanks to Guanghui Ma of Bentley University. I follow Korean romanization for concepts that pertain to Chosŏn and Jeong's works. When putting both together, I put Korean before pinyin.

4. I rely upon Seong (1991) when referencing *Mencius* and upon Seong (1990) when referencing Confucius's *Analects* in this chapter.

5. Typically, "five human relations" (*wulun* 五倫) are considered fundamental for Confucian society. The other three relations are between ruler-minister, old-young, and friend-friend.

6. The *Zhuzijiali* 朱子家禮 is one of the best known.

7. Early Chosŏn Confucians followed the ancient custom of China, which allowed a feudal lord to "take at one time nine women, a minister or a great officer one wife and two concubines, and a common officer one wife and one concubine" (Deuchler 1992, 233).

8. Women, however, were strictly prohibited from having any sexual relations other than with their husbands. For example, a wife of a high official who committed adultery was decapitated as a model in 1423 (Deuchler 1992, 259).

9. Indeed, for both men and women, not marrying was "socially inconceivable" (Deuchler 1992, 243).

10. Lower-class women were exceptions, as they had to participate in the public realm for their own and their families' survival. However, they were not exempt from patriarchal ideology.

11. I rely primarily on Tu Wei-ming's interpretation of the Confucian self in what follows.

12. *Ren* appears 105 times in 58 chapters of the total 499 chapters of the *Analects* (Chan 1955, 296) and assumes different roles.

13. This is W. Chan's translation (1963).

14. I rely upon Seong (1998) when referencing the *Zhongyoung* in this chapter.

15. This is Tu's translation (1986).

16. I rely upon Seong (1998) when referencing the *Daxue*.

17. In referencing the *Xiao Jing*, I rely upon Seong (1998).

18. This, however, does not imply selfless altruism, as it is a process undertaken for the sake of none other than the realization of one's "authentic" self (Tu 1979, 25). In other words, "considerateness to others is . . . essential to our own self-cultivation" (Tu 1986, 179).

19. I shall later argue that this duty need not be so strict in the contemporary Confucian world.

20. For a Western argument in favor of this point, see Okin (1989).

21. Fortunate mothers have their relatives, particularly their own mothers, to help them with childcare. It should be noted that even in such cases it is almost without exception *female* relatives who assume childcare responsibilities.

22. For a survey of how *min* was used in various Confucian sources, see Hall and Ames (1987, 140–44).

23. Jeong's numerous works written in Chinese were compiled into fourteen books entitled *Sambongjip* in 1486 by the order of King Seong 成宗. In reconstructing his theory, I rely on its Korean translation (2006) as well as the exegesis provided by Han (1999).

24. On trustee politics, see *Analects* 12.7, 12.19, 14.44, 19.19, 20.1; *Mencius* 4A.7, 4A.9, 7B.14, 1A.7. Tu calls it a "fiduciary community" that is "based on trust, rather than on contract" (1986, 176).

25. Chan (2006) states, for example, that "Confucianism may not contain any democratic ideas." See also Huntington (1991).

References

Chan, Joseph. 2006. Political philosophy, Confucian. In *Routledge encyclopedia of philosophy* (Internet version), ed. E. Craig. London: Routledge.

Chan, Sin Yee. 2008. Gender and relationship roles in the *Analects* and the *Mencius*. In *Confucian political ethics,* ed. D. Bell, 147–74. Princeton: Princeton University Press.

Chan, Wing-tsit. 1955. The evolution of the Confucian concept *jen*. *Philosophy East and West* 4 (4): 295–319.

——. 1963. *A source book in Chinese philosophy*. Princeton: Princeton University Press.

Cua, A. S. 1996. The conceptual framework of Confucian ethical thought. *Journal of Chinese Philosophy* 23 (2): 153–74.

Deuchler, Martina. 1992. *The Confucian transformation of Korea: A study of society and ideology*. Cambridge: Harvard University Press.

Fung, Yu-lan. 1948. *A short history of Chinese philosophy*, ed. D. Bodde. New York: Macmillan.

Goldin, Paul. 2000. The view of women in early Confucianism. In *The sage and the second sex*, ed. Chenyang Li, 133–62. Chicago: Open Court.

Hall, David, and Roger Ames. 1987. *Thinking through Confucius*. Albany: State University of New York Press.

Han, Young-Woo. 1999. *The architect of the Chosōn dynasty: Jeong Do-Jeon* (in Korean). Seoul, Korea: Ji-shik-san-eop.

Herr, Ranjoo Seodu. 2003. Is Confucianism compatible with care ethics? A critique. *Philosophy East and West* 53 (4): 471–89.

———. 2008. Confucian democracy and equality. Unpublished manuscript.

———. 2009. Democracy in decent nonliberal nations: A defense. *Philosophical Forum* 40 (3): 309–37.

Huntington, Samuel. 1991. Democracy's third wave. *Journal of Democracy* 2 (2): 12–34.

Jeong, Do-Jeon. 2006. *Sambong Jeong Do-Jeon Mun-jip*, part 1 (bks. 1–3), part 2 (bks. 4–9), and part 3 (bks. 10–14), translated into Korean by the Association of Min-jok-Munhwa-Chujin. Seoul, Korea: Hanguk-haksul-jeongbo.

Jeong, Tae-Hyeon. 1998. *Xiao Jing: Complete Korean translation with the original Chinese text*. Seoul, Korea: Association for Traditional Culture Studies.

Koh, Byong-ik. 1996. Confucianism in contemporary Korea. In *Confucian traditions in East Asian modernity*, ed. Tu Wei-Ming, 191–201. Cambridge: Harvard University Press.

Lai, Whalen. 1991. In defense of graded love. *Asian Philosophy* 1 (1): 51–60.

Nylan, Michael. 2000. Golden spindles and axes. In *The sage and the second sex*, ed. Chenyang Li, 199–222. Chicago: Open Court.

Okin, Susan Moller. 1989. *Gender, justice and the family*. New York: Basic Books.

Raphals, Lisa. 2000. Gendered virtue reconsidered. In *The sage and the second sex*, ed. Chenyang Li, 223–48. Chicago: Open Court.

Seong, Baek-Hyo. 1990. *Analects: Complete Korean translation with the original Chinese text*. Seoul: Association for Traditional Culture Studies.

———. 1991. *Mencius: Complete Korean translation with the original Chinese text*. Seoul: Association for Traditional Culture Studies.

———. 1998. *Daxue/Zhongyong: Complete Korean translation with the original Chinese text*. Seoul: Association for Traditional Culture Studies.

Tu, Wei-ming. 1979. *Humanity and self-cultivation: Essays in Confucian thought*. Berkeley: Asian Humanities.

———. 1986. An inquiry in the five relationships in Confucian humanism. In *The psycho-cultural dynamics of the Confucian family: Past and present*, ed. Walter H. Slote, 175–190. Seoul: International Cultural Society of Korea.

———. 1989. *Way, learning, and politics: Essays on the Confucian intellectual*. Singapore: Institute of East Asian Philosophies.

Wawrytko, Sandra. 2000. Prudery and prurience. In *The sage and the second sex*, ed. Chenyang Li, 163–98. Chicago: Open Court.

PART TWO

RAISING CONSCIOUSNESS

CHAPTER FOUR

Mindfulness, *Anātman*, and the Possibility of a Feminist Self-consciousness

KEYA MAITRA

> Without mindfulness . . . consciousness itself would break
> in[to] pieces, become fragmentary.
> —SOMA THERA, *THE WAY OF MINDFULNESS*

THIS CHAPTER aims to explore the role of Buddhist mindfulness in developing a feminist conception of self-consciousness. The main argument will be put forth in two phases. The first phase will offer an articulation of feminist self-consciousness. The second will delve into the applicability of consciousness-centering Buddhist meditative practices, such as mindfulness, for feminist self-consciousness. The point of departure is going to be a careful discussion of the concept of feminist consciousness and the role that the notion of feminist self-consciousness plays in it. I will show that, although largely unrecognized in the relevant scholarly literature, feminist *self*-consciousness is an essential component of feminist consciousness, and, as such, the political activity of feminist consciousness-raising is dependent on the development of a distinctively feminist self-consciousness.

Feminist consciousness is not a topic that has attracted the attention of many feminist theorists, as echoed in Sandra Bartky's lamentation that feminist consciousness remains largely unaddressed even by Marxist feminists (Bartky 1995, 398). Further, even the few feminists who do discuss feminist consciousness (for example, Barkty, de Lauretis, and Rich) do so in the context of "consciousness-raising," which is a political activity that aims at "partial or total liberation of women" (399). In this regard, feminist consciousness is conceived as a consciousness that emerges when a woman becomes a feminist. As

Bartky writes, "to become a feminist is to develop a radically altered consciousness of oneself, of others, and of what, for lack of better term, I shall call 'social reality'" (397). So the question of consciousness here is framed in the *social* space in the form of women's emerging consciousness of their common experience of oppression and sexism in being a woman and their apprehension of the real possibility of change in their status within that social reality. This understanding of feminist consciousness creates a unique problem when trying to articulate a theory of feminist self-consciousness. Ordinarily, at least in analytic philosophy of mind, self-consciousness stands for the idea of the consciousness that one has of one's own self (and mental states), which most commonly is located in the privacy of one's own mind. Thus one of the debates in the philosophy of mind literature focuses on whether consciousness implies self-consciousness, that is, whether having a thought automatically means being conscious of having that thought. But given the previous characterization of feminist consciousness in communal and social terms, the exact role or even the viability of self-consciousness understood in terms of privacy becomes unclear. The task for a feminist philosopher of mind, then, will be to articulate a self-consciousness that is not purely private, which, I argue, is a necessary step for any robust articulation of feminist consciousness *tout court*.

However, we need not start from scratch. The Buddhist philosophical tradition offers a detailed account of self-consciousness that is not dependent on an individualistic, asocial, transcendent, or essentialist notion of the self. One of the well-known aspects of Buddhist ontology is its denial of an essentialist conception of self (Sanskrit: *ātman*) in favor of a conception that posits *no* abiding self (Sanskrit: *anātman*). The Buddha clearly rejected any essentialist or traditional notion of self even though such a notion was in wide use in the philosophical dialogues of Brahmanism of his time. One of the central arguments the Buddha gives against the thesis of an essentialist self is that no such self ever becomes available in our experience. In denying this conception of self, however, the Buddha is not proposing a purely materialist view of the self either. In keeping with the methodology of the middle path, his *anātman* thesis proposes to understand self as a middle point between the two extreme ontologies of Brahmanical essentialism and a materialist theory of self. According to the Buddha's view, the self is a continuous series of causally connected time slices.

The essentialist notion of self is thus replaced by an explanation of self in terms of a mixture of different factors that include bodily form as well as consciousness, perception, sensations, and volition.

These central Buddhist ideas highlight the need to acknowledge and understand the impermanent, fleeting, and dependent nature of human experience. They thus require training in overcoming the essentialist ways of conceiving ourselves and our realities. Mindfulness is the training of the mind to be present at a given moment without any preconception. What mindfulness ultimately does is enable us to see the inherent selflessness and interconnectedness of our experiences. Techniques used to cultivate mindfulness can help us articulate and attain a feminist self-consciousness that takes into account the particular situations, contexts, and positions of individual women and does not homogenize them in one group in an essentialist fashion. In other words, the Buddhist conception of mindfulness can help to construct a conception of feminist self-consciousness that can account for differences between women, such as race, class, and nationality, in a meaningful way.

Feminist Consciousness

Feminist consciousness refers to the consciousness that a woman has in being and becoming a feminist.[1] Thus specific aspects and characteristics of this consciousness can be captured in comparing it with a woman's simple consciousness of herself. What characterizes feminist consciousness is its underlying grasp of the possibilities of change, transformation, and eventually liberation. As Bartky clarifies,

> Women have long lamented their condition, but a lament, pure and simple, need not be an expression of feminist consciousness. As long as their situation is appreciated *as* natural, inevitable, and inescapable, women's consciousness of themselves, no matter how alive to insult and inferiority, is not yet feminist consciousness. *This consciousness . . . emerges only when there exists a genuine possibility for the partial or total liberation of women.* This possibility is more than a mere accidental accompaniment of feminist consciousness, rather, *feminist consciousness is the apprehension of that possibility.*
> (399, EMPHASIS ADDED).

We can enumerate several features of feminist consciousness from Bartky's characterization: 1. feminist consciousness is transformative since it effects a shift in a woman's cognitive, emotional, and physical behavior; 2. it is at least partially liberatory, because it establishes change and liberation as real goals; and 3. in its active moral dimension, this consciousness is not focused merely on the self, but essentially on the world beyond. As a result of feminist consciousness, feminists do come to view themselves differently, but only *in terms of* their arising awareness of the entire structure of socioeconomic and cultural systems operational in women's oppression. Therefore, feminist consciousness is not simply a different awareness about a woman's own conditions, but it is also constituted by an awareness of the powers and structures that have worked to limit women to those conditions. Further, as Bartky observes, feminist consciousness allows feminists to understand *what* they are and *where* they are "in the light of what [they] are not yet" (399). Thus the full extent of the transformative force of feminist consciousness is also empowering, since it is ultimately reflected in feminists' sense of agency in relation to their struggle. An important aspect of this transformative agency is the realization that even though this project of transformation starts with women's given locations, it ultimately must be other directed in that it is aimed at changing the wider structures of social reality.

The two conditions that Bartky identifies as necessary for the emergence of this consciousness are: "the existence of what Marxists call 'contradictions' in our society and . . . the presence, due to these same contradictions, of concrete circumstances which would permit a significant alteration in the status of women" (397). Some concrete examples of such contradictions include the development of inexpensive contraceptives, the steady increase of women (including middle-class white women) in the workforce, and the emergence of the civil rights, antiwar, and student movements of the sixties. What makes these events contradictory is that they all help to question the "prevailing conception about women's function and destiny" (398). For example, the steady increase of white women in the service industries of post–World War II America clearly contradicted the socially prescribed role for these women as "wife, mother, and homemaker." Thus they offered concrete locations of change where the social "facts" about women's relative wage, role within the family, and continuing subjugation are turned into "contradictions" that become the foci for the transformative projects of the emergent feminist consciousness. Following Marxist theory, Bartky argues that the possibility of social change becomes real only when existing patterns of social interactions come into conflict with new and emergent social relations. These contradictions thereby provide concrete locations for transgression of the social "facts" and the transformative projects of feminist politics. The emergent feminist consciousness is not merely an awareness of the existence of these contradictions, but, more importantly, it is an awareness of the transforming potentials that empower feminist agency to new social realities.

The most central aspect of this consciousness is its altered mode of engagement, in the sense that feminist consciousness engenders being differently aware, which is enabled by primarily seeing oneself (and one's world) as an agent of change and transformation.[2] As Bartky writes, "Coming to have a feminist consciousness is the experience of coming to see things about oneself and one's society that were heretofore hidden. This experience, the acquiring of a 'raised' consciousness, in spite of its disturbing aspects, is an immeasurable advance over the false consciousness which it replaces" (404). While both might be aware of unequal and oppressive social arrangements for women, it is only the raised consciousness that incorporates the real possibility of change and transformation. Hence "false consciousness" is a consciousness that is false only in its relation to the transformative and liberatory project of feminism.

An interesting point about Bartky's conceptualization of feminist consciousness is the level of generality attributed to the emerging consciousness. Even though Bartky locates the emergence of feminist consciousness in the "profound *personal* transformation" (Bartky 1995, 396, emphasis added) that a woman goes through in the process of becoming a feminist, her discussion of the conditions under which such consciousness emerges as well as of the characteristics of such a consciousness remain general. Thus, for example, her characterization of feminist consciousness as a "consciousness of victimization" focuses on the form of victimization and not on its content in the sense of how a particular woman *experiences* such a victimization. In fact, Bartky acknowledges as much when she writes, "Feminist consciousness is consciousness of *victimization.* . . . Victimization is impartial, even though its damage is done to each one of us personally. One is victimized as a woman, as one among many. In the realization that others are made to suffer *in the same way* I am made to suffer lies the beginning of a sense of solidarity with other victims" (400, emphasis added).

Here the emergence of feminist consciousness is articulated in terms of apprehending the *fact* of victimization. The focus, therefore, is on capturing the commonality within the experience of victimization and the "solidarity" that it provides rather than on identifying the diverse individual locations where such victimization occurs. She is suggesting that what is involved in feminist consciousness is this general feeling of victimization "as a woman" where being a woman is conceived without its differences or particularities.

Now the general nature of her discussion may not be surprising given the fact that feminist consciousness is conceived here in the political and therefore, public space. Bartky's characterization of feminist consciousness thus follows from the feminist theme that the "personal is political" where no explanation, theorizing, or engagement with consciousness can happen in the purely private "personal" space. While this politicization of consciousness is understandable given the feminist suspicion of the false dichotomy between the private (and personal) and political, we need also to be mindful of the exact import of the claim the "personal is political." Are we suggesting an equation between these two, where either the personal is collapsed into the political and thus taken as the sole source of meaning and value or the political is collapsed into the personal and thus taken as the sole source of meaning and value? Teresa de Lauretis rightly rejects their equation and instead advocates that we recast the notion that the personal is political by maintaining "the tension between them precisely through the understanding of identity as multiple and even self-contradictory" (de Lauretis 1986, 9). What seems to be missing in Bartky's account of feminist consciousness is an acknowledgment of the fact that there are different manners and experiences of victimization associated with diverse locations.

Interestingly, while further characterizing the consciousness of victimization as a "divided consciousness," Bartky writes, "the awareness I have of myself as victim may rest uneasily alongside the awareness that I am also and at the same time enormously privileged, more privileged than the overwhelming majority of the world's population" (400). What is interesting about this comment is that Bartky is here cognizant of the different locations of a woman's experience of victimization, including the simultaneity of "oppressor" and "feminist." The "divided" nature of this experience thus refers to the fact that while a white woman experiences herself as a "victim," she also experiences herself as being "implicated in the victimization of others" (400). However, it remains unclear whether Bartky takes this as a necessary feature of feminist consciousness. Moreover, even in this point, she fails to address the issues of whether this "consciousness divided" is experienced by each relatively privileged feminist in identical ways (such as middle-class white women) and of whether it is similarly experienced by feminists of color. Her silence in relation to the subjective or private location of the experience of consciousness is intriguing and telling, especially since she aims to provide a "phenomenology" of feminist consciousness.

Another way of articulating Bartky's project might be that even though feminist consciousness is located within each individual, what gives rise to the emergence of that consciousness is the rise of the awareness of one's victimization "as a woman," that is, as a member of the group "women." For example, in sharing one's experiences of domestic abuse with other women in consciousness-raising and by speaking what is not allowed to be spoken in patriarchal culture, an individual woman begins to realize that her situation is not so unique, and that it is more a result of her being a woman in patriarchal culture than it is her being herself. Of course, the role of community of other women is undeniable in feminist consciousness-raising. My point is not to rule out the role of community, but to draw attention to the fact that there has to be more to it. In other words, feminist consciousness-raising is predicated on a woman's coming to see the implicit social structure of patriarchy that oppresses, but it has to acknowledge one's own positionality in relation to the patriarchal structure as well. What is also problematic in this is the fact that by overlooking different individual locations, feminist consciousness also generalizes the variety of feminist experiences and thus, in an essentialist fashion, fails to speak for every feminist's consciousness in any robust sense. In failing to speak for all feminists, it becomes unclear whether such a consciousness speaks for any feminist's consciousness at all.

The transformative project of feminist consciousness depends on a feminist's ability to see herself as an agent of change and transformation. But does feminist consciousness conceived in general terms allow for such an agency? It does not seem so since such an agency has to be located within the individual self for it to be a source of transformative actions. This is not simply because only the individual can be the source of such a transformation, but, more important, because only the individual can be the *location* of such transformation, whatever the impetus. Further, as Nancy J. Hirschmann argues, a feminist analysis of agency should not only consider "external factors" like domestic abuse, but must also consider the "internal factors" relating to "the ways in which cultural structures actually produce 'women'" (Hirschmann 1998, 347). My worry here is informed by de Lauretis's point that woman's subjectivity is produced "by *one's personal, subjective engagement* in the practices, discourses, and institutions that lend significance (value, meaning, and affect) to the events of the world" (de Lauretis 1984, 159). If this conception of subjectivity is at the heart of feminist consciousness, as it has to be given the fact that it enables agency, then what Bartky's conception overlooks in its generalized form is the explanation of how this articulation of feminist consciousness features in a particular woman's identity. To counterbalance the generality of feminist consciousness, I want to introduce the concept of feminist self-consciousness.

Feminist Self-consciousness

De Lauretis characterizes the notion of self-consciousness within feminist theorizing in the following terms: "The Italian feminists call it '*autocoscienza*,' selfconsciousness, and better still, self consciousness. For example, Manuela Fraire: 'the practice of self consciousness is the way in which women reflect politically on their own condition'" (1984, 185). According to this view, feminist self-consciousness, in first approximation, refers to the individual feminist's personal engagement with factors of her social reality. It is a mode of self-analyzing and self-reflection that serves as the point of departure in every feminist's arrival at feminist consciousness. Thus, it precedes feminist consciousness and facilitates the emergence of feminist consciousness by allowing for the specificity that each feminist has with factors of her social reality in the construction and critical revision of her identity. When Linda Alcoff observes that [feminist] consciousness needs to be "reconstructed through the process of reflective practices" (Alcoff 1988, 425), I believe she is alluding to the important role played by feminist self-consciousness. This entails "a fluid interaction in constant motion and open to alteration by self-analyzing practice" that is at the heart of woman's subjectivity and thereby also of feminist consciousness (425).

This notion of self-consciousness is assumed in Alcoff's reading of de Lauretis on subjectivity:

> Lauretis claims that an individual's identity is constituted with a historical process of consciousness, a process in which one's history "is interpreted or reconstructed by each of us within the horizon of meanings and knowledges available in the culture at given historical moments, a horizon that also includes modes of political commitment and struggle." . . . Lauretis formulates a subjectivity that gives agency to the individual while at the same time placing her within "particular discursive configurations" and, moreover, conceives of the process of consciousness as a strategy.
>
> (425)

Alcoff's main argument here is that the concept of woman needs to be articulated in terms of "a gendered identity as positionality" (422). Although Alcoff does not articulate her point in terms of self-consciousness, it is this notion that enables her to incorporate the individual feminist's positionality because self-consciousness indeed is the location for a woman's self-reflective, self-altering opportunities. So the need to focus on self-consciousness and not just on feminist consciousness seems to be at least twofold: first, what grounds and gives content to the strategy of feminist consciousness is feminist self-consciousness and, second, a focus on self-consciousness seems to provide a complete, nuanced, and effective sense of feminist consciousness. Thus, as de Lauretis writes while commenting on the role of feminist consciousness in feminist politics, "Consciousness raising is a 'critical method,' a specific mode of apprehension or 'appropriation' of reality . . . the social and subjective impact of a practice—the collective articulation of one's experience of sexuality and gender—which has produced, and continues to elaborate, a radically new mode of understanding the subject's relation to social-historical reality. Consciousness raising is the original critical instrument that women have developed toward such understanding, the analysis of social reality, and its critical revision" (1984, 185).

However, consciousness as such must necessarily travel through self-consciousness, which allows the role of individual self to serve as a location where the analysis and the reflective and critical revisions take place. What I am further suggesting is that the specificities of these individuals shape and color the resultant consciousness in an important manner. In other words, feminist self-consciousness is this moment within the process of feminist consciousness where a particular feminist's specific experiences shape and give meaning to her awareness of her identity.

Even if one is persuaded by this argument for feminist self-consciousness, any articulation of the nature of such self-consciousness needs to respond to the question: *whose* self-consciousness? My point here is that a concept of woman on which the feminist notion of self (and therefore of self-consciousness) can be predicated is hard to come by. What complicates the matter is that the dominant conception of self, popular in mainstream philosophy, relies on what Wendy Lee-Lampshire (1992) and others call "a transcendental subject" that goes beyond the materialist and physicalist vision of an individual. This view presupposes mind-body dualism, where mind (with which self is identified) comes to be equated with a transcendental entity. Feminism has tried to avoid affirming this dualistic view of personhood because, among other things, this dualism has been instrumental in the devaluation of women. By equating women with the body and thus the realm of emotions and irrationality, this dualism limits women's moral, social, and political aspirations. Thus feminists have by and large resisted the urge to locate consciousness in the transcendental subject or the immaterial mind. "Cultural feminism" and "postmodernist/poststructuralist feminism" are two emergent movements within feminist theorizing that have resisted and offered alternatives to this prevalent conception of self (Alcoff 1988).

Essentialism is a real worry, especially in terms of Bartky's characterization of feminist consciousness, because of its focus on capturing the generality of feminist experience. More specifically, when Bartky argues that feminist consciousness is a consciousness of victimization and locates the consciousness at the level of the group, she is overlooking the multitude and diversity of victimizations as experienced by feminists. She is also overlooking the simultaneity and intersectionality of victimizations as in the case of women of color and other minorities who experience victimization on multiple fronts. In so doing, Bartky offers a universalist conception where she is, however unintentionally, privileging one kind of experience of victimization in her conception of feminist consciousness. What results, as in any case of essentialism, is "a homogenous, unproblematized, and ahistorical conception" of woman that seems utterly ineffective for feminism (Alcoff 1988, 413). In addition, this conception is extremely problematic since it valorizes one attribute and thereby precludes the future possibility of developing a different attribute under changed socioeconomic conditions. If the transformative project is truly at the heart of feminist consciousness as Bartky contends, then a universalizing, essentialist conception cannot provide for a sustained feminist movement. It might be useful to add in this regard that when Adrienne Rich (1979) articulates what she calls the political, aesthetic, and erotic "female consciousness" in opposition to a "culture of passivity," her characterization draws on the female body as the "innate female essence" (Alcoff 1988, 412). What connects Rich's essentialism to Bartky's discussion of feminist consciousness is the latter's articulation of the defining features of feminist consciousness in terms of women's shared, common, and therefore undifferentiated experience of victimization. While I agree with Bartky regarding the centrality of the experience of victimization to the emergence of feminist consciousness, I also believe that the essentialism of her account follows from its assumption of the single dimensionality of the texture of such experiences.

These essentialist worries highlight the difficulties faced in developing a viable feminist theory of self. It is important to have such a viable notion because without it we cannot even talk about feminist self-consciousness. Furthermore, and more significantly, "the concept and category of woman is the necessary point of departure for any feminist theory and feminist politics, *predicated as these are on the transformation of women's lived experience in contemporary culture and the reevaluation of social theory and practice from women's point of view*" (Alcoff 1988, 405, emphasis added). It is in developing this viable theory that Alcoff introduces her conception of women's identity as positionality. As noted before, positionality is articulated in terms of the dynamism between the network of relations in which a woman finds herself as well as her ability for self-creation through self-reflection and self-analysis. I believe this is what de Lauretis has in mind when she discusses feminist consciousness and self-consciousness not in terms of a subject's private possession but in terms of a "process"; thus consciousness for her and Alcoff is not something "fixed" that is waiting to be discovered, but something that is being created (de Lauretis 1986, 8). This different sense of consciousness is expected, given the feminist understanding of self and subjectivity. But it is here, I want to argue, that the role of feminist self-consciousness becomes central in embedding the self-analysis and self-reflection that positionality takes to be of such importance. Especially if one articulates the concept of self in a nonessentialist, possibly positional way à la Alcoff, then a woman's ability to engage, analyze, and reflect critically on her positionality in the network of social reality in which she finds herself would constitute her self-consciousness. This point is captured when de Lauretis writes, "As a form of political critique or critical politics, feminism . . . has effected a *habit-change* in readers, spectators, speakers, etc. And with that *habit-change* it has produced a new social subject, women. *The practice of self consciousness, in short, has a constitutiveness as well as a constituency*" (1984, 185–86, emphasis added).

What captures the heart of feminist self-consciousness in enabling a new feminist subjectivity is this aspect of "habit-change" that de Lauretis is alluding to. I argue that what enables this habit change are not only the opportunities for self-reflection, self-analysis, and self-revision that feminist writers commonly point to; more important, it is the self-centering aspect of self-consciousness that underwrites this habit change in feminists. The self-centering aspect does not hesitate to ground the self and its identities within its given intersectionalities. Such grounding allows this consciousness to not fixate privately and narrowly on the self. As a result, instead of being merely self-critical, a feminist becomes comfortable and accepting of her self. Such a consciousness thus is aware of one's positional intersectionalities, but is no longer defined or limited by them. In fact, in the next section, I want to argue that it is this self-centering aspect that provides the grounding for feminist self-consciousness. The technique of Buddhist mindfulness becomes relevant to the development of feminist self-consciousness in helping us enhance the self-centering aspects of self-consciousness.

Let me also speak to the issue of the relation between feminist consciousness and feminist self-consciousness. I am not suggesting that these two states are independent in the sense that one can exist without the other. The main reason for the focus of my discussion on feminist self-consciousness is not to identify it as a separate process and/or state from feminist consciousness but to highlight its role in a well-developed account of feminist consciousness. The specific suggestion of this chapter is that, procedurally, feminist self-consciousness has to be identified as a necessary step within any discussion of feminist consciousness. Buddhist themes are relevant to this discussion because one prevailing Buddhist theory analyzes the relationship between self-consciousness and consciousness in terms of reflexivity (MacKenzie 2007). That is to say, consciousness and self-consciousness are reflexively related; in being aware of x, a subject is also aware of being aware of x. In what follows I offer a more nuanced and inclusive account of feminist consciousness than has been previously given by applying this Buddhist theory of reflexivity to the discussion of feminist consciousness and relying on it to articulate the dynamics between feminist consciousness and self-consciousness.

Buddhist Mindfulness and Feminist Self-consciousness

Theoretical crossovers between Western feminism and Eastern meditative practices may help explain yoga's particular appeal to women; most yoga centers in Britain report over sixty percent of their membership as consisting of women (Newcombe 2007; Warner 2009). What has been argued in Western popular culture is that yoga's general ability to improve physical and mental well-being, including fostering a positive self-image, holds special appeal to Western women. These affinities provide an important precedent for the idea that mindfulness practices to center the self can be particularly relevant to feminist activism. It is no wonder then, as Anne Klein attests, that Buddhist practice has encouraged women throughout the United States to assume "formative leadership roles in developing Buddhist communities, both as scholars and as meditation teachers" (Klein 1995, xvi). I argue that the phenomenon of Buddhist mindfulness and the meditative practices associated with attaining mindfulness not only make the attainment of feminist consciousness possible but also allow us to articulate another dimension of feminist self-consciousness, namely, self-centering, which is an aspect that is starkly absent in Western feminist discussions of self, subjectivity, and consciousness.

Just as Bartky and Alcoff argue that the emergence of feminist consciousness does not require acquisition of new facts but rather a new way of engaging one's social reality, I want to argue that feminist self-consciousness arises through "a new sensibility about subjectivity" and the self (Klein 1995, 61). What underlies this new sensibility is a dimension of the mind that is not discursive or purely conceptual, but, rather, is captured in its ability to be fully present. As Klein elaborates, "Buddhist epistemologies . . . emphasize that one's mind has a dimension that is neither primarily gained nor governed through language. The mind's capacity for clarity, for example, is simply part of its collateral or natural dynamic" (61). Mindfulness practices aim to reinforce this "capacity for clarity." The function of mindfulness thus is not to alter the contents of one's mind "but to change the *tone* of consciousness" (82). In *Anguttara Nikāya*, Buddha says, "If one thing, O monks, is developed and cultivated, the body is calmed, the mind is calmed, discursive thoughts are quieted, and all wholesome states that partake of supreme knowledge reach fullness of development. What is this one thing? It is mindfulness directed to the body" (Thera and Bodhi 1970, 9). As I will note shortly, it is not at all accidental that Buddha singles out mindfulness directed toward the body as the sole source of ultimate wisdom.

The primary meaning of mindfulness in the context of meditation practices refers to the Pāli term *sati*, which is variously translated as mindfulness and "bare attention." While it is hard to describe mindfulness in words, it is not an artificial or exotic or even difficult thing; rather, it is an experience that can be experienced by anyone at any waking moment. It is the simple act of focusing one's entire attention on the present moment. It is bare not because it is devoid of content; rather it is bare due to the absence of emotional reaction of either pleasure or aversion, like or dislike. In mindful meditation the object of one's attention might change from breath to any visualized image to any part of one's body or mind; it is the *manner* of engagement, namely, the bare attending, that makes them all mindful. What lies at the heart of mindful meditation is this ability of the mind to be fully present, its ability to "notice with bare attention" (Norsworthy 2004,

110); this noticing is not channeled through the mediation of inter-pretation, layers of meaning, or various forms of mental reactivities that normally accompany our everyday attention. It is simple, pure, and complete attending that gives rise to not only a calm but also a clear insight about the nature of reality and ultimately the final deliv-erance from suffering. Mindful meditative practices strive to cultivate the "capacity of attending to the content of our experiences as it be-comes manifest in the immediate present" (Thera 1967, 3).

A classic Theravada Buddhist source and manual, *The Way of Mind-fulness: The Satipatthana Suta and Its Commentary*, lays out in detail the meditative practices that are central to the methodical cultivation of the "faculty of mindfulness" and also the different objects that an aspirant is encouraged to focus on in gradual and comprehensive "arousing" of mindfulness. The first item of "contemplating the body in the body" is quite illuminating because it attests to the fact that mindfulness ultimately stands for participatory observation where the divide between the mind (spectator) and body (object) fades away. How does one do this? The Buddhist response is to focus on any one of the fourteen different exercises, including "mindfulness of breath-ing," "attention to the posture," among others, that many different Pāli Buddhist texts outline. When an aspirant focuses her attention on each breath as she breathes, not only is her breathing stabilized, but ultimately an awareness rises that consciousness is never a fully disembodied experience. By treating the body not in terms of its es-sential otherness from the mind but in terms of living the body as the ground of mind, mindfulness thus reveals that mind and body are "functions in constant communication, always shaping and re-sponding to the other 'like a drum and the sound of a drum'" (Klein 1994, 119).[3] Further, by focusing on the "contemplation of the body" as the first step, Buddha here emphasizes the fact that "meditative comprehension of the impermanent, painful, and selfless nature of bodily processes forms the *indispensable basis* for a corresponding comprehension of mental processes" (Thera and Bodhi 1970, 9, em-phasis added).

Some basic characteristics of mindfulness should already be emerg-ing. In focusing one's entire attention on the object, the mind attains a kind of unmediated, impartial objectivity that is both nondiscursive and nonjudgmental. As Bhante Gunaratana says, mindfulness "is the ability of the mind to observe without criticism" (Gunaratana 1999,

134). Further, instead of becoming oppressive, this objectivity is cel-
ebrated as ultimately liberating since it not only frees one from the
egotistical and critical voices inside but also because it "alone has the
power to reveal the deepest level of reality available to human observation" (138). Mindfulness is the avenue through which every aspiring Buddhist is able to see the inherent selflessness of everything
including the truth of the no-abiding self (*anātman*) theory. The continuous and sustained focus on the arising and passing of mental and
bodily events and states allows one to realize how what we consider
independently existing objects are results of an arbitrary process that
bundles certain perceptions together, thereby differentiating them
from "the rest of the surging flow of experience" (142). This arbitrary
process not only gives rise to conceptions of enduring objects but also
to the theme of mind-body dualism, along with the notion of a transcendental subject. In coming to see mind and body more as a part
of an interrelated and interdependent complex series of experiences
in which they both participate, one comes to experience a centeredness and internal coherence that provides the self with a "unified
strength" (Klein 1994, 122).

One might detect a kind of paradox here as the increasing sense of
grounding in one's present experience is accompanied by the rise of
a proportional awareness of the conventional and constructed nature
of one's reality including one's self. But as Klein clarifies, this paradox is "only in description, not in the experience" (Klein 1995, 67). At
the level of experience, a clear simultaneity between the constructed
and grounded natures of our reality comes to the foreground, which
becomes the location for a renewed sense of agency. Indeed, by not
being mediated through discursive attention, the centeredness and
unified strength of self come to signify a "visceral"—rather than an
intellectual or conceptual—"sense of continuity" (66). "When one is
strongly mindful, one plants one's consciousness deep in an object
like a firm post well sunk in the ground, and withstands the tempestu-
ous clamour of the extraneous" (Thera 1967, 10). In this way mindfulness qualifies an attitude of the mind and not its contents. To be fully
present, the mind does not have to know every detail about the object
of its attention. Rather, what marks this presence is the availability
of the coherent mind's undivided and, more important, nonreactive
attention, thereby automatically providing a centered calm within
one's consciousness.

The most important aspect of emergent mindfulness from the perspective of my project is the multidimensional sense of self that it allows. We have already noted the centrality of the notion of self for feminism in both theory and practice. In this regard the self-centering abilities of Buddhist mindfulness allow an improved way of envisioning the self. In its explicit acceptance of the physical grounding of our mental being, mindfulness allows us to articulate what remains merely a hint in Alcoff's and de Lauretis's conceptions of feminist subjectivity. If the self is viewed through its constructedness in the conceptual space—either by multiple narratives or by the networks of positionalities—what we get is a picture of consciousness that turns out to be, to use Klein's term, "inappropriately flat," which becomes "a crucial factor in making the [resultant] self seem too 'thin' or insubstantial to be a basis for feminist agendas" (Klein 1995, 84). In this regard, I want to conclude with Klein, "Buddhist understandings depict a self that is strong, not limited or overgeneralized by essentialist or other concepts, and a type of coherence not marred by recognition of the self's constructed nature. It offers the subject a sense of her mind as an extensive, even inexhaustible, resource of strength and fresh perspectives. This subjectivity is of particular interest to women, because women are today explicitly concerned with finding modes of expression and reflection that are as free as possible from the internalized cultural restraints on women's being" (86).

Mindfulness practices ultimately come to empower the self through self-cultivation and self-acceptance. Through its focus on the cultivation of self through mindfulness, Buddhism gives us a new way of understanding self-cultivation. While such cultivation is impossible in the postmodernist framework because no self is left to be cultivated, even in the essentialist framework such cultivation becomes limiting and oppressive. If we acknowledge the dual nature of feminist empowerment, following Patricia Hill Collins, then the role of self-cultivation through mindfulness becomes quite pertinent. Collins has argued that the empowerment attained through "critical consciousness" has two dimensions (Collins 2000, 286). First, in coming to recognize the social system of hegemony, it enables the feminist to criticize hegemonic ideologies.[4] However, this critical ability is only necessary and not sufficient for true empowerment and liberation because such critiques are merely "reactive." Thus the second dimension consists of the "construction of new knowledge." Mindfulness can enable this constructive dimension in its simplicity, nonreactivity, and ability to be open to new perspectives while being grounded in the present moment. Such openness further allows a "sphere of freedom" by creating a safe space where new meanings and revisions can be explored without losing one's anchor (285). What is more useful in this openness is the compatibility between self-acceptance and self-revision that it enables. If a feminist is no longer imprisoned by her specific intersectionalities, or a particular perspective, but is ready to see every experience as a fresh one, then she can truly work toward developing a freed consciousness. Such cultivation could also result in the kind of permanent habit change that de Lauretis talks about.

The force of mindfulness in the personal dimension draws from the fact that it ultimately allows its practitioners to gain a clear insight into the nature of things, including the constructed and grounded nature of their selves. However, what is important for our purpose is the social dimension of mindfulness. A common worry in this regard is that the Buddhist theme of liberation, based on the ideas of "detachment" and "indifference," can only lead to the removal of oneself from the social realm. However, as the story of the Buddha's own life would attest, this detachment can free one up to devote oneself truly to society instead. "As we step away from attachment to the things that bind and limit us, we can begin to see deeply into both inner and outer conditions and to move in harmony with the demands of the moment" (Boucher 1988, 260). The social dimension of mindfulness emerges through two avenues. First, mindfulness enables us to appreciate the interconnectivities that bind each one of us to others and thus acknowledge our shared conditions, goals, realities, and destinies. Second, the self-acceptance aspect of mindfulness fosters acceptance of others. Sandy Boucher provides a useful example of this social dimension when she writes, "In my own experience, my Buddhist practice and my political activism have formed a loop, carrying me out into action and back into meditation—the one informing the other—and at some moments the two are one. In jail after antinuclear demonstrations, my Buddhist practice helped me to tolerate and at times transform the frustrations and indignities" (261).

But it might be asked how this social dimension relates to *feminist* activism. By way of responding to this question, I want to make two related points. First, as Kathryn L. Norsworthy writes, "Both feminist therapy and Engaged Buddhism include an emphasis on activism as a source of growth and healing" (Norsworthy 2004, 112). Discussing the relevance of Buddhist themes to feminist therapy, Norsworthy further argues that the equanimity that comes from attending to and accepting one's present location "is an important, empowering aspect of the healing process for the woman trauma survivor" (111). The importance of arriving at the moment of equanimity can be further articulated by referring to the "paranoia" Bartky talks about, "especially when the feminist first begins to apprehend the full extent of sex discrimination and the subtlety and variety of the ways in which it is enforced. Its agents are everywhere, even inside her own mind, since she can fall prey to self-doubt or to a temptation to compliance" (402). One can argue that for feminist mental well-being as well as the transformative project of feminism, the calm, equanimity of mindfulness, and being in the present moment can be extremely fitting and effective in the political and social projects of feminism. Second, as Klein clarifies, "Mindfulness departs from the urge to master, override, rein in, or otherwise manipulate the self. It avoids treating the self as a territory to be conquered, governed, or colonized by ideals. Insofar as the relationship to oneself sets the tone for one's relationship to others, it is crucial to have models of self-engagement that do not denigrate or otherwise oppress. A mindful person is attentive, interactive, and nonoppositional. She is also autonomous in that she need not depend on some external goal to galvanize her mindful collateral energies" (80). Where this nonjudgmental and self-accepting attitude becomes really helpful is in combating the issue of self-hatred that many women, including many feminists, struggle with. In being noncritically aware of weakness, defect, or confusion in me or others, I am finally relieved from the need to have to fight it or deny it. Such a self-acceptance not only encompasses an acceptance of others but also provides a solid ground for feminist solidarity in its awareness of our interrelated and interpenetrating realities.

Now, am I suggesting that a feminist must be a Buddhist in order to grasp or develop self-consciousness? To the contrary, my discussion of feminist self-consciousness shows that any person, from any location, can develop self-consciousness. There is nothing intrinsically Buddhist about mindfulness because this faculty of mind is not restricted to Buddhists by any means. However, the Buddhist discussion does enable us to highlight an ability of the mind, namely, mindful attending, that often goes unnoticed and unrecognized. Further, when Hirschmann and others argue that the "act of choosing" is only necessary but not sufficient for feminist agency and that we need the ability to create new choices that are not circumscribed by patriarchy, I believe a feminist self-consciousness that is developed through mindfulness could be the location where such new formulations could begin. Moreover, in developing cosmopolitan feminism (Reilly 2007) and global feminism, where the primacy is on "authentic" cross-cultural and cross-boundaries dialogue, I believe this feminist self-consciousness can go a long way in providing the starting point and set the tone for such a dialogue by enabling unprejudiced listening, attentive understanding, and honest collaborating and negotiating. This not only results in better readiness to forge connections with others but also in arriving at "a global feminist standpoint" without requiring a "homogeneity of identity or experience or even an ongoing consensus among women across a range of issues" (Reilly 2007, 187). This attests to the immense potentials that feminist self-consciousness has in contemporary feminist theories and activisms.

In summary, a viable feminist theory requires a sustained development of the notion of feminist consciousness. Only such a notion can ground feminist activism. I have argued that a necessary step in the articulation of feminist consciousness is feminist self-consciousness, which provides the specific locations for transformation and liberation. Finally, I have articulated a notion of feminist self-consciousness informed by the Buddhist notion of mindfulness—both in theory and practice—that enables us with a sense of agency suitable for global feminisms.

Notes

1. It might appear that nothing in principle would preclude a man from having a feminist consciousness. However, I have limited my discussion of feminist consciousness to women's consciousness because transformation of *women's* consciousness was the principal goal of the consciousness-raising movement that brought the conception of feminist consciousness to the forefront.

2. The same idea is expressed by Linda Alcoff when she writes, "When women become feminists the crucial thing that has occurred is not that they have learned any new facts about the world but that they come to view those facts from a different position, from their own position as subjects" (Alcoff 1988, 434).

3. See also Buddhaghosa (1976, 690).

4. Though in her argument Collins focuses on black feminists, I believe the import of her argument naturally extends to all feminists.

References

Alcoff, Linda. 1988. Cultural feminism versus post-structuralism: The identity crisis in feminist theory. *Signs* 13 (3): 405–36.

Bartky, Sandra L. 1995. Toward a phenomenology of feminist consciousness. In *Feminism and philosophy: Essential readings in theory, reinterpretation, and application*, ed. Nancy Tuana and Rosemary Tong, 396–406. Boulder: Westview.

Boucher, Sandy. 1988. *Turning the wheel: American women creating the new Buddhism.* San Francisco: Harper and Row.

Buddhaghosa. 1976. *Path of purification* (*Visuddhimagga*). Trans. Bhikkhu Nyanarnoli. Berkeley: Shambhala.

Collins, Patricia Hill. 2000. *Black feminist thought: Knowledge, consciousness, and the politics of empowerment.* New York: Routledge.

Fraire, Manuela. 1977. La politica del femminismo. *Quaderni Piacentini* 62/63:195.

Gunaratana, Bhante Henepola. 1999. Mindfulness. In *Voices of insight: Teachers of Buddhism in the West share their wisdom, stories, and experiences of insight meditation*, ed. Sharon Salzberg, 133–42. Berkeley: Shambhala.

Hirschmann, Nancy J. 1998. Western feminism, Eastern veiling, and the question of free agency. *Constellations* 5 (3): 345–68.

Klein, Anne C. 1994. Presence with a difference: Buddhists and feminists on subjectivity. *Hypatia* 9 (4): 112–30.

———. 1995. *Meeting the great bliss queen: Buddhists, feminists, and the art of the self.* Boston: Beacon.

Lauretis, Teresa de. 1984. *Alice doesn't.* Bloomington: Indiana University Press.

———, ed. 1986. *Feminist studies/critical studies.* Bloomington: Indian University Press.

Lee-Lampshire, Wendy. 1992. Moral "I": The feminist subject and the grammar of self- reference. *Hypatia* 7 (1): 34–51.

MacKenzie, Matthew. 2007. The illumination of consciousness: Approaches to self-awareness in the Indian and Western traditions. *Philosophy East and West* 57 (1): 40–62.

Newcombe, Suzanne. 2007. Stretching for health and well-being: Yoga and women in Britain, 1960–1980. *Asian Medicine* 3:37–63.

Norsworthy, Kathryn L. 2004. Integrating feminist theory and engaged Buddhism. In *Buddhist women and social justice: Ideals, challenges, and achievements*, ed. K. L. Tsomo, 101–16. Albany: State University of New York Press.

Reilly, Niamh. 2007. Cosmopolitan feminism and human rights. *Hypatia* 22 (4): 180–98.

Rich, Adrienne. 1979. *On lies, secrets, and silence.* New York: Norton.

Thera, Nyanopanika, and Bhikkhu Bodhi, trans. 1970. *Anguttara Nikāya: Discourses of the Buddha, an anthology.* Part 1. Kandy: Buddhist Publication Society.

Thera, Soma, trans. 1967. *The way of mindfulness: The Satipatthana Sutta and commentary.* Kandy: Buddhist Publication Society.

Warner, Judith. 2009. Being and mindfulness. *New York Times*, March 9.

CHAPTER FIVE

Liberating Anger, Embodying Knowledge
A Comparative Study of María Lugones and Zen Master Hakuin

JENNIFER MCWEENY

IN RECENT decades, feminist philosophers have become increasingly attuned to the liberatory aspects of anger. Audre Lorde, Naomi Scheman, Marilyn Frye, Uma Narayan, Elizabeth V. Spelman, Sue Campbell, Wendy Donner, María Lugones, Diana Tietjens Meyers, and Sylvia Burrow all ask us to reconsider dominant views of our angers, which see them as irrational, unjustified, hypersensitive, and morally and epistemologically unproductive. In so doing, these philosophers encourage us to understand our angers as lucid and appropriate responses to institutionalized oppression. Such feminist analyses of anger are often grounded, either explicitly or implicitly, in the radical idea that *angry experience is a kind of knowing experience.*[1] Our angers empower us, because within them we *know* our own agency and self-worth (Frye 1983; Narayan 1988; Spelman 1989; Burrow 2005), we *know* we have been wronged (Frye 1983; Spelman 1989), we *know* the patterns and functions of the oppressive structures that work on us (Frye 1983; Narayan 1988; Campbell 1994; Lugones 2003; Meyers 2004), and we *know* revolutionary strategies for enacting different, liberatory kinds of existence (Lorde 1984b; Donner 2002; Lugones 2003).

My aim in this chapter is to strengthen the theoretical ground of feminist analyses of anger by focusing on the epistemological mechanisms of angry experience. Rather than argue *that* angry experience must involve knowing experience, I offer a description of *how* and, by extension, *why* the angers of the oppressed are ways of knowing. In agreement with the idea that traditional pictures of self and mind have difficulty accommodating the emotionality of the oppressed (Scheman 1980; Meyers 2004), I situate my description between two extraordinary philosophers whose respective accounts of anger emerge within unorthodox ontological frameworks. Specifically, I compare María Lugones's account of "second-order anger" with Zen Master Hakuin Ekaku's descriptions of self-less anger.[2] Against the backdrops of Latina feminism and Rinzai Buddhism, we are able to make out two thoroughly embodied kinds of anger that do not vie for intelligibility within the confines of prevailing interpretations of reality. In virtue of their bodily and insubordinate characters, these angers are able to take stock of the ways in which cognitive content is and is not linked to the orienting perspective that renders that content visible, sensible, and expressible. As such, second-order and self-less angers constitute epistemological transformations in the angry person, and hence they also create possibilities for her liberation.

After first establishing Lugones's and Hakuin's respective theories, I go on to delineate the epistemological mechanisms of these angers by developing a perceptual theory that draws from Maurice Merleau-Ponty's notion of operative intentionality. I then show how my "operative view" of anger can explain why the angers of the oppressed are ways of knowing without succumbing to some of the problems generated by the pluralistic ontologies of Lugones and Hakuin. In the final section, I explore various parallels between this epistemology of anger and the feminist comparative methodologies employed throughout this book.

Lugones: Second-Order Anger

In her essay "Hard-to-Handle Anger," Lugones writes of a kind of knowing anger that remains concealed to us if we consider it within the framework of an ontology that affirms a unitary self who is independent from an objective world. She explains this special type of "second-order" anger by contrasting it with "first-order" anger, which is more conducive to this traditional "one self/one world" ontology. According to Lugones, "first-order" anger is a communicative anger that vies for respect from the oppressor in the "official world of sense" (Lugones 2003, 108). First-order angers include the angers discussed by Frye and Spelman: righteous anger about having been treated unjustly or unfairly (Frye 1983, 85–86), demanding anger that asks you to respect my domain and social position (87–90), and judgmental anger that blames another for wrongdoing (Spelman 1989, 266). As assertions of agency and claims to respect, first-order angers want *uptake*, that is, they want to be included and heeded in the prevailing world of sense. While first-order angers are epistemologically important because their successes and failures at getting uptake map our own social positions and those of others, they also express a certain futility in oppressive contexts. When a woman in a sexist society is angry in a first-order way, she is asking to be heard by the very world that marks her angers as inaudible precisely because they issue from a woman—a perceived subordinate who is expected to lack agency and respectability. First-order angers thus accommodate a one self/one world ontology, because the angry person attempts to fit her self into the given world by demanding respect and fair treatment from that world. Perhaps as a result of the connection between first-order angers and traditional ontology, most people are likely to identify their angers as first-order, and our philosophical accounts of anger reflect this bias.

In contrast to first-order anger, Lugones describes "second-order" anger as a separatist, uncommunicative anger that recognizes that the angry self and the metaphysical presuppositions of the official "'world' of sense" are mutually exclusive.[3] Here, we must remember that Lugones rejects a one self/one world ontology and instead subscribes to a pluralistic metaphysics where selves are multiple, as are the worlds that they inhabit and move between. Lugones's metaphysics is based on a conception of space as "multiple, intersecting, contemporaneous realities" (Lugones 2003, 16) and on a conception of the oppressed person as a "'world'-traveler" who journeys between realities and selves in order to survive (16–26, 88–90). Within this fresh ontological apparatus, we are led to understand an experience of intense anger not as a stepping outside of ourselves, but as "the anger of a self different from the one who is trying to make sense within the confines of official reality, a self who is doing the work of resistance" (104). Hence, the "second-order" label is appropriate for this type of anger, not because it is anger about being angry (as one entrenched in a one self/one world ontology might suspect), but because it is the anger of a different, "second" self. The very existence of this second self is fundamentally incompatible with the first world and with the first, *subordinate* self who survives in that world.

Lugones readily acknowledges that her pluralism is "ontologically problematic" (89–91). On the one hand, Lugones claims that each person consists in a multiplicity of different selves and experiences these selves *as different*. On the other hand, although Lugones denies the existence of any "underlying I," she affirms that a person is somehow able to identify each different self as "me." In addition, Lugones observes that "'worlds' of sense" are distinct from one another and that these differences are real and not simply a matter of interpretation (16). And yet, worlds of sense are permeable since they intersect, overlap, and trespass upon one another, and since people can inhabit more than one world at the same time (16, 88). We can now see that the problem generated by Lugones's ontology is a problem that accompanies any nonsolipsistic ontological pluralism: how do we make sense of a self that is at the same time both one and many without erasing one ontology in the other? Although Lugones intentionally leaves this question unanswered (89), we may nonetheless observe that her criteria for distinguishing one world from another should place her view somewhere between a strong pluralism that holds that worlds are numerically distinct and a weak pluralism that believes that simply having a "different take" on reality is a sufficient condition for defining a world.[4]

Given that Lugones's pluralism is neither strong nor weak, I argue that it is reasonable to identify what Lugones means by "'world' of sense" with another of her concepts, namely, "structure." In "Structure/Anti-Structure and Agency Under Oppression," Lugones defines a structure as the patterned arrangements of practices, roles, concepts, and institutions within a given society that function as a means of construing and constituting persons (60). For example, one structure could construe women of color as passive subordinates whereas another structure could construe them as active subjectivities. Because the practical demands of a structure constitute the "emotions, beliefs, norms, desires, and intentions" of the people who move within that structure, when a person shifts structures she also becomes a different self (60). Not only can a person live in more than one structure at the same time, she can also go in between structures and be without structure (61).

Thus described, Lugones's ontological pluralism beckons us to explore the spatiality of second-order anger: Where, in relation to the multiplicity of worlds, is second-order anger located? And which of our multiplicity of selves is capable of this emotion? At first glance, Lugones seems to be saying that second-order anger is the anger of a resistant self who inhabits a "'world' of sense" that is different from, or even opposed to, the structure that authorizes her oppression. However, upon closer examination, we find that the self of second-order anger is *not* a fully-formed self. Rather, the angry self is an "in-between self" who is without structure and not yet tied to a world. Unlike first-order anger, second-order anger "decries the sense of the world that erases it" and begins to travel to alternative spaces apart from "harmful sense" (111–14). The location of second-order anger, then, is *across*, rather than within, "'worlds' of sense" (33, 111, 115). We can thus infer that the self of second-order anger must inhabit what Lugones calls "the limen," a gap between universes of sense (59). The limen is a "creative preparation" and a "way of life" (Lugones 2006, 79, 83); it is the space/moment where we are most aware of our own multiplicity and where we are best able to see different structures critically (Lugones 2003, 59). Temporally, second-order anger is forward looking as it moves to create new liberatory sensibilities. Spatially, second-order anger lies between the first world of the dominators and the third world of the oppressed: it is a borderland territory that resists assimilation to either side.

When Gloria Anzaldúa writes of the "intimate terrorisms" of domestic abuse, sexual assault, and colonial violence, she is expressing second-order anger. Her words are enraged and enflamed by her own bodily oppression and by the oppression of others:

> The dark-skinned woman has been silenced, gagged, caged, bound in servitude with marriage, bludgeoned for 300 years, sterilized and castrated in the twentieth century. For 300 years she has been a slave, a force of cheap labor, colonized by the Spaniard, the Anglo, by her own people.... For 300 years she was invisible, she was not heard. . . . she concealed her fire; but she kept stoking the inner flame. . . . The spirit of the fire spurs her to fight for her own skin and a piece of ground to stand on, a ground from which to view

> the world—a perspective. . . . Battered and bruised she waits, her bruises throwing her back upon herself and the rhythmic pulse of the feminine.
>
> (ANZALDÚA 1999, 44–45)

The anger of the dark-skinned woman begins with various forms of collective bodily violation, which include bludgeoning, sterilization, silencing, and erasure. Colonization and imperialism, at the hands of both outsiders and intimates, cut off parts of the queer mestiza's body/body of expression. Her subjectivity/objectification and existence/nonexistence are erased by the patterned logics and material practices of noncontradiction, excluded middles, and either/or. Her anger is about being erased and disempowered by one or more "'worlds' of sense" (Lugones 2003, 114). The bruises that are the material and symbolic indications that her communications have received no uptake in prevailing structures throw her back on herself in isolation as she fights to inhabit a different, not-yet-formed "'world' of sense" (and to find a different practice of expression) that is compatible with her own flourishing.

Attending to the spatiality of second-order anger helps us to see why Lugones would conceive of this anger as fundamentally epistemological. Second-order anger embodies a shift in perspective that allows us to perceive objects and their situating backgrounds differently than we do with the unitary vision of the official "'world' of sense." In the limen we experience objects as contextual and tied to "worlds" rather than as simply given. In this respect, second-order anger embodies what Anzaldúa calls *la facultad*: "*La facultad* is the capacity to see in surface phenomena the meaning of deeper realities, to see the deep structure below the surface. It is an instant 'sensing,' a quick perception arrived at without conscious reasoning. It is an acute awareness mediated by the part of the psyche that does not speak" (Anzaldúa 1999, 60). In contrast to arrogant perceptions and either/or reasonings that seek the destruction and assimilation of whatever is different or contradictory, second-order angers are fresh perceptions whose content depends on our openness to uncertainty, indeterminacy, unruliness, and surprise. Indeed, risking our senses of self and the "ossified" meanings that make up their concomitant worlds are necessary conditions for experiencing second-order angers (Lugones 2003, 26). Consequently, the way of knowing that is enacted in second-order anger is a kind of "traveling"; it is a shift from being one self to being a different self (89). This epistemic process "isolates the resistant self in germination" (103), since cognitive content is rarely "cognitively straightforward" as it moves across worlds of sense (116–17). However, the separatist, incommunicative character of second-order anger is oriented by a hope for transformation and connection: the angry self's willingness to create new meanings that elude the logic of oppression is a condition for the possibility of coalition-building activities like "world"-traveling, "complex communication" (Lugones 2006), love, and liberation.[5] By placing us in the limen, second-order angers give us the chance to renegotiate perceptual, social, and linguistic meanings to better accord with the fullness and complexity of reality, which includes its back side (even though this back side is invisible when viewed from the dominant, habitual perspective). Here the angry self participates in a way of knowing that does not drive a wedge between the experiences of our resistant, germinating selves and the languages of their expression.

Hakuin: Anger Without Self

Let us now travel to eighteenth-century Japan, where we will find depictions of a similarly insightful kind of anger in the writings of Zen Master Hakuin. Whereas we would expect a Buddhist to think of anger as a poison that binds a person to the delusions of the ego and other independent objects, Hakuin instead believes that some angers are actually conducive to enlightenment (Japanese: *satori*) and "liberation from suffering" (Sanskrit: *nirvana*).[6] This seeming inconsistency in Hakuin's account of anger is less pronounced when situated in the context of his Rinzai Buddhism.[7] The Chinese Buddhist Linji (ca. 810–866), for whom the school of Rinzai Buddhism is named, is famous for incorporating thundering shouts, blows from his staff, physical beatings, and crude, evocative language into his teachings. In light of Zen's emphasis on the primacy of compassion within the teacher-student relationship, we should not jump to the conclusion that Linji's pedagogical techniques are themselves expressions of anger. Alternatively, these methods are potentially ways of provoking and evoking anger in students so that they may learn. As such, Rinzai pedagogy reflects an awareness that, in certain situations, emotions can be more effective than discourse or scripture at disrupting those habitual psychological patterns that bind a person to independent objects and to the wheel of *karma*.

In the *Orategama*, Hakuin tells the story of the Zen priest Gudō Toshōku who goes to visit the monk Yōzan Rōshi to discuss his understanding of Zen.[8] As the story goes, Yōzan responds to Gudō's query promptly with verbal abuse and beatings. At this, Gudō becomes quite angry: "Angered, Gudō went one very hot day to a grove of bamboo and sat in meditation without a stitch of clothing covering his body. At night great swarms of mosquitoes surrounded him and covered his skin with bites. Fighting at this time against the hideous itching, he gritted his teeth, clenched his fists, and simply sat as though mad. Several times he almost lost consciousness, but then unexpectedly he experienced a great enlightenment" (Yampolsky 1971b, 66). In *Orategama Zokushō*, Hakuin again associates anger with enlightenment when he writes that the person who does not get angry "even when reviled" and who does not care "even if he is rejected" is a "torn rice bag, bloated from gorging himself on the swill of swine, an ignorant blind fool" (Yampolsky 1971b, 135). While this person without anger may mistakenly think his dispassion indicates an enlightened disavowal of the ultimate reality of the self, Hakuin points out that he is quite far from realizing no-self in any robust way. Hakuin's portrayal of anger in these passages raises several questions: What is the nature of the relationship between Gudō's anger and his enlightenment? What kind of self is realized within this anger? And, how is Gudō's anger related to his embodiment?

We are likely familiar with one or more variants of the basic Buddhist idea that the unenlightened person and the enlightened person perceive reality differently from each other. The unenlightened person partakes in *samsāra*, which is the cycle of daily repetitive existence that entails suffering, reincarnation, birth, and death. This person is committed to the existence of independent objects that persist through time, such as trees, pots, rocks, bodies, and selves. By contrast, the enlightened person experiences *nirvāṇa* by attending to the interrelatedness, impermanence, indeterminacy, nonduality, and emptiness of all things. In other words, the enlightened person sees the individuations that divide reality into self-contained, persistent objects as illusions. Practitioners of Rinzai, like other Mahayana Buddhists, believe that ultimately *nirvana* is *samsara*. This claim of identity avoids the hypocrisy that Hakuin believes is entailed by simultaneously advocating nondual perception and positing a duality between ordinary life and enlightened life (Yampolsky 1971b, 75). Ethically speaking, it also discourages students from believing that it is possible to transcend, and therefore withdraw from, worldly existence. However, in positing the identity of *nirvāna* and *samsāra,* Buddhist metaphysics encounters an ontological problem similar to the one generated by Lugones's ontological pluralism: How can reality be both unitary and plural at the same time? Unlike Lugones, Rinzai Buddhists address this problem by abandoning ontological pluralism in favor of an epistemological pluralism: *nirvāna* and *samsāra* are not two different realities, but are instead two different ways of engaging/perceiving one reality.

In contrast to some Buddhist schools, Rinzai Buddhists believe that all people are "originally enlightened" (Japanese: *hongaku*), but many are unable to "see into their own nature" (Japanese: *kenshō*), which is the indeterminate, relational, nondual nature of reality (Yampolsky 1971b, 114). Thus, for Hakuin, enlightenment is not an uncommon state of mind that is attained through meditation; it is rather the interminable epistemological process of recognizing that you are not the self that you have come to believe you are. Hakuin repeatedly teaches that this recognition cannot be explained or transmitted and that instead it is "just like knowing for yourself by drinking it whether the water is hot or cold" (145). This view of enlightenment not only highlights the role that embodied experience plays in reaching *nirvana* but also emphasizes the Rinzai idea that there is no necessary causal connection between Zen teaching and practice and being enlightened. Rinzai Buddhists believe that enlightenment comes suddenly and spontaneously, as in Hakuin's many examples of people who experience enlightenment at the very moment of breaking a leg, cutting off an arm, being dehydrated by severe diarrhea, suffering from a spinal tumor, or being knocked on the head with a broom (Yampolsky 1971b, 65–67; Waddell 2001, 33–34).

Once a person first achieves nondual perception, however, he must undertake "post-*satori* practice" in order to help him continually enact this enlightened way of perceiving in the face of considerable pressure to fall back into old habits of thinking dually (Waddell 2001, 48–62). Linji thus describes how no-self is realized within enlightenment: "He has neither form nor shape, neither root nor trunk; nor does he have a dwelling place; he is as lively as a fish leaping in the water, and performs his function in response to all situations. Only, the place of his functioning is not a locality" (Schloegl 1976, 30). This place of lively, spontaneous responsiveness is "no-place," because it is an indeterminate landscape that is fashioned by the coexistence of opposing ideas, words, and identities.[9] Lacking determinate, individuated meanings, no-place is a place rich with epistemological possibilities, fluid and in motion, out of which a leaping fish could spring. Even though no-place is terrifying because the continued existence of independent identities, including that of the self, finds no foothold, here we are "in a position to move in any direction" (Yampolsky 1971b, 59, 135).

When we better understand what Hakuin means by enlightenment, we are able to see that he is associating the kind of anger that is not attached to an individuated self (what, for brevity, we might term *self-less anger*) with the shift in perspective that is established through a person's nondual apprehension of reality, that is, through his inhabitating of no-place. In this respect, Gudō's anger functions in much the same way that *kōan* study does in the instruction of the Zen student to frustrate dualistic thinking through the use of paradox, contradiction, and non sequiturs. Examples of widely used *kōans* in the Rinzai tradition include Hakuin's famous question "Two hands clap and there is a sound, what is the sound of one hand?" and others, such as "What is your original face before your mother and father were born?"[10] When pursued assiduously, *kōan* study can constitute an important break in the habit of committing to the dualistic either/or ontologies that are entailed by the more conventional ways in which we use language. In addition, *kōan* practice eschews the "retrospective reconstruction of reality" inherent in representational languages, concepts, and thoughts and places the Zen student in the immediacy of the present moment (Kasulis 1981, 60). For this reason, enlightened understandings of *kōans* are rarely given in analysis, but are instead *demonstrated* through shouting, hitting, grasping the master's staff, and other activities. As instantiations of spontaneous responsiveness, improvisation, presentness, and openness to the flow of the world, these bodily orientations cut against the grain of dualistic logics and, as such, enact the student's position at no-place that is both *nirvāṇa* and *samsāra*. Therefore, *kōan* practice is best conceived as an *expres-*

sion of the nondual perspective that is enlightenment rather than as a cause of or a means to that enlightenment.

Like *kōan* study, Gudō's anger rejects dualistic thinking, either/or ontology, and the linguistic practices that are laced through both. In defiance of the slow-moving meditative practices that Hakuin contemptuously refers to as "dead-sitting" or "silent-illumination Zen," Gudō's anger, like a leaping fish, is a swift and present response that throbs with life and movement. As an embodied practice, Gudō's anger is his letting go of his need to grasp the enlightened perspective through language and analysis. As such, Gudō's anger is his demonstrated ability to move beyond *samsāra* and its concomitant epistemological framework that sets the knower in opposition to the known. In this way, Gudō's anger is his becoming involved in the experiential flow of the world and his perceiving, as the heat and mosquitoes mix his insides with the outside, the relationality of all things. Like a *kōan*, his anger eats at the subject/object duality that is his skin. Gudō's anger is the very incarnation of the lack of boundary between self and world; it is the place where the self is transformed and no-self is realized. Naked in the bamboo grove, Gudō becomes one with the world in the same sense that the Zen student "becomes one" with a particular *kōan* and lets its nondual perspective constitute his every activity (Yampolsky 1971b, 33–34).

The great insight that animates Hakuin's account of self-less anger is that striving for the extirpation or suppression of our passions can sometimes heighten, rather than diminish, our capacities for dualistic thinking. This is why Hakuin tells us that "the very objects of the senses will be Zen meditation, and the five desires themselves will be the One Vehicle" (Yampolsky 1971b, 36). Mindful of the identity of *nirvāṇa* and *samsāra*, Hakuin teaches that we must perceive the plurality and the unity, that is, the determinacy and indeterminacy, of experience at the same time. We best express our grasp of this whole and present reality within our everyday bodily practices, instead of through thoughts, language, or concepts that are seen as separable and temporally removed from experience. Self-less anger is thus a liberatory anger because, although it engages the same world that the unenlightened person engages, it does so in a nondualistic way that is incompatible with object-attachment, karmic bondage, and worldly suffering.

The Operative View of Anger

Having acquainted ourselves with Lugones's and Hakuin's accounts of anger and their respective ontologies, we are now well positioned to consider the epistemological mechanisms of these angers. Second-order anger is a knowing anger because it is a practical mode of traveling between cognitive frameworks and hence it is a way of seeing the deep structures that constitute meanings and sense. Selfless anger is a knowing anger because it demonstrates, or embodies, being fully present in and mindful of the whole of reality, including those aspects of reality that exceed dualistic logics, languages, and actions. Although notably different in many respects, both angers are knowing experiences because they are insubordinate to conventional ways of being and thinking, and both angers are tied to transforming selves who come to know precisely because they engage fresh perspectives. In what follows, I suggest that thinking of these angers as perceptions that proceed in virtue of what Merleau-Ponty terms "operative intentionality" (2002, xx, 158) can provide a more detailed description of their epistemological mechanisms.[11] This in turn can help feminists explain *how* and *why* the angers of the oppressed are ways of knowing.

Merleau-Ponty rejects the idea that our minds' directedness toward objects is a kind of mental state and instead claims that intentionality is, at base, an interactive, bodily process whereby meaningful perceptions of determinate objects emerge from indeterminate, ambiguous experience. Merleau-Ponty believes that intentionality arises because we are oriented toward a specific aspect of the world in a practical way; we are trying to accomplish something like going for a walk, feeding ourselves, or communicating with another. The practical orientation that is entailed by our particular project, whatever it may be, is necessarily a taking up of a particular perspective with our bodies. In taking up this perspective with our bodies, we situate the intended aspect of the world against a certain background or "horizon" (Merleau-Ponty 2002, 78, 117). Once this aspect is situated, "objects" such as a snake in the path, the drips of water from the faucet, or the frown of another become perceptible. When a determinate object has thus emerged, the dynamic process of creating its meaning then becomes "sedimented" as a result of maintaining our practical orientations over time and in virtue of the object's capacity to cohere with the rest of our determinate, unified perceptions (150). Hence we often forget that the object is a meaning we negotiated through practical engagements that are situated by temporal, historical, social, cultural, and anatomical backgrounds and so we experience the object as a thing-in-itself viewable from any perspective. However, we are not always able to sustain the perceptual constancy of an object. The snake we perceived in the path turns out to be a coil of rope, the drips from the faucet are later identified as acorns falling on the tin roof, and another's frown is soon recognized as an expression of pensive agreement. As our perceptions of Necker cubes and duck-rabbit pictures illustrate, reality is able to sustain multiple determinations and perspectives, although none can be sustained exhaustively and no two contradictory perspectives can be sustained at exactly the same time (36).

In contrast to our sedimented perceptions of physical objects, we should locate angry perceptions on the fluid, emergent side of Merleau-Ponty's spectrum of intentionality. Unlike sedimented objects, thoughts, and words that possess definite boundaries, our angers are those original moments where meaning is *negotiated* (not discovered or created) through the coming-into-contact of body and world. Although other emotions and perceptions also involve meaning-negotiating activity, anger is distinctive due to the peculiar character of the activity that it entails. In particular, anger surfaces when there is *a lack of fit* between a certain bodily orientation (along with its concomitant cognitive perspective) and the "world of sense" within which this orientation/perspective is framed. In cases of second-order and self-less angers specifically, the lack of uptake is far more profound than that of other angers because the bodily subjectivity of the angry person presents an overwhelming challenge to the logic and sensibility of its situating world of sense. Fueled by the implausibility of reconciliation between self and world, these angers separate the angry person's experience of reality from her available frameworks for understanding that reality; they are *borderland perceptions* where no one framework of meaning is able to get a foothold in sensibility at the expense of any another. Second-order and self-less angers thus lead us to negotiate new worlds of sense, new senses of self, or both.

Just as the operative character of perception best reveals itself when unified perceptions break down, as is the case with the experimental conditions and illnesses that Merleau-Ponty so frequently describes, second-order and self-less angers surface most easily in oppressive situations where the very subjectivity of the angry person contradicts the official world of sense. For example, the queer mestiza speaks English at school, or else she is rapped on the knuckles with a sharp ruler (Anzaldúa 1999, 75). In this instance, the mestiza's way of moving her mouth, pronouncing her own name, and conceptualizing her own identity when speaking Spanish receive no uptake from the "American" world of sense. The queer mestiza's anger at this incompatibility is her experiencing the irresolvable tension between who she is and what the official world of sense will allow. Likewise, when the Zen master redirects the bodily orientation of his students with shouts and beatings, the master calls the student to be fully present in his body; he helps his student to *feel* the tension between his experience of reality as interrelated and impermanent (his experience of no-self) and the frameworks that the student possesses for describing and understanding that reality. Located in the limen and no-place, these angers grope around in the dark to find alternate comportments and subversive, bodily perspectives from which to better see, resist, and thrive. This feature of our angers explains why angers usually feel urgent and preoccupying: they are our struggles to make determinate what is unsettling and has yet to be decided.

The operative view of anger as I have described it explains *how*, that is, by what process, our angers constitute ways of knowing and thus also helps us to see *why* we should think of our angers as fundamentally epistemological in nature. As experiences of disharmonies between our bodily orientations and the uptake they receive from their situating world of sense, our angers are our *realizations* of these dissonances, in the double sense of "realization" as "awareness" and "instantiation." Our angers thus demonstrate what we know when we attend to the tension and slack of those intentional threads that embed our practices within a world. As operative cognitions, these angers are fluid and structurally open enough to account for those aspects of reality that are multiple, complex, and indeterminate. And, because they are contemporaneous with what they seek to illuminate, angry cognitions do not risk distortion by being temporally removed from the experiences of reality that they intend. Moreover, the mechanisms of our angers centrally involve the epistemologically valuable skills of openness to surprise, inquisitiveness, responsiveness, body-trust, experimentation, improvisation, and creativity.

We should not, however, misconstrue our angers to be mere causes of knowledge or mere dispositions to acquire knowledge. In taking up the practical struggles inherent in making sense of a self who over-flows the boundaries of her situating framework, our angers embody the knowing that is formed by being *in touch* with reality, fully present and attuned to its constitutive relationships. While all our angers are ways of knowing in this respect, second-order and self-less angers are *doubly* epistemological in nature because they specifically intend the deep structures of reality. In virtue of their ability to travel between worlds of sense, these angers function on a meta-epistemological level as witnessing players in the relational interactions that build objects and conceptual frameworks in tandem with one another. The angry self's inhabitating of these liminal locations reorients her practical perspective and thus effects a radical epistemic shift in her percep-tion. There is, quite literally, a *world* of difference between thinking of objects, people, and meanings as already determined or amenable to dualistic thinking and thinking of them as negotiable, in-process, and always partially in excess of any retrospective reconstruction of them.

Let us now consider how this operative view of anger can bolster many of the claims articulated in contemporary feminist analyses of anger. According to the operative view, our angers realize the lack of fit between a practical orientation and a world of sense and conse-quently expose the constitution of the world of sense in question. As such, first-order and second-order angers reveal the harmfulness and hypocrisy of the oppressive structures that work on us and the wrongs that have been done to us within the limits of a particular world of sense. In addition, the active, practical orientations that our angers entail fully express our obvious claims to agency and self-worth, even if our situating world of sense does not acknowledge these claims. We can also see why oppressed people would be especially prone to the practical struggles that constitute our angers: in a society where members of certain groups are thought to lack agency and respect-ability, most of the practices these individuals undertake *as active sub-jects* will be out of sync with the society's established cognitive frame-works. Hence the operative view can help strengthen feminist views like Narayan's that associate the emotionality of the oppressed with an epistemic privilege in regard to the nature of oppression (Narayan 1988). Finally, Lorde's and Lugones's claims that within our angers we know revolutionary strategies for enacting liberatory languages, selves, and existences are easily accommodated by the operative view. Since the dissonance between a person's subjectivity and its world of sense is so profound that a reconciliation of the two is not pursued, the practical struggles involved in second-order and self-less angers entail traveling to places of possibility that are without structure and between worlds.

Comparing Angers

The methodology that informs my articulation of the epistemology of anger presented here is one that practices this very epistemology. The philosophical juxtaposition of Lugones and Hakuin is itself a journeying to an in-between space that is crisscrossed by many borders: East/West, North/South, man/woman, self/other, teacher/student, past/present, fact/value, mind/body, theory/practice, politics/spirituality, and reason/emotion. As such, this methodology, which is aptly termed feminist comparative philosophy, demonstrates the spatiality of second-order and self-less angers by insubordinately trekking through undisciplined, epistemologically fertile places. Recognizing the incompatibility of her specialized disciplinary training and the diversity of human experiences, the feminist comparative philosopher takes up the project of renegotiating the philosophical structures of meaning, sense, and approbation that encapsulate her expression in order to make collective liberation possible.

There are abundant advantages to using feminist comparative methodologies when theorizing, not the least of which is that they emphasize the culturally dependent nature of ideas in a central way. Moreover, when resisting established logics, views, and disciplines, there is strength and strategy to be found in the diverse numbers entailed by unconventional coalitions. For example, exposing parallels between Lugones's and Hakuin's philosophies renders us less able to dismiss each in turn as "extremist," incomprehensible, or outrageously religious or political. These important similarities include the beliefs that there is more than one way to know reality; that worldly suffering is tied to dualistic, individuating ways of knowing that are temporally removed from experience; that the self is acutely habituated to this either/or way of knowing and being; that the self can be liberated from this habituation by assuming unconventional, or insubordinate, practical orientations; and that the place of self-transformation is precarious and indeterminate, yet also the ground of future liberation. However, once put into conversation, it is the differences (both subtle and incommensurable) between these philosophies that spur our imaginations and push us further in our theoretical understandings. The in-between self of Latina feminism is not Zen Buddhism's no-self, the limen of the borderlands is not kenshō's no-place, forward-looking anger is not a self-less anger that is entirely within the present moment, "liberation" and "suffering" do not possess identical meanings in both contexts, and receiving "compassionate beatings" from a Zen master is *not at all* comparable to being beaten in the context of domestic abuse.

Situated by the juxtaposition of Lugones and Hakuin, we are not only able to see how the angers of the oppressed are ways of knowing, but we are also better able to maneuver the impasse that is suggested by the ontologically problematic nature of ambiguous subjectivities. As we observed earlier, Lugones's philosophy is ontologically problematic because it claims *both* that a person is a multiplicity of distinct selves, each of whom inhabits a different "world," *and* that there is something that recognizes this plurality of selves as "me" and allows worlds to intersect spatially and temporally. Hakuin's Buddhist account of anger provides us with an important key to this feminist problem because it indicates that by changing our habitual, bodily orientations we can learn to be fully present to the nondual, ambiguous aspects of reality and thus we can learn to perceive the world differently. When we juxtapose the enlightened and unenlightened selves of Buddhism with Lugones's resistant and oppressed selves, we are led to construe a self as a *system* of internally coherent, practical, bodily orientations.[12] Given this notion of "self," it seems perfectly permissible to conceive of a person as having more than one self and as possibly having selves that are different from and contradictory to one another. The oppressed self is different from the resistant self because carrying out the actions of a subordinate person involves engaging the body in a system of orientations (for example, comportments of deference, surrender, invisibility, and so on) that are exactly contrary to the system that sustains liberatory actions. We can then rely on Merleau-Ponty's theory of perception to help us understand how habitually engaging different systems of practical orientations actually constructs different determinate worlds for us out of indeterminate ambiguous experience. By conceiving of selves as *essentially* embodied, we move beyond Lugones's ontological impasse: systems of practical orientations do create different selves and different worlds, but these distinct entities are connected through our bodies, which are those liminal spaces where our experiences of reality first get paired with a perspective, that is, with a framework for understanding that reality. Since our emotions are our primary ways of being present in our bodies, they are thus important ways of knowing the contours of what is real.

We have only just begun to explore the fruitfulness of the comparison between Lugones and Hakuin. Many more significant questions remain to be explored: Are "second-order" ways of knowing that take stock of the depth of reality always preferable to first-order ways of knowing? How should we choose among multiple or competing ways of knowing? How does the operative view of knowing support or complicate other epistemological theories, such as reliabilism, virtue epistemology, externalism, and epistemic contextualism? Which kinds of forces, specifically, motivate us to assume one practical orientation rather than another? Are there contexts where the knowing that comes with anger could be antithetical to the angry person's liberation and/or to collective liberation? Is the operative view of anger too dependent on suffering as a means to knowledge, transformation, and liberation?[13] And does the inclusion of the Western, canonically "legitimate" theories of Merleau-Ponty support or frustrate the feminist comparative methodology that guides this chapter? Since feminist comparative philosophy cannot be sustained if it is practiced by only a few "undisciplined" thinkers, I leave these and other questions as urgent invitations to engage in comparative feminist projects.

Notes

I would like to thank Ashby Butnor, Vrinda Dalmiya, Bradley Park, Dianna Taylor, Brenda Wirkus, David Allamon, and two anonymous reviewers for their helpful and insightful comments on earlier drafts of this essay. I am also thankful for conversations with Charles Goodman and James Behuniak Jr., each of whom helped me to understand some of the finer points of Buddhist philosophy. Lastly, this essay benefited greatly from the ensuing discussions when I presented initial versions at the Second Annual Roundtable on Latina Feminism in Cleveland, Ohio (April 2007) and at the Annual Meeting of the Society of Asian and Comparative Philosophy in Pacific Grove, California (June 2007).

1. Although the feminist philosophers mentioned do associate *particular* kinds of anger with knowing experience, many hesitate to make the stronger claim that *all* angers are epistemic all of the time. For example, see Lorde (1984a, 152) and Lugones (2003, 105).

2. Hakuin Ekaku (1685–1768) is one of Japan's greatest Zen masters. He is most famous for his innovative reforms of Zen practice, which led to a widespread reversal in the decline of the Zen movement that occurred during Japan's medieval period. His best known achievements include developing a way to formalize *koan* practice within the Zen curriculum and bringing Zen to the masses through his insistence that Zen be practiced by people from all ranks of society. For a historical account of Hakuin's life and ideas, see Dumoulin (2005, 367–99).

3. For more on Lugones's conception of a "'world' of sense," see the introduction to this volume.

4. The phrase "different take" comes from Ortega (2001, 11).

5. For more on the practice of "world"-traveling, see the introduction to this volume.

6. I am grateful to Graham Parkes for introducing me to Hakuin's unorthodox theory of the emotions and sparking my initial interest in Rinzai Zen (Parkes 1995).

7. For excellent discussions of the place of anger in the wider tradition of Buddhism, see Goodman (2002, 366–68), and Vernezze (2008). See also Hershock (2003) for a thorough discussion of the role of emotion in Buddhism.

8. Gudō Toshōku (1579–1661) was a Zen priest of the Rinzai tradition whose lineage of Zen heirs can be traced directly to Hakuin (Yampolsky 1971a, 12).

9. The phrase "no-place" is used in Ruth F. Sasaki's translation of this passage in place of Schloegl's "not a locality" (Sasaki 1975, 15). See also Parkes's commentary on this passage (Parkes 1995, 222).

10. I cite G. Victor Sōgen Hori's translations of these popular koans (Hori 2000, 289–90).

11. Although perceptual theories of emotion are not yet widespread in emotions theory, they have come to greater prominence in recent years. See, for example, Cataldi (1993), Mazis (1993), Charland (1996), Döring (2003), and Prinz (2004). In contrast to my view, however, most of these theories understand perception as a fundamentally representational, rather than practical, affair. Cataldi's and Mazis's theories are exceptions to this trend.

12. This idea is implicated in Lugones's work through her emphases on embodiment and praxis. See especially her essay "Tactical Strategies of the Streetwalker/*Estrategias Tácticas de la Callejera*" in Lugones (2003, 207–37).

13. I am grateful to Dianna Taylor for first posing this question to me.

References

Anzaldúa, Gloria. 1999. *Borderlands/La Frontera: The new mestiza*. 2d ed. San Francisco: Aunt Lute.

Burrow, Sylvia. 2005. The political structure of emotion: From dismissal to dialogue. *Hypatia* 20 (4): 27–43.

Campbell, Sue. 1994. Being dismissed: The politics of emotional expression. *Hypatia* 9 (3): 46–65.

Cataldi, Sue L. 1993. *Emotion, depth, and flesh: A study of sensitive space*. Albany: State University of New York Press.

Charland, L. 1996. Feeling and representing: Computational theory and the modularity of affect. *Synthese* 105:273–301.

Donner, Wendy. 2002. Feminist ethics and anger: A feminist Buddhist reflection. *American Philosophical Association Newsletter on Feminism and Philosophy* 1 (2): 67–70.

Döring, Sabine A. 2003. Explaining action by emotion. *Philosophical Quarterly* 53 (211): 214–30.

Dumoulin, Henrich. 2005. *Zen Buddhism: A history*, vol. 2: *Japan*. Trans. James W. Heisig and Paul Knitter. Bloomington: World Wisdom.

Frye, Marilyn. 1983. *The politics of reality*. Berkeley: Crossing.

Goodman, Charles. 2002. Resentment and reality: Buddhism on moral responsibility. *American Philosophical Quarterly* 39 (4): 359–72.

Hershock, Peter D. 2003. Renegade emotion: Buddhist precedents for returning rationality to the heart. *Philosophy East and West* 53 (2): 251–70.

Hori, G. Victor Sōgen. 2000. Kōan and *kenshō* in the Rinzai Zen curriculum. In *The kōan: Texts and contexts in Zen Buddhism*, ed. Steven Heine and Dale S. Wright, 280–316. New York: Oxford University Press.

Kasulis, T. P. 1981. *Zen action/Zen person*. Honolulu: University of Hawaii Press.

Lorde, Audre. 1984a. Eye to eye: Black women, hatred, and anger. In *Sister outsider*. Berkeley: Crossing.

———. 1984b. The uses of anger: Women responding to racism. In *Sister outsider*. Berkeley: Crossing.

Lugones, María. 2003. *Pilgrimages/peregrinajes: Theorizing coalition against multiple oppressions*. Lanham: Rowman and Littlefield.

———. 2006. On complex communication. *Hypatia* 21 (3): 75–85.

Mazis, Glen A. 1993. *Emotion and embodiment: Fragile ontology*. New York: Peter Lang.

Merleau-Ponty, Maurice. 2002. *The phenomenology of perception*. Trans. Colin Smith. New York: Routledge.

Meyers, Diana Tietjens. 2004. Emotion and heterodox moral perception: An essay in moral social psychology. In *Being yourself: Essays on identity, action, and social life*, 137–57. Lanham, MD: Rowman and Littlefield.

Narayan, Uma. 1988. Working together across difference: Some considerations on emotions and political practice. *Hypatia* 3 (2): 31–47.

Ortega, Mariana. 2001. "New Mestizas," "'world'-travelers," and "dasein": Phenomenology and the multi-voiced, multi-cultural self. *Hypatia* 16 (3): 1–29.

Parkes, Graham. 1995. Nietzsche and Zen Master Hakuin on the roles of emotion and passion. In *Emotions in Asian thought*, ed. Joel Marks and Roger T. Ames, 213–34. Albany: State University of New York Press.

Prinz, Jesse J. 2004. *Gut reactions: A perceptual theory of emotion*. New York: Oxford University Press.

Sasaki, Ruth Fuller, trans. 1975. *The record of Lin-chi*. Kyoto: The Institute for Zen Studies.

Scheman, Naomi. 1980. Anger and the politics of naming. In *Women, language, and society*, ed. Sally McConnell-Ginet, Ruth Borker, and Nelly Furman, 174–87. New York: Praeger.

Schloegl, Irmgard, trans. 1976. *The Zen teaching of Rinzai*. Berkeley: Shambhala.

Spelman, Elizabeth V. 1989. Anger and insubordination. In *Women, knowledge, and reality*, ed. Ann Garry and Marilyn Pearsall, 263–73. Boston: Unwin Hyman.

Vernezze, Peter J. 2008. Moderation or the middle way: Two approaches to anger. *Philosophy East and West* 58 (1): 2–16.

Waddell, Norman, trans. 2001. *Wild ivy: The spiritual autobiography of Zen Master Hakuin*. Boston: Shambhala.

Yampolsky, Philip. 1971a. Introduction: Hakuin and Rinzai Zen. In *The Zen Master Hakuin: Selected writings*. Trans. Philip Yampolsky. New York: Columbia University Press.

——, trans. 1971b. *The Zen Master Hakuin: Selected writings*. New York: Columbia University Press.

PART THREE

PLACES OF KNOWING

CHAPTER SIX

What Would Zhuangzi Say to Harding?

A Daoist Critique of Feminist Standpoint Epistemology

XINYAN JIANG

THE DAOIST Zhuangzi, who lived in ancient China during the fourth century BCE, is well known for taking perspectives and circumstances of knowers into account in knowledge claims. His epistemological insights on the nature of dominant norms and contempt for conventional values are still very much appreciated by many Chinese today. Contemporary feminist epistemologists have posed formidable challenges to dominant Western epistemologies by arguing that knowers and their knowledge claims are socially situated. These feminists point out that the so-called universal subjects of knowing are often male epistemic agents and that so-called universal knowledge claims are mainly made from male perspectives. If Zhuangzi and feminist epistemologists could know each other, they would be surprised to find what close allies they could be in struggling against pseudo-universalism in epistemology. There are vast bodies of literature on Zhuangzi's view of knowledge, on the one hand, and feminist epistemology, on the other. However, the striking similarities and interesting differences between the two have not been studied. This chapter aims to begin this important dialogue by undertaking a critical analysis of one formulation of feminist epistemology—Sandra Harding's standpoint theory—through the lens of Zhuangzi.

The Situatedness of Knowledge

Regardless of the differences between feminist epistemologies, every feminist theory of knowledge examines the ways in which gender influences what epistemic agents take to be knowledge, what can be known, and who counts as a credible epistemic agent. Feminist epistemology is in part motivated by the recognition that each epistemic agent occupies a position in one or more social groups (Webb 1995, 85). While feminist epistemologists focus on the gender identity of the knower as the central social aspect of their analyses, gender is usually investigated in connection to other social identities, such as class, race, and culture.[1] In general, these theorists are critical of the idea of an abstract epistemic agent, that is, one who is totally autonomous in his reasoning and who can be impartial and disembodied (Code 1993, 16). Such a critique is crucial in order to show that all knowledge claims are socially situated and also that so-called universal truths are usually not value-neutral, but androcentric in disguise.

In her standpoint epistemology Harding argues strongly for the situatedness of knowledge. According to her, each epistemic agent is located somewhere in society, and this location is classified into various groups with differing statuses and interests. Therefore, knowledge claims are inevitably limited by social locations and colored by values. As Harding puts it:

> In societies where power is organized hierarchically—for example by class or race or gender—there is no possibility of an Archimedean perspective, one that is disinterested, impartial, value-free, or detached from the particular, historical social relations in which everyone participates. Instead, each person can achieve only a partial view of reality from the perspective of his or her own position in the social hierarchy. And such a view is not only partial but also distorted by the way the relations of domination are organized.
> (HARDING 1991, 59)

Since each knowledge claim is partial and distorted, no one's knowledge claim can be considered the "absolute truth" that exactly corresponds to the way reality is. These claims should be considered *partial* because they are made from somewhere from which epistemic agents cannot see the whole of reality, as well as *distorted* because they are affected by the values and interests of epistemic agents in hierarchical societies.

Zhuangzi would agree with Harding that all knowledge claims are perspectival and situated. However, he would not connect universalist epistemologies to masculinity and androcentrism. Interestingly, in China, "universalist," disembodied epistemologies have never been well-developed, although China has been a patriarchal society for thousands of years and men's oppression of women there has been some of the worst on earth. An emphasis on rationality and universality does not have the same association with masculinity in Chinese philosophy as in Western philosophy. On the contrary, characteristics that are usually associated with femininity in Western philosophy, such as emphases on relationships and caring and the appreciation of intuition and emotions, are highly regarded in Chinese philosophy, though all important figures in Chinese philosophy are male.[2] To explore the reason why Chinese male domination in epistemology in particular and in philosophy in general does not take the same form in China as in the West is beyond the scope of this chapter. But to mention the Chinese situation as such will at least show that the "universalist," disembodied characteristics of many Western epistemologies have a lot to do with the structure of Western society and culture and are not simply caused by male domination per se. If Zhuangzi could encounter these types of Western epistemology, he might criticize them as flawed philosophically because they are not wise enough to realize that knowledge claims are perspectival. However, for him, these trends in Western epistemology would not be problematic on account of their association with masculinity.

According to Zhuangzi, all knowledge claims make some distinctions between things. However, all distinctions between things have to be made from certain perspectives. For example, whether an object is large is dependent on who views it. Similarly, whether a thing is "this" or "that" is dependent on the position of a knower in relation to that thing. It could be "this" for me if I am close to it and be "that" for someone else who is at a distance from it. Therefore, a thing can be "that" and "this" at the same time. He illustrates this point in the following passage:

There is nothing that is not the "that," and there is nothing that is not the "this." From the point of view of the other, a thing cannot

be perceived as "this," but from the point of view of the thing itself, the thing is clearly known as "this" . . . "This" is "that," and
"that" is "this." "That" has its own criterion of right and wrong, and
"this" has its as well. Is there really a distinction between "that"
and "this"? Or is there not such a distinction at all? From the axis of
Dao (the Way),[3] "this" and "that" are not opposites. The axis is the
center of the circle that responds to infinite changes.
(ZZ, CH. 2, 10)[4]

Zhuangzi's concept of an epistemic agent is in clear contrast to the
Cartesian universal knower who perceives truths as absolute. Instead,
Zhuangzi's knower is thoroughly situated.[5] Such a knower is unable to
see the whole picture of reality, accurately understand the real nature
of what he sees, and see clearly what he is perceiving due to his presupposed values and prejudices. In this sense, his knowledge claims
are not only partial but also distorted. It is because Zhuangzi understands this so well that he believes that the dominant moral norms
and legal institutions of a society are not embodiments of universal
and neutral truths, but actually express what the dominant members
of a society believe and what will best serve that group's interests.
He observes "petty thieves are put in jails, while big thieves have become kings. So-called people of benevolence and rightness work for
big thieves" (ZZ, ch. 29, 199). On this same point, he asks, "Is there
any so called 'sage' who is not a guard of big thieves?" (ZZ, ch. 10, 59).

Zhuangzi's knower is not only situated in society but in the natural world as well. As a Daoist, he infers the situated knower from the
existence of various perspectives in nature and bases his arguments
for situated knowledge in the existence of an ultimately naturalistic
universe. How a knower perceives things is dependent not only on his
location in society but also his location in the cosmos. Due to different
positions in the universe, different species naturally have different
perspectives. Zhuangzi argues that they are all entitled to have their
knowledge claims:

If a human being sleeps in a damp place, he will have a pain in his
loins and feel half his or her body paralyzed. Is that true of eels? If
a human being lives up in a tree, he will be frightened and trem-
ble. Is that true of monkeys? Which of the three knows the right

place to live? Human beings eat the flesh of animals, deer eat grass, centipedes enjoy snakes, and owls and crows enjoy mice. Which of the four knows the right taste? Dog-headed male *pianju* 猵狙 mate with female apes,[6] the buck mates with the doe, and eels mate with fishes. Mao Qiang and Li Ji were considered by human beings to be beauties, but at the sight of them fish dove deep to the water, birds flew high, and deer ran away. Which of the four knows the right kind of beauty?

(ZZ, CH. 2, 15)

Zhuangzi's attention to other species provides the logical reasons for his perspectivalism.[7] Harding only says that a particular group of human beings cannot claim to be representatives of all humankind and know all truth, while Zhuangzi goes further and holds that all knowledge claimed by the human race can only be perspectival—that is, from human perspectives alone. Therefore, there is no ultimate justification for believing in the absoluteness of human knowledge claims. Given the lack of a theistic view of the world, Zhuangzi does not presuppose an inherent value hierarchy in nature. All beings in the universe are part of the natural world and thereby equal in value with equally valid perspectives. As Chad Hansen puts it, "none has any special status or warrant from the point of view of the universe" (Hansen 1983, 35). But how about different perspectives among human beings? Are they also equally valid? To this, Zhuangzi and Harding have different answers.

The Privileged Vantage Point for Knowledge

Although Harding holds that all knowledge claims are situated and can neither be impartial nor completely accurate accounts of reality, she does not think that all knowledge claims are equally valuable. For her, some social locations, such as the lives of women, are epistemologically advantaged starting points for knowledge seeking (Harding 1993, 56). Just as Marx claims that the social location of the proletariat is epistemologically privileged in a capitalist society, Harding holds that perspectives from women's lives have such a privilege in a patriarchal society. This idea is clearly expressed in the following passages:

Standpoint theories argue for "starting off thought" from the lives of marginalized peoples; beginning in those determinate, objective locations in any social order will generate illuminating critical questions that do not arise in thought that begins from dominant group lives. Starting off research from women's lives will generate less partial and distorted accounts not only of women's lives but also of men's lives and of the whole social order. (56)

Thus the standpoint claims that all knowledge attempts are socially situated and that some of these objective social locations are better than others as starting points for knowledge projects challenge some of the most fundamental assumptions of the scientific world view and the Western thought that takes science as its model of how to produce knowledge. (56)

Harding believes that women's lives, unlike women's experiences, are better locations to serve as starting points for knowledge seeking. Starting off from the lives of women may produce more objective knowledge. Like many feminist epistemologists, Harding does not want to give up objectivity in her standpoint theory. On the contrary, she believes that standpoint epistemology will enable knowers to achieve more objectivity. As she puts it:

The socially situated grounds and subjects of standpoint epistemologies require and generate stronger standards for objectivity than do those that turn away from providing systematic methods for locating knowledge in history. The problem with the conventional conception of objectivity is not that it is too rigorous or too "objectifying," as some have argued, but that it is not rigorous or objectifying enough; it is too weak to accomplish even the goals for which it has been designed, let alone the more difficult projects called for by feminisms and other new social movements. (50–51)

To maximize the objectivity of knowledge, one should start from the lives of women and other oppressed groups. But how can such a starting point offer a privileged vantage point for knowledge?

Harding has proposed a number of reasons why women's lives provide epistemologically privileged starting points for knowledge seeking. The most compelling are: 1. since dominant knowledge claims have been mainly based on the lives of men and women's lives have been devalued and neglected, starting from women's lives can decrease partialities and distortions in "the picture of nature and social life provided by natural and social sciences" (Harding 1991, 121); 2. since women have been excluded from the "design and direction of both the social order and the production of knowledge" (124), they are valuable strangers or outsiders who may be more capable of objectively perceiving things;[8] 3. as members of oppressed groups, women "have fewer interests in ignorance about the social order and few reasons to invest in maintaining or justifying the status quo than do dominant groups" (126), therefore their perspectives more easily produce "fresh and critical analyses" (126); 4. "women's perspective is from daily life" and can better recover the actual process of the formation of social life (128–29); 5. women's double duty and women's activities of production and reproduction bridge nature and culture in a way men's activities cannot, hence, starting from women's activities, we can better understand why and how social and cultural phenomena have taken their current forms (131).

What would Zhuangzi say to Harding about this privileged vantage point for knowledge? He would clearly disagree with her. For Zhuangzi, there is no epistemological ground for anyone to compare different perspectives and starting points for knowledge. Since all knowers are positioned somewhere and all knowledge claims are situated, no one can neutrally rank which perspectives are better. Whenever one judges others' views, one will inevitably bring his value and partiality with him. Zhuangzi clearly illustrates this as follows:

> If you and I argue with each other . . . is really one of us right and the other wrong? Or are both of us right or both of us wrong? Neither you nor I can know, and others can't know either. Whom should we ask to make a right judgment? Should we ask someone who agrees with you? Since he agrees with you, how can he make a right judgment? Should we ask someone who agrees with me? Since he agrees with me, how can he make a right judgment? Should we ask someone who agrees with both you and me? Since he agrees with both of you and me, how can he make a right judgment? Should we

ask someone who disagrees with both you and me? Since he disagrees with both you and me, how can he make a right judgment?
(ZZ, CH. 2, 17)

Zhuangzi obviously would say that Harding's claim that women's lives
are the epistemologically privileged starting point for knowledge
seeking is in itself partial, biased, and not really objective. Actually,
Harding herself admits that her claim about the epistemic advantage
of perspectives from women's lives is situated (Harding 1991, 185).
She insists that all knowledge claims are situated and perspectival,
and some of them are indeed better, but she does not offer epistemological grounds for such a claim.

Harding's specific arguments for the epistemic privilege of women's
lives cannot offer a justification at an epistemological level. When she
gives these arguments, she seems to presuppose that there is a reality that can be revealed and that research starting off from women's
lives can discover that reality and grasp universal and absolute truths
better than research starting off from somewhere else. For example,
Harding claims that because women and other oppressed groups have
less interest in obscuring and hiding those conditions that produce hierarchical relations in society, starting from their lives will produce
less false views (59). This entails that (1) there is a social reality to be
understood, (2) truth about such a reality is objectively valid to all, and
(3) some perspectives see such reality better and obtain more truth
about it. But Harding clearly denies that she holds any assumptions
about universal and absolute truth. Furthermore, she claims that the
standards for knowledge claims are changeable and situated too. As
she says: "Of course the standard for what counts as 'less false' can be
at issue or change over time. The standards for knowledge claims, too,
are provisional and tend to change over time. We need not avoid the
useful notion of 'less false' claims just because we turn away from the
absolutist standards of modernism" (Harding 2004, 260). Then, after
all, according to what criterion, can she claim some perspectives and
knowledge claims are epistemologically better than others? It seems
that she cannot avoid presupposing some impartial standard. As one
of her critics rightly points out:

All of Harding's talk of "less false stories," "less partial and per-
verse account," and more "objective" research necessarily presup-

poses a shared discourse—a metanarrative, even—that establishes standards by which these judgments can be validated. . . . Comparative statements such as those Harding advances require shared standards of judgment; no such standards bridge the gap between feminist and masculinist science. It is ironic that Harding's polemic against the metanarrative of masculinist science ultimately relies on the reconstruction of a similar standard for its validity.

(HEKMAN 2004, 233)

Zhuangzi would agree with such criticisms of Harding. For him, if we do not have a neutral standard to judge different knowledge claims made from different perspectives, we cannot objectively rank them. We can only legitimately say that all perspectives are equally valid.

Harding's insistence on the superiority of some perspectives is motivated by her belief in the objectivity of knowledge that offers epistemological justification for the feminist struggle for women's liberation. To this, Zhuangzi might say that admitting the equality of all perspectives may not necessarily lead to a total denial of objective knowledge claims, since truths are plural and contextual. If all epistemic agents must occupy certain positions in certain contexts and make knowledge claims from various perspectives, then it is plausible to say that sometimes they are equally right when they give different knowledge claims about the same object. These different claims might be compatible and complement each other. When two knowers describe the same thing at different times, compare the same thing with different references, or emphasize different aspects of the same thing, their statements about the same thing may look contradictory at face value but be equally true (Jiang 1992). For example, person A may say "mountain X is high" when she compares it with the marshes nearby, while person B may say "mountain X is not high" when she compares the mountain with the marshes in a high land. Both of their statements could be true at the same time. Similarly, if person A says "person Y is a genius" in relation to Y's great talent in mathematics and person B says "person Y is not a genius" in relation to Y's mediocre ability in literature, they may both be right. Zhuangzi's famous example about a huge strange-looking tree makes the same point. Such a tree is regarded as useless by a carpenter for making furniture, but its "being useless" is extremely useful for preserving its life (since people will not cut it down for making furniture). Such a tree is not less valuable than other trees from some perspectives, although from other perspectives it is. Therefore, "this tree is useful" and "this tree is not useful" could be equally valid when they are made from different perspectives (ZZ, ch. 4, 27–29). One can judge it only in the context in which the sentence is uttered. In this way, contextual truths can be objective even though they are tied to a concrete situation and a concrete perspective.

Feminist Elites and Daoist Sages

For Harding, all types of women's lives are good places to begin knowledge seeking, including those defined by different races and classes. She says: "Standpoint theory argues that each of these groups of women's lives is a good place to start in order to explain certain aspects of the social order. There is no single, ideal woman's life from which standpoint theories recommend that thought start. Instead, one must turn to all of the lives that are marginalized in different ways by the operative systems of social stratification" (Harding 1993, 60). However, given the diversity of human lives, are all women's lives epistemologically privileged starting points compared to all men's lives? For example, are the lives of working-class African men worse starting points for knowledge seeking than the lives of upper-class white women? Perhaps in recognition of this problem, Harding has increasingly associated epistemically privileged standpoints with "marginalized lives," rather than "women's lives" in her writing (Pels 2004, 277).

Furthermore, according to Harding, although the lives of women and other oppressed groups are the epistemologically advantaged starting points for knowledge seeking, not all women and members of the oppressed actually look at things from the perspectives of their own lives. For example, what a woman actually thinks and says does not necessarily embody a perspective of women's lives. It is possible that she looks at her society according to what the dominant norm in her society has taught her. Therefore, "it cannot be overemphasized that the epistemic privilege oppressed groups possess is by no means automatic" (Harding 2004, 9). Harding distinguishes the perspectives of actual members of oppressed groups and the perspectives of marginalized lives. Although she does not directly say that the latter is equivalent to the standpoint of the oppressed, she clearly indicates this idea when she talks about the relation between a standpoint and women's lives:

> For a position to count as a standpoint, rather than as a claim—equally valuable but for different reasons—for the importance of listening to women tell us about their lives and experiences, we must insist on an objective location—women's lives—as the place from which feminist research should begin. . . . And who is to do this "starting out"? With this question it becomes clear that knowledge-seeking requires democratic, participatory politics. Otherwise, only the gender, race, sexuality, and class elites who now predominate in institutions of knowledge-seeking will have the chance to decide how to start asking their research questions.
>
> (HARDING 1991, 123)

According to Harding, the term *standpoint* in its technical use is not exactly the same as *perspective*, although many authors in feminist epistemology use them synonymously. In her writing, *standpoint* refers to "an achieved (versus ascribed) collective identity or consciousness, one for which oppressed groups must struggle" (Harding 2004, 14n11). A standpoint is an achievement that does not automatically arise from one's social location (8). Since perspectives of women's lives are not the automatic perspectives of actual women, we may regard them as women's standpoints. Only when a woman understands the nature of her social location and has her feminist consciousness awakened does she achieve a woman's standpoint. Her experience as a woman will help her achieve such a standpoint, but political engagement and critical thinking are necessary conditions. This is similar to Marx's idea that members of the working class need to gain class consciousness so as to achieve their proletarian standpoint. According to Harding, gaining a political consciousness is essential because the dominant ideologies have blocked the critical insight of the oppressed and obscured its understandings (9).

Harding's view thus implies that ordinary women need to be educated to achieve standpoints of women. The standpoint of women in this sense is actually a feminist viewpoint. Feminists are usually women intellectuals—that is, elite women (Pels 2004, 280–81). They are spokespersons of women who represent the interests of women and perceive the world from the perspectives of women's lives. However, a man can take the standpoint of women and be a spokesperson of women if he does reflexive analysis of his social location and starts his knowledge seeking from the perspective of women's lives. In other words, the standpoint of women does not require womanhood, just as a nonproletarian can take the standpoint of the proletarian. John Stuart Mill, Karl Marx, and Friedrich Engels are examples of men who were able to look at things from the perspective of women's lives (Harding 1993, 67). This means that one's standpoint does not have to be determined by one's actual social location, although one's material location affects one's standpoint to a great degree. This is to say that ordinarily limitations and inaccuracy of one's knowledge claims are decided by one's social location, but once one understands how social location may affect knowledge claims, one can take a better epistemic position and make one's knowledge claims less partial and less distorted.

If this is the case, a knower will not be limited by her original social location but instead be able to choose standpoints to begin knowledge seeking. Then epistemic agents are still situated, but they can freely decide where to be situated. As Dick Pels points out, "Consciousness is decisive, not situation or place. Knowledge, or critical thought, may in principle emancipate itself from all situational determination" (Pels 2004, 284). Therefore, in theory, epistemic agents can be everywhere, though not at the same time. At last, the situatedness of one's knowledge claims is not decided by one's actual location but by one's critical thinking. Hence, according to Pels, standpoint theory approaches "the conventional transcendental view that it originally set out to criticize" and "the radical epistemological impulse of standpoint thinking is effectively eradicated" (284).

Zhuangzi would agree with the aforementioned criticism of Harding. For him, shifting one's perspective or standpoint (they are the same in the *Zhuangzi*) without changing one's actual epistemic location is impossible. Such an idea is well illustrated in the following saying: "Morning bugs who are born in the morning and dead in the evening can't know what a month is like; and summer cicadas who are born in summer and dead in autumn or born in spring and dead in summer can't know four seasons" (ZZ, ch. 1, 2). Of course, when one's epistemic location has changed, one's perspective will change too. Zhuangzi makes this point in a conversation between He Bo, the

Lord of the River, and Beihai Ruo, the God of the North Sea. The Lord of the River thought that his river was the greatest until he saw the ocean. Their dialogue proceeds as follows: Beihai Ruo said, "You can't discuss the ocean with a well frog—it's limited by the space it lives in. You can't discuss ice with a summer insect—it's limited by its life-span. You can't discuss Dao with an ignorant and ill-informed person—he's limited by his education. Now you have come out beyond your river and have seen the great sea—so you realize your own meagerness. From now on it will be possible for me to talk to you about the Great Principle" (ZZ, ch. 17, 100).

The change in one's perspective can be explained in terms of the change in one's epistemic location. Epistemic locations are not limited to class, gender, and racial identities, but also include those places that are associated with these identities or exist in between these identities. Therefore, the change of epistemic location does not have to be externally visible to others. It could be one caused by the change in experience or relationships. Zhaungzi's story about Li Ji demonstrates this idea. When Li Ji, the most beautiful woman in the state of Li, was captured by the duke of Jin, she was extremely sad so that "she wept until the front of her garment was drenched with tears" (ZZ, ch. 2, 16). But she regretted that she was so upset after she started sharing a good life with the duke. Her perspective changed after she lived with the duke, because her situations before being captured and after were very different. Similarly, we may explain why Mill became a firm feminist after he was deeply involved with Harriet Taylor. Through his relationship with Taylor, he was located somewhere from which women's lives were much more clearly perceived and women's intellectual capacities more visibly presented to him than before. One may change one's standpoint by changing one's epistemic location, not simply by enhancing one's consciousness. However, the change in one's epistemic location is not a matter of individual choice. If Harding takes a view such as Zhuangzi's, she may avoid the trouble that Pels has pointed out above.

A question that one who is familiar with Zhuangzi's philosophy may ask is whether Zhuangzi's Daoist sage is an epistemic agent who views all from everywhere or nowhere. To answer this question, a brief description of the Daoist sage portrayed by Zhuangzi is in order. According to Zhuangzi, a sage assigns equal value to all perspectives without attaching to any of them (ZZ, ch. 2, 17). Therefore, he is totally free from any worldly worries and conventional values. He views the world from the viewpoint of Dao—which is not a limited perspective but the total of all perspectives.[9] He calls such a person a "perfect person" (zhiren 至人). "The perfect person uses the heart like a mirror; he does not escort things as they go or welcome them as they come; he responds but does not store" (ZZ, ch. 7, 51). Such an ideal person is neutral to all and simply responds to things without evaluating them. He lives naturally and spontaneously (Graham 1989, 193). Zhuangzi used the concept of the perfect person to symbolize the highest ideal (Allinson 1989, 111).

Zhuangzi's perfect person seems to be an impartial and ideal epistemic agent who is situated nowhere. However, he should not be considered an epistemic agent in the ordinary sense. A knowledge claim involves making some distinction between things; an epistemic agent seeks the proper distinction between things. However, a Daoist sage does not distinguish things nor even describe them (since description involves distinction). Therefore, he does not seek what we define as knowledge and does not make knowledge claims in the ordinary sense. That is why Fung Yu-lan says that such a Daoist sage has "knowledge that is not knowledge" (Fung 1989, 143).[10] It is because Zhuangzi's sage is not an epistemic agent that Zhuangzi's claim that all knowledge statements are perspectival and all epistemic agents are situated is valid.

Given Zhuangzi's ideal of the perfect person, he would definitely be critical of Harding's feminist attitude to politics and social reform. Although he and Harding share a similar attitude to authority in the sense that he holds that the existing authority and dominant ideology might not really possess more truth than others and might not be as legitimate as claimed, he does not try to establish new authority and change the existing social structure. For him, a new social structure will not be better than an old one—it cannot be. As a consequence of this view, true liberation comes from inside. One is truly free when one stops craving worldly goods. Behind his apolitical veil of indifference and detachment, Zhuangzi is a strong critic of people's craving for conventional values, especially those advocated by the dominant members of society. Zhuangzi sees how the pursuit of conventional goods, such as power, fame, and wealth, has led to human suffering;[11] how hypocrisy has corrupted society in the name of morality; and how the ruling class has created conventional norms to maximize its own interests. It seems that it is his dissatisfaction with the existing social situation and his understanding of the origin of evil that motivated him to discard all conventional values and stay away from politics. He embraces perspectivalism and demonstrates the relativity of all conventional values in order to correct people's excessive craving for worldly goods. If all perspectives are equally valid, then it is reasonable to advocate detachment from all conventional values. Such detachment will help people return to nature and live simply and peacefully. In this sense, his perspectivalism is a kind of medicine for social ills.

Zhuangzi, like other Daoists, is well known for promoting living according to nature. For him, naturalness is most desirable. "The duck's legs are short, but to lengthen them will make the duck suffer. The crane's legs are long, but to shorten them will bring the crane grief. Therefore, what is naturally long should not be shortened, while what is naturally short should not be lengthened" (ZZ, ch. 8, 54). For him, if people are detached from conventional values and live according to nature, human society will be well ordered and human beings will be in harmony with their environment. As he puts it: "Let your mind excurse in simplicity and indifference, make no distinction between yourself and the world, and follow the nature of all things without selfish thought. Then, the world will be in good order" (ZZ, ch. 7, 49). Once this order and harmony are achieved, we will not need to struggle for equality and justice. Therefore, Zhuangzi advises people to stay away from political centers and live a hermit-like life.[12]

Perspectival Knowledge and Universal Truth

Although Zhuangzi's perspectivalism may serve as a useful tool for criticizing and improving Harding's standpoint theory, it itself is certainly not immune to criticism. One difficulty with his perspectivalism is that it is logically dependent on the existence of universal truth. To claim that all perspectives are equally valid is itself to assert a universal truth. If "all perspectives are equally valid" is relative and perspectival, then the claim is no better than those claims made from a particular perspective and Zhuangzi would no longer have any justification for advocating his theory. Furthermore, to believe that everyone's knowledge claim is limited and relative is to presume the existence of the objective entirety of reality to which everyone at best has only partial access. This is to assert a universal truth about reality. As a matter of fact, Zhuangzi does talk about such a whole of reality. "All things are united as one via Dao" (ZZ, ch. 2, 10). Such oneness in itself does not contain separable parts and objective distinctions in value: "Dao has no distinctions" (ZZ, ch. 2, 13). All separations are not the way things really are, and value judgments do not correspond to reality. Here he is asserting another universal truth that existence is oneness and value free. The way of such existence is natural and not artificial. Therefore, any distinction imposed on existence is unnatural. He does not stop here but further asserts that naturalness is better than unnaturalness. Then he makes another universal claim that naturalness is universally best. Moreover, such a claim also presupposes some neutral and universal truth that can serve as a criterion to rank naturalness over unnaturalness. Like other Daoists, Zhuangzi also believes that the highest state of human life is the one in which a person grasps Dao and truly lives a natural life. For Zhuangzi, living according to nature means discarding all conventional values and identifying with the universe. Such an existence understands that all value judgments are not objective truths but opinions made from certain perspectives and therefore not worth following. "All things are united as oneness. Once we understand this and identify ourselves with the one, we will regard our bodies as nothing but dust and dirt, life and death, and beginning and end as nothing but the succession of day and night, which cannot disturb our hearts at all. Then, how could worldly gain and loss, and good fortune and misfortune matter to us?" (ZZ, ch. 20, 131–32). This is the ideal that Zhuangzi wants people to realize: "Forget life and death. Forget right and wrong. Freely wander in the realm of the infinite and abide there forever" (ZZ, ch. 2, 17). After all, his perspectivalism is aimed at justifying such a Daoist ideal life. Up to this point, we can obviously see that Zhuangzi cannot justify his perspectivalism without taking some universal truths for granted; he cannot establish the Daoist ideal of natural life as the most desirable way for human beings to follow if he denies that there is any shared criterion for knowledge and value. It seems that what he actually argues against are not all universal truths but rather what is commonly taken to be universal truth in society.

The necessary connection between Harding's feminist standpoint epistemology and universal truth is even more obvious than in Zhuangzi's philosophy, although Harding overtly denies universal truth. First of all, as discussed early on, in her epistemology, the belief in the privileged vantage point for knowledge entails some universal standard for ranking different perspectives. Otherwise, the privileged vantage point is not really better. Second, the political and moral goal of her epistemology determines its dependence on universal values. Her feminist standpoint epistemology as a means to women's liberation must justify women's cause and struggle to keep people *attached* to this goal. But, this requires demonstrating that sexual oppression is objectively wrong. To do so, one has to presuppose some criterion shared by all human beings. Without some shared concepts, such as that of universal human rights or respect, criticisms of sexual oppression will be groundless. Therefore, logically, Harding cannot give up some basic enlightenment values, such as freedom and equality, no matter whether she endorses their associated universalist epistemologies or not. Although Harding openly denies the existence of universal truths, her epistemology logically entails their existence. Under such an analysis, the disagreement between her standpoint theory and "universalist" epistemologies no longer lies in the question whether there are universal truths, but rather in the question whether what people usually claim to be a universal truth is actually a universal truth. This means that differences between feminist standpoint epistemology and Zhuangzi's perspectivalism are not as dramatic as they may at first seem.

Neither Zhuangzi nor Harding can establish a coherent epistemology without presupposing some universal truths. Furthermore, their strong denial of nonperspectival knowledge seems to indicate that they have not paid enough attention to the fact that human beings, regardless of differences in class, gender, and culture, share a lot in common and therefore their perspectives overlap to a great degree. The fact that people can communicate across genders, races, and cultures and reach many mutual understandings suggests that there are universal human concerns and needs. Such common ground makes perspectival and nonperspectival knowledge claims united in many cases and justifies the existence of universal truths and values. To be critical of one's own society and to improve social conditions requires admitting the existence of both perspectival knowledge and universal truth. To admit the former will enable us to see that many prevailing norms in our society are not universal truths, but mere ideologies to serve the ruling classes. To admit the existence of universal values and truths will enable us to justify our criticism of those norms that solely serve the interests of the ruling class. For example, in traditional China obedience was regarded as a major virtue of women. For a long time "women ought to obey men" was considered an unquestionable rule of conduct. One would realize that such a moral norm was not a universal moral truth but a tool to favor men's interests if one understands that knowledge claims are usually socially constructed and therefore partial and distorted. However, to justify the abolition of such a norm, one needs to appeal to the universal validity of the ideal of equality. Simply pointing out that this norm serves men's interests is not sufficient for claiming that the norm should be abolished. Only when one can show that the claim that women's and men's interests should be treated equally is a universal moral truth can one show that a sexist norm is truly wrong and should be abandoned. Clearly, there is no intrinsic contradiction in upholding both perspectival knowledge and universal truth. If we label perspectival knowledge *relative truth* and universal truth *absolute truth,* their relationship may be just like some Marxists put it: the two are not separate—absolute truth is embodied in relative truth, and the total of relative truths amounts to absolute truth (Lenin 1988, 323). The more perspectival knowledge we obtain, the more progress we will make toward universal truth.

Notes

I would like to thank the editors of this volume, my colleague Kathie Jenni, and several other readers for their valuable suggestions and comments on earlier versions of this essay.

1. Feminist epistemology does not claim that gender affects knowers more than other social aspects, such as class or race, but it does focus its study on the relationship between gender and knowledge.

2. For discussions of these characteristics of Chinese thought and their association with so-called femininity, see Lin (1988, 62–67), Li (1994, 70–89), and Jiang (2009, 237–38).

3. The meaning of *Dao* 道 (Way) in Daoism is complicated and controversial. I agree with the following interpretations: 1. Dao is the source of all beings from which all come to be (Fung 1948, 95–96); 2. Dao is the universal law of Nature, i.e.,

the natural way all things are (Zhang 1982, 20; Chan 1963, 136); and 3. Dao is the totality of spontaneity or naturalness of the world (Fung 1989, 7).

4. ZZ refers to the *Zhuangzi*. All translations in this chapter are my own and are made from *Zhuangzi Jijie* 庄子集解, edited and annotated by Wang Xianqian and Yi Wu (1990). Some existing translations, such as those by Yu-lan Fung (1989), Wing-tsit Chan (1963), Burton Watson (1964), and A. C. Graham (1981), are consulted.

5. Chad Hansen (1983) has argued that for Zhuangzi the existence of different perspectives is due to the fact that we perceive the world through language. Different ways of using language present people with different conceptual schemes and different ways, therefore, of seeing the world. Although I agree that Zhuangzi has addressed the correlation between the multiplicity of languages and the multiplicity of perspectives, I believe that textual evidence shows that Zhuangzi associates the multiplicity of perspectives more with differences in time and location between different knowers.

6. It is said that *pianju* is a kind of animal similar to an ape except its head is doglike. Male *pianju* tend to mate with female apes. See ZZ (15).

7. I borrow this term from Chad Hansen to refer Zhuangzi's perspectival view of knowledge (Hansen 1992, 268).

8. The Chinese saying "outsiders can see clearly" (*pangguan zhe qing* 旁观者清) may well express Harding's point.

9. I do not consider the viewpoint of Dao as a particular perspective, since a particular perspective in the *Zhuangzi* is associated with a limited angle from which one perceives the world. The viewpoint of Dao that synthesizes all perspectives and sees things from all angles has no limitations and is therefore not a perspective for Zhuangzi.

10. Although Zhuangzi sometimes claims that such a perfect person has true knowledge, his use of the term *knowledge* does not refer to knowledge claims commonly understood in these cases. To obtain true knowledge is to achieve the mental state in which one makes no distinctions and judgments.

11. For a discussion of how Zhuangzi connects human suffering with the human pursuit of conventional values, see Watson (1964, 4).

12. Zhuangzi was married and had children and friends. In that sense, he was not a hermit. But he was not involved in political and social activity and refused to take office in government. In this sense, I label him "hermit-like."

References

Allinson, Robert E. 1989. *Chuang-Tzu for spiritual transformation*. Albany: State University of New York Press.

Chan, Wing-tsit, trans. 1963. *A source book in Chinese philosophy*. Princeton: Princeton University Press.

Code, Lorraine. 1993. Taking subjectivity into account. In *Feminist epistemologies*, ed. Linda Alcoff and Elizabeth Potter, 5–48. New York: Routledge.

Fung, Yu-lan. 1948. *A short history of Chinese philosophy*. New York: Macmillan.

———. trans. 1989. *Chuang Tzu*. Beijing: Foreign Languages Press.

Graham, A. C., trans. 1981. *Chuang-Tzu: The inner chapters*. Indianapolis: Hackett.

———. 1989. *Disputers of the tao*. Chicago: Open Court.

Hansen, Chad. 1983. A tao of tao in Chuang-tzu. In *Experimental Essays on Chuang-tzu*, ed. Victor H. Mair, 24–55. Honolulu: University of Hawaii Press.

———. 1992. *A Daoist theory of Chinese thought*. Oxford: Oxford University Press.

Harding, Sandra. 1991. *Whose science? Whose knowledge?* Ithaca: Cornell University Press.

———. 1993. Rethinking standpoint epistemology: What is "strong objectivity"? In *Feminist epistemologies*, ed. Linda Alcoff and Elizabeth Potter, 49–82. New York: Routledge.

———. 2004. Introduction: Standpoint theory as a site of political, philosophic, and scientific debate. In *The feminist standpoint theory reader: Intellectual and political controversies,* ed. Sandra Harding, 1–15. New York: Routledge.

Hekman, Susan. 2004. Truth and method: Feminist standpoint theory revisited. In *The feminist standpoint theory reader: Intellectual and political controversies,* ed. Sandra Harding, 225–241. New York: Routledge.

Jiang, Xinyan. 1992. The law of non-contradiction and Chinese philosophy. *History and Philosophy of Logic* 13:1–14.

———. 2009. Confucianism, women, and social contexts. *Journal of Chinese Philosophy*, 36 (2): 228–42.

Lenin, Vladimir. 1988. *Complete works of Lenin*. Vol. 18. Beijing: People's Press.

Li, Chenyang. 1994. The Confucian concept of *jen* and the feminist ethics of care: A comparative study. *Hypatia* 9 (1): 70–89.

Lin, Yutung. 1988. *The Chinese*. Hangzhou: Zhejiang People's Press.

Pels, Dick. 2004. Strange standpoints; or, how to define the situation for situated knowledge. In *The feminist standpoint theory reader: Intellectual and political controversies,* ed. Sandra Harding, 273–89. New York: Routledge.

Watson, Burton, trans. 1964. *Chuang Tzu: Basic writings*. New York: Columbia University Press.

Wang, Xianqian, and Yi Wu, eds. 1990. *Zhuangzi Jijie* 庄子集解 (*Zhuangzi*). vol. 3 of *Zhuzi Jicheng* 诸子集成 (*A collection of many schools*). Beijing: Zhonghua Shuju 中华书局.

Webb, Mark Owen. 1995. Feminist epistemology and the extent of the social. *Hypatia* 10 (3): 85–98.

Zhang, Dainian. 1982. *Zhongguo zhexue dagang* 中国哲学大纲. Beijing: Zhongguo Shehui Kexue Chubanshe 中国社会科学出版社.

CHAPTER SEVEN

"Epistemic Multiculturalism" and Objectivity

Rethinking Vandana Shiva's Ecospirituality

VRINDA DALMIYA

WHEN CONTEMPORARY environmental movements link themselves to religious worldviews, their motives can be theoretical or strategic. Deep ecology and ecofeminisms, for example, have regularly looked to the metaphysics of pagan and Eastern spiritualities to construct ecologically embedded theories of being human. Arne Naess's Vedānta-inspired deep ecology (Naess 1986) and Vandana Shiva's *prakriti*-based ecofeminism (Shiva 1989) are cases in point. Moreover, we regularly find secular organizations engaging in the political theater of invoking religious rituals to mobilize popular sentiments for environmental agendas. For example, during a drought in 2004, activists in Maharashtra, India staged a *pani yatra* (water pilgrimage) to raise consciousness about water conservation. This secular march featured a water pot decked out in traditional Hindu religious symbols to draw the crowds (Nanda 2005a, 67). Madhu Kishwar also speaks of a *jhadu puja* (worship of the broom) that helped politicize street vendors in Delhi against routine harassment by civic authorities on charges of their perpetuating urban filth (Kishwar 2004). Here a new goddess called Swachhnarayani (Goddess of Cleanliness) was invented specifically to reinforce the ecological importance of urban hygiene.

Such intertwining of environmentalism and religiosity, however, has recently come under trenchant critical scrutiny because of instances of misanthropic violence conniving with earth-based spiritualities. Bron Taylor, for instance, documents how ecospirituality motivated some members of the radical environmental group Earth First! to view acts of sabotage (like monkeywrenching) as a "form of worship" and encouraged a few to take "even the KKK into the movement if they put earth first" (Taylor 2002, 27). Michael Zimmerman has also highlighted the easy alliance between ecospirituality and fascism in describing National Socialism as a "Green version of neopaganism" (Zimmerman 2000, 172).

In the context of India, the issue of a (broadly) religion-inspired environmentalism intertwining with socially regressive and authoritarian agendas surfaces in Meera Nanda's strident critiques of Vandana Shiva's ecofeminism (Nanda 2002, 2003). According to Nanda, Shiva's invocation of a mythico-religious Nature as a Goddess is problematic because it promotes neoconservative Hindu fundamentalism (*Hindutva*). Nanda supports her critique through a careful analysis of how conservative farmers' movements in contemporary India actively gloss over class and caste distinctions within the rural population to form a powerful vote bank for Hindutva-aligned parties. Even though such movements serve the interests of the rural elite, Nanda shows that they successfully maintain a multiclass membership by appealing to traditional symbols of nature goddesses and a romanticized "agrarian myth" signifying cultural authenticity and true Indianness. Shiva's revival of indigenous worldviews thus gets hijacked from its explicit environmental purpose to provide the ideology needed to cement a heterogeneous group into a "homogenous peasantry" with a highly conservative political voice (Nanda 2003, ch. 10). Such ease of "political bricolage" between radical environmental agendas and various forms of social violence, racism, and fascism, both in the West and in India, calls into question the very desirability of framing environmentalism in terms of spirituality.

My purpose in this chapter is not to exonerate all forms of ecospirituality from alleged complicity with fanaticism. Rather, I argue that Shiva's activism suggests a nuanced deployment of earth spirituality that can resist these worries. I analyze the mixing of environmentalism and religion in Shiva's work to explore the larger question of whether the admittedly hierarchical and premodern religious elements of a postcolonial society can be used to critique inequities bred by the modern state without spawning even more violent forms of preexisting oppressions. This, as Shiv Visvanathan poignantly puts it, is the question whether it is ever possible to "take the best of Indian civilization and at the same time keep [my] modern, democratic imagination alive" (Visvanathan 2000). Thus my purpose is to explore whether and how the nature-based spirituality explicitly developed in Shiva's earlier work (1989) still has a role in her newly articulated vision of an "Earth Democracy" (2005a). The broader significance of this specific discussion is, of course, the general relevance of the mystical for the political or the efficacy of enabling a democracy through spirituality.

Now, any analysis of Shiva's ecospirituality involves an engagement with the foundational notion of *prakriti*. Of course, prakriti, what Shiva has infamously called the "Feminine Principle" (1989), has been justifiably criticized as an essentialist characterization of women and/or of Indian women (Agarwal 1992; Jackson 1995; Salleh 1991). It is also interesting that Shiva's recent work has tended not to mention prakriti, almost as if she had taken seriously Ariel Salleh's suggestion to let the concept "sleep in a footnote" (Salleh 1991, 214). My attention to prakriti, therefore, could well seem anachronistic. However, by refocusing on this much maligned notion, I try to show that essentialist discourses associated with it can be avoided by concentrating on how it *functions* in Shiva's environmental activism.

To anticipate my conclusion: prakriti as a marker of ecospirituality can serve as a bridge between science and social justice and need not hark back to biological or civilizational essences. Ecofeminist spirituality is used by Shiva to democratize cognitive space, and prakriti serves as a tool for democracy by securing *epistemic justice* and citizenship. Of course, scholars like Meera Nanda readily agree that prakriti has epistemological significance, but they construe that function in terms of making visible "Indian" (Vedic) ethnosciences. Thus Nanda claims that prakriti-spirituality results in an "epistemic multiculturalism" (Nanda 2005c, 149), which easily lends itself to a relativism at odds with the scientific temper. According to her, "epistemizing" ecospirituality also ends up "sacralizing" local knowledges, which serves to shield them from critical scrutiny. Arguing against this interpretation of the epistemic significance of ecospirituality, I show that reclaiming prakriti does not amount to abandoning scientific rationality, but is a way of rethinking critical inquiry along feminist lines. The mystical here helps us come closer to a democratic future by deconstructing deep structures of epistemic power in a globalized world.

Such an understanding emerges from the work done by the (broadly mystical) concept of prakriti in environmental politics.

Reductionisms and the "Logic of Colonization"

To unravel the complex and multilayered use of prakriti by Shiva, it is best to begin with a close look at the problem that it is meant to counter. Shiva identifies a "logic of colonization" at the heart of exploitative relationships—between the first world and the rest of the world, between national elites and the rural poor, between men and women, and between humans and nature. Her basic point is that an "ontology of dichotomization generates an ontology of domination, over nature and people" (Shiva 1989, 41). Here Shiva concurs with standard ecofeminist analyses, though she inflects the "logic of domination" (Warren 1990) and the "logic of dualism" (Plumwood 1993) with the specific history of India's colonization. Briefly put, her point is that a conceptual framework that plots nature and women lower than culture and men (respectively) also places the first world and national elites in a hierarchical relationship to the rest of the world and the rural poor (respectively). Thus the exploitation of both the third world and of the rural poor within the global South is intertwined with the twin oppressions of nature and women.

On the level of practice, such a colonizing "logic" is enacted by the independent Indian state in its push toward development and its participation in various international policies of economic globalization. Shiva points out that these state policies are grounded in the ideology of modern science, which in turn revolves around the two basic "reductionisms" of knowledge and productivity. Reductionism of knowledge articulates understanding as a process of breaking up a complex whole into its discrete parts and considers the laboratory to be the only site for knowledge production. Reductionism of productivity disassociates the concept of creativity from processes that satisfy needs and sustain life and links it exclusively to processes involved in the production of commodities for profit.

Contemporary "scientific" forestry in India clearly illustrates the link between these two reductionisms, on the one hand, and natural and social devastation on the other. The discipline of forestry studies a "forest" only as a source of timber, thus "managing" out of existence its food-producing and regenerating capabilities, which are central to village life. According to this narrow construction of what a forest is, anything that does not have market value is labeled "waste" or "weeds." The fact that such alleged waste is the wealth of biomass that helps maintain the water and nutrient levels of the soil is ignored (reductionism of knowledge) and the fact that the so-called weeds are a source of food, fuel, fodder, fertilizer, and medicine that produce and maintain life at the fringes is overlooked (reductionism of productivity). The practices of (scientific) forestry thus have an adverse effect on nature and on poorer rural populations. In the same way, intellectual property rights (IPRs) reflect the prioritizing of technological manipulation and "ownership" of genes over the natural preservation of biodiversity in traditional farming practices. Diverse species, such as multiple strains of rice and wheat, form the basic materials for genetic engineering, and their access in research is due to centuries of agricultural labor in subsistence economies. Intellectual property rights, however, privilege and reward laboratory research and the interests of multinational corporations ("gene giants") that fund genetic research. This is at the literal expense of poorer farmers who are not only *not* given any credit for their wisdom, which has preserved genetic diversity over the centuries, but are also cornered by the government-corporation nexus into paying higher prices for engineered seeds that are possible only because of *their* historical labor and knowledge. The narrow categories of science and the narrow goals of capitalism together constitute what Shiva calls a "market fundamentalism" (Shiva 2005b, 57). In its current, full-blown form of economic globalization, this ends up disrupting both the organic unity and sustainability of the various subsystems within nature and harming the peoples whose lives depend upon it.

Shiva reclaims the ancient metaphysical notion of prakriti—the "primordial energy which is the substance of everything, pervading everything," the "feminine and creative principle of the cosmos," and the *shakti* that manifests itself as both animate and inanimate nature—as a corrective to the above scenario (Shiva 1989, 38). She sidesteps a host of ontological subtleties that any scholar of Indian philosophy would raise here: *Which* prakriti? Of Vedanta, Samkhya, or Tantra? What *kind of relation* between prakriti and nature? Instead, Shiva is satisfied by simply emphasizing the figuration of this panentheistic principle into a Goddess and the framework of "reverence" toward nature it sustains. Thus a broadly religious attitude toward all manifestations of a primordial energy—worshipping forests, relating to rivers as goddesses, maintaining sacred groves—is what is retained as "ancient Indian culture" and as what rural women in India have an intimate access to.

What is interesting about this analysis is that prakriti, in religious and metaphysical terms, is posited as a *solution* to oppression spelled out in socioeconomic terms. So, on the face of it, the problem and what is proposed to fix it appear to belong to two completely different discourses: the problem is socioeconomic and the solution is metaphysical. An adequate understanding of prakriti, therefore, must bridge this divide. In other words, whatever else prakriti-spirituality might be, it needs to be read as a strategy for dismantling the exploitative structures that Shiva identifies as the cause of oppression.

Various Functions of Prakriti

In this section I explore three different ways in which prakriti-spirituality can be imagined as an effective intervention in the distribution of socioeconomic power. Shiva gestures toward each of these in her writings, and I suggest that in them we get three different and progressively richer interpretations of prakriti-spirituality. I briefly discuss these alternatives, but only to make room for yet another, relatively unnoticed way in which prakriti becomes relevant for countering the logic of colonization.

Prakriti as an Ontological and Monistic "First Principle"

Shiva's prakriti perspective clearly introduces an ontological continuity between nature, humans, and the divine. A mystical awareness of such metaphysical monism leads to a reenchantment of nature that, in turn, can ground ecological and nonhierarchical lifestyles. By reclaiming the common transcendental source of all creation, prakriti resists both an anthropomorphic domination over the natural world and an androcentric schism within society. We are all *equally*—men and women, animals, rocks, and plants—expressions of the divine prakriti. This unity grounds the central moral imperative that no one of these categories should claim superiority or ownership over the others.

Such a straightforward parsing of ecospirituality, however, is too thin. A simple monism cannot ultimately sustain the kind of political intervention Shiva desires. Empirical evidence shows that metaphysical monisms do not automatically translate into ecological behavior and that Goddess worship is ineffective in redressing exploitive patriarchal structures. As Nanda repeatedly points out, focusing on the identity of the social with the divine does not disrupt social hierarchies. Rather, dualisms tend to become naturalized and entrenched when they are seen as sacred. But, most important, Shiva's own activism does not sit well with a metaphysical merging of multiplicity into a prepersonal First Principle. Her engagement in antiglobalization movements points to the crafting of politically sensitive webs of *interpersonal* and *intercommunal* alliances that require attention to particularities and differences in power. To enable such sensitivity, prakriti-spirituality must be much more than the retrieval of a monism that simply emphasizes sameness. Shiva's activism is clearly based on recognition of difference rather than on a metaphysics of identity.

Prakriti as a Form of Rural Life

Shiva often speaks of the spirituality she has in mind as being neither an organized religion nor a learned grasp of metaphysical principles, but a form of rural life, particularly that of village women in India. Poor women's *work* of sustaining life (and not their biological essence) forces them into kinds of interactions with natural resources that are very different from those the market economy has with nature. This helps rural women carve an "earth-identity" that actually enacts the metaphysical wisdom of prakriti as First Principle. The practices within which such interactions with Nature are embedded aim at harmonizing "intellectually, emotionally and spiritually with nature's rhythms and patterns" (Shiva 2005b, 22). Shiva generalizes this (of course, problematically) into an "Indian" ethos of *aranya sanskriti* (culture of the forest) where "diversity, harmony and self-sustaining nature of the forest formed the organizational principles that guide Indian civilization" (21). Prakriti-spirituality now amounts to reclaiming the lifestyles and work of rural women in order to rec-reate a premodern Indian rural ethos that models itself both on the harmony in and with nature.

However, this interpretation of the prakriti perspective fares no better than the first. Village communities themselves are rife with horrific inequities of class and caste and the very access to natural resources that women have and Shiva valorizes are mediated through these exclusionary social structures. Moreover, emphasizing women's nonmonetized subsistence work only reinforces the invisibility of their labor and entrenches gender oppression in a monetized econ-omy. Thus recovering prakriti by returning to peasant life is at best a "retro-romantic" creation of a myth and cannot be the import of an ecospirituality meant explicitly to be a corrective to injustice in the contemporary globalized world.

Prakriti as a "Standpoint" for Categorical Change

As noted earlier, the logic of colonization in Shiva's analysis is kept in place by the twin reductionisms of modern science, that is, by nar-row notions of productivity and knowledge. To be viable as a solu-tion, prakriti-spirituality would thus need to resist these reductions of "complex ecosystems to a single component and a single compo-nent to a single function" (Shiva 1989, 24). In fact, Shiva explicitly says that prakriti

(a) "allows a *redefinition of growth and productivity* as categories linked to production, not the destruction of *life*" (13, emphasis added), and
(b) "involves an *epistemological shift* in the criteria of assessment of the rationality of knowledge" (28, emphasis added).

This makes it abundantly clear that the monistic principle revered as a Goddess (the first sense of prakriti), the veneration of which is re-flected in the lifestyles of the rural poor (the second sense of prakriti stressed here), is used by Shiva primarily as a device to rethink no-tions of productive labor and knowledge: Earth *spirituality* thus func-tions to reconceptualize both economic categories and concepts of rationality. How is this possible?

Feminist standpoint epistemology, often used to frame Shiva's work, is helpful here. Life at the rural margins, which is a practical realization of prakriti metaphysics, can be cast as a "location" from where alternatives to reductionist science become visible. Struggles for survival of poor, disenfranchised, rural women force them into different kinds of interactions with nature. When feeding an entire family on meager resources is at stake, the "forest" is not constructed as a "timber factory" to be owned by a lucky few, but becomes a common source for meeting nutritional and medicinal needs and providing housing supplies. As the only available resource, it also needs to be preserved as self-renewing. Shiva's point could well be that a "spiritual" orientation to Nature (in the first and second senses of prakriti) is the site through which alternative and indigenous *understandings* of and relations to nature are reclaimed. In this way prakriti-spirituality becomes an "epistemic standpoint," and rural women who live that life become "intellectual gene pools of ecological categories of thought and action" (Shiva 1989, 46). Now, remember that Shiva traces exploitation to state policies of "development," supported by "science," and that science, in turn, is based on reductionist definitions of knowledge and productivity. Thus prakriti as a means of accessing *local knowledges* that are keyed into broader and more holistic approaches to understanding and creativity can be a solution to the problems spawned by narrow, reductionist science.

Nanda, however, fears a pernicious form of cultural relativism in such an epistemological reading of prakriti-spirituality. The retrieval of indigenous wisdom in the form of local knowledge systems becomes, according to her, a route to both reviving alternative "Hindu" ethnosciences and to *rejecting* science constructed now as an "ethnoscience of the West." Abandoning science leaves us with no transcultural universals to critique retrieved local frameworks and the host of social prejudices they harbor. Prakriti-spirituality thus devolves into a facile "epistemic multiculturalism" and loses its liberatory political teeth.

As Nanda has been repeatedly criticized for her gloomy take on epistemological pluralism, I will not reiterate those objections here (see Maffie 2005a). Rather, I ask whether elevating indigenous knowledges to the status of "ethnosciences" is the only way that first-order theories can intervene in systemic hierarchies. The imperialism associated with practices of modern science Shiva discusses is undeniable, but Nanda's appreciation of the critical power of enlightenment rationality and its ability to maintain secular structures in third world societies is also important. The challenge is to show whether the cognitive function of prakriti-spirituality can carve out an intermediate space between these two poles. In the next section I present a reading of prakriti-spirituality that encourages culturally situated understandings of nature while aspiring for transcultural scientific objectivity.

Prakriti-Spirituality in the Service of Objectivity

All criticisms of science do not necessarily amount to rejections of it. Nanda herself says that the value of science is that it has "progressively learned how to learn better, or how to correct itself through socially institutionalized ways" (Nanda 2005b, 99). Could the critique of science inherent in prakriti-spirituality improve our learning how to learn? The argument for an affirmative answer to this question hinges first on the claim that prakriti-spirituality can function to redress certain injustices in the scientific community. Recent work in feminist epistemology, however, shows that intervening in imbalances of power is not simply a political move, but ensures the *objectivity* of science itself. Thus prakriti, even as it engages with political normativity, and perhaps because it does so, has a deeply epistemological function in making science more objective. Of course, both steps here can be contentious. How does prakriti make the epistemic community more *just*? And why should this affect the *objectivity* of science? I begin with the latter by discussing the coimplication of politics and objectivity.

The authority of science is underwritten by its claims to objectivity. Attributions of objectivity commend a statement as being worthy of being accepted by diverse groups, including those outside the scientific community. Naomi Scheman takes this a step further and identifies *trustworthiness* as a crucial enabler of (universal) acceptability (Scheman 2001). In other words, whatever is labeled objective is also considered *worthy of appropriate trust*. The conditions of trustworthiness, however, include more than a statement's being true or it being generated by reliable, truth-conducive research mechanisms. The workings and structures of social institutions within which truth-producing mechanisms are embedded as well as *their* trustworthiness are crucial for the credibility of the theories they produce. For instance, if someone or some institution is known to have an interest in harming me, or is known not to be concerned about my well-being, I will be, justifiably, dismissive and wary of their pronouncements. To ensure objectivity, understood as underwriting the universal acceptability of scientific statements then, we must pay attention not only to their truth-value but also to whether they or the practices that generate them can be trusted.

Associating objectivity to conditions of trustworthiness in this way amounts to widening the scope of the epistemic to include the ethical and the political. Trust is a thicker notion than truth, and *mistrust* can be justified even when we speak the truth. Since the importance of epistemic objectivity lies in its justifying universal acceptance, and since such acceptance can be undermined by conditions that vitiate trust, the conditions of objectivity must include minimal conditions of trustworthiness also. Because trustworthiness depends on the quality of the sociopolitical relations within which scientific claims are generated, scientists are required to engage with injustices in their pursuit of objectivity. Simply put, when norms that yield objectivity are widened beyond the narrowly epistemic (that is, truth conduciveness) to include the broadly moral and political (that is, being worthy of trust), then an engagement with messy social arrangements within the institutions of science is necessary to secure the objectivity of its products.

Within this framework, Shiva's antiscience rhetoric and valorization of prakriti-spirituality acquire new meaning. The colonial history of science and its more recent complicity with corporate capitalism makes it *untrustworthy* in certain segments of the world, irrespective of its truth-securing features. The inherently trust-eroding structures of contemporary scientific practice are brought into sharp focus by Scheman's question: "Who, for a start, are the 'we' who put in place the mechanisms meant to ensure the integrity of scientific results?" (Scheman 2001, 34). Her observation that "those who have been authorized knowers have been, in subtle and complex ways, dependent on those whom *they would not have acknowledged . . . as their peers*; and those forms of dependency have gone unacknowledged and unaccounted for" further marks the credibility-undermining features of scientific communities (41, emphasis added). Moreover, Shiva's claim that the needs of the rural poor do not usually figure in profit-and-capital-driven research agendas amounts to a reason why this population is justified in being skeptical of scientific progress. Her discussion of IPRs underscores how cognitive contributions of entire groups are erased, even though, ironically, scientific research depends on them. The systemic exclusions and denied dependencies inherent in scientific culture that Shiva unearths explain a *mistrust* of science. And, given Scheman's construal of epistemic objectivity, such mistrust translates into a critique of its objectivity.

Even if this is so, can prakriti-spirituality ensure a more inclusive scientific community? Can Shiva's retrieval of alternative, indigenous theories help *build* trust and reestablish scientific credibility and objectivity? To see how this might happen requires us to appreciate that making local knowledges visible (which seems to be one of Shiva's proximate political goals) reverberates through multiple registers. Of course, it straightforwardly introduces new hypotheses and theoretical content into the discussion. But it also does something crucial for the *agents* who are associated with these hypotheses. Retrieving hitherto ignored knowledge systems is also a process of including excluded *knowers* into the epistemic community, hence beginning to rectify the injustices of marginalization and erasure.

To flesh this out further, it might be useful to read prakriti as a way of addressing forms of what Miranda Fricker has recently called "testimonial injustice" (Fricker 2007). Fricker explains how we routinely construct certain identities as not capable of producing knowledge. Stereotypical prejudices against women as irrational and intuitive, for example, enable us to guiltlessly discount their contributions to the cooperative cognitive endeavor. Testimonial injustice is this erasure of participation in inquiry because of prejudicial identity constructions. Now it is easy to see how the twin reductionisms that Shiva has identified as the pillars of contemporary scientific practice also cause testimonial injustice. The activities of the rural poor fail to have any cognitive significance in a social imagination where knowledge and creativity are construed in terms of profit generation alone. Thus the two reductionisms of knowledge and productivity function as social prejudices that prevent individuals at the economic fringes from being considered epistemic agents. Scientific practice now becomes reductionist in yet another sense of "excluding other knowers" (Shiva 1989, 22).

Injustice (in general) and testimonial injustice (in particular) lead to a loss of trust. A condition for the scientific establishment to win back trust, therefore, "would be to work to make the institutions in question and the broader society within which they exist more genuinely just, more truly worthy of everyone's trust" (Scheman 2001, 38). The assumption is that, to prove itself trust*worthy* to a skeptical audience, science needs to seriously engage with the *reasons* that led this audience to withdraw their allegiance. On Shiva's analysis, the reasons for withdrawal of trust are forms of testimonial injustice that erase the rural poor in institutions—universities, corporate research departments, and governmental agencies—within which scientific research agendas are formulated and executed. Thus taking the views of these disenfranchised groups as serious theoretical options corrects for such marginalizations and combats the identity prejudices that sustain them. In doing so, it disrupts the links between social and economic power, on the one hand, and epistemic or testimonial power, on the other.

On this interpretation, the importance of local knowledges lies not just in the possibility that they may well be true but also in the fact that they are retrieved at all. Shiva's critical engagement with alternative knowledges could well be an invitation to the establishment to also take these alternatives seriously and thereby consider their proponents as *knowers* and epistemic participants. This would be a small but significant step by mainstream science toward rectifying a serious systemic injustice in the global scientific community and, consequently, of earning back the trust of the disenfranchised. Since establishing objectivity is tantamount to maintaining relationships of trust, this gesture would amount to making cross-cultural scientific objectivity a real possibility.

It should now be clear that Shiva is distrustful of traditional science not on the a priori grounds that anything "Western" is bad, but because of multiple levels of violence inherent in its reductionist ideology. It should also be clear that Shiva upholds indigenous knowledges not to isolate them from critical investigation, but to open them up for serious discussion. For instance, the aim of Navdanya, a movement launched by Shiva to save seed diversity in farmers' fields, is to "build a program in which farmers and scientists *relate horizontally rather than vertically*, in which conversation of biodiversity and production of food go hand in hand, and in which farmers' knowledge is strengthened, not robbed" (Shiva 2005a, 92, emphasis added). In principle, Shiva is not even opposed to transcultural epistemological universals. After all, the prakriti principle for her is "transgender" and, as an alternative to the logic of colonization, comes with a claim to its being adopted across the board. What is problematic for Shiva is the way in which Western science goes about the business of "learning" about the world and its practice of claiming universal status by making some forms of dissent, some agendas, and some agents disappear.

The diversity that Shiva ensures through prakriti is not simply a plurality of first-order theories and hypotheses about the world or even a cultural diversity of alternative perspectives on the world. What Nanda derisively terms "epistemic multiculturalism" is a way of expanding epistemological citizenship for marginalized groups. The insertion of indigenous first-order theories into cognitive space tangles with power by changing who gets to speak and who is heard when articulating research agendas, thereby strengthening the objectivity of prevailing scientific claims. The ecospirituality of Vandana Shiva, therefore, has profound epistemological significance because it has political significance and vice versa.

Prakriti-Spirituality and Hindu Fundamentalism

A question about the *tactical* or pragmatic appropriateness of prakriti-spirituality in a postcolonial society like India still remains. After all, prakriti could well become one more avenue of making *Hindu* symbols—the markers of a majority religion—visible in a public sphere that intends to serve other minority religions as well. Can our case for prakriti-spirituality as a form of epistemological egalitarianism resist a fundamentalist, Hindu appropriation of spiritual-environmentalist rhetoric?

Nanda's reminder to "those of us who trade in ideas" is that we "have a responsibility to ensure that our ideas should do no harm" (Nanda 2003, 159). Dubbing this the "No Harm Principle," James Maffie rejects it as being too stringent (Maffie 2005b, 69): we obviously cannot guard against all possible misappropriations of a theory and so need not feel responsible for politically pernicious manipulations of it. However, the "harm" associated with religious environmentalism for Nanda is quite specific, and it is unfair to read her cautionary admonition as a decontextualized epistemic principle. Nanda rightly forces an intellectual responsibility on postmodern and feminist scholars who blithely go about "picking and choosing those aspects of the non-Western world that help them fight their own battles against modern science, without adequate awareness of the role local knowledges play in sustaining traditional power structures in non-Western societies" (Nanda 2005c, 164). This is an important warning when "picking and choosing" prakriti-based ecospirituality to critique science because, once retrieved, spiritualized agency can work in multiple and unexpected ways on the ground to reinforce the very oppressions that its retrieval was meant to counter. Given the misuses of ecospirituality that I pointed to at the beginning of this chapter, it is important to show how and why a prakriti-based theory is *not* hospitable to such misappropriations. Over and above arguing for its positive potential, can we argue that prakriti-spirituality does not end up fanning Hindu nationalism and might even stem the spread of such fanatical violence?

Though Bron Taylor points out how violence is sometimes justified in ecospiritual terms by some members of Earth First! even he concludes his ethnography of the movement on a contrary note: "Earth First! simply does not provide suitable habitat for racist (or sexist) ideologies" (Taylor 2002, 62). According to Taylor, the "militantly egalitarian, anti-hierarchical and feminist" rhetoric he finds in the environmentalist subcultures makes long-term cross-fertilizations between radical environmentalism and the green racist right extremely "unlikely." These are liable to be weeded out by the inherently progressive strains within environmentalist movements themselves. Something similar could be said about the fear of lasting alliances between prakriti ecospirituality and Hindu fundamentalism. After all, Shiva is not silent about the dangers of cultural fundamentalism: her rhetoric is openly and fervently anti-Hindutva. While Nanda sees the retrieval of "Indian"/Hindu metaphysical roots as resulting in fundamentalist nationalism, Shiva sees such fundamentalism as sustained by growing economic globalization. Prakriti-spirituality, according to Shiva, explicitly attempts to unravel globalization and consequently aims at removing an important condition for the rise of Hindutva. Note Shiva's prizing apart of "Indian" and "Hindutva," linking the latter to Cartesian (read reductionist) science when she says: "The new ideology of Hindutva is not Indian. It is molded by Cartesian

philosophy and amounts to the colonization of our minds by categories of division, separation, and exclusion. It is doubly alien: first, it
has no place for nature, ecology, and the land; second, it creates a
fictitious "culture" that has no rooting in nature or the land. It is also
alien because it replaces our capacity to live and think nondualisti-
cally" (Shiva 2005b, 160). We do find political parties in India resorting to idiosyncratically defined notions of Indianness to gain a popular power base. But, on Shiva's analysis, this is traced to the weakened
hold that national governments have on their own economic policies
because of their participation in global economic trends.

A stronger claim can be made, based on the epistemological function that I have tried to tease out of Shiva's use of prakriti-spirituality.
Prakriti, on this interpretation, focuses on establishing the trustworthiness of science, which involves engaging with actual past and present as well as possible future injustices in scientific practice. Guarding
against such injustices requires a self-reflexivity on multiple fronts.
It involves an attention to the criticisms of one's performance, to injustices (perceived or real) that one's performance gets embroiled in,
and to the acknowledgment of one's own privileges that engender
and exacerbate these injustices. My suggestion is that this methodology retrieved through prakriti—a continuous socially and materially grounded critical awareness about the consequences of power in
knowledge seeking and the constant modulation of scientific practice
in light of this awareness—can encompass the very standpoint from
which it is imposed. Prakriti, as a socially grounded self-reflexivity
about the workings of power, can loop back to illuminate its own complicity in the trust-eroding consequences of its very *own* location. The
moves to address this could well result in changes to that location
itself.

Since reclaiming prakriti is a gesture toward a being-in-the-world
that is also a specific strategy for reflecting critically on the social
world, the hope is that it has the resources to stem the slide of spiritual environmentalism into Hindu fundamentalism. Remember that
prakriti-spirituality is consistent with the existence of other ways of
world making, making them visible and taking them into account in
our reflective practice. Thus, living by the prakriti principle, as interpreted here, would include taking seriously the possible locations
from which it (the use of the prakriti-spirituality itself) might look
politically suspicious to some. This would involve engaging with the

reasons for the suspicion and trying to redress them, which ultimately permits a readiness to give it up altogether if that is required for building trust. Prakriti-spirituality as a form of valorizing "situated knowing" becomes a form of "situated reflection." In no way can prakriti-spirituality consistently support hegemony of the dominant cultural-religious institutions and symbols because its very adoption leaves room for its possible withdrawal. Interpreted as a form of situated knowing, then, prakriti-spirituality becomes a form of embedded and responsible "*situated* devotionalism" as well.

Note

I am grateful to Ashby Butnor and Jennifer McWeeny for comments on an earlier draft. The criticisms and points raised by them were of great help in clarifying my argument.

References

Agarwal, Bina. 1992. The gender and environmental debate: Lessons from India. *Feminist Studies* 18: 119–58.

Fricker, Miranda. 2007. *Epistemic injustice: Power and ethics of knowing.* Oxford: Oxford University Press.

Jackson, Cecile. 1995. Radical environmental myths: A gender perspective. *New Left Review* 210: 124–43.

Kishwar, Madhu. 2004. When religions claim superiority, preconditions for genuine interfaith harmony. *Manushi* 145: 4–10.

Maffie, James, ed. 2005a. Science, modernity, and critique. Special issue of *Social Epistemology* 19 (1).

——. 2005b. The consequences of ideas. *Social Epistemology* 19 (1): 63–76.

Naess, Arne. 1986. The deep ecological movement: Some philosophical aspects. *Philosophical Inquiry* 8 (1–2): 10–31.

Nanda, Meera. 2002. Breaking the spell of dharma: A case for Indian enlightenment. In *Breaking the spell of dharma and other essays,* 103–83. New Delhi: Three Essays Collective.

——. 2003. *Prophets facing backward: Postmodern critiques of science and Hindu nationalism in India.* New Brunswick, NJ: Rutgers University Press.

——. 2005a. Hindu ecology in the age of Hindutva. In *The wrongs of the religious right: Reflections on science, secularism and Hindutva,* 66–95. Gurgaon: Three Essays Collective.

——. 2005b. Making science sacred: How postmodernism aids Vedic science. In *Wrongs of the religious right: Reflections on science, secularism and Hindutva*, 93–118. Gurgaon: Three Essays Collective.

——. 2005c. Response to my critics. *Social Epistemology* 19 (1): 147–91.

Plumwood, Val. 1993. *Feminism and the mastery of nature*. London: Routledge.

Salleh, Ariel. 1991. Review of *Staying alive*. *Hypatia* 6 (1): 206–14.

Scheman, Naomi. 2001. Epistemology resuscitated: Objectivity as trustworthiness. In *Engendering rationalities*, ed. Nancy Tuana and Sandra Morgen, 23–52. Albany: State University of New York Press.

Shiva, Vandana. 1989. *Staying alive: Women, ecology and development*. London: Zed.

——. 2005a. *Earth democracy: Justice, sustainability, and peace*. Cambridge: Southend.

——. 2005b. *India divided: Diversity and democracy under attack*. New York: Seven Stories.

Taylor, Bron. 2002. Diggers, wolves, ents, elves and expanding universes. In *The cultic milieu: Oppositional subcultures in an age of globalization*, ed. Jeffrey Kaplan and Helene Loow, 26–74. Walnut Creek, CA: Altamira.

Visvanathan, Shiv. 2000. Environmental values, policy, and conflict in India. Transcript, Carnegie Council on Ethics and International Affairs, 21.

Warren, Karen. 1990. The power and promise of ecological feminism. *Environmental Ethics* 12 (2): 125–46.

Zimmerman, Michael. 2000. Possible political problems of earth-based religiosity. In *Beneath the surface: Critical essays in the philosophy of deep ecology*, ed. Eric Katz, Andrew Light and David Rosenthal, 169–94. Cambridge: MIT Press.

PART FOUR

CULTIVATING ETHICAL SELVES

CHAPTER EIGHT

Confucian Care

A Hybrid Feminist Ethics

LI-HSIANG LISA ROSENLEE

EVER SINCE Sara Ruddick published "Maternal Thinking" in 1980, care ethics has emerged as a significant contender in the field of ethics, serving as a viable feminist alternative to the Kantian-liberal approach to normative ethics. Carol Gilligan's *In a Difference Voice* (1982) and Nel Noddings's *Caring* (1986) paved the way for later fruitful discussions on issues such as the compatibility between care thinking and justice thinking, the limited applicability of the mother-child dyadic relationship, and the stereotyping of care thinking as feminine in nature. In its early stages, discussions surrounding care ethics were by and large confined to Western theories. Then, in 1994, Chenyang Li's pioneering essay on the compatibility between care ethics and the Confucian concept of *ren* 仁 (often translated as "benevolence") extended the scholarly engagement in the field of care ethics beyond the confines of Western theories for the first time. Li's initial effort to bring about positive engagement between Confucianism and feminism has sparked some excitement as well as critical objections. This criticism culminates in Virginia Held's publication of *The Ethics of Care* (2006) where she briefly but decisively rejects the compatibility between Confucianism and feminism in general. As Held writes, "A traditional Confucian ethic, if seen as an ethic of care, would be a form of care ethics unacceptable to feminists" (Held 2006, 22). However, Held is mistaken on this point. It is my contention that a Confucian ethics of *ren* is not only compatible with care ethics, but, more important, contemporary feminist care ethics will be rendered more plausible by the inclusion of *ren*. For one thing, a Confucian ethics of *ren* is immediately able to resolve two perennial problems haunting contemporary care ethics: the limited application of care-based ethics to strangers and the lack of a structural analysis of political institutions. In this chapter I will show how a Confucian ethics of *ren* is able to provide a normative basis for the ethical extension of care from one's loved ones to the world at large as well as a familial care-based analysis of political authority.

The Issue of Compatibility Revisited

Held's rather hasty dismissal of Confucianism is, in my view, indicative of the narrow application of contemporary care ethics, on the one hand, and its implicit colonialist overtones in assessing non-Western traditions, on the other. Although Held's objection to the compatibility between Confucianism and care ethics is quite brief, its significance is twofold. First, Held is one of just a few prominent care ethicists who actually engage Confucianism in their writings and, therefore, Held's mention of Confucianism could serve as an important starting point for dialogue between Confucianism and the feminist community. Second, even with the rise of Western scholarship on Confucianism, positive assessment of Confucianism in the context of gender and feminism remains marginal. Held's blunt characterization of Confucianism as patriarchal and antifeminist serves as a fresh reminder of the colonial politics of feminism at play within the Western academy where we find non-Western intellectual traditions frequently judged as ethically unworthy. This colonialist assumption is at the heart of the discourse of normative ethics in the nonfeminist community and, unfortunately, also gets duplicated in the feminist community where imperialistic hegemony is supposedly rejected. As Held reminds her readers, "Great care needs to be taken to avoid the imperialism in thinking and in programs that postcolonial feminists discern in many feminists from the global North" (Held 2006, 164). However, Held's conscious rejection of imperialism is inconsistent with her exclusion of non-Western intellectual traditions in her theoretical construction of feminist care ethics.

In the case of Confucianism, Held is only one among many who reject its compatibility with feminism. As Terry Woo observed back in 1999, the relationship between Confucianism and feminism "has largely been a one-sided affair: feminists criticizing the status and treatment of women determined by Confucianism" (Woo 1999, 110). In Western eyes, third world women victimized by their uniformly patriarchal traditions are often thought to exist outside the progressive world.[1] This Western imperialistic assessment of third world culture is well reflected in earlier versions of feminism, such as in Simone de Beauvoir's perception of Chinese women as living in a state of slavery since the beginning of time. As she writes in *The Second Sex*, albeit only in a footnote and not fit for a more lengthy discussion, "The history of woman in the East, in India, in China, has been in effect that of a long and unchanging slavery" (Beauvoir 1989, 81). Beauvoir's characterization of the East is situated in the long tradition of Western colonialist perceptions of its colonized. Uma Narayan explains this precisely in her critique of the politics of Western feminism: "From the viewpoint of colonizing Western power, an important 'difference' between 'Western culture' and various colonized cultures was the alleged singular openness of 'Western culture' to historical change—cast, not surprisingly, as 'progress.' Colonized cultures were conversely often represented as victims of a static past of unchanging custom and tradition, virtually immune to history" (Narayan 1997, 16).

As a result, any change that occurs in these "traditional" societies, such as the rise of feminist consciousness, is invariably read as a sign of "Westernization." In this way, the West's monopoly of the world, from natural resources to feminist consciousness, is fostered. But if this imperialistic attitude in the theoretical landscape is intolerable, then it is necessary for ethicists in general and feminists in particular to reassess the ethical worthiness of non-Western traditions, including Confucianism. As improbable as this claim might sound to some Western feminists, I do believe that there is a viable form of care ethics that is Confucian and feminist at the same time.

Li's 1994 essay on the compatibility between Confucian *ren* and feminist care ethics can be seen as the first step in changing the terms of the one-sided conversation between feminism and Confucianism. The main tenet of Li's argument is that the Confucian concept of *ren* that takes filial care (*xiao*孝) in the parent-child relationship as the basis of its moral paradigm shares significant common ground with feminist care ethics, which anchors its moral paradigm in noncontractual maternal thinking. Li then concludes with the following optimistic note: "Since, as we have shown, Confucianism and feminism share important common grounds, it is possible to reconstruct Confucianism to be feminist. If this is the case, then it seems more likely for feminism to prevail in a form of new Confucianism" (86). Although Li did not elaborate on this new form of Confucianism, his pronouncement of a Confucianism that is also *feminist* is radical if it is placed against the prevailing assumption of the patriarchal nature of Confucianism found in the feminist community.

Li's reconciliatory effort has been met with intense interest as well furious objections within the sinologist community, but has been virtually ignored within feminist communities, which by and large remain immune to the influence of non-Western, philosophical traditions. In this respect, Held's dismissal of Confucianism is nevertheless a welcome starting point of engagement. Held's rejection of the compatibility between Confucianism and feminism is familiar. Citing both Lijun Yuan (2002) and Daniel Star's (2002) objections to Li's article, Held characterizes Confucianism as essentially hierarchal and patriarchal and hence incompatible with feminism. Even if Li is correct in arguing for theoretical common ground between Confucian *ren* and care ethics, Held believes that it is unacceptable to call Confucianism "feminist." Held is not so much disputing whether Confucian *ren* is a form of care ethics, but what matters to her is that Confucianism does not merit the label *feminist*. In fact, for Held, care ethics is the *only* ethical theory that merits the name *feminist* since it explores what all others fail to notice by giving moral weight to women's experience in caring activities such as mothering. Moreover, care ethics exposes the patriarchal root of all other moral theories, like Aristotelian virtue ethics and Kantian liberalism, that take men's experience in the public realm as paradigmatic of moral thinking. According to Held, "to establish that the experience of women is as important, relevant, and philosophically interesting as the experience of men" is an important achievement of feminism (Held 1996, 22). Thus, to incorporate "non-feminist versions of valuing care," such as Confucian *ren*, into care ethics would be to take away what Held regards as the feminist achievement of care ethics (22).

Ironically, Yuan, whom Held cited in support of her objection to the compatibility between Confucianism and feminism, also objects to the status of care ethics as genuinely feminist. As Yuan writes, "Insofar as the concept of care is similar to *jen* [*ren*], it may be a culturally feminine feature of morality but is very questionable as feminist ethics" (Yuan 2002, 108). Quoting from Marilyn Friedman's criticism of early forms of care ethics, Yuan rejects both Confucian *ren* and care ethics: "care ethics [the concept of *jen*, too] 'does not (yet) constitute a sufficiently rich or fully liberatory *feminist* ethics'" (119). Interestingly, Held does not discuss Yuan's objection to care ethics' feminist status, yet boldly denies the feminist potential of Confucianism. Indeed, what constitutes a feminist liberatory theory is far from being settled, and therefore it is certainly worthwhile to revisit the possibility of a feminist theory anchored in Confucian *ren*.

In rejecting Li's optimistic, conciliatory effort to bring together Confucianism and feminist care ethics, critics such as Yuan provide familiar objections to both care ethics and Confucianism. For Yuan, Confucianism *is* a form of care ethics, but care ethics and Confucianism are bad for women. In her view, both care ethics and Confucianism encourage unnecessary self-sacrifice and silencing, fail to address the issue of justice within the family, focus on women's roles instead of women's rights, and, finally, fail to provide adequate conceptual tools to criticize all forms of male dominance (125). In contrast to Yuan, Star, whom Held also cited in support of her argument, maintains that care ethics is distinct from Confucian ethics, which he calls "role-focused virtue ethics." In Star's view, Confucian *ren* is not compatible with feminism due to the Confucian emphasis on hierarchal role-based relationships and its reliance on patriarchal tradition, as seen in constant references to the father-son relationship (Star 2002, 93).

In sum, Li, Yuan, and Star respectively represent the following three responses to the possibility of a Confucian feminist care ethics: 1. Confucian *ren* is a form of care ethics and is compatible with feminism; 2. Confucian *ren* is a form of care ethics, but is not compatible with feminism; and 3. Confucian *ren* is not a form of care ethics and is not compatible with feminism. Although Held has not explicitly spelled out her position on whether Confucianism can be considered a form of care ethics, she has made it abundantly clear that Confucian ethics of *ren* is *not* feminist.

Setting aside whether Confucianism is a form of care ethics or not, it is worthwhile to examine what makes a theory "feminist": Is care ethics a "feminist" theory? And in what respects is Confucian *ren* "feminist"? According to Held, a genuine feminist ethics must take caring experiences and activities in intimate relationships as the basis for our normative moral thinking. If one adopts Held's criterion for a feminist theory, then I would argue that Confucian *ren* is *feminist* through and through. For first of all, unlike the dominant moral theories based on a masculine model of abstract reasoning, force, and confrontation, which Held criticizes, Confucianism takes seriously the activity of reciprocal care in unchosen relations such as those between parents and children. As sinologists generally agree, Confucianism bases its moral core in the private realm of filial affection and familial responsibility, not in the public realm of state or commerce. Akin to Held's care ethics, Confucian *ren* stresses the codependent nature of human existence, which is embodied in the Confucian ideal person, *junzi* 君子, for whom filial care for her parents is indicative of her basic humanity. In Confucianism, since the private familial virtue of filial piety (*xiao* 孝) is not seen as different in kind from the public virtue of *ren*, reciprocal care and relational personhood have *always* been taken as paradigmatic.

Furthermore, for Held, moral thinking must begin with the standpoint of human children whose survival must presuppose the activity of care being performed (Held 2006, 66). Held claims that the value of care is, therefore, empirically and ontologically prior to all other values (73). Similarly, in Confucianism the importance of filial care is justified on the ground that we were cared for by our parents when we were young. As Confucius says to his disciple in the *Analects*, he who questions the necessity of observing the mourning ritual for his deceased parents really neglects the fact that he was cared for by his parents when he was young (*Analects* 17.21).[2] Therefore, similar to Held's care ethics, Confucianism, with its emphasis on filial care as the basis for its highest virtue of *ren*, cannot be said to neglect the work of care in unchosen private relations or the relatedness of human existence. In sum, Confucian *ren* parallels feminist care ethics in that it takes the work of care in these situations as the core of our moral thinking.

Of course, not everyone agrees with Held's definition of a feminist theory. Liberal critics, in particular, argue that a theory that derives its moral core from caring activities that are typically performed by women, as shown in the mother-child dyadic relationship, is not yet a *feminist* theory that aims at liberating women from oppression. For instance, in addition to Yuan, Martha Nussbaum, Ann Cudd, Claudia Card, and Marilyn Friedman all argue that the sole emphasis on caring activities is not a sufficient condition to foster liberation for women unless the questions of justice and equality are also adequately addressed. For one thing, as critics argue, women's caregiving roles have been historically performed under a patriarchal structure in which a disproportional amount of caring labor is done by women alone. Such a structure fails to address women's own needs for a full-range of self-development and reciprocal care. The common criticisms against care ethics can be summarized as follows: first, care ethics is silent on the moral imperative to care for oneself and to be reciprocally cared for by one's equals; second, care ethics is unable to deal with the issue of violence due to its emphasis on the caring relation regardless of the quality of the relations; third, care ethics neglects wider social, economic, and political institutions due to its emphasis on the mother-child dyadic relationship. All in all, as Friedman puts it, care ethics might do more harm than good to women by bolstering "some of the practices and conceptions that subordinate women" (Friedman 1993, 151). To account for these shortcomings, Friedman argues that a fully liberatory feminist ethic must address all of these concerns (155–56).

Care ethicists, such as Held, are well aware of such objections and seek not to eliminate but rather to incorporate other moral values into care ethics. For instance, in Held's all-encompassing metaphor of the moral tapestry, care forms the overall framework of our moral thinking, within which specific moral values like justice can be incorporated into certain domains, such as that of the law. As she writes, "It is plausible to see caring relations as the wider and deeper context within which we seek justice and, in certain domains, give it priority" (Held 2006, 158). It is in this spirit that I seek to incorporate Confucian *ren*, with its emphasis on the spiritual pursuit of self-cultivation and ritualized reciprocal obligation, into feminist care ethics' overarching moral tapestry and further strengthen its theoretical grounding in order to respond to these objections.

The Political Extension of *Ren*

Similar to care ethics, Confucian *ren* begins its moral thinking from the dyadic relationship between parent and child in the private realm.

However, Confucianism extends the spiritual discipline of one's whole self outward from the family to the community, the state, and beyond. Thus Confucian *ren* is both a familial virtue of filial piety and, at the same time, a civil virtue of benevolent governance. *Ren* is a caring ideal, but also a perfect virtue that encompasses all other particular excellences such as courage, wisdom, righteousness, and trust. *Ren* represents a full range of human excellences (including filial care and political harmony) that is able to provide a moral imperative for women to care for themselves and to actualize their utmost potential as exemplary persons. In Confucianism a person of *ren* is not just a filial child to her parents but also a *junzi*, a political leader, who leads by virtuous examples. One's political authority hangs on one's moral cultivation in effecting caring relations. Confucian *ren* extends caring relations naturally outward and therefore it is, at the same time, personal, political, and global.

Confucian *ren* begins with a familial, parent-child dyadic relationship; however, it also emphasizes the outward movement of caring relations from the personal to the global, as it has been well articulated by numerous contemporary Confucian scholars such as Roger Ames (1987), Tu Wei-ming (1985), Chenyang Li (1994, 2000, 2002), and Julia Po-Wah Lai Tao (2000). In the *Analects* Confucius takes filial responsibility as the root of *ren* and urges his disciples not only to be filial at home and deferential in the community, but also trustworthy in one's words and capable of "lov[ing] the multitude broadly" (*Analects* 1.1, 1.6). Mencius, the second Confucian master, in his advice to King Xuan of Chi on becoming a true king, grounds political authority in the practice of this gradual extension of the caring relation. As Mencius says, "Treat the aged of your own family in a manner befitting their venerable age and extend this treatment to the aged of other families; treat your own young in a manner befitting their tender age and extend this to the young of other families, and you can roll the Empire on your palm" (*Mencius* 1A.7).[3] Past sage kings, according to Mencius, were able to rule over the empire because they practiced *ren* and took good care of the vulnerable: old men without wives, old women without husbands, old people without children, young children without parents (*Mencius* 1B.5, 1B.12, 3A.3, 4A.1, 4A.13, 6B.7, 7A.15, 7A.22). In other words, one's capacity to care for one's family and to extend that same caring capability to all is the key to good governing.[4] This intermingling of familial love with political authority has provided

Confucian *ren* the theoretical capacity to articulate larger social and political problems within the framework of caring relations.

In fact, some contemporary Confucian scholars such as Li and Lai Tao believe that, compared to early care ethics as theorized by Nel Noddings, *ren* is much better equipped to deal with larger social problems. *Ren* is not just limited to one's intimate loved ones, but is also a social ideal, a common good that describes the Great Society (*datong* 大同) in which all are cared for by all. This ideal Confucian society is depicted in the following passage from the *Book of Rituals* (*Liji* 禮記):

> When the great *Dao* prevailed, the world belonged to the general public (*tianxia wei gong*). They chose the worthy and capable, were trustworthy in what they said and cultivated harmony. Therefore, people did not love only their own parents (*bu du qin qi qin*) and did not treat only their own children as children (*bu du zi qi zi*). Thus the aged could live out their lives, the grown-ups all had their function, the young could be reared, and the widowed, the lonely, the orphans, the crippled, and the sick all found their care. Men had their roles, and women their homes. They hated casting away goods, but not necessarily to keep them for themselves. They hated leaving their strength unemployed, but not necessarily to employ it for themselves. Therefore, scheming had no outlet, and theft, rebellion, and robbery did not arise, so that the outer doors were left unlocked. This is called the Great Community (*datong*).
>
> (LAI TAO 2000, 226–27)

In sum, Confucian *ren* as both filial love and a common good, by its very nature, dictates the natural outward extension of care and love from near to far. And *ren*'s natural outward extension of love and care can help resolve the so-called domesticity objection often raised against early care ethics that seems to confine caring activities to one's intimate relationships (Card 1990; Dalmiya 2009).

Even though Confucian ethics, like care ethics, is thoroughly relational, I believe that the sociopolitical dimension of *ren* forestalls some of the problematic issues that have plagued care ethics. For example, the concept of ritual propriety (*li* 禮) is central to the expression of *ren* insofar as our exemplary natures are performed through ritualized norms. Moreover, *li* is coupled with shame to provide an immediate response to the issue of violence and women's needs for

reciprocal care. For Confucius, ritual propriety structured with reciprocal obligation and role appropriation is capable of minimizing social
discord (*Analects* 2.3, 12.11), since one's failure to embody those social
excellences invites communal shame, which in turn functions as an
effective corrective to the issue of violence and neglect. Of course,
this is not to say that Confucianism has been effectively dealing with
violence and neglect in historical reality. This empirical shortcoming,
however, is common to all ethical theories. For this reason, it should
not be used to undermine the theoretical validity of Confucianism
per se.

Despite the promise of *ren* and *li*, feminist theorists (of any sort)
remain largely suspicious of communal norms, especially those based
on gender. In agreement with Samantha Brennan, Star writes, "it
has been important for women to say, and be able to say, that they
are more than someone's daughter, or someone's wife, to assert that
one's identity transcends the roles assigned to women" (Star 2002,
94). Additionally, Yuan cites numerous disparaging passages toward
women in Confucian writings to substantiate her claim of the patriarchal nature of Confucianism, such as the well-known passage in the
Analects in which women are compared with petty men (17.25) as well
as neo-Confucian Zhu Xi's rigid attitude toward the issue of remar-
riage for women (Yuan 2002, 114–16). In general, Confucianism's emphasis on communal norms, tradition, and social roles is incompatible
with feminists' general distrust of them (Star 2002, 85). As Friedman
puts it, "Communitarian theory, in the form in which it condones or
tolerates traditional communal norms of gender subordination, is
unacceptable from any standpoint enlightened by feminist analysis"
(Friedman 1993, 234). Additionally, Star is concerned about a communitarian, role-based ethic because care is then limited to socially prescribed relationships rather than the particular needs of individuals.

It appears that this feminist critique of Confucianism is misguided
and perhaps even paradoxical. It is true that hierarchal relationships
form the core of Confucian *ren* and the concept of ritual (communal
norms and social roles) plays a prominent role in a Confucians' daily
conduct. But it is not clear to me that maternal care as exhibited in
the mother-child relationship is incompatible with Confucian role-
based care. For one thing, the mother-child relationship that typifies
moral thinking in feminist care ethics is *hierarchal* and *role-based*. Second, maternal care itself is often considered nothing but a remnant of

the patriarchal past in which women were often assigned the role of self-sacrificing caregiver in the family. Third, care ethics' rejection of the (masculine) autonomous self and its embracing of the relational self in fact mirrors a communitarian model of ethics that, as Star and Friedman point out, is often tradition bound and hence incompatible with feminism. If a feminist care ethics can incorporate and/or overcome these features in its development, then it surely seems possible for a Confucian ethic to do the same.

Some critics, such as Star, might still argue that the mother-child relationship in care ethics is markedly different from the patriarchal relationship between father and son in Confucianism. It is true that the language and concepts employed in Confucianism are inescapably patriarchal and sexist, but that patriarchal and sexist tendencies are common to all traditions, whether they originated in the East or West, North or South. Rampant sexist practices and remarks are not an exclusively Confucian invention; they are part of a shared human past. The real issue here, as I see it, is whether we can acknowledge Confucianism's inevitable shortcomings in the discourse on gender, race, and class and, at the same time, appreciate what is valuable in it. On a philosophical level, the father-son relationship in Confucianism, though patriarchal in form, can be extended to cover all sorts of parent-child relationships in the contemporary world. This extension of the Confucian care originated in the father-son dyadic relationship parallels the extension of care originated in mother-child relationships of care ethics. Care ethicists would certainly argue that care, although originated in maternal thinking, is not limited to women per se, nor does it condone any sort of patriarchal oppression of women. In the same way, although Confucian ren arises out of the father-son relationship and is dependent on communal rituals, it by no means is limited to the patriarchal relationships of men, nor is it synonymous with oppressive communal practices against women.

In fact, Confucianism, unlike a particularistic form of care ethics, does contain within itself a corrective to the kinds of oppressive practices that became contingently interwoven in its rituals and social norms. The concept of yi 義 (appropriateness in context) allows Confucians to deviate from prevalent communal norms and thereby reform them with the aim of approximating the ideal of ren as caring comprehensively for all. Although Confucian ren allows for contextualized moral thinking, rule-breaking in Confucian ren in accordance with *yi* is done with the aim of revising the communal norms and rituals, but not challenging the normative status of rituals in general (Star 2002, 89). In contrast, nonprinciple-based moral thinking in feminist care ethics is derived from the context-dependent needs of the cared for, particularly in the relationship between mother-child. Confucian *ren*'s involvement in communal practices is not a weakness, but is rather a theoretical and practical strength insofar as the question whether Confucian *ren* can be efficacious in changing social practices is concerned. As Star acknowledges, Confucianism is much more effective in changing social norms than care ethics, because the latter is deeply particularistic (89). And if the end for feminism is to bring about social changes in favor of gender parity, it seems preferable and logical that care ethics embrace Confucian *ren* along with its communal involvement. In other words, Confucian *li* (ritual) can provide a necessary corrective to what liberal feminists, such as Friedman, call the lack of institutional analysis and the particularistic tendency in care ethics. Certainly, care ethics, as a feminist normative ethic, seeks to achieve that goal.

In the end, Confucian *ren,* with its natural extension of caring relations to the world at large, its employment of *yi* to correct oppressive communal rituals in restoring social harmony, its demand for reciprocity in all human relations, and, last, its grounding of the political in the personal, is able to provide a stronger theoretical grounding for feminist care ethics to meet the objections of its liberal critics. A person of *ren*, at the most basic level, must be able to sustain harmonious relationships in both the intimate familial realm and the public political realm. Therefore, *ren* is not only compatible with the notion and the practice of care ethics, but, more important, is able to extend familial (maternal) care into the wider social and political realm.

Confucian Care: A Hybrid Feminist Ethics

Without a doubt, Confucianism was not originally a feminist tradition, nor did it take particular interest in promoting women's well-being. But, if any theory contaminated with patriarchal practices is deemed unworthy of the name *feminist,* then what is being advocated is an exclusive, purist version of feminism. And that exclusion will have to be extended not only to all theories, Western and non-Western, but also to the very notion of care as well. For one might argue that the practice of (maternal) care has been historically performed under a patriarchal social structure and therefore must in some way contribute to the continuous oppression of women, functioning as a major impediment to women's autonomy and liberation. In fact, this suspicion is shared by numerous feminists. Held is well aware of that objection and argues that "practices of care to be recommended were not those conducted under patriarchal oppression but those to be sought in postpatriarchal society" (Held 2006, 64). If the practice of (maternal) care can be separated from the social conditions in which it has historically found itself, then the same thing can be done for Confucianism. To arbitrarily deny Confucianism this theoretical move is to participate in the very structures of imperialism that Held warns against. On a philosophical level, Confucianism, just as any other system of ideas, should be granted the ability to distinguish the ideal from its empirical applications. Regardless of how Confucianism has been used throughout history, its theoretical validity should still be assessed independently. To argue otherwise is to condemn Confucianism to an immanent status inapplicable and irrelevant to this progressive world while making Western theories, such as care ethics and liberalism, ideals unbound to their own empirical pasts.

The ability to rethink and to transcend what is given to us is also a hallmark of feminist thinking. As Held points out, feminist philosophy "is a rethinking of thinking in the history of philosophy about how to live and organize our worlds and what we take as true and what our values are" (60). Held believes that feminist thinking can reorient our conventional thinking guided by the masculine model of autonomous individuals and can begin to find what is valuable in women's experiences. As she writes, "One often fails to find what one is not looking for, and scientific research that has been looking for female weaknesses and passivities has often failed to pay attention to women's strengths. Feminist thinking is changing what is looked for and what is found" (60). In the same spirit, I would argue that feminists must look beyond the confines of Western canons and change what is looked for and what is found in non-Western philosophies in order to foster a genuine cross-cultural dialogue. This kind of genuine openness to diversity will pave the way for an inclusive feminism that views non-Western traditions not as antitheses of feminism but as viable liberatory moral theories in their own right.

The construction of a hybrid feminist care ethics has now become clear. A feminist normative ethics that is informed by Confucian *ren* will, first of all, retain the basic structure of care ethics in which caring activities that arise out of noncontractual familial relationships are the starting points of moral thinking. An interpretation of Confucian *ren* that takes the standpoint of human children in need of care to justify the subsequent ethical demands of reciprocating one's parents with filial affection makes the notion of care both ontologically and ethically prior to other values. One cares for one's family not only because it is good in itself as part of the virtue of *ren* but also because of the recognition that without parental care one would not be able to survive in the first place. Reciprocal care at home will be seen as indicative of one's most basic humanity.

Second, a feminist Confucian *ren* will then extend the demand of familial reciprocal care to the wider society to which each has a corresponding social excellence governed by communal rituals. Without a doubt, there are certain communal rituals not worth keeping, but every social reform must begin with the involvement of society, not just the mere rejection of it. With its dual familial and civil nature, Confucian *ren* will enable feminists to move from familial relationships to civil ones while addressing the issue of gender parity. Gender disparity is not essential to Confucian *ren*, and hence all existing ritual practices can be revised in compliance with the ideal of *ren* in which all are cared for comprehensively, as depicted in the ideal Confucian Great Community (*datong*). Gender-based social roles and communal rituals can certainly be revised in light of the changing social conditions through the application of *yi*. And this change is not only consistent with but also *necessary* from the standpoint of ritual, since any ritual providing an aesthetic and cultural identity to members of a given community must be relevant to the material conditions of the community or it will cease to be practicable.

Last, beyond the personal and the communal, a feminist Confucian *ren* will provide a care-oriented analysis of political authority in which politics is nothing but an extension of familial care to distant others. Familial care and reciprocal affection is not only the foundation of a harmonious household and a caring community but also the very foundation of good governance for world citizens. A familial world grounded in Confucian *ren* will have much less need for constant military domination and reckless market consumption, since the aim is not to accumulate as much wealth or resources for one's own, but to extend the same filial affection to strangers whom one does not necessarily care for naturally but must care for ethically.

All in all, Confucian *ren* is not only compatible with care ethics but also able to provide the kind of conceptual and practical grounding that care ethics needs to strengthen its theoretical foundation and extend its applicability to the world at large. This hybrid care ethics is simultaneously Confucian and feminist. It is a kind of normative ethics infused with Confucian *ren* that dictates an outward extension of care from the family to the world community *and* it is a kind of feminism that seeks structural changes to foster a cooperative environment in which reciprocity and mutual trust characterize all human relationships in private as well as in public. Indeed, a Confucian will not only care, but will care rather efficaciously without borders, as a feminist should.

Notes

1. See chapter 11 in this book for a detailed discussion of how the tendency to see third world women as victims supports colonialist and imperialist projects.

2. I rely upon the Ames and Rosemont translation of Confucius's *Analects* in this chapter (1998).

3. I rely upon D. C. Lau's translation of the *Mencius* in this chapter (1970).

4. For a discussion of the political importance of *ren*, see chapter 3 in this book, which also argues for the compatibility of Confucianism and feminism.

References

Ames, Roger. 1987. *Thinking through Confucius*. Albany: State University of New York Press.

Ames, Roger, and Henry Rosemont, trans. 1998. *The Analects of Confucius: A philosophical translation*. New York: Ballantine.

Beauvoir, Simone de. 1989. *The second sex*. New York: Vintage.

Card, Claudia. 1990. Caring and evil. *Hypatia* 5 (1): 101–6.

Dalmiya, Vrinda. 2009. Caring comparisons: Some thoughts on comparative care ethics. *Journal of Chinese Philosophy* 36 (2): 192–209.

Friedman, Marilyn. 1993. *What are friends for? Feminist perspectives on personal relationships and moral theory*. Ithaca: Cornell University Press.

Gilligan, Carol. 1982. *In a different voice: Psychological theory and women's development*. Cambridge: Harvard University Press.

Held, Virginia. 2006. *The ethics of care: Personal, political, and global*. New York: Oxford University Press.

Lai Tao, Julia Po-Wah. 2000. Two perspectives of care: Confucian *ren* and feminist care. *Journal of Chinese Philosophy* 27 (2): 215–40.

Lau, D. C., trans. 1970. *Mencius*. New York: Penguin.

Li, Chenyang. 1994. The Confucian concept of *jen* and the feminist ethics of care: A comparative study. *Hypatia* 9 (1): 70–89.

———, ed. 2000. *The sage and the second sex: Confucianism, ethics and gender*. Chicago: Open Court.

———. 2002. Revisiting Confucian *jen* ethics and feminist care ethics: A reply to Daniel Star and Lijun Yuan. *Hypatia* 17 (1): 130–40.

Narayan, Uma. 1997. *Dislocating cultures: Identities, traditions, and third-world feminism*. New York: Routledge.

Noddings, Nel. 1986. *Caring: A feminine approach to ethics and moral education*. Berkeley: University of California Press.

Ruddick, Sara. 1980. Maternal thinking. *Feminist Studies* 6: 342–67.

Star, Daniel. 2002. Do Confucians really care? A defense of the distinctiveness of care ethics: A reply to Chenyang Li. *Hypatia* 17 (1): 77–106.

Tu, Wei-ming. 1985. *Confucian thought: Selfhood as creative transformation*. Albany: State University of New York Press.

Woo, Terry. 1999. Confucianism and feminism. In *Feminism and world religions*, ed. Arvind Sharma and Katherine K. Young, 110–47. Albany: State University of New York Press.

Yuan, Lijun. 2002. Ethics of care and concept of *jen*: A reply to Chenyang Li. *Hypatia* 17 (1): 107–29.

CHAPTER NINE

The Embodied Ethical Self

A Japanese and Feminist Account of Nondual Subjectivity

ERIN MCCARTHY

IN THIS chapter, I articulate the ideal of an embodied ethical self by bringing together Japanese and feminist philosophy. I say "ideal," rather than "idea," because the final aim is not merely to explain an unfamiliar concept of self, but, further, to inspire a moral ideal—one we are prevented from realizing when certain common assumptions about the self are taken as models for living. The assumptions about self challenged here are those that follow from a dualistic conception. A view is dualistic in my sense if it conceives of the self in terms of the dichotomies of mind and body, self and other, and so on. Dualists locate the self in some subset of the elements of human being (such as reason, individual consciousness, the brain, or an individual soul) and believe these core elements to be more authentically human than others and thereby worthy of more weight, authority, or value. Accordingly, cultivation of these elements of the self is essential to becoming fully human in a way that the development of other elements is not. This sort of position takes the remaining elements to be, if not inimical, at best ancillary to human development. Examples of dualist conceptions of self span various metaphysical and ontological commitments. Ontological dualism is a clear example of this, since it involves the separation of mind from body, but physicalists can be, and often are, equally dualist in my sense of the term. It is worth noting that dualism need not imply a rationalist conception of the self. For example, someone who pits passion against reason is no less dualistic than someone who pits reason against passion. And while individualism is a dualistic position, since it sees the ethical self as prior to and separate from its communal roles, to take communal relations to be wholly constitutive of selfhood is also dualistic.

Nondualism, on the other hand, rejects these sharp distinctions between body and mind, self and other, and subject and object. In each case it is a matter of a both/and rather than an either/or relation. That is, nondualism allows for difference to be retained even as it is transcended. On this view, self is constituted by both mind and body at the same time, yet neither is more important nor more fundamental to the ethical self than the other. Similarly, and particularly for the philosophers examined in this chapter, a nondualistic concept of self sees each person's ethical identity as integrally related to that of others. Both self and other are seen as inseparable from one another, instead of opposed to or exclusive of one another as well as from ethical identity itself.

Interestingly, philosophers from the disparate traditions of Japan and contemporary Western feminism have each criticized dualism as a way of viewing the condition of human beings in the world and called for a nondualistic alternative—one that does not flatten out difference under the guise of universality or neutrality, but creates a space for it (McCarthy 2008). Despite their different philosophical, geographical, and historical foundations, Japanese philosophers Watsuji Tetsurō (1889–1960) and Yuasa Yasuo (1925–2005) and contemporary feminist philosophers Elizabeth Grosz and Luce Irigaray interpret much of Western philosophy as promoting dualistic conceptions of the self, thus placing unnecessary conceptual limitations on the fullness and complexity of human experience. For each of these philosophers, self, body, and ethics are intimately interrelated. In other words, selfhood is inseparable from embodied ethical selfhood and thus is not comprehensible within the bounds of dualistic frameworks. The striking similarities between the Japanese and feminist traditions are rooted in the fact that both urge an understanding of the ethical self from a nondualistic perspective, which is both more accurate to moral experience as it is lived than traditional models of the self and, moreover, contributes to the realization of certain ideals of ethical relations between people.

While similar in their belief in a nondual basis of the self, these traditions can share significant insights with one another. For example, Irigaray and Grosz call for and point toward a nondualistic way of conceptualizing selfhood that includes both embodied and ethical dimensions in order to overcome the subordination of women as "other" or inferior. However, they nevertheless struggle to articulate such a framework. The philosophies of Watsuji and Yuasa, particularly their concepts of self (Japanese: *ningen* 人間), betweenness (Japanese: *aidagara* 間柄), and cultivation (Japanese: *shugyō* 修行), can help respond to the feminist call for a nondual subjectivity that can sustain difference and distinction. This is due to the scarcity of conceptual resources in the Western philosophical tradition from which to draw. Watsuji and Yuasa, I argue, provide the necessary conceptual resources required for describing the nondualistic subjectivity Irigaray and Grosz seek. Thus, I claim their philosophies can enrich the project of feminist philosophy.

In reconceptualizing body, self, and ethics here, I do not seek to provide a strictly philosophical theory of the body along the lines of, for example, Maurice Merleau-Ponty. Rather, I seek to characterize and call for a way of living, one that is to be cultivated through experience that is not easily classified as mental or physical, spiritual or corporeal, cognitive or noncognitive, or psychic or somatic. My claim is that in bringing together these Japanese and feminist philosophical voices we can be motivated to pursue an ideal that is richer than any attainable by either tradition on its own. Attending to the striking resonances and important differences between these two traditions of thought, I develop the implications of living as an embodied, ethical self. I urge such an ideal of selfhood as a means of promoting the recognition of different perspectives and offering a distinctive way of looking at and shaping the world in which we live.

Self as *Ningen*

If we turn to modern Japanese philosophy, particularly Watsuji's theory of self as *ningen* and Yuasa's models for self-cultivation and bodymind knowledge, we find examples of ethical selfhood and embodiment that do not have dualism at their foundation and that, as we will see later, can help feminists move further beyond that horizon. A nondualist framework is one that allows for body and self to be conceptualized without the prioritization and consequent devaluation of various aspects of the self. In nondualistic philosophies, such prioritization does not occur, for, "although there may be mind-aspects and body-aspects within all lived experience, the presence of either one includes experientially the presence of the other" (Shaner 1985, 42–43). In the Japanese philosophical tradition, the body is not considered inimical to knowledge but, rather, necessary for its attainment. As a result, much of Japanese philosophy emphasizes lived experience, including the significance of the body. On this view, the entire person is taken into account, rather than locating selfhood in a rational (or other) part set against other elements of the self. This nondualistic perspective, the notion of "bodymind," figures prominently in the Japanese tradition. The term *bodymind* reflects the idea that body and mind are interdependent; in fact, they are "inseparably connected" (ch. 2).

In Watsuji's philosophy, the body is inseparable from being-in-the-world right from the outset, for it is an integral part of his nondualistic concept of selfhood, or *ningen*. There is never a moment where the body is *naturally* abstracted from the rest of one's self-identity. Any such separation is contrary to the human condition as it is actually experienced. Watsuji's philosophy is based on his concept of human being as *ningen* 人間. The Japanese character for *ningen* is made up of two characters: the character for *individual*, 人; and for *between*, 間. This signifies that, as *ningen*, we are both individual and social *at the same time*. As Watsuji conceives it: "*ningen* is the public and, at the same time, the individual human beings living within it. Therefore, it refers neither merely to an individual 'human being' nor merely to 'society.' What is recognizable here is a dialectical unity of those double characteristics that are inherent in a human being" (Watsuji 1996, 15). For Watsuji, this dialectical unity means that the self is dynamic insofar as it comprises both individual and social aspects and, as *ningen*, one continually moves back and forth between these two characteristics. This dialectical unity means that, due to the community or social aspect of *ningen*, we merge with others, they are part of us, yet, due to the individual aspect of *ningen*, we emerge out of that relation, transformed in some way as individuals, only to move back again into relationship. In fact, *ningen* literally means "between persons," which is actually a very helpful way to think about Watsuji's concept. For him, *ningen* is not to be understood as a thing or substance but more like a place or space, yet not a fixed place. It is more like a shifting network of relations that are continually configured and reconfigured in time and space.

For Watsuji, ethics emerges from this intimate interconnection to other human beings in "betweenness" (*aidagara* 間柄). The locus of ethical problems, he tells us, "lies not in the consciousness of the isolated individual, but precisely in the in-betweenness of person and person" (Watsuji 1996, 10). By this, he means to say that ethics is the study of human beings, or *ningengaku* 人間学: humans not only as individuals but also as social beings residing in the betweenness among selves in the world. There is no notion of individuality applicable to selves that can be understood without considering the individual's relations to others. Watsuji maintains that ethics exists in this betweenness. *Ningen* is a dynamic self, one that is in continual becoming, moving constantly back and forth between individual and community: "The subject is not something static like a mirror, whose only business it is to contemplate objects, but includes within itself the connections between oneself and the other" (31). We see here how this concept resists dualism—one is not *either* an individual *or* in relation, rather one is *both* an individual *and* in relation at the same time. To be "one" requires that one is also "other" simultaneously, and neither element is subordinate or more essential to the self. Indeed, to talk of these as separate elements is misleading if pressed too far. As a result of being in betweenness with others, we are deeply interconnected to others and they are a part of who we are and how we live our lives.

Thinking of human being as *ningen* already considers the self as embodied, for the relations between people are not merely relations between minds, but between embodied human beings. Watsuji tells us, in fact, that "bodily connections are always visible wherever betweenness prevails" (62). As Yuasa observes, "Watsuji's concept of betweenness, the subjective interconnection of meanings, must be grasped as a carnal interconnection. Moreover, this interconnection must not be thought of as either a psychological or physical relatedness, nor even their conjunction" (Yuasa 1987, 47). If this is hard to grasp, it is because Watsuji's understanding of the body goes beyond our inherited either/or dualistic frameworks. He challenges us to think differently about corporeal boundaries and how they figure into ethics and our conception of ethical human beings. Watsuji explains the nondualism of body and mind between human beings as follows:

> To hold the view that the relationship between one human body and another is a psychological relation as well is common enough. To account for this relationship as though it were merely a psychological relationship without giving heed to the relationship between one human body and another is an obvious error. To whatever extent a mental element is involved, human bodies are attracted by and related to each other. These connections are neither merely physical nor merely psychological or physical/psychological.
> (WATSUJI 1996, 66)

Watsuji implies, in fact, that we don't even have the vocabulary to express these nondualistic ways of conceiving of bodymind. The final sentence of this passage also illustrates the idea that nondualism allows us to transcend yet maintain difference. For example, the connections that Watsuji discusses above do not discount the existence of the physical or the psychological. Both are part of the relation and attraction between human bodies, yet this is not simply a matter of adding the physical to the psychological. Watsuji's concept of embodied betweenness is nondualistic in allowing for both the physical and psychological relations between people to mirror the concept of *ningen* itself.

Throughout *Ethics*, Watsuji gives everyday examples of how false mind-body dualism is to human ethical experience. He observes that, upon meeting a friend, we never have to stop and think that this person is made up of an objective body and a mind. We do not touch our friend thinking that this "material solid is put into motion by my friend's mind" (64). We do not have to work to differentiate the body of the friend we meet by the fountain from the fountain itself. We do not need to work to distinguish the person-matter from the nonperson matter; rather, we see our friend there by the fountain as a mind-body complex from the outset (64). In fact, there is, he says, "no momentary period of time in which a human body is experienced as a mere material solid" (64). Furthermore, "there is no distance between a subject and a human body" (65). So Watsuji's notion of *ningen* provides us with a model of self that is not dualistic. It is an embodied self, and, moreover, an embodied *ethical* self, for betweenness deeply links our identity as ethical beings to other human beings since we are all part of each other as *ningen*.

The betweenness that Watsuji evokes in *ningen* goes beyond the model of intersubjectivity found in Western phenomenology. When considering the interactions between *ningen*, activity inherent in their consciousnesses "is not merely a reciprocal activity in that one-way conscious activities are performed one after another but, rather, that either one of them is at once determined by both sides; that is, by itself and by the other" (69). Here Watsuji seems to be responding to Husserl's phenomenology in particular. Husserl recognizes that in encounters with another human being part of what we understand about her *and* ourselves comes by way of the body of the other. But, for Husserl, this contribution to understanding does not go beyond the bodily comportment of the other person. Husserl does not recognize even a sense of connection with the other body, which is key for Watsuji. On Husserl's view, we transfer the physical aspects of ourselves to the understanding of the other and vice versa. That is, we understand her only by analogy with ourselves, rather than by connecting with her. We recognize not only that this other person has a body like mine, but "there also belongs . . . the interiority of psychic acts. In this connection it should be noted that the point of departure is here, too, a transferred co-presence: to the seen Body there belongs a psychic life, just as there does to my Body" (Husserl 1989, 174). We see, for all his departure from Descartes, a holdover of dualism in Husserl's concept of the "interiority of psychic acts" and its contrast to the exterior, observable body. For him, the mind is the locus of the self, and it resides behind the scenes as it were—inside the body in a way others cannot get at directly. Furthermore, for Husserl, bodies and their minds remain fundamentally separated and distinct from each other. We can *liken* the other minds to ourselves, but each self remains locked in its own subjectivity. For Watsuji, this falls far short of the experience of true betweenness.

In Yuasa's philosophy, the phrase "the oneness of bodymind" (*shinjin ichinyo* 身心一如), borrowed from medieval Zen Master Eisai, best expresses the nonduality of bodymind. In Japanese thought, even though nonduality is an inherent part of *ningen*, it is still an experience or way of relating that requires cultivation. The practice of cultivation leads to wisdom that is neither lodged in a purely intellectual faculty (it is not propositional in nature) nor in purely physical dispositions (it is not merely a motor skill), nor in any straightforward combination of the two. For Watsuji and Yuasa, it is through cultivation that the human being comes to attain (and thus experience) the wisdom that integrated bodymind requires—body and mind come to know together, as an integrated whole. Yuasa devotes a chapter of *The Body* to the question "What Is Cultivation?" The Japanese term for cultivation, *shugyō* 修行, is also the term for Buddhist practice. Central to this notion is the idea of training the mind through the body in order to reach the ultimate goal that is the attainment or experience of their oneness. The attainment of oneness, the nonduality of bodymind, is also the same moment of dissolution of the duality between self and other: it is the moment at which we become selfless, open, and ethical. Self-cultivation, on Yuasa's view, is a physical practice— be it through Daoist practice, traditional Chinese medicine, martial arts, the art of the sword, yoga, poetry, or developing self as *ningen* in one's relations with others—and involves cultivation of *ki* energy (気), a vital force that pervades all life.

As Shigenori Nagatomo explains in the introduction to Yuasa's *The Body, Self-Cultivation, and Ki Energy*, *ki* energy (in Japanese, simply *ki*) has a broad scope and "can include, for example, a climatic condition, an arising social condition, a psychological and pathological condition. It also extends to cover a power expressed in fine arts, martial arts, and literature" (Nagatomo 1993, xi). According to Yuasa, *ki* energy has "a *psychophysical* character that cannot be properly accommodated within the dualistic paradigm of thinking" (xii). Thus the cultivation of *ki* cannot be understood in terms of the Western distinction between body and mind. *Ki* is not something that is understood or experienced *only* intellectually. In fact, the point is that in order to truly understand *ki* and be able to harness this vital force, one must realize that "it is not arrived at merely through intellectual abstraction, but is derived also from the observation of empirical phenomena detectable both experientially and experimentally in and around the human body" (xii). Mastery of *ki* is not mastery of a conceptual definition or a matter of having a set of true beliefs about it. It is mastery of a way of being. It is the cultivation of something that is within our embodied selves, but also extends beyond our bodies even as it remains connected to them. *Ki* is all encompassing; it permeates our entire way of being-in-the-world. In this interpretation, the cultivated self simply cannot be viewed as bodily matter attached to an isolated mind. Yuasa puts it this way: "The scientific study of *ki*... suggests through its biological and physical energy measurement of the living human body that there latently exists an invisible exchange of life between the living human body and the environment, that is, between a human being and the world, which transcends the surface relation established through consciousness and sensory perception" (Yuasa 1993, 1). This exchange of life also occurs between human bodies as well: this is the nondual betweenness of which Watsuji writes. The connections and attractions between human beings go beyond the idea of simply adding the physical to the psychic.

On Yuasa's view, the knowledge attained through cultivation is wisdom about how to conduct oneself as an integrated bodymind. Cultivation is practice and knowledge simultaneously—it is lived, embodied knowledge. In cultivating oneself, one is also becoming ethical, for, one is developing wisdom that allows for the knowledge of how to live in the world. According to Buddhism, this is "seeing the true profile of Being in no-ego . . . when one becomes, as it were, an authentic self, the person comes to command a new perspective on openness" (Yuasa 1987, 98). Cultivation leads to authentic selfhood, which for Yuasa is inseparable from ethical selfhood. Hence self-cultivation provides a way of approaching the problem of how to realize and live the ideal of embodied ethical selfhood.

Realization of this sort of ethical self requires cultivation of all dimensions of human being-in-the-world. It also requires empathy and attention to interconnectedness in a way that is not open to selves living as isolated egos. Watsuji's betweenness structure of human being as *ningen* acknowledges the experience of a nondualistic merging of consciousnesses in human relationships—one in which neither subject becomes subsumed by the other. As we will see, this is one of the primary points of contention between feminists and dualist philosophies, namely the position of women on the undervalued side of dualistic frameworks. In much of the history of Western philosophy, what this has meant is that both women and bodies have been dismissed as philosophically insignificant.

Feminist Subjects

Although mind-body dualism is usually associated with Descartes, we can find its roots as far back as Plato. In the *Republic*, for example, the body was seen as something contrary to knowledge. As many feminist philosophers have pointed out, women were considered by Plato to be the most attached to their bodies and thus considered incapable of attaining philosophical knowledge. For Plato, the body is appetitive, not cognitive, and must be controlled by reason (the mind) lest the appetites overtake us. Elizabeth Spelman notes: "According to Plato, the body, with its deceptive senses, keeps us from real knowledge; it rivets us in a world of material things which is far removed from the world of reality; and it tempts us away from the virtuous life" (Spelman 1982, 111). The soul, not the body, is that which attains knowledge. The ethical self, for Plato, is also situated in the soul—if not identified *as* soul—and the body is merely subjugated to it. In Plato, we see the beginning of the hierarchy that gets established by these dualisms: a dichotomy of mind/body mapped onto the homologous hierarchical dichotomies of male/female, reason/emotion, and so on. In these dichotomies each side is set up in opposition to the other, the second term in the pair always devalued or subordinated. As Spelman continues,

> What we learn from Plato . . . about knowledge, reality, goodness, beauty, love, and statehood, is phrased in terms of a distinction between soul and body, or alternatively and roughly equivalently, in terms of a distinction between the rational and the irrational. And the body, or the irrational part of the soul, is seen as an enormous and annoying obstacle to the possession of these desiderata. If the body gets the upper hand (!) over the soul, or if the irrational part of the soul overpowers the rational part, one can't have knowledge, one can't see beauty, one will be far from the highest form of love. And the state will be in utter chaos.
> (113)

Over and over again, Plato holds up women as objects of ridicule because they are connected to their bodies and thus irrational, weak, emotional, and incapable of philosophical reflection. In book 3 of the *Republic*, Plato discusses the training, mentoring, and education of the future (male) members of the guardian class. Here, we see that, above all, young guardians should never take women as examples to emulate. Note what is seen as not worthy of imitation and identified as female, that is, emotion and the body: "Then, we won't allow those for whom we profess to care and who must grow into good men, to imitate either a young woman or an older one, or one abusing her husband, quarreling with the gods, or bragging because she thinks herself happy, or on suffering misfortune and possessed by sorrow and lamentations, and even less one who is ill, in love, or in labor" (*Republic* III, 395d–e).[1] Women are here portrayed as irrational and hysterical, and are especially not to be emulated when their bodily connection is most pronounced, such as in childbirth. For Plato, "the body is seen as the source of all the undesirable traits a human being could have, and women's lives are spent manifesting those traits" (Spelman 1982, 118).

Elizabeth Grosz agrees with Spelman's diagnosis of a deep-seated somatophobia that has permeated much of Western philosophy. She writes, "It could be argued that philosophy as we know it has established itself as a form of knowing, a form of rationality, only through the disavowal of the body . . . and the corresponding elevation of mind as a disembodied term" (Grosz 1994, 4). And, of course, even reactions against this (for example, those celebrating the passions over reason) merely reinforce the dichotomizing way of thinking. As a result of these assumptions about the relation of mind and body and its implications for gender relations, Grosz argues that there are two ways in which femininity is represented: "Either mind is rendered equivalent to the masculine and body equivalent to the feminine (thus ruling out women a priori as possible subjects of knowledge, or philosophers) or each sex is attributed its own form of corporeality. However, instead of granting women an autonomous and active form of corporeal specificity, at best women's bodies are judged in terms of a 'natural inequality,' as if there were a standard or measure for the value of bodies independent of sex" (14).

Thus, women have been denied access to philosophy, largely due to the perception that they are more attached to their bodies than men. This attachment, it is assumed, means that women are incapable of attaining the kind of rationality deemed necessary for philosophizing. However, as Grosz points out, even if each sex is granted its own corporeality, women still get denied access to philosophizing as the standard for the ideal body is the male body. The female body is seen as inferior despite the fact that without women's bodies no bodies would come into being. Irigaray points out that the "womb is never thought of as the primal place in which we become body" (Irigaray 1993b, 16). Taken over, as Grosz has described, by a dominant male subjectivity that tries to silence, dismiss, and disembody women, women's bodies become not the place of love or of power to be respected, but an inferior silent place—a place without a voice.

We need only look to book 5 of the *Republic* to see that, for Plato, even when women supposedly share equally in the governance of the ideal city and the pursuits of men, they remain nonetheless always inferior to men: "Then there is no way of life concerned with the management of the city that belongs to a woman because she's a woman, or to a man because he's a man, but the various natures are distributed in the same way in both creatures. Women share by nature in every way of life just as men do, but in all of them women are weaker than men" (*Republic* V, 455d). So, we see how, as Grosz contends, women are relegated to the sidelines of philosophy practically from its beginnings. Judging by this quotation, it seems that even if the rational part of women's souls could manage to gain control over their bodies, they would still be at a disadvantage. For even if they were able to philosophize, according to Plato they would still be inferior to men in the practice of philosophy. Here we see the beginnings of women's exclusion.

Luce Irigaray maintains that this dualism of mind and body renders an adequate view of both female subjectivity and ethics impossible. The primary point of contention with dualism for Irigaray, as for Grosz, is that it tends to lead to the subjugation of one of the two terms: mind over body, subject over object, man over woman, and self over other. This subjugation can occur in several ways: the second term is subsumed into the first term; the first term becomes the norm, with the second becoming the "other"; the first term is taken as "neutral" and either denies the second term its own subjectivity or makes its purpose the flourishing of the first term. If woman is always the other—that is, on the devalued side of the binary opposition, subsumed by the supposed neutral male subject and defined only as that which is not male—then she has no subjectivity of her own. Irigaray argues that the philosophy out of which ethics arose has been based on and rooted in this dualistic system and, as a result, has not taken the female subject into account. The philosophical world, which claims to be neuter—in the sense of being stripped of its identification with any gender—has in fact, she maintains, been man's alone (Irigaray 1993b, 122). Irigaray argues that we need to construct, or reconstruct, ethics if a genuine female subjectivity is to be established: "A revolution in thought and ethics is needed if the work of sexual difference is to take place. We need to reinterpret everything concerning the relations between the subject and discourse, the subject and the world, the subject and the cosmic, the microcosmic and the macrocosmic. Everything, beginning with the way in which the subject has always been written in the masculine form, as *man*, even when it claimed to be universal or neutral" (6). We need, in other words, to establish a female subjectivity before we can have an ethics for all subjects.

On my view, Irigaray seeks a nondualistic framework for women's subjectivity. She challenges us to imagine a subjectivity that is not based on the dualism of mind and body. She urges us to create a new language, one that, as she puts it, "speaks the body." We must "keep our bodies even as we bring them out of silence and servitude" (19). Women have been denied their voice, in part, because their bodies have been denied their voice, relegated to mere object status and viewed as tools that reproduce but are not productive themselves (Grosz 1994, 8–10). This hierarchy has led to both bodies and women being subordinated in philosophy. To establish female subjectivity, we have to eliminate the hierarchy inherent in dualistic frameworks that support the structures of patriarchy. Due to the repeated association of women with the body then, this project also requires that we renegotiate gender subjectivity such that the body is no longer identified solely or merely with women and both body and woman are brought back into philosophy. We need to seek new ways of conceptualizing female subjectivity that include the body so that female subjectivity is creative in itself, has its own voice, its own language. It is interesting that, after *An Ethics of Sexual Difference*, when Irigaray turns to articulating what this female subjectivity involves (Stone 2006, 39), she eventually looks to Asian philosophy for inspiration.

Grosz also calls for the sort of feminist corporeal philosophy Irigaray imagines. Grosz seeks "an account of [embodied subjectivity or *psychic corporeality*] which refuses reductionism, resists dualism, and remains suspicious of the holism and unity implied by monism—a notion of corporeality, that is, which avoids not only dualism but also the very problematic of dualism that makes alternatives to it and criticisms of it possible" (Grosz 1994, 22). In short, Grosz and Irigaray both call for a new foundation for ethical philosophy, for "altogether new conceptions of corporeality" (22). More important for my purposes here, they suggest that the way to develop this new foundation is to "use the hints and suggestions of others . . . [to] move beyond the overall context and horizon governed by dualism" (22). While Grosz does not use the term *nondualistic* (she seems to imply that the only alternative to dualism is monism), she clearly advocates a move beyond dualism. As we will now see, the nondualistic models provided in Japanese philosophy can help this project while also avoiding the spurious unity of holism found in monism of which both Grosz and Irigaray are critical and suspicious.

Nondual Subjectivity

Nondualism does not mean that difference is annihilated (McCarthy 2010). The idea that nondualism is nondifference lies behind Grosz's fear of the holism implied in monism. Irigaray too fears this. In fact, when questioned about nondualistic frameworks as an answer to her criticisms of dualism, Irigaray is critical of the very term, claiming that "overcoming the subject-object categories is not suitable" (Irigaray 2008a, 41) and, later, "the subject-other relationship has to remain potentially dualistic in all its modalities" (47). These responses rightly express a concern; if differences are merely ignored, one subject would be subsumed by the other and denied its own distinctive subjectivity. However, I claim that the kind of nondualism found in Watsuji's concept of *ningen* is *not* the sort of nondualism Irigaray and Grosz rightly resist. To the contrary, it is precisely the sort of notion that can provide a workable framework to respond to their concerns about Western notions of self and ethics. Therefore, Irigaray's notion of the "in-between" is in fact a nondualist notion, one of the very sort that we find in Watsuji and Yuasa, yet one that has significant feminist implications so far left unconsidered.

In the introduction to *The Way of Love* Irigaray discusses the place that arises when two really do come together in genuine relation or betweenness: "The constitution of such a place, always becoming, calls for a relation between subjective and objective where the one could never assume nor integrate the other because the one and the other are two, and turn round for each subject in the passage from the subjective to the objective, from the objective to the subjective. What henceforth represents the absolute to be attained is the perfection of the relation—never accomplished" (Irigaray 2002b, 9). In the relation that Irigaray imagines, one subject does not surrender her subjectivity to the other. Rather, there is reciprocity, a dynamic movement of give and take where each subject moves from the subjective to the objective and back again. However, there is also a place of relation that remains open and never perfected or completed, thus never subjugating one to the other. This movement reflects the dynamic nature of *ningen*—an embodied, ethical self that moves continually back and forth between self and other.

In *Sharing the World* Irigaray again discusses the encounter with another: "Through such a gift [the encounter], which each offers to the other as a result of recognizing him, or her, as other, we are both two and one. Each has to be oneself and return to oneself in one's otherness in order for unity to exist" (Irigaray 2008b, 50). Here we see that the place of relation may be a place of union, but not one of monolithic subjectivity. Rather, in her expression "both two and one," we see Watsuji's nondualistic notion of "dialectical unity" reflected. For, in the encounter Irigaray describes, one is not *either* one's own individual self *or* in union with the other, but one is *both* oneself *and* in union with the other in a continual movement.

The betweenness that is required for such becoming finds conceptual articulation in Watsuji's concept of *ningen*. The betweenness (*aidagara*) of *ningen* foregrounds the social aspect of the self, although not at the expense of a loss of all individuality. The betweenness of *ningen* is precisely the space that allows each subject to maintain his own individuality yet nevertheless enter into betweenness with others. As Robert Carter reminds us, Watsuji's concept of *ningen* does not eliminate difference or deny individuality: "He cautions that it is imperative to recognize that a human being is not just an individual, but is also a member of many social groupings. We are individuals, and yet we are not just individuals, for we are also social beings; and we are social beings, but we are not just social beings, for we are also individuals. Many who interpret Watsuji forget the importance which he gave to this balanced and dual-nature of a human being" (Carter 2004).

In reading Watsuji, we see that he insists on the need to continually move between the poles of subject and community, and between the poles of self and other in relations such as marriage and friendship. If one is truly being *ningen,* the individual is not subsumed by either another individual or the community in these relations. Watsuji characterizes this as a movement of negation comprised of three dynamically unified moments: "fundamental emptiness, then individual existence, and social existence as its negative development" (Watsuji 1996, 117). This movement is the movement of becoming where one moves back and forth between individuality and community, never being stuck in one place. For as soon as one arrives and asserts one's individuality, one negates it by asserting oneself as a part of a community. And, likewise, as soon as one merges with the community and negates the individual self, that too must be negated and the process continues.

The fundamental emptiness in this movement of betweenness inherent in Watsuji's *ningen* has its roots in Zen Buddhism. In Zen Buddhism, emptiness is not a nihilistic idea. Rather, it is at the root of everything that exists; it is beyond even the dualism of individual and social. As Thomas Kasulis puts it: "Emptiness—the logical interdependence of opposing terms—lies at the basis of all philosophical distinctions" (Kasulis 1981, 24). The particular distinctions in the negation inherent in *ningen* are individual and social. This is both fundamental emptiness *and* wholeness, but not the holism feared by Grosz and Irigaray. For the individual does not subsist in herself, nor does the whole subsist in itself, but, as Watsuji explains, the whole "appears only in the form of the restriction or negation of the individual" (Watsuji 1996, 99). We, and all things, on the Zen Buddhist view, arise *co-emergently* out of this emptiness "that is the ground of all distinctions, yet that itself is without distinction" (Carter 1996, 332).

As Watsuji puts it, "the movement of the negation of absolute negativity is, at the same time, the continuous creation of human beings" (Watsuji 1996, 118). So, in a true encounter with the other, we enter into a space of betweenness, a space where we each negate, for a moment, our individual subjectivity but then return back to ourselves, each transformed by this encounter with the other. Then the process begins again. There is no end point; there is no absolute knowledge or truth, no final stage of becoming. As Irigaray puts it above, the relation is never perfected; it never comes to an end. As Watsuji tells us, "When this movement comes to a standstill in one way or another, the association itself collapses. Thus, if an individual, as the negation of emptiness, sticks to this negation in such a way as to refuse to allow the negation of negation to occur as well, then that association disintegrates on the spot. Likewise, if an individual submerges herself in the whole and refuses to become an individual again, then the whole perishes at the same time" (117–18).

For Irigaray, patriarchy has meant that women have, in fact, been forced to be submerged in the whole and not permitted to emerge out of it to become individual subjects. This has meant that half of humanity has been denied its subjectivity. It seems to me that Watsuji's *ningen* structure of selfhood and relationality can be used to address what Irigaray is after. Combined with her concern for female subjectivity, we now see how the *ningen* model can provide a philosophical framework in which the female subject could enter into genuine relation without, however, losing her own subjectivity. I maintain that Watsuji's nondualistic framework for *ningen* can be expanded to include not simply self-other relations but also male-female relations. Through the lens of the *ningen* framework, thereby not based on oppositional dualisms, we see, first, that woman is no longer on the devalued side of the dualism; rather, each "side" is weighted equally. Second, as we have seen earlier, dualisms often lead to one side (woman) being subsumed by the other side (man). However, the fact that this *ningen* betweenness relation is never completed means that woman will not lose her subjectivity because of the dynamic dialectical unity that is a part of betweenness relations. Because she is always moving back and forth between being in relation and being an individual subject, her subjectivity remains an integral element of this being-in-relation. In the nondualism espoused by Watsuji and Yuasa—and unlike the forms of nondualism Irigaray and Grosz both caution against—one's individuality and subjectivity are not lost. To the contrary, in this model both female and male subjectivity are continually preserved and transformed.

The nondualism we find in Yuasa and in Watsuji's *ningen* can supplement, support, and inform the ethical frameworks Irigaray and Grosz call for, including those that take feminist philosophical concerns into account. For example, Watsuji's notion of *ningen* can be read through the lens of Irigaray to provide an analysis of gender relations and encourage the kind of encounters she envisages. Integrating feminist ideas into Japanese philosophy can also temper the patriarchal slant that unfortunately exists in this tradition. Watsuji's writings on marriage and the family, for example, reflect some hierarchical Confucian and Japanese values (Watsuji 1996, 87–91). Yuasa recognizes that the "power of femininity has failed to function" in the West, where "the power of masculinity has been a solo runner, fortifying rationalism as well as promoting the opposition and competition between 'I' and 'other'" (Yuasa 2001, 17–18). And yet he could not understand how his philosophy could be applied to feminist concerns. When I interviewed Professor Yuasa in the summer of 2001, I explained my understanding of feminism and how I saw his philosophy as supportive of the work of feminist philosophy. However, I was not able to convince him that feminism was more than an ideology, despite his views on the feminine in his own work. I remain convinced, however, that Yuasa's philosophy has, unbeknownst to him, a feminist slant. For once one sees the resonance between, for example, Yuasa's and Irigaray's criticisms of dualism, it becomes clear that they are working toward similar goals, which involve allowing for all human beings—men and women—to flourish in both body and mind.

Irigaray has recently begun to turn toward Eastern philosophy for nondualistic alternative frameworks, most notably in *Between East and West*.[2] There she explores the implications of yoga for a nondualistic understanding of human subjectivity and how we might use it to cultivate such a subjectivity through its practice (Irigaray 2002a, xi). Again, this resonates with what we find in Yuasa's work. In his introduction to *The Body*, he discusses how theoretical understanding of bodymind is not enough to attain wisdom, for "true knowledge cannot be obtained simply by means of theoretical thinking, but only through 'bodily recognition or realization' (*tainin* or *taitoku*), that is, through the utilization of one's total mind and body" (Yuasa 1987, 25). Irigaray's philosophy, too, claims that ethical learning takes place through one's total mind and body. She discusses the cultivation of the breath in the practice of yoga and gestures toward the necessity of self-cultivation for developing nondualistic subjectivity: "In this becoming the body is not separated off from the mental, nor is consciousness the domination of nature by a clever know-how. It is a progressive awakening for the entire being" (Irigaray 2002a, 8). We find the notion of self-cultivation also discussed by Grosz when she writes: "Knowledges are not purely conceptual nor merely intellectual; they are not governed by a love of truth or a will to comprehension. The self-images of knowledges have always been, and remain today, bereft of an understanding of their own (textual) corporeality. Knowledge is an activity; it is a practice and not a contemplative reflection" (Grosz 1994, 37).

Japanese philosophy and feminist philosophy can again come together here, for both are firmly rooted in traditions that view knowledge in terms of the cultivation of praxis and as fundamentally connected to activity in the world. Imagining the forms of bodymind practice that would cultivate embodied ethical selfhood is work that remains to be done in the future. Creating such practices opens up new possibilities and provides new motivation for comparative feminist philosophy.

Notes

1. I rely upon G. M. A. Grube's translation of Plato's *Republic* (Plato 1992).

2. It should be noted that this is a problematic work in Irigaray's corpus, especially from a comparative perspective, and has been subject to much critique. There is a tendency to romanticize "the East" in this work, and she cites no Indian philosophers, let alone Indian feminist philosophers, in her discussion of yoga. However, she is also careful to note that her incorporation of Indian thought in her work emerges out of her own embodied practice of yoga. For more on this, see Deutscher (2003).

References

Carter, Robert E. 1996. Strands of influence. In *Watsuji Tetsuro's Rinrigaku: Ethics in Japan*, trans. Yamamoto Seisaku and Robert E. Carter, 325–54. Albany: State University of New York Press.

——. 2004. Watsuji Tetsuro. http://plato.stanford.edu/entries/watsuji-tetsuro/.

Deutscher, Penelope. 2003. Between East and West and the politics of cultural "ingenuité": Irigaray on cultural difference. *Theory, Culture, Society* 20 (3): 65–75.

Grosz, Elizabeth. 1994. *Volatile bodies: Towards a corporeal feminism*. Bloomington: Indiana University Press.

Husserl, Edmund. 1989. *Ideas pertaining to a pure phenomenology and to a phenomenological philosophy. Second book: Studies in the phenomenology of constitution.* Trans. R. Rojcewicz and A. Schuwer. Dordrecht: Kluwer.

Irigaray, Luce. 1993a. *An ethics of sexual difference.* Trans. Carolyn Burke and Gillian C. Gill. Ithaca: Cornell University Press.

———. 1993b. *Sexes and genealogies.* Trans. Gillian Gill. New York: Columbia University Press.

———. 2002a. *Between East and West: From singularity to community.* Trans. Stephen Pluhacek. New York: Columbia University Press.

———. 2002b. *The way of love.* Trans. Heidi Bostic and Stephen Pluhacek. New York: Continuum.

———. 2008a. *Conversations.* New York: Continuum.

———. 2008b. *Sharing the world.* New York: Continuum.

Kasulis, Thomas. 1981. *Zen action/Zen person.* Honolulu: University of Hawaii Press.

McCarthy, Erin. 2008. Towards peaceful bodies. In *Philosophieren über den krieg. War in Eastern and Western philosophies,* ed. Hans-Georg Moeller and Günter Wohlfart, 147–64. Berlin: Parerga.

———. 2010. *Ethics embodied: Rethinking selfhood through continental, Japanese and feminist philosophies.* Lanham, MD: Lexington.

Nagatomo, Shigenori. 1993. Translator's introduction to *The body, self-cultivation, and ki-energy* by Yuasa Yasuo, ix-xxxvi. Albany: State University of New York Press.

Plato. 1992. *Republic,* trans. G. M. A. Grube, rev. C. D. C. Reeve. Indianapolis: Hackett.

Shaner, David Edward. 1985. *The bodymind experience in Japanese Buddhism: A phenomenological study of Kukai and Dogen.* Albany: State University of New York Press.

Spelman, Elizabeth. 1982. Woman as body: Ancient and contemporary views. *Feminist Studies* 8 (1): 109–31.

Stone, Alison. 2006. *Luce Irigaray and the philosophy of sexual difference.* Cambridge: Cambridge University Press.

Watsuji, Tetsuro. 1996. *Watsuji Tetsuro's Rinrigaku: Ethics in Japan.* Trans. Robert E. Carter and Yamamoto Seisaku. Albany: State University of New York Press.

Yuasa, Yasuo. 1987. *The body: Toward an Eastern mind-body theory.* Ed. T. P. Kasulis. Trans. Nagatomo Shigenori and T. P. Kasulis. Albany: State University of New York Press.

———. 1993. *The body, self-cultivation, and ki-energy.* Trans. Shigenori Nagatomo and Monte S. Hull. Albany: State University of New York Press.

———. 2001. *Cultivation of the body in Japanese religions.* Trans. Shigenori Nagatomo. Unpublished manuscript.

CHAPTER TEN

Dōgen, Feminism, and the Embodied Practice of Care

ASHBY BUTNOR

DESPITE THE fact that we live much of our lives in a nontheoretical mode, absorbed in daily activity, philosophers tend to privilege a narrow subset of human experience that includes conceptual thought, reflection, and calculation. This priority even permeates the realm of ethics, which has to do with action and interaction between persons. To correct this bias, I explore those practical dimensions of our lives characterized by full immersion in activity—what is usually referred to as *know-how*—as well as their ethical significance. While many may characterize such behavior as thoughtless, there is a growing appreciation of the depth of this mode of being and the central role the body plays in ethical and political life. Thus we need to look more closely at our how our bodies communicate at this unspoken, and often unthought, level of ethical experience.

When cultivated, the synchronicity between mind, body, and environment found in know-how allows for the development of ethical expertise. However, there is certainly the risk of ethical failure here too. It is easy to imagine examples in which people are simply not in tune with their situations, never mind other people. This inattention may be to the physical needs of another at a particular moment (such as help with a door), to their emotional states (such as anxiety, fear, or embarrassment), or to greater concerns that frame another's perspective of herself and her place in the world. Such inattention is typically not a "one-time thing"; rather, it is reinforced and sedimented through patterned histories of interaction, or lack of interaction.[1] These examples suggest that we have a moral responsibility to cultivate ethical habits and work to transform unethical ones. I believe this task begins with an examination of our embodied situatedness.

I see our ethical development related to our bodies in two general ways: 1. our actual *embodiment* of particular habits, including sedimented habits of perception, affect, and action; and 2. the embodiment, or *embeddedness*, of these skills in particular social and cultural frameworks. In discussing both avenues and obstacles to ethical expertise residing in our bodies, I take a feminist comparative approach by drawing on resources from multiple traditions—specifically, here, Zen Buddhism and feminist theory. I first turn to Dōgen (1200–1253), founder of the Sōtō ("just sitting") school of Zen. Dōgen emphasizes how dismantling sedimented and harmful habits in the body is a necessary step in the cultivation of both self-awareness and other-awareness—what Buddhists often call "mindfulness." After diagnosing our self-perpetuating obstacles to mindfulness, I will highlight Dōgen's discussion of meditative practice in *enhancing* our perceptual receptivity, empathetic connection, and compassionate responsiveness to the needs of another.

While Dōgen is instructive regarding the process of ethical transformation through the body, a sociopolitical analysis is largely absent from his work. Thus, second, with the help of some feminist insights, I look at how the "worlds" in which we reside influence our ability to be morally skilled. I am particularly interested in the ways in which negative values, or *dis*values, from our social, cultural, and political environments become inscribed within the body via the process of sedimentation. These disvalues come to affect our social environments as well as our ability to be ethically responsive. My general claim is that we can improve our ethical skills by seeking solutions in both the cultivation of our somatic possibilities (as exemplified in Buddhist practice) and a restructuring of social contexts that frame moral behavior (as discussed in feminist theory).

Embodied Know-How and Its Ethical Significance

A discussion of embodied activity has not been absent in philosophical discourse. In fact, in Asian philosophical traditions, such activity is widely discussed as an achievement of self-cultivating practices. In the West we see it discussed by such thinkers as John Dewey (1922), Maurice Merleau-Ponty (1945), Martin Heidegger (1962), and, more recently, Francisco Varela (1999). These philosophers are correcting a long-held (Western) misconception regarding the priority of abstract, rule-guided behavior in our everyday lives. Dewey is credited with being the first to make the distinction between "knowing-how" and "knowing that": "We may . . . be said to *know how* by means of our habits. . . . We walk and read aloud, we get off and on street cars, we dress and undress, and do a thousand useful acts without thinking of them. We know something, namely, how to do them. . . . If we choose to call [this] knowledge . . . then other things also called knowledge, knowledge of and about things, knowledge that things are thus and so, knowledge that involves reflections and conscious appreciation, remains of a different sort" (Dewey 1922, 177–78, emphasis added). Embodied know-how, as Dewey describes it, takes precedence in our day-to-day activities and can be seen to underlie all human activity. In addition, know-how reflects a fundamental situatedness within our local environments. When we "walk and read aloud, get on and off street cars, and dress and undress," we are engaging with the basic objects of our lives and maneuvering our way in the world. Yet, we do not simply walk, read, eat, or drive. Instead, we walk through our neighborhood parks, read the daily news online, eat pad thai with chopsticks, and drive cars down busy interstates. In their performances, these embodied activities are never decontextualized. Rather, they occur by means of a well-coordinated balancing act between agent and environment.

We can see such activity as demonstrative of the cultivation and culmination of body-mind-environment interaction and thus the basis for our advanced forms of skill. For all skills, the pinnacle of achievement is "expertise"—dexterous, intuitive coping with the world in a fluid and wholly engaged manner. Consider the skillful use of chopsticks. At this level of expertise, "what must be done, simply is done" without calculation, analysis, and comparison of alternative possibilities (Dreyfus 1992, 6). For example, one simply eats. Reflection upon the activity itself, such as consideration of the way in which the chopsticks are balanced between the fingers or how the food moves from the bowl to the mouth, is not prevalent; rather there is simply proper performance. Hubert and Stuart Dreyfus explain that "an expert's skill has become so much a part of him that he need be no more aware of it than he is of his own body" (Dreyfus and Dreyfus 1986, 30). This embodied know-how results from the "deep situational understanding" of particular contexts, with particular opportunities, movements, challenges, and possibilities, that result from accumulated experience and practice. The cultivation of such expertise, then, results from a holistic engagement—perceptually and bodily—with the task and its environment.

It is my claim that this kind of embodied, engaged activity is ethically significant. Just as Dewey, Heidegger, and Merleau-Ponty claim that abstract reflection is derivative from a more primordial mode of practical activity, I see much ethical theorizing as derivative from, and thus secondary to, our engaged, ethical activity. This is not to dismiss the value of ethical theory, but, rather, to point to the significance of much ethical action at the embodied level. Perhaps the relationship between ethics and know-how is difficult to see if our examples are limited to riding streetcars, hammering nails, and eating at a table. However, the ethical significance is apparent as soon as we allow for some degree of *intersubjectivity* to come to the forefront in our examples. As soon as we realize that our environments are, in fact, filled with significant others, beyond trolleys, hammers, and tables, then the ethical dimension becomes more apparent.

In considering human interaction as a form of embodied know-how, I am most interested in the phenomenological level at which we perceive, attune, and respond to the subtle bodily cues of another. This, however, does not radically change our conception of know-how. We must still aim to achieve a deep situational understanding of the context, with its own particular opportunities, challenges, and possibilities, and rely upon our accumulated experience and practice of such contexts in order to respond well. One difference, though, is the fact that we are not merely comporting ourselves to a physical environment, but, rather, another sentient being. Thus, the shared embodied resonance of that relationship is paramount.

The most distinctive component of ethics-as-practice (as opposed to ethics-as-theory) is the role of the *body*. In thinking about ethical activity, it is helpful to understand the great significance of our embodied situatedness. We rely upon our embodied awareness to tell us a great deal about our current situation, including the needs of other people. I am particularly interested in three central elements of this ethical attunement: primary intersubjectivity, empathy, and care. "Primary intersubjectivity" is foundational here, for it sets the necessary groundwork for the development of empathy and care. Primary intersubjectivity can be understood as one way to describe our basic connections to one another through a form of "body reading" (instead of "mind reading"). Rather than intuit what another may be thinking, we pick up dozens of cues through a basic understanding available to us via our shared embodiment. In his discussion of primary intersubjectivity, Shaun Gallagher claims, "Before we are in a position to form a theory about or to simulate what the other person believes or desires, we already have specific pre-theoretical knowledge about how people behave in particular contexts" (Gallagher 2001, 90). We attain this knowledge from our embodied engagement with others, which comes across through things like "gestures, intentions, and emotions, and in terms of what they see, what they do or pretend to do with objects, and how they act toward ourselves and others" (91). This is a basic feature of what it means to be an embodied human being among other embodied human beings.

Primary intersubjectivity is thus the basis for the accumulation of embodied knowledge that is necessary for the development of ethical skill. Let us consider a simple example: "You are in your office. The conversation is lively and a topic comes up that embarrasses your secretary. You immediately perceive that embarrassment and turn the conversation away from the topic with a humorous remark" (Varela 1999, 5). Here we see the significance of a basic embodied resonance to attain knowledge of the other and to act appropriately. The ability to *even notice* the secretary's embarrassment is dependent upon the reading and understanding of subtle, embodied cues such as the reddening of her cheeks or the chewing of her bottom lip. This understanding need not be formulated propositionally. Rather, it is simply by virtue of having a body that reacts to the world in similar ways to similar situations that allows for an embodied knowing. In one sense, we perceive others with all our capacities—sight, hearing, smell, touch, etc.—often operating unbeknownst to us. Furthermore, our shared understanding of embodied experience—for example, of pain or discomfort, sheer joy, or awkwardness—gives us an understanding of the other that is necessary for embodied ethical practice. This does not preclude propositional knowing (a knowing that); rather, it demonstrates the developmental primacy of embodied resonance.

Primary intersubjectivity can be seen to serve as the foundation for more advanced forms of embodied connection such as empathy and care. Although there are many ways to discuss empathy, here I simply refer to empathy as a form of *emotional* participation with another that establishes an interest and a concern for the other's well-being. This basic interest is what allows for moral perception, that is, the ability to be perceptive to the suffering of others. In *Perception, Empathy, and Judgment* Arne Johan Vetlesen argues that "to 'see' suffering as *suffering* is already to have established an *emotional bond* between myself and the person I 'see' suffering" (Vetlesen 1994, 159). Here, the ability to view situations as *moral* situations (involving the weal and woe of others) does depend on the moral subject playing an active, participatory role in constituting the world around her. The moral subject must be openly empathetic: "Moral perception has its source in human receptivity, in the primordial capacity of human beings to be attentive to, to be alert to. It is thanks to this underlying active receptivity, this *sensuous-cognitive-emotional openness to the world*, that moral perception is provided with a direction, is 'tuned in' to deal with specific features of specific situations" (162). Here Vetlesen stresses the cognitive-emotional *activity* of the moral subject. The subject must enact a particular kind of self that is able to empathize sufficiently to recognize the moral saliency of her worlds. We see this kind of emotional participation in the example of the secretary. If the agent is not receptive to the embodied presence of others, she may not even notice the subtle cues that exhibit embarrassment or distress. Unfortunately, this probably happens more often than not. Without this emotional participation, one is unable to fulfill basic moral obligations to those around her and thus risks ethical failure.

In addition to primary intersubjectivity and empathy, care can be viewed as another dimension of our intersubjective connections. I like to leave the term *care* sufficiently vague so as to capture a wide variety of our engagements with one another. However, beyond the idea of simply "caring about," I do take care to be an *embodied* practice, a form of practical know-how that directs many of our intersubjective relationships. Oftentimes care must be demonstrated in actual hands-on work. Maurice Hamington describes caring habits as those "physical practices of knowledge held in the body" that specifically express one's caring knowledge (Hamington 2004, 4). As a complex practice involving many different forms of expression, caring habits consist in a variety of embodied activities—ranging from our snuggles with partners or pets, warm embraces of old friends, physical play with children, to our bodily comportment and engagement in work meetings and out and about in our communities.

The body, of course, plays an important role in these activities. However, we often do not recognize its significance. As in other forms of practical know-how, the body recedes into the background of our awareness when we are fully engaged in an activity. As with all habits, the tools we use, including our own bodies, are not objects of reflective awareness when we are engaged fully in an activity. Returning to our example of the embarrassed secretary, part of the caring response is the deflection of the conversation with a "humorous remark." While such wit is certainly skillful, we can also imagine the gentle placement of a hand on the secretary's shoulder or a sudden jump out of one's chair to redirect the discussion or activity elsewhere. These embodied gestures are no less skillful than the wit they accompany. However, given the tendency for such skilled habits to slip out of view, I want to highlight them and investigate the factors that contribute to their successful development. If we are interested in cultivating our everyday habits as empathetic and caring habits, or skills, such attention to our embodied engagement with others is necessary.

Buddhism and the Cultivation of Embodied Care

A Buddhist analysis of embodied intersubjectivity is most helpful for providing guidance in cultivating attention through mindfulness.[2] Cultivated mindfulness promotes a thoroughgoing realization of the embodied interconnection between persons that produces a wellspring of compassion. While offering mind and body training to this end, Buddhists also do much work in diagnosing issues of moral inattention and failures of care that lie at the root of our collective human suffering (Sanskrit: *duhkha*). Buddhists diagnose the problem of inattention in terms of craving and attachment—to objects of desire, relationships with others, and one's own sense of self. For example, we grasp onto things that please us, reject things that cause uneasiness, and remain indifferent to that which does not interest us. We remain closed off to really understanding our situation or the causes and conditions of our reactions. Robert Carter thus describes this everyday mode of living: "We are so mesmerized by our own way of seeing the world that there is, by and large, not a single doubt about our life-pattern, our actions, or our assumptions. We take them all as fact, as 'givens'" (Carter 2001, 78). However, the problem is that these "givens" often stand in conflict to reality—that is, there is sometimes a mismatch between expectations, assumptions, perceptions, and actions, on the one hand, and the actual functioning of the world, on the other.

It is easy to see how problematic this everyday approach to life can be when placed in the context of our relationships to others, especially the intimate relationships we have with family, friends, and children. If we become attached to our ideal of the perfect relationship or the perfect child, the reality of our situation will always disappoint us and cause suffering. This does not imply that we should not care deeply or love passionately, as some may assume when "attachment" is denied. Rather, it is pernicious forms of attachment that should be eradicated—that is, those that are perpetuated by our habitual tendencies to perceive, feel, act, and react in familiar and often harmful patterns. Buddhists certainly advocate love and care for others, as long as we are continuously mindful of the reality of our relationships and their ever-evolving nature. Part of the Buddhist project, then, is to relinquish attachments to unrealistic ideals, absolute control, and habitualized behaviors. Instead, we should strive to address and alleviate the suffering that we help to create and perpetuate in our relationships and be more attentive to the dynamic interconnections that constitute our lives.

Consider this example of perpetuating harmful patterns of interaction: I am rushing to finish an important lecture and a student interrupts with what seems to be a quite confused and inarticulate reflection on his own personal experience. It is easy to become frustrated by many elements of this situation, and my obvious annoyance is directed toward the student. However, much of that irritation has nothing to do with the student and everything to do with my own expectations regarding professorial authority, proper methods of analysis and dialogue, and attachment to an arbitrary schedule for the course. By attaching to my own idea of what should be happening at that moment, I am unable to listen to this student, empathize with his struggle to articulate crucial links between theory and practice, or help him make sense of his own experience. I am shutting down all fruitful interpersonal as well as pedagogical possibilities in favor of a stubborn hold on a self-centered and self-promoting reaction to the situation.

To counter such patterns of disconnection, Buddhists engage in a variety of practices devoted to cultivating our capacity to be attentive to, or mindful of, our selves, relationships, and extended situation. In the following passage, Ken McLeod describes the role of attention in overcoming self-imposed sources of suffering: "Attention is used to dismantle the wall that separates us from what we are. This wall consists of *conditioned patterns of perception, emotional reactions, and behaviors.* The wall has many components: conventional notions of success and failure, the belief that I am a separate and independent entity, reactive emotional patterns, passivity, an inability to open to others, and misperceptions about the nature of being" (McLeod 2001, 16). By reorienting the body and mind in attention, we can begin to unravel the conditions that prompt this view of the world and our wholehearted interest in preserving it. When we divest ourselves of self-centeredness, we are able to be more fully present to the dynamic relationship between self and world, as well as self and other. In the previous example, if I simply let go of absolute control and a vision of how this class session is going to wrap up, I may begin to listen to the student, perhaps as I never had before. This is the first step to true engagement with another human being.

Buddhist meditation techniques are embodied practices designed to cultivate attention, or mindfulness, so that we can become more attuned to the reality of our lives, thereby aiding in the process of overcoming suffering and its support system. It is one thing to *conceptually* understand how we maintain the conditioned patterns and perceptual habits that perpetuate our own suffering, but it is quite another to *embody* that knowledge. Attention to the body is paramount, for within it we can find the means to enhance our capacity for attention, increase our perceptual receptivity, and promote ethical action through an embodied connectedness with others. To narrow this discussion of Buddhist meditation and its somatic and ethical possibilities, I focus on the teachings and writings of Zen Master Dōgen and one of his contemporary interpreters, Shigenori Nagatomo. Dōgen's emphasis on the body, or, more appropriately, the *bodymind* (*shinjin* 身心), in enlightening practice makes him especially relevant to this discussion.

Dōgen is known for his advocacy of a nondualistic achievement of bodymind and the "oneness of practice-enlightenment" (*shushō-ichinyo* 修證一如). Given our tendencies to "live in our heads" and associate our senses of self with our ideas and beliefs, we often become disassociated from our bodies and the knowledge and habits that reside there. To correct this tendency, in *Shinjin Gakudō*, Dōgen writes, "To study the way with the body means to study the way with your own body. It is the study of the way using this lump of red flesh" (Tanahashi 1985, 91). However, this "lump of red flesh" is integrally linked with our minds. The trick, then, is to bring together, or "harmonize," body-and-mind. By reuniting those parts of us deemed "physical" and those deemed "mental," we can become more attuned to our situation. In *Gakudō Yōjin-shū* Dōgen explains: "We can see that breaking bones or crushing marrow is not difficult, but to harmonize the mind is most difficult. Again, the practice of prolonged austerities is not difficult, but to harmonize bodily activities is most difficult. . . . Brilliance is not primary, understanding is not primary, conscious endeavor is not primary, introspection is not primary. Without using any of these, harmonize body-and-mind and enter the Buddha way" (38).

For Dōgen, enlightening practice is not achieved by bodily austerities and regimens, nor is it attained through distinctly cognitive exercises. Rather than prioritizing mind or body, Dōgen writes of "casting off" or the "dropping away" of body-mind (*shinji-datsuraku* 身心脱落)—that is, casting off the dualistic tendency to separate the two. For Dōgen, mind and body are fundamentally intertwined, and thus both must be brought to bear on spiritual practice. By developing a phenomenology of meditative practice (*zazen* 坐禅), Dōgen demonstrates how such harmonization is centrally important in overcoming self-centered attachments and attuning ourselves to our surroundings.

While meditative practice, or "just sitting," is the most efficient way to harmonize body-and-mind, Dōgen claims that it can also have serious implications for reorienting and reengaging us with the world. Shigenori Nagatomo, in *Attunement Through the Body*, discusses the mechanisms of meditation via the following passage from Dōgen: "The role of [Zen cultivation] is to avert the path of intellectual understanding by eradicating the root of all mental functions by means of [just] sitting. This, I maintain, is an expedient means of guiding a beginner's mind. Afterwards, [an aspirant] casts off body and mind and discards delusions and *satori*. This is the second step. If one were to eradicate the root of all mental functions by means of sitting, eight or nine out of ten people would be able to see the way instantly" (Nagatomo 1992, 110). Here Dōgen advises the beginner to "avert the path of intellectual understanding." I see this as a call to "get out of our heads" and be more attentive to our embodied being-in-the-world. Only so much can be accomplished, ethically, spiritually, or otherwise, through conceptual thought. In *Fukanzazengi* Dōgen tells us to "think not thinking" by moving "beyond thinking." Rather than thinking, or taking the opposite stance of refusing to think at all, Dōgen urges us to sit and pay attention. Anyone who has attempted to simply sit without getting enthralled with one's own thoughts, plans, and daydreams knows how difficult the command to "just sit!" really is. However, the point is not to shut down the mind and to plunge oneself into nothingness; rather, the point is to not attach ourselves to or identify with our thoughts. However, this remains a struggle for most of us, because self-centered desires, cravings, and attachments fuel our "everyday perceptual ego-consciousness." It is this everyday consciousness that must be modified in order to attain the epistemological and ethical reorientations that characterize enlightened existence (112–13). The extent to which we are successful at dismantling desire and attachment through meditation determines our capacity to become more perceptive and more responsive to the world.

Dōgen's most famous passage from *Genjokoan* summarizes his key message on nonattachment and perceptual receptivity: "To study the Buddha way is to study the self. To study the self is to forget the self. To forget the self is to be actualized by myriad things. When actualized by myriad things, your body and mind as well as the bodies and minds of others drop away" (Tanahashi 1985, 70). For Dōgen, with the realization of no-self (the "forgetting of self") comes a concurrent realization of our surroundings and all the "myriad things" therein. Given the interdependence of selves, Dōgen claims that absolute distinctions between persons erode in enlightening activity—that is, "your body and mind as well as the bodies and minds of others drop away." When the self, as primary subject, erodes, the world, including others, emerges more clearly into full perceptual attention.

Fully engaging the body and mind in perception and casting off our dysfunctional habits transforms the act from a single subject-centered experience to what Nagatomo calls the experience of "intercorporeality," which is similar to the phenomenological notions of primary intersubjectivity and empathy discussed earlier. However, the notion of intercorporeality can be understood to exhibit more depth than either insofar as it is the lived feeling of enlightened awareness in which there is a subtle intermingling with *all* things. This is the unfolding of intimacy; the path of mutual assistance and mutual responsiveness of practitioner and her flesh-and-blood surroundings that comes when the boundaries of the self dissolve and are felt to be more fluid. As we can see, this actualization is not simply a break from our ordinary cognitive awareness; rather, it is a whole body event, a perceptual revolution. This perceptual shift results in what Nagatomo calls "felt inter-resonance" (*kannō dōkō* 感応同交), or, in my translation, "intersecting paths of responsive feeling"—an affective sense of connectedness with one's situation (Nagatomo 1992, 147–53). Because felt inter-resonance is an achievement attainable through sustained practice, its effects are transformative.

Though transformative and thoroughgoing, felt inter-resonance need not refer to anything extraordinary. Rather, we can see a shared intimacy in the most basic of interactions. If we return to our examples of the embarrassed secretary or the inarticulate student, we see the possibility for true engagement as soon as we background our own self-interest and self-promoting agenda. As soon as I "forget myself," I can simply be present and open to the situation and all its possibilities. If I am mindfully attentive to my surroundings, which is more likely if I have cultivated my bodily sensitivities to others, noticing the subtle distress of another or how my behavior is hurting someone is not an overwhelmingly difficult task. By opening myself to the world, experiencing through my body, and resonating with other embodied beings, these truths will speak to me. The goal, however, is to be "self"-aware (or *bodymind*-aware) enough so that our actions do not perpetuate suffering in the first place. When we have achieved an "intimacy" with our environment, there is less chance of ethical failure, more directedness of ethical attention, and an increased potential for care and compassion for oneself and others. The transformation of dysfunctional embodied habits allows for this new power of acuity and results in a more intimate seeing *and* feeling (146–47). This full-bodied and now enlightened participation in the world is what allows for attunement to situation and thus a skillful and immediate responsiveness to the needs that emerge within it.

Feminism and the Social Embeddedness of Care

We have just considered how our own perceptual and affective comportment affects the extent to which we attend to others. The complexity builds, however, when we consider our larger social, cultural, and political worlds and our place within them or what I call our "social embeddedness." We are embedded in social worlds in countless ways that influence how we view ourselves, how we view the world, and how others view us—with various, intersecting degrees of privilege and subordination derived from differences in gender, race, class, ability, education, and so on. To further complicate this analysis, I am interested in how we embody this complexity of social status and meaning and how that embeddedness comes to mold our bodily comportment in telling ways. This may make no significant difference in how we board trolleys, hammer nails, or manage our chopsticks, but it will make all the difference in our expressions of care to one another and how well or poorly we express that care. Because of the ethical implications of our often subtle embodied habits, I believe it is necessary to more thoroughly examine the embodiment of social values or *dis*values.

This issue is particularly relevant following a discussion of Buddhist meditation, somatic transformation, and the cultivation of mindful attention. There are many questions a feminist may ask about the ability and desirability of the sort of body-body resonance that is being promoted by Buddhism and Buddhist practice. For example, one problem with inter-resonance is that it occurs at a very basic level: our bodily existence. The other's body is a body like mine—similarly structured, commonly experiencing the world, and, at this level, interchangeable in its corporeality. While realizing the depth of shared human embodiment in a thoroughgoing way is necessary, it is important to recognize the variety of social influences that come to affect bodies in particular ways, even affecting the ways we experience them. Looking at social contexts, especially oppressive social contexts, adds a new dimension to moral perception and its cultivation that I find generally absent in the Buddhist tradition.

Let us take the examples of tacit racism and internalized oppression to demonstrate the ways that social disvalues are defined and incorporated. What is particularly insidious about these biases is the way in which they are taken up and enacted through embodied practices.

This is important to highlight because the embodied performances of disvalues are often inconsistent with consciously held beliefs and values and hence often go unrecognized. As Iris Marion Young observes, one can see tacit racism in individuals who profess racial equality and yet "enact bigotry" in the presence of people of color "by becoming jittery or by keeping their distance" (Young 1990, 80). Similarly, Sandra Bartky and Diana Meyers point to women's embodied inferiority: "By satisfying feminine body norms, women homogenize their own looks, constrict their own agency, and deprive themselves of the individuality and freedom that full persons should enjoy" (Meyers 2004, 80; cf. Bartky 1990, 71–74). In this case, women who consciously believe in their own equality, strength, and freedom may actually embody inequality and self-loathing by conforming to traditional feminine norms of appearance or demeanor—such as embodying an obsession with thinness or displaying a demure personality.

These analyses may help us to more fully understand the various perspectives in our prior examples. For example, are the embarrassed secretary's overcompensating smile and batting eyelashes resultant from her gendered socialization to "play nice"? Is my "blood boiling" annoyance at an African American male student a result of my incorporation of the racist tendencies of childhood caregivers? The primary difficulty with embodied disvalues is they are often very difficult to diagnose, even within oneself. Thus these embodied disvalues create a disconnect and an ambivalence in psychocorporeal identity—"so innocent in a way, yet so politically treacherous"—that needs to be recognized and resolved in order to overcome oppressive tendencies that are literally "in the flesh" (Meyers 2004, 80–81).

In these examples we see how social context plays itself out on different bodies and how detrimental habits come to be formed and sedimented through a history of interaction within particular environments. Vetlesen describes this social phenomenon and its particular influence on our capacity to be morally perceptive: "Individuals are not free to pick just any moral objects they would like. Perception does not start from scratch; it is guided, channeled, given a specific horizon, direction, and target by society. Society, not the single individual, selects the appropriate objects of moral concern and the like, other objects it rules out, conceals from view, demanding that the individual do so as well" (Vetlesen 1994, 194). Social values affect our moral perception and how we answer, or fail to answer, the demands of our environment. By unknowingly repeating the practices of prejudice, our everyday activities become tainted by these implicit biases and assumptions. For example, we may not recognize certain forms of suffering as suffering if we have been *trained to be inattentive* to their existence. It is easy to see how embodied disvalues work to perpetuate oppression through their covert operations. Regardless of conscious, intellectual rejection of prejudices, we may still embody, and thus perpetuate, these habits of prejudice without explicit awareness.

I see these embodied disvalues as having major ethical ramifications. First, contrary to the aims of enlightened practice, we are unable to be fully present to particular others given these biases and prejudices. They affect our ability to care well, whether for ourselves, an intimate, or a stranger. In order to enact our empathetic and compassionate responsiveness, we must be able to attune with and be receptive to another. By enacting these socially directed prejudices, we often remain inattentive to specific others and larger social problems. The second point, however, is more significant and the one that will be developed here. That is, through our performance of social disvalues, we often unknowingly perpetuate oppressive behaviors through the practice of care itself. If we consider the examples of racism and sexism, we can recognize these as prejudices we are taught that we, over time, come to incorporate in our embodied habits. Clearly, this affects our conception of care, insofar as it has the potential to be paradoxical and politically dangerous.

One telling example of the embodiment of noncaring habits is found in the maternally sanctioned promotion of violent bodies. Raised in postindependence Israel, philosopher Bat-Ami Bar On describes her experience of embodying violence.

> When I was about four years old, I came home one day crying because some children in the neighborhood with whom I was playing had hit me. My mother responded to my crying rather harshly, saying that since my father left her and I had no brothers, I had no one to defend me but myself. She proceeded to send me back to the streets to learn to fight. Though far from an obedient daughter even then, sensing her desperation at what she took as the fact that I had no protection other than what I could devise, I did as I was told. This began the construction of my body as a ready-to-fight

body and, as such, a violent body, a body habituated to use violence or, more precisely, a body habituated to act violently.

(BAR ON 2001, 63)

Of particular interest here is 1. the purposeful promotion of violent habits, 2. the parental sanction of these habits, and 3. the possibility that the cultivation of these habits is an act of care in itself. This example brings into play one of the requirements of practical knowhow: skillful coping with the demands of one's environment. Given the Israeli nationalist project of producing ready-to-fight bodies in all of its citizens, Bar On's mother is confronted by a society that promotes an unorthodox picture of care. This example shows how disvalues are inscribed in the flesh and become embodied—thereby affecting not only one's bodily posture toward the world but also how one thinks, feels, experiences, plans, and projects oneself into the future. No doubt, these disvalues come also to affect our moral lives and the capacities we have to care for ourselves and others.

As an adult, Bar On reflects on this habituation as well as her conscious and continued maintenance and reproduction of her body as violent. While the creation of Bar On's ready-to-fight body appears to meet Sara Ruddick's three demands of maternal care insofar as it is in service both to self-defense (and thereby fostered her *preservation* and *development*) and to the larger goals of society (thereby meeting the needs of *social acceptability*), it is quite complex (Ruddick 1980). For example, we may ask if the continued cultivation of these embodied habits is ethically justified. Further, we may consider whether her psychocorporeal agency is inalterably damaged by the embodiment of these supposed disvalues of violence, war, and harm. Years later, Bar On writes of her ambivalence about her violence-habituated body. She says, there is an "anxiety about and a need for innocence, a need to be as clean-handed as the pacifist that I feel that I cannot be, burdened as I am by the materiality of my violent body" (Bar On 2001, 64). She also points to the transgression of maintaining a specifically female body that is ready-to-fight and highlights that this gendering may alter the moral significance of her embodied habits. She asks, "Might it be the case that my violent body is ethico-politically acceptable while a man's violent body is not?" (65). Perhaps we can see Bar On's violent body as representative of the possibility for change. She may no longer be viewed as embodying disvalues per se, but, rather, practices of ambiguity, transgression, and resistance as she grapples to redefine and reshape her embodied practices.

There are a number of significant insights we can glean from Bar On's example. First, we see the ambiguity of care in her mother's transmission and support of violent practices. These can be understood as directed by the particular environment and context in which her childhood unfolded—that is, her social embeddedness. Second, we see Bar On's critical reflection on embodied habits and the possibility for change and revision. Importantly, though, Bar On cannot escape the weightiness of her habituated body. One cannot start anew simply by realizing how one comes to embody values and disvalues. Rather, like any embodied practice, one must take the time and effort to retrain various aspects of one's bodily comportment. This leads us to a third insight. In this example, we see the possibility of the continual emergence of meaning, including revised meanings, as one's environment and the needs of that environment change. While Bar On cannot escape her body and the embodied knowledge it contains, she can work to revise that meaning and its implications for her current life and its direction. As a mother herself now, a revised understanding and enactment of her habituated body will have even greater significance as she shapes her daughter's life with *her* practices of care.

Because moral values are inscribed in the body and are expressed within and through the body, prioritizing ethical embodiment is a step in overcoming and transforming the harmful ways in which we have become socially embedded. Furthermore, this transformation assists in the practice of care insofar as these values that are passed down and these embodied practices that are demonstrated are more supportive of flourishing in place of oppression. As many feminists have pointed out, we learn care from being cared for ourselves. Thus to introduce care to one who has been raised in the absence of care or with an ambiguous depiction of care is a difficult task. Unfortunately, one cannot simply pull out a manual on caring and teach oneself the techniques. As an embodied practice between individuals, one typically has to learn the skill through embodied engagement with others. Thus a person lacking the habits and skills necessary for a meaningful understanding of good care must struggle in an uphill battle to learn new incorporated habits, develop emotions necessary for care, and transform her psychocorporeal identity. Though difficult, retraining and cultivating somatic potential is possible (as seen in Buddhist practice and other embodied therapies). However, one's environment must be sufficiently supportive for this cultivation to be realized.

Embodied Potentials

This pluralistic investigation of ethical know-how has endeavored to provide an account of our moral lives and experiences that is more compatible with the kinds of beings we are and the kinds of worlds we inhabit than those accounts that focus mainly on reflective consciousness and propositional attitudes. From this view, ethics is not something that only occurs in the mind as a cognitive exercise divorced or detached from concrete lived experience. Rather, much of what comprises moral activity occurs below the surface of reflective awareness in the interplay of embodied persons embedded in social worlds. It is the embodied situatedness of moral practice that concerns me as well as the question of how these embodied dimensions can be brought to light and deliberately improved and developed.

It is important to recognize these embodied and embedded dimensions of moral agency and how they can serve as impediments to ethical expertise. However, the purpose of this chapter has not been to focus exclusively on our moral failures. Instead, I am also interested in the ways in which bodies can serve as avenues for moral transformation. I see Buddhism and feminism serving as models for how both embodied and embedded aspects of moral development can be addressed. As models, I am not claiming that needed resources can only be found in these two traditions. Instead, I see these traditions as exemplary in recognizing and discussing these central aspects of moral personhood as well as putting in place practical strategies for tackling them. While both Buddhism and feminism take the coconstitution of self and world seriously, I see different emphases in each tradition. For example, Buddhism serves a necessary role by focusing on the "self" and the habits of perception, cognition, affect, and action that block moral subjects from adequately addressing their situation, including the embodied persons therein. Buddhists recognize how harmful patterns of interaction may limit necessary access to our situation—most especially, to those around us. Failing to acknowledge our own shortcomings generates suffering for ourselves and others. Likewise, feminism is exemplary in analyzing the fundamental role of social structures and institutions in the habits that shape our daily lives. Feminist phenomenologists are especially acute in their examination of power and privilege in everyday experience as well as moral experience. Together, I see Buddhism and feminism giving us a more well-rounded view of how moral experience takes shape in these very bodies and in these very worlds we inhabit and, importantly, how our embodied know-how can be revised for the better.

Simply recognizing the embodied dimensions of ethical life is important for reconceiving moral experience. However, if we are interested in the mindful cultivation of our ethical potentials, then we need to think more systematically about how this may be accomplished. For example, in "Moral Mindfulness," Peggy DesAutels supports a radical revision of our embodied situation in the world: "Moral attentiveness requires *active* structuring of our social environments, habits, and practices in ways that facilitate seeing and responding to the moral features to which we are committed" (DesAutels 2004, 72). Thus moral progression requires a threefold process to aid in the development of our own moral personhood and the communities in which we live: 1. a thoroughgoing process of self-examination, including our embodied practices, habits, values and commitments; 2. a recognition of the resonance of shared embodiment and the cultivation of mindful attention therein; and 3. a keen insight into the ways that oppression and injustice are inscribed on variously positioned social bodies and how this affects our ethical embodiment. Exploring Buddhism and feminism together can help us shape this complete picture of moral progression. It is through a process of cultivating our way of both seeing and being in the world that we may refine our ethical skills and begin to approach something akin to ethical expertise.

Notes

I would like to thank Jennifer McWeeny and Matt MacKenzie for their invaluable feedback on this chapter. I am fortunate to have such brilliant philosophers as best friends. Thanks are also due to Vrinda Dalmiya, Charles Goodman, Kathryn Norlock, Bradley Park, and Graham Parkes for their insights on various formulations of these ideas. Additionally, this chapter benefited greatly from questions and discussion following presentations at Binghamton University (2006), a panel for the Society for the Advancement of Asian Philosophy and Asian-American Philosophers at the central meeting of the American Philosophical

Association (2009), the annual meeting of the Association of Feminist Ethics and Social Theory (2009), and the University of Colorado at Denver (2011).

1. See chapter 1 in this volume for a detailed discussion of sedimentation in Buddhist philosophy and postmodern feminism.

2. See chapter 4 in this volume for a detailed discussion of mindfulness in the early Buddhist tradition.

References

Bar On, Bat-Ami. 2001. Violent bodies. In *Feminists doing ethics*, ed. Peggy DesAutels and Joanne Waugh, 63–75. Lanham, MD: Rowman and Littlefield.

Bartky, Sandra Lee. 1990. *Femininity and domination: Studies in the phenomenology of oppression*. New York: Routledge.

Carter, Robert. 2001. *Encounter with enlightenment: A study in Japanese ethics*. Albany: State University of New York Press.

DesAutels, Peggy. 2004. Moral mindfulness. In *Moral psychology: Feminist ethics and social theory*, ed. Peggy DesAutels and Margaret Urban Walker, 69–82. Lanham, MD: Rowman and Littlefield.

Dewey, John. 1922. *Human nature and conduct: An introduction to social psychology*. London: Allen and Unwin.

Dreyfus, Hubert. 1992. What is moral maturity? Towards a phenomenology of ethical expertise. In *Revisioning philosophy*, ed. James Ogilvy, 111–31. Albany: State University of New York Press.

Dreyfus, Hubert, and Stuart Dreyfus. 1986. *Mind over machine: The power of human intuition and the expertise in the era of the computer*. New York: Free Press.

Gallagher, Shaun. 2001. The practice of mind: Theory, simulation or interaction? In *Between ourselves: Second-person issues in the study of consciousness*, ed. Evan Thompson, 83–108. Charlottesville, VA: Imprint Academic.

Hamington, Maurice. 2004. *Embodied care: Jane Addams, Maurice Merleau-Ponty, and feminist ethics*. Chicago: University of Illinois Press.

Heidegger, Martin. 1962. *Being and time*. Trans. John Macquarrie and Edward Robinson. New York: Harper and Row.

McLeod, Ken. 2001. *Wake up to your life: Discovering the Buddhist path of attention*. New York: HarperCollins.

Merleau-Ponty, Maurice. 2002. *The phenomenology of perception*. Trans. Colin Smith. New York: Routledge.

Meyers, Diana Tietjens. 2004. *Being yourself: Essays on identity, action, and social life*. Lanham, MD: Rowman and Littlefield.

Nagatomo Shigenori. 1992. *Attunement through the body*. Albany: State University of New York Press.

Ruddick, Sara. 1980. Maternal thinking. *Feminist Studies* 6 (2): 342–67.

Tanahashi Kazuaki, trans. 1985. *Moon in a dewdrop: Writings of Zen master Dōgen.* New York: North Point.

Varela, Francisco J. 1999. *Ethical know-how: Action, wisdom, and cognition.* Stanford: Stanford University Press.

Vetlesen, Arne Johan. 1994. *Perception, empathy, and judgment: An inquiry into the preconditions of moral performance.* University Park: Pennsylvania State University Press.

Young, Iris Marion. 1990. *Justice and the politics of difference.* Princeton: Princeton University Press.

PART FIVE

TRANSFORMING DISCOURSE

CHAPTER ELEVEN

De-liberating Traditions
The Female Bodies of Sati and Slavery

NAMITA GOSWAMI

> We are each of us both shorelines
> A left country where time suffices
> And the right land . . .
> Joined our bodies have passage into one
> Without merging . . .
> And while the we conspires to make secret its two eyes
> We search each other's shores for some crossing home.
> —AUDRE LORDE, "BRIDGE THROUGH MY WINDOWS"

THE CONSTITUTION of the female body is a central and often over-determined aspect in both postcolonial and African American feminist analyses of the status of the subject. Despite the obvious advantages of a comparative approach to this area, there remains a paucity of feminist dialogue across and between these feminisms. In other words, in spite of the hard-won gains of postcolonial and African American feminisms in the U.S. academy, their theories often adhere to traditional disciplinary boundaries, overdetermined social groupings, and historical academic practices. The reasons for this separation, as well as the relations between these fields, are sufficiently complex. Historically, postcolonial and African American feminisms have been conflated in terms of their opposition to, or difference from, Anglo-American and French feminisms.[1] Feminist theory, furthermore, is marginalized within traditionally masculinist postcolonial and African American studies programs.[2] Postcolonial theory, however, thematically aligns itself with poststructuralism, deconstruction, postmodernism, and psychoanalysis and, as a result, has been privileged in relation to African American studies.[3] Such hierarchies within feminist theorizing are emphasized in Ann DuCille's challenging observation: "In American feminist studies, the enslavement and breeding of African women is yesterday's news. . . . Widow burning, on the other hand, is not simply history: it is story" (DuCille 1996, 123–24).

My response to DuCille's statement is to refuse to further entrench the hierarchy between postcolonial and African American feminisms. This hierarchy as formulated by DuCille presumes their compatibility as theorizing by women of color, yet also acknowledges the minor status accorded to African American feminism in what Barbara Christian terms the "race for theory" (Christian 1987). I undermine the hierarchical positioning of these fields through a comparative analysis of two female bodies and what these bodies tell us about agency, co-option, and the emergence of various feminist discourses. Specifically, this chapter conducts a comparative analysis of Roop Kanwar's *sati* in 1987 and the display and dissection of Saartjie Baartman (the "Hottentot Venus") in London and Paris from 1810–1815. Despite the temporal and geographical disparity between Kanwar and Baartman, the religious and nationalist debates that emerged after Kanwar's sati echo and provide access to colonial discourses of sati occurring in British India in the early nineteenth century. These colonial discourses on sati and Baartman's display are concurrent phenomena, marked with the death of Baartman in 1815 and the official abolition of sati in 1829 by Lord William Bentinck. After examining how Kanwar's Hindu female body and Baartman's African female body were treated differently in colonization, I argue that the minor status of African American feminism in comparison to postcolonial feminism is partly due to the differential legacy of these female bodies. As mentioned earlier, DuCille figures this hierarchal status as the difference between "yesterday's news," which has already been forgotten, and "history" that is as novel and interesting as a "story."

I argue that those feminisms that fail to recognize the legacy of differential treatment of these female bodies repeat colonialist material and symbolic practices as they seek to undermine them. This repetition occurs when feminist theory affirms the colonialist notion that the body is a signifier of agency because it embodies "free will." Insofar as postcolonial and African American feminisms presuppose free will to be a concrete entity, or an actual, existing thing that must be recuperated, they then de-liberate the bodies they aim to liberate. Such feminist restorative history *obliges* Kanwar and Baartman to occupy this space of fully intending subjects so that their status as sheer victim *can* be refuted (Spivak 1999, 211, 214). Paradoxically, according to this methodology, Kanwar and Baartman are reduced to the "interchangeable (female) body" qua victimization; in other words, they are already "yesterday's news." Yet, they are also somehow endowed with a personal will that animates this fully determined body; in other words, they are also "history" and "story." In this way postcolonial and African American feminist theories repeat cultural prejudice because they presuppose the anthropomorphic nature/culture dichotomy and equate personhood with embodied free will, which is rendered a universal feature of all (human) bodies and therefore not historical.

Such a restorative methodology attempts to provide reparation for a free will deferred or denied but neglects how the imperialist *constitution* of free will is fundamental to what Gayatri Spivak calls the *mechanics* of the constitution of the Other (1999, 207), which displaces the "female subject *in life*" (235) in order to dissimulate the imperialist "appropriation of a role in gendering" (227). Rather than adhere to this overdetermined dialectic of subject-object, which evacuates the very colonialist history that feminist theorists seek to interrupt, Spivak examines the ideological manipulation of gendering implicit in presupposing the body as a signifier of agency. In contrast to the explanatory model just described, Spivak's philosophical model shifts feminist examination toward contemporary ideological investment in embodied free will, which can function as an alibi for appropriation of the subaltern in the name of (women's) history (239). Yet even Spivak neglects to use a comparative methodology, which could further guard against the dangers of the explanatory model. A comparative approach at once reveals the dangers of repeating colonialist discourses within feminist theory and enables solidarities among women of color by helping us to admit and therefore subvert the hierarchy between postcolonial and African American feminisms.

Roop Kanwar and Saartjie Baartman

Roop Kanwar was a nineteen-year-old Rajput widow immolated on her husband's funeral pyre before five thousand spectators in Deorala in 1987.[4] Her death provoked the outrage of feminists, activists, and academics in India and abroad who were horrified at yet another example of women's victimization by tradition in "underdeveloped" nations. Rajput communalists, however, interpreted Kanwar's act differently: Kanwar was a goddess, and sati is an intrinsic part of Rajput culture. Moreover, Kanwar should have the right to commit sati (Kumar 1993, 174). Given the intensity of these disputes, as Rajeswari Sunder Rajan points out, Kanwar's imputed identity depends on the ideological conviction through which these factions understand her death (Sunder Rajan 1993). Predominant postcolonial feminist analyses of Kanwar's death state that she could not have freely chosen to commit sati; either she was forced against her will or her choice was determined by patriarchal ideologies (Kishwar and Vanita 1988; Sarkar and Butalia 1995). Sunder Rajan also examines the ambivalence of the Prevention of *Sati* Ordinance of November 1987, which conflates sati with suicide such that a woman is punishable for her failed sati. And yet, if she is successful, the participants are prosecutable for abetment, not murder (Sunder Rajan 1993, 24). Vasudha Dhagamwar notes that the 1987 act passed by the central government punishes the woman for the offense of sati with lesser punishment only if coerced. According to the act, sati is inherently voluntary: the woman *commits* sati; the family/community does not burn a woman (Dhagamwar 1988, 38). Communalists also rely on essentialist understandings of Hinduism as timeless in origin and perennially subjugated. They believe that sati should occur, in fact, can only occur, when *satt* (truth) emerges ("evidence" for *satt* includes, for example, a glowing complexion and "miracles" such as the pyre lighting itself). *Satt* implies transformation without individual choice because the individual never existed; she was merely the material form of the goddess. Yet, as KumKum Sangari and Sudesh Vaid argue, *satt* is a legal alibi for the perpetrators (Sangari and Vaid 1989, 249–61).

The construction of Kanwar as goddess or victim recreates static binaries such as tradition versus progress, ritual versus crime, and secularism versus Hindu nationalism. Spivak argues that these constructions of sati function within colonial scripts; women either become objects of rescue for colonizers and benevolent indigenous patriarchies or they are self-determining and thereby transparent subjects (Spivak 1988, 271–302). The goddess Kanwar becomes the appropriate site for communalists to imagine a nation with rigid caste

(Brahmin), gender (male), and religious (Hindu) demarcations. The victim Kanwar allows feminists to condemn exploitation by transnational corporations, infanticide, low literacy rates, the condition of widows, increasing women's participation in Hindu and Muslim fundamentalism, and waning legal and property rights. Sati remains caught between spirituality and victimization: women have the right to commit sati or to be protected from sati. This struggle for signification attempts to resolve the disparity between an archaic "practice" in postcolonial India and a timeless and regressive patriarchy in a modern secular state; the *roop* (Hindi: manifestation) of Kanwar's death is the victorious narrative that names the *post* in postcolonial India.

Saartjie Baartman's display and dissection is similarly caught within colonialist scripts. Baartman won the right of return on January 29, 2002, when the French senate voted unanimously to repatriate her remains to South Africa for proper burial by her descendants after 186 years of possession.[5] Her naked body cast and skeleton had stood by the entrance to the gift shop in the lobby of the Musée de l'Homme until 1982 (Lindfors 1985, 134). Sharpley-Whiting states that her body cast "caused such excitement among museum visitors (one of the female tour guides was allegedly sexually accosted, and the molding itself had become the object of touching and many amorous masturbatory liaisons) that its exhibition was discontinued" (Sharpley-Whiting 1999, 31).

Baartman, whose original name is unknown, was born in Kaffraria in approximately 1788. Ironically, she was not a "Hottentot." In 1810 Baartman, an indentured female servant of a Boer farmer, Peter Cezar, in the Cape of Good Hope (Young 1997, 701), was taken to London by naval surgeon Alexander Dunlop and Cezar's brother, Hendrik. Cezar capitalized on "curiosity" about this new African colony that the British occupied in 1806 and on the "fame" of the "Hottentots" (Sharpley-Whiting 1999, 23).[6] British missionaries fought for and won special protection of the Khoikhoi as legal wards from the Boers in 1809. As a result, the Khoikhoi could not own land, had to perform service and carry work passes, and were restricted in their movement (Strother 1999, 22). Abolitionist protest in England against her exhibition continued this infantilizing of the Khoikhoi through colonial nationalism against the Boers who, as "savage, lazy, and cruel," were unnatural patriarchs because they "kept" Baartman as an "animal" (Jolly 1994, 3). According to this line of thinking, the civilized English and not the Boers or the working class could (naturally) colonize her body (Wiss 1994, 15–16), which became the alibi for what Spivak terms a race-divisive historiography (Spivak 1999, 230). The abolitionists could stage an intervention because Baartman was identified with sheer victimhood; yet the court was centrally concerned about "indecent exhibition . . . of a body already constituted as indecent" (Wiss 1994, 16–17). The African Association, founded in the early nineteenth century by Scottish-Jamaican Robert Wedderburn to fight against racism and slavery, petitioned to "release" Baartman due to possible physical/sexual abuse by Cezar (Young 1997, 703). This ideological *constitution* of free will, therefore, displaced Baartman as a "female subject *in life*" (Spivak 1999, 235) and dissimulated imperialism as patriarchal protection.

The attorney general pleaded Baartman's case on November 24, 1810. Cezar claimed that he "obtained" her from the Boers and received government permission to bring her to England (Lindfors 1985, 138–40). He presented a "contract," most likely drawn after the case was filed, which stated that she agreed to be exhibited and to serve as a domestic.[7] During occupation, however, the Dutch considered contracts not made before a magistrate invalid (Young 1997, 704), and the court record makes no mention of Baartman's signature on the document (Fausto-Sterling 1995, 29). Baartman had the "liberty," Cezar claimed, to choose her employment because her body was her private property. The "legalistic fixation" on consent belies the dependence on "extraction": her body, as anthropologist Rosemary Wiss argues, *is* the use the Boers, the court, and the abolitionists make of it, even during *her* confession (Wiss 1994, 18, 37). In other words, Baartman's "confession" is inherently a testimony of her "will." Baartman, however, was never mentioned by name in court proceedings or public discourse. Yet her testimony was translated as consent (Young 1997, 703–5).[8]

Subsequently, Baartman was exhibited in London for more than eight months and then in the provinces (Lindfors 1985, 134). She was brought to Paris in September 1814, abandoned by Cezar, and exhibited by an animal trainer named Réaux in a shed for eleven hours a day for fifteen months (Wiss 1994, 23; Sharpley-Whiting 1999, 17–21).

Although in England she was cast simultaneously as victim and agent, in France her body was an object of scientific curiosity. In March 1815 zoologists, anatomists, and physiologists examined her for three days at the Jardin du Roi; the "findings" were published (Sharpley-Whiting 1999, 33, 22).[9] Baartman took very ill in November 1815 and could no longer be exhibited. She died either on December 29, 1815, or January 1, 1816. The same scientists who keenly desired to expose her genitalia, that is, her (one) "secret," showed little concern for her illness. Her body was "naturally degenerating"; hence her death was "natural" as well (Wiss 1994, 28), even though she suffered from smallpox, pleurisy, and alcohol poisoning (Young 1997, 705–6; Fausto-Sterling 1995, 29). Georges Cuvier received permission from the police prefect to dissect her body. In the early 1800s, the work of de Blainville and Cuvier helped others establish the field of comparative anatomy, morphology, and modern zoological taxonomy (Fausto-Sterling 1995, 37, 23).[10]

Bodies That (Do Not) Matter

Feminism Inverted: Kanwar as Subaltern

Spivak argues that subalternity in the case of sati requires an examination of *how* it is possible for someone to want to die by ritually burning oneself as an act of mourning for the deceased husband; this question is not equivalent to discerning free will or coercion (Spivak 1999, 282). The fact that the historical archive does not account for the gendering of this female subject results in a compensatory object constituted by free will as a signifier of embodied agency (283). Thus when Sangari and Vaid regard *satt* as the *legal* alibi for coercion, they establish Kanwar's fate as the *natural* consequence of her gendering as a subject without free will. Similarly, Sunder Rajan's shift from "objective spectacle" to "subjective pain" or from "*sati*-as-death" to "*sati*-as-burning" (Sunder Rajan 1993, 19) avoids the question of embodied agency that necessitated her (re)formulation in the first place. The crucial aspect of Spivak's analysis is that subalternity does not refer to ultimate victimization. Instead, the subaltern's gendering, and her life, is what remains irretrievably heterogeneous (Spivak 1999, 270).

Instead of recuperating signs of free will from a silent archive, Spivak plots a history to discern what could have made this (final) sentence—"White men are saving brown women from brown men"—possible *as a sentence* that granted what she terms "honorary whiteness" to colonial subjects who colluded (Spivak 1999, 284, 285). Spivak emphasizes that this elided history has a double origin. Honorary whites enabled the British to manipulate "Hindu" India's Vedic past, as found in the Ṛg Veda and the Dharmaśāstra. These maneuverings led to the British abolishing sati in 1829 (286). The widow shuttles between "hyperbolic admiration" and "pious guilt," as the sentence is met with another sentence, which was formulated by nationalists: "The woman wanted to die." The latter, however, legitimates the former by reversal. One cannot find the woman's voice consciousness in the two sentences that are pitted against one another. Such a voice consciousness would allow for another sentence, which could be pitted against the two sentences (British and Indian) that pass for the extent of the historical deliberations (287). For Spivak, the recuperation, against these two sentences, of embodied agency, thus personhood, thus "free will," thus (woman's) voice consciousness, causes the further retreat of the subaltern. Spivak is careful to explain precisely what she means by the paradoxical scapegoating of the subaltern by way of granting her free will. She is not saying that seeing signs of a refusal to commit sati is putting words in someone else's mouth. She is also not saying that refusal alone demonstrates that the woman has free will. Instead, any understanding of free will is based on the negotiations a subject can undertake while choosing an interested action. We do not choose to act, nor is an action justified by a free will that is free by virtue of being disinterested (287n135). Indeed, disinterested free will and, hence, free will per se is impossible to discern, as any discernment is *already* interested.

Spivak turns, therefore, to colonial history to examine the interested constitution of disinterested free will that led to the imperialist and nationalist sentences. The British institute the spirit of the law of noninterference in Hindu custom by breaking the letter of the law. The Ṛg Veda and the Dharmaśāstra allow a woman to commit suicide on her husband's pyre as an exceptional signifier of her will. Similarly, this "sanctioned transgression" is the singular event of the protection of women from their ritually sanctioned singularity because "woman" emerges as (an) *exception* to the rule of suicide (Spivak 1999, 235). Sati or suttee (British transcription) leaped from private to public spheres; this crossing turned it from "ritual" into "crime" (287–88).

For the widow, her "own" desire to exceed the *general* conduct ritually stipulated for a widow is exceptional, and she thus desires to *be* exceptional. If the widow does decide to be exceptional by exceeding ritual prescription, turning back is a transgression punishable by specific penance (235). Turning back was *not* a choice akin to exceeding the letter of ritual. The tautological sanctioning of this suicide, therefore, manifests the woman's will through praising her for choosing to die by burning (293), due to which she emerges as exception to the rule of suicide, that is, as "woman," in the first place. In comparison, as the British instituted a distinction between legal and illegal sati based on free will, they assumed that the woman *had* no will, which manifested itself *only* when she was dissuaded by the officer present to ascertain the legality of the sati. The British construct suttee as metonym for (radical) cultural difference, which means that India was patriarchal until India is incorporated within an imperialist (now transnational) economy (291n142). Imperialism (now globalization) becomes the creation of a "good" (not just civil) society through championing (the) woman as needing protection from her own kind (brown men and not honorary whites). This image of imperialism dissimulates how professing to give women free choice (now "financialization" and "aid" agencies), and hence subject status, is a patriarchal British strategy (291). The nationalist, or the bad Hindu, with a proclivity for savagery (297), constructs a "counternarrative of woman's consciousness, thus woman's being, thus woman's being good, thus the good woman's desire, thus woman's desire" (235) against this construction.

What's important about Spivak's analysis is that she questions the *mechanics* of the constitution of free will within the colonial-nationalist historical dialectic. These mutually reinforcing simulacrums of either deprivation or possession of free will fill the (empty) place of the widow. Spivak emphasizes that within these two ostensibly competing narratives choosing sati or being rescued grants the woman subject status by nationalists and imperialists, respectively. Between these two poles, the place where the subaltern's free will actually lives is effaced, as is any possible agency this living subject may have had (235). One patriarchal discourse proffers will as exception (to suicide, to letter of ritual) at the moment of the husband's death, whereupon the woman can manifest her "will" to commit sati; to turn back is a transgression, which results in prescribed penance. Another patriarchal discourse also proffers will as exception because in this ritual prescription (or exceptional interference) to be rescued or dissuaded, which presumes the hapless woman was persuaded/ forced, demonstrates that choosing freedom is the only real choice and *not* a transgression (235). As a result, sati is either "victimage" or "cultural heroism" (293).[11]

What can free choice *mean* on this register? Nationalists used over-determined figurations of strength of character to justify the full objectification of the widow as an appropriate punishment for relinquishing her right to be courageous and hence her ascension to subject status (295n151). If dissuasion for the British was a demonstration of a choice signifying freedom (296), then this figuration also completely identifies (exceptional) good wifehood with self-immolation. Thus (the prohibition of) suttee was not (re)defined as British patriarchy, that is, natural patriarchy, but as a *crime* against "reasonable humanity" (303). The objects of protection are *legally* innocent and "punished for no *offense* but the [natural] physical weakness which had placed them at [unnatural] *man's* mercy" (296, emphasis added).[12] Through suttee the British turned imperialism into social mission, while nationalists turned sati into reward (296): both transcriptions are patriarchal strategies in which woman is always victim of those who forced her to commit suttee and those who prevented her from committing sati (291). Therefore, examining sati through Spivak's analysis of the shifting "diagnosis" of what constitutes free will for the female subaltern manifests the constant displacement of woman as (empty) signifier (307n171). When Sunder Rajan and Dhagamwar criticize the legal rendering of sati as inherently voluntary, or when Radha Kumar describes her encounter with "hostile" women at a pro-sati procession in New Delhi (Sunder Rajan 1993, 174), they speak of this history of displacement. This displacement is a story of gendering that results in a "feminism inverted" (Basu 1995, 159): recuperating free will paradoxically causes the further retreat of (women's) irretrievably heterogeneous history.

Le Cadavre d'une Femme Connue à Paris[13]

Wiss points to the contradictions inherent in the staging of Baartman's "testimony": she was "free to be a knowing subject of her own
desires and condition, free to speak as a colonized person within a colonial discourse, free to make rational decisions though . . . primitive,
bestial, and irrational" (Wiss 1994, 17). Therefore her enslavement
and display are of her own doing. Her emphasis on "lip-reading,"
however, belies a similar script of embodied free will. Due to Baartman's ventriloquism during her "confession," this free will could not
be heard, but existed as an actual historical entity. This "freedom,"
apparently, continued to shock and awe Bernth Lindfors, a scholar
of African literature who presents Baartman's experience in court as
the "courting" of the "Hottentot Venus": "She *freely* elected to continue working, *no doubt* believing that she stood to benefit. . . . Given
the opportunity to quit show business . . . she *chose* to remain. . . .
She was *willing* to collaborate in her own degradation . . . she *could
not* have failed to comprehend what the conditions of her employment were. . . . She *may* have been the victim of the cruelest kind
of predatory ruthlessness, but her collusion . . . is *unmistakable*. She
wanted the show to go on. . . . She *wanted* to capitalize on Western curiosity" (Lindfors 1985, 147–48, emphasis added). Lindfors emphasizes
the "depths" to which Baartman descended to attain "*her* objective"
(148, emphasis added), thereby making victims out of the Boers and
the British. Baartman, according to unquestioned accounts, became
a prostitute and this "way of life" led to "self-destruction" because
"she *swore* before witnesses that she was perfectly happy and under
no restraint. Taking her at *her* word, the magistrate . . . was *compelled*
to rule that . . . she was *already* free" (148, emphasis added).

Anthropologist Carmel Schrire continues this presupposition of the
inviolability of grossly violated personhood. "Saartjie explained the
situation *as she saw it*. . . . Today . . . Times Square . . . affords views of
working women offering their words and wares in cages or booths . . .
all part of a working girl's life . . . a more varied and amusing way to
pay the bills. It is likely that the pleasures of life in London far out-
stripped the alternative . . . she *surely* saw more diverting sights . . .
as she traveled. . . . But chilly Europe was not the sultry Cape, and
in due course, she took ill and died" (Schrire 1996, 348–50, emphasis

added). DuCille terms these textual gestures toward black women an "intentional phallacy." An intentional phallacy occurs when an author expressly wishes to avoid appropriation and objectification but nonetheless produces a text that perpetuates such appropriation and objectification (DuCille 1994, 620). As feminist theorists note, these accounts reify a melodramatic fiction of complicity (Young 1997, 699), valorize sexual objectification, and trace the subtleties of tautology (Matus 1991, 473): Baartman was *already* free.[14] Yet, both Jill Matus, a Victorian scholar, and Jean Young, an African American scholar and filmmaker, focus on the self-serving ideological manipulations through which exploitation, coercion, and silence are recast as free will, ostensibly to prevent recommodification and reobjectification. As a result, they ironically reestablish Baartman as "scapegoat": she is the product of a desire that tautologically *seeks* subject-status for what it signifies by *obliging* the "sexed subject" to occupy the space of embodied agency to then refute her sheer victimization (Spivak 1999, 283, 211, 214). Art historian Z. S. Strother, for example, notes that the painting of Baartman at the Jardin du Roi, depicts her "mocking" Cuvier. Baartman prohibits Cuvier from accessing what he most wanted to see. Thus Baartman's "free will" negotiates Cuvier's intrusion upon her fundamental inviolable personhood, which *is* her free will: Cuvier reports how his team meticulously observed Baartman so as to "describe even her pubic hair"; however, Strother sees how Baartman "*refuses* to enact fully the body Hottentot" by compressing her thighs (1999, 35, emphasis added). In its zest for aesthetic meticulousness, Wiss notes how this painting also omits Baartman's facial markings. This omission renders her the prototype of a (culturally constructed) "race" in its (culturally constructed) "natural" state (1994, 26).

Scholars have examined Baartman as racial type and specimen or as a freak and example of pathological difference.[15] Many have focused on her as a "highly sexed" (Strother 1999, 30) object whose overdetermined name and apotropaic staging allowed the scientist and the layperson to *directly* participate in resolving the anxieties and ambivalences of colonialism: the world lay inert on the dissecting table or could be controlled through extracting choreographed performances.[16] Although African American feminist scholarship has examined Baartman as a black female body "trapped in an image of itself" (Sharpley-Whiting 1999, 10), very few of its scholars question the categories of the human and animal upon which this body was constituted. Instead, they use her exhibition "as an animal" to demonstrate the presumption of her lack of will, as one would assume of animals, naturally, or to demonstrate the deprivation of her will, as one would deprive the will of an animal, naturally.

Baartman's body was "naturally unnatural" (Wiss 1994), yet also culturally unnatural. Baartman was what Fausto-Sterling calls a "primitive primitive" but not because her body was animal-like and hence naturally inferior. By being the "link" to nature she became the natural/cultural alibi for the separation from a nature conflated with animal bodies. Because animal bodies are naturally capable only of bodily existence, such bodily existence is a signifier of *lack* of free will. However, this signification of animal bodies is a cultural ideology rather than based on natural fact. In other words, to not have free will is to be an animal. Why is *animal* an appropriate name for radical alterity? Why is "to be" to have free will? Thus, if Baartman is already free—*naturally*, one must ask why the exhibitors, scientists, and audiences fell prey to *their* context in spite of the force of reason/history behind them? Why did Georges and Frédéric Cuvier, Geoffrey Saint-Hilaire, and Henri de Blainville refuse to be scientists when they *most* needed to be?

Liberating Traditions: The Personal Is Political

Iconographic and textual representations of sati and the Hottentot Venus indicate that both phenomena were crucial to strategies of colonization by imperial powers. Despite this similarity, the status of the Hindu female body differed from that of the black female body. For the British, the presence of a Hindu tradition and a large body of Sanskrit texts indicated that India possessed civilization and glory to some extent, even if this civilization no longer existed. Africa, with the exception of Egypt, had never been granted a civilization worth redeeming. While the Hindu female body elicited pity and awe, the black female body elicited repulsion and fear. The Hindu female body remained remote and inaccessible because sati is construed as an act of *wifely* devotion, and the women in question are ritual (non)actors. The Hindu female body, therefore, materializes as an (in)appropriately *gendered* rather than a biologically determined body, because the body is the (im)material vessel for the essential goddess. Due to its spectacular violence, this (non)gendering renders the banal normalcy of a widow's wretched life invisible (Spivak 1999, 299–300). This (non)gendering stages the unnaturalness of Indian patriarchy qua culture (Hindu men burn their women; European men rescue them) as well as the (un)natural individual uniqueness of the woman who burned. As a retired Rajput military officer stated, "Yes, in those days of Rajput kings, before British times, before independence, those women who became satis, they knew how to die like men" (Courtright and Goswami 2001, 224). Unlike the Hindu female body of sati, the black female body did not enter into predominant conceptions of femininity. The black female body, in a spectacular excess similar to the Hindu female body, remained a *type*, classified according to the biological characteristics that became colonialism's *gendered* alibi. This female body remained ungendered, even as this gendering staged the absence of indigenous patriarchy qua culture as well as the (un)natural lack of individual uniqueness among the females who were considered indistinguishable from the countryside; in their sloth they simply copulated, indifferently fed their offspring, and "exposed" themselves for an insignificant amount of chewing tobacco.

In contrast, the public appearance of the Hindu *female* body of sati, which is its uniqueness, is also the point of its public (dis)appearance because the volition presumed simultaneously with *satt* (truth) stages its gendering. The Hindu female body is invisible precisely when it is most visible in its singularity, if only as the unique vehicle for divinity. This gendering not only abstracts the very materiality of being a body but also renders this literal dematerialization through burning alive compatible with liberal notions of individual will: Kanwar wanted to die. Yet, for the British, this will appeared at the moment of dissuasion when the woman claimed the right to not commit sati; for indigenous patriarchs this will is manifest at the moment of decision to claim the right to commit sati. The black female body materializes as matter *plus*, hypervisible and overdetermined, even as this body's *blackness* and *femaleness* renders it simultaneously opaque in its literalness and transparent in its readability and fixity. The black female body materializes at the point of its public (dis)appearance because the volition presumed simultaneously with conjured bestiality, pathology, and degeneracy stages its gendering. This gendering not only abstracts the very materiality of being a body but also renders this literal dematerialization through overmaterialization as display compatible with liberal notions of individual will: Baartman wanted to display herself. Baartman and Kanwar, therefore, demonstrate the irrationality of rationality: they are expected to answer on the terms of the discourse from which, as (non)bodies, they are constitutively excluded.

I would like to suggest that this de-liberating legacy of female embodiment has led to what Darlene Clark Hine terms the "culture of dissemblance" within *both* African American and postcolonial feminisms (Hine 1995, 380–87). In Janell Hobson's terms, "wounded black female bodies" may increase horror but they also perpetuate the identification of black women with "hypersexuality—as victim or as seducer" (Hobson 2005, 49–50). The death-by-culture argument that constitutes a "colonialist stance" toward sati has led postcolonial feminists to shy away from explicit discussions of sexuality in order to focus on grand narratives of culture, nation, and (post)colonialism as metonyms for gender.[17] By contrast, African American feminism is reduced to a hyperparticular narrative of hyperparticular sexuality assumed to have little bearing on the study of gender and, therefore, of culture, nation, and (post)colonialism. African American feminism counters the nature versus culture binary that renders "nature" black women's "culture." Postcolonial feminism struggles against the cultural/social versus political dichotomy that renders "culture" Indian women's "nature" (John 2004, 60). Both the female bodies of sati and slavery are hypersexualized and fixed as *female* bodies to counter the ambivalence that lay at the heart of the colonizing mission and the conquest of nature. Given that the black female body is its matter plus while the Hindu female body is its patriarchal protection, African American feminism becomes political plus: simultaneously much too political as hypervisible excess and, hence, prepolitical at ground zero, yet not really figuring in its invisibility.

On the basis of this comparative analysis, I argue that the cultural prejudices of both postcolonial and African American feminisms render the female bodies of sati and slavery simply cultural texts to be read for patriarchal strategies that deprive them of free will. Instead, these differential legacies can be used to create the imaginative possibility for a generalized history with what one might term *philo-sophical* implications for understanding embodied agency. Specifically, the gendering strategy of objectification is the basis on which culture is consolidated as culture per se through the presumed actuality of free will as the principle of separation from nature. Postcolonial and African American feminisms risk de-liberating the female body if this body is rendered a transparent textual effect from which to deduce (once again) the mechanisms of the constitution of culture. These feminisms should examine the anthropomorphic nature/culture dichotomy that constitutes this culture in the *first* place (qua place). If postcolonial and African American feminisms repeat rather than question the presumed actuality of free will as the principle of separation from nature, then they cannot assume the stance of being cultural criticism par excellence. In other words, postcolonial and African American feminisms risk neglecting the problem of creating a philosophical space from which a criticism of culture can be launched. These (now self-evident) bodies may be used as explanatory pivots for critique of hegemonic cultures. However, these feminisms may also use these bodies to dismantle cultural prejudice. This cultural prejudice allows for the constitution of (a) culture to begin with via the ostensible separation of the human from an ill-understood and stereotypically posited nature.

This cultural prejudice leads to at least two consequences. First, if postcolonial and African American feminisms neglect the female body's philosophical dimension, then they neglect their conceptual framework's historical dimension. This neglect of the historical dimension occurs because these feminist theories accept the anthropomorphic nature/culture dichotomy, such that culture is human nature and personhood is equated with embodied free will. A feminist postcolonial imaginary premised on a subject who intends to resist attempts to reconcile a privileged identity (gender) with abstract personhood renders the subaltern what is incommensurable in our subjectivity. The subaltern becomes "that which needs cultural intervention" (Gabrielpillai 2000, 289, 293). The subaltern, however, is not the shadow of a *better* cultured woman, nor is she a threshold to be crossed for theory to be "successful" or "inclusive." The subaltern's body does not mark an undomesticated or unincorporated space, but constitutes what is properly real.

Second, if postcolonial and African American feminisms neglect this historic dimension, which is also a philosophical dimension, then postcolonial and African American feminisms are already the projects of establishing (oppositional) historical difference. This project of establishing historical difference, however, is undertaken in the interest of constituting cultural difference from exclusionary culture. Thus postcolonial and African American feminisms deduce better (less exclusionary) culture from the historical difference of the female bodies of sati and slavery, respectively. The conflation of historical and cultural difference constitutes a philosophical difference between the mechanisms of exclusive culture and the mechanisms of feminism. The female bodies of sati and slavery become the *feminist* object of study for (a) better culture. However, postcolonial and African American feminisms cannot claim cultural or historical difference if they neglect the philosophical charge of their enterprise—even if they persuasively argue against the female body's victimization within patriarchal structures. This charge is not to accept an already naturally differentiated body, in the beginning, from presupposed nature, which must be restored only to its proper cultural lineaments (free will). Rather, it is to challenge the nature/culture dichotomy that has led to the erstwhile fixing, destruction, and invisibility of all other bodies (*in* nature *qua* nature). The anthropomorphic nature/culture dichotomy, therefore, is in fact a process of dematerialization of bodies through free will. This dichotomy presupposes a debased relationship to nature and other biological species, and thus to ourselves, as the very possibility of culture. In the name of this culture (now "sustainability"), imperialism turned *all* bodies into bodies that do not matter.

The neglect of the philosophical dimension, therefore, occurs because the female bodies of sati and slavery are further dematerialized. In other words, this dematerialization occurs in the very process of foregrounding how culture renders these bodies fully determined yet animated by embodied personal will. The philosophical dimension of the female bodies of sati and slavery, therefore, is paradoxically its materiality that both inclusive feminism and exclusive hegemonic culture write over in their historically different cultural interests. The materiality of the living body is irretrievably lost even before its literal death under the burden of its representation and the selectively preserved historical archive. However, the materiality that is lost is also the living body that can be substituted for all bodies because this body is a part of nature. This writing over takes place, that is, establishes the contemporary moment of critique, on the basis of further consolidating the pastness of the past ("yesterday's news"). As a result, the question of embodied agency is refigured as a *political* problem for the contemporary theorist taking the *personal* place of Kanwar and Baartman ("history" and "story").

The common cultural prejudice of these feminisms, furthermore, evacuates the historical differences between the constitution of the Hindu female body and the black female body in the imperialist project. Ironically, postcolonial and African-American feminisms become compatible as women of color theorizing that preserves cultural prejudice by upholding the ostensibly liberating notion of free will. The lack of a comparative framework prevents an adequate cultural critique of the victimization of the female body due to the absence of an adequate historical framework. Thus an inadequate attention to historical difference leads to the inability of postcolonial and African American feminisms to foreground the philosophical and therefore historical valence of sati and slavery, respectively.

Posthumous Subjects

This comparative analysis does not attempt to (re)situate the female bodies of sati and slavery within apparently authentic precolonial representations and/or indigenous theories of the body. Such a restoration inevitably constitutes authenticity on the basis of an ideological desire and evacuates the very history of violence these bodies in fact embody. This chapter, moreover, deploys analyses provided by notable scholars whose class privilege may allow for transnational and/or cross-cultural dispersal of their theorizing, a problem that is well-documented and examined in the annals of both postcolonial and African American feminisms. Nonetheless, a comparison of their theories may provide the theoretical tools to avoid the slippage from cultural prejudice to culturalism (a brown theory of the body versus a black theory of the body). It can also challenge what both postcolonial and African American feminisms have explicitly argued against: a global feminism that dissimulates abjectly medieval systems of production while promulgating a transnational gender bonding that is in fact debt-bondage of the poorest nations (Spivak 1995, 243). The feminist comparative methodology used here reorients an explanatory model of hierarchal colonial figurations to a philosophical model that attempts to render Roop Kanwar and Saartjie Baartman meaningful through the theoretical issues they present us with rather than making them the occasion for liberal outrage. This approach also challenges conventional Western versus non-Western comparative methodologies. African American feminism as *American* feminism is ostensibly privileged in comparison with feminism emerging from even metropolitan India. However, postcolonial theory's consolidation as a "model minority" discourse paradoxically renders African American feminism non-Western in relation to postcolonial theory's Eurocentrism.

This examination thus reveals the profound loneliness that haunts an empty cremation ground in Deorala and the empty spot where skeleton number 1603 (third from the right in the third row) hung in a dark and dingy room in the Musée de l'Homme. As neither subject nor object, Kanwar and Baartman are the *imaginative* possibility for something else besides. Their names mark a (non)passage to the historical ground of feminist inquiry whose historical density cannot be retrieved. This historical density constitutes, nonetheless, the ground beneath our feet. Thus representational desire is marked by a fundamental paradox. When representation is assumed to be an enabling task, the history that needs to be dealt with for representational accuracy ("true" representation) or representational stasis ("impossible" representation) is precisely the history that is evacuated. Representation requires the literal foreclosure of most of the world in order to create the historical ground upon which representation (true or impossible) can be representational. Kanwar and Baartman as specters of suffering never quite suffice to instigate a call to arms for the object of one's political beneficence, because such a calling emerges through recollection of the historical ground upon which this contact takes place and not through the presentist instrumentalism of fixing a problem. A theory of the body that does not de-liberate on the representation of the body itself as a telescoped and condensed standing-in for the *meaningful* body already constitutes an ability to represent that is not in our name. This otherwise name is the distance we must travel to become that which is left behind. Only then has the personal truly become political.

Notes

1. For example, Naomi Zack conflates postcolonial, transnational, and African American feminisms while criticizing Anglo-American feminism's Eurocentrism in *Inclusive Feminism: A Third Wave Theory of Women's Commonality* (2005).

2. For examples of works on this marginalization, see Cole and Guy-Sheftall (2003), Lewis (1996), McClintock (1995), Chow (1993), hooks (1989), and Hull, Scott, and Smith (1982).

3. For examples of works on this privileging, see Bahri (2003), Davies (1994), hooks (1990), and Spivak (1996).

4. For details of this case and firsthand interviews with Kanwar's father-in-law and witnessing neighbors, see Courtright and Goswami (2001). During this 1999 visit to Deorala, I also met a "living sati" in nearby Triveni whose sati had been stopped by the police in 1985. She refused to speak to us further when my mother asked her why she did not want to die her own death.

5. For discussions of how Baartman's remains became a diplomatic and aboriginal rights issue, see the Associated Press (2002) and Koch (1995, 1996).

6. Within sixty years of Dutch settlement in the Cape (1652), the Khoikhoi were extinct due to smallpox and genocide. The Bushmen, Khoisan, and the Khoi were physically similar, but culturally different, even though in the eighteenth and nineteenth centuries *Hottentot* became interchangeable with *Bushman* (Fausto-Sterling 1995, 22–23). The Khoikhoi (people of people) were nomadic pastoralists, but turned into an impoverished migrant laboring class. Due to representations of them as savage, congenitally stupid, lazy, and without proper language (Strother 1999, 3–14), *Hottentot* became the metonym for radical otherness (Thomson 1997, 71).

7. None of the scholars I have researched have seen this contract, if it ever existed.

8. See Strother (1999, 41) for Baartman's "testimony."

9. See Cuvier and St.-Hilaire (1824) and Cuvier (1864).

10. De Blainville's report, given to the Société Philomatique de Paris, orally (1815) and in the society's proceedings (1816), compares her to "Negroes" and the orangutan. Cuvier's detailed dissection report renders her similarity to mandrills and baboons somehow unlike that of all *homo sapiens* (Fausto-Sterling 1995, 33–34, 37).

11. Spivak asks if this question of gendering is the memory of (another) time from within rationalized gender and therefore no longer patriarchal but freed (Spivak 1999, 291). She invokes the "atrophy of classical learning" and the resulting impossibility of asking the "radical questions" (292). See Shetty and Bellamy

(2000) for an analysis of Spivak's argument that the precolonial archive is the postcolonial archive.

12. Spivak is citing Edward Thompson's influential colonial account, *Suttee: A Historical and Philosophical Enquiry Into the Hindu Rite of Widow-Burning* (Thompson 1928, 132).

13. This is a reference to the title of an article by Georges Cuvier (1817).

14. Lindfors notes, "Her insistence upon her right . . . became the subject of countless jokes, cartoons, and newspaper doggerel" (Lindfors 1985, 144).

15. Baartman's sexual difference was "extreme" racial difference (Wiss 1994, 11). In order to present Baartman as a "typical specimen" (Strother 1999, 33), Cuvier omits de Blainville's references to her unease and her refusal to reveal her genitals at the Jardin du Roi. Schrire continues this venerable tradition: "The specimen resembled a marine creature, an exsanguinated polyp, drifting in a pale, topaz sea. It carried no personal title other than 'Hottentot Venus,' but, given *her* fame, that was more than enough" (Schrire 1996, 348, emphasis added). Strother notes, "The sobriquet ["Hottentot Venus"] neutralizes (temporarily) the tension between freak and type. . . . Baartman represents . . . a rare and desired form of the type. . . . As a 'freak,' . . . [she] normalized the spectator as an individual. . . . [As] an ethnographic 'type,' [she] normalizes and legitimates the British colonial project . . . even 'freaks' in Europe are more attractive" (Strother 1999, 25–30).

16. In the "enacted ethnography" of Baartman's exhibition, which was the first major ethnological exhibition in the nineteenth century, her body was an "unusual object of 'natural history'" and a "signifier of the real, the authentic" (Strother 1999, 35–37).

17. For more on the "death-by-culture argument," see Narayan (1997, 41–118). See also Puri (1999) for a response to this absence.

References

Associated Press. 2002. France returning remains of African. *New York Times*, January 30.

Bahri, Deepika. 2003. *Native intelligence: Aesthetics, politics, and postcolonial literature*. Minneapolis: University of Minnesota Press.

Basu, Amrita. 1995. Feminism inverted: The gendered imagery and real women of Hindu nationalism. In *Women and the Hindu right: A collection of essays*, ed. Tanika Sarkar and Urvashi Butalia, 158–80. New Delhi: Kali for Women.

Chow, Rey. 1993. *Writing diaspora: Tactics of intervention in contemporary cultural studies*. Bloomington: Indiana University Press.

Christian, Barbara. 1988. The race for theory. *Feminist Studies* 14 (1): 67–79.

Cole, Johnetta B., and Beverly Guy-Sheftall. 2003. *Gender talk: The struggle for women's equality in African-American communities*. New York: One World.

Courtright, Paul B., and Namita Goswami. 2001. Who was Roop Kanwar? *Sati, law, religion, and postcolonial feminism*. In *Religion and personal law in secular India: A call to judgment*, ed. Gerald James Larson, 200–25. Bloomington: Indiana University Press.

Cuvier, Frédéric, and Geoffrey Saint-Hilaire. 1824. *Histoire naturelle des mammifères, avec des figures originales coloriées*. Paris: Belin.

Cuvier, Georges. 1817. Extrait d'observations faites sur le cadavre d'une femme connue à Paris et à Londres sous le nom de Vénus Hottentote. *Mémoires du Muséum d' histoire naturelle* 3: 259–74. Paris: Mémoires.

——. 1864. *Discours sur les revolutions du globe: Études sur l'ibis et mémoire sur la Vénus hottentote*. Paris: Passard.

Davies, Carole Boyce. 1994. From "post-coloniality" to uprising textualities: Black women writing the critique of empire. In *Black women, writing, and identity: Migrations of the subject*, 80–112. New York: Routledge.

Dhagamwar, Vasudha. 1988. Saint, victim, or criminal. *Seminar* 342: 34–39.

DuCille, Ann. 1994. The occult of true black womanhood: Critical demeanor and black feminist studies. *Signs* 19 (3): 591–629.

——. 1996. *Skin trade*. Cambridge: Harvard University Press

Fausto-Sterling, Anne. 1995. Gender, race, and nation: The comparative anatomy of "hottentot" women in Europe, 1815–1817. In *Deviant bodies*, ed. Jennifer Terry and Jacqueline Urla, 19–48. Bloomington: Indiana University Press.

Gabrielpillai, Matilda. 2000. Postcolonial identity as feminist fantasy: A study of Tamil women's short fiction on dowry. In *Faces of the feminine in ancient, medieval, and modern India*, ed. M. Bose, 287–96. New York: Oxford University Press.

Hine, Darlene Clark. 1995. Rape and the inner lives of black women in the middle West: Ruminations on the culture of dissemblance. In *Words of fire: An anthology of African-American feminist thought*, ed. Beverly Guy-Sheftall, 380–87. New York: New Press.

Hobson, Janell. 2005. *Venus in the dark: Blackness and beauty in popular culture*. New York: Routledge.

hooks, bell. 1989. *Talking back: Thinking feminist, thinking black*. Boston: South End.

——. 1990. Third world diva girls: Politics of feminist solidarity. In *Yearning: Race, gender, and cultural politics*, 89–102. Boston: South End.

Hull, Gloria T., Patricia Bell Scott, and Barbara Smith, eds. 1982. *All the women are white, all the blacks are men, but some of us are brave*. New York: Feminist Press.

John, Mary E. 2004. Feminism in India and the West: Recasting a relationship. In *Feminism in India: Issues in contemporary Indian feminism*, ed. Maitrayee Chaudhari, 52–68. New Delhi: Women Unlimited and Kali for Women.

Jolly, Margaret. 1994. Introduction. *Australian Journal of Anthropology* 5 (1–2): 1–11.

Kishwar, Madhu, and Ruth Vanita. 1988. The burning of Roop Kanwar. *Manushi: A Journal About Women and Society* 42–43: 15–25.

Koch, Eddie. 1995. Bring back the Hottentot Venus. *Mail and Guardian*, June 15.

——. 1996. New bid for body parts. *Mail and Guardian*, May 3.

Kumar, Radha. 1993. *The history of doing: An illustrated account of movements for women's rights and feminism in India, 1800-1900.* New York: Verso.

Lewis, Reina. 1996. *Gendering orientalism: Race, femininity and representation.* New York: Routledge.

Lindfors, Bernth. 1985. Courting the Hottentot Venus. *Africa* (Rome) 40:133–48.

Lorde, Audre. 1997. Bridge through my windows. In *The collected poems of Audre Lorde,* 9. New York: Norton.

Matus, Jill. 1991. Blonde, black and Hottentot Venus: Context and critique in Angela Carter's "Black Venus." *Studies in short fiction* 28 (4): 467–76.

McClintock, Anne. 1995. *Imperial leather: Race, gender, and sexuality in the colonial contest.* New York: Routledge.

Narayan, Uma. 1997. *Dislocating cultures: Identities, traditions, and third-world feminism.* New York: Routledge.

Puri, Jyoti. 1999. *Woman, body, desire in post-colonial India: Narratives of gender and sexuality.* New York: Routledge.

Sangari, KumKum, and Sudesh Vaid. 1996. Institutions, beliefs, ideologies: Widow immolation in contemporary Rajasthan. In *Embodied violence: Communalising female sexuality in South Asia,* ed. Kumari Jayawardena and Malathi de Alwis, 240–296. London: Zed.

Sarkar, Tanika, and Urvashi Butalia. 1995. Introductory remarks. In *Women and the Hindu right: A collection of essays,* ed. Tanika Sarkar and Urvashi Butalia, 1–9. New Delhi: Kali for Women.

Schrire, Carmel. 1996. Native views of Western eyes. In *Miscast: Negotiating the presence of the Bushmen,* ed. Pippa Skotnes, 343–53. Cape Town: University of Cape Town Press.

Sharpley-Whiting, T. Denean. 1999. *Black Venus: Sexualized savages, primal fears, and primitive narratives in French.* Durham: Duke University Press.

Shetty, Sandhya, and Elizabeth Bellamy. 2000. Postcolonialism's archive fever. *Diacritics* 30 (1): 25–48.

Spivak, Gayatri. 1988. Can the subaltern speak? In *Marxism and the interpretation of culture,* ed. Cary Nelson and Lawrence Grossberg, 271–313. Urbana: University of Illinois Press.

———. 1995. At the planchette of deconstruction is/in America. In *Deconstruction is/in America: A new sense of the political,* ed. Anselm Haverkamp, 237–49. New York: New York University Press.

———. 1996. Transnationality and multiculturalist ideology: Interview with Gayatri Spivak. In *Between the lines: South Asians and postcoloniality,* ed. Deepika Bahri and Mary Vasudeva, 64–92. Philadelphia: Temple University Press.

———. 1999. *The critique of postcolonial reason: Toward a history of the vanishing present.* Cambridge: Harvard University Press.

Strother, Z. S. 1999. Display of the body Hottentot. In *Africans on stage: Studies in ethnological show business,* ed. Bernth Lindfors, 1–61. Bloomington: Indiana University Press.

Sunder Rajan, Rajeswari. 1993. *Real and imagined women: Gender, culture, and post-colonialism*. New York: Routledge.

Thompson, Edward. 1928. *Suttee: A historical and philosophical enquiry into the Hindu rite of widow-burning*. London: Allen and Unwin.

Thomson, Rosemarie Garland. 1997. *Extraordinary bodies: Figuring physical disability in American culture and literature*. New York: Columbia University Press.

Wiss, Rosemary. 1994. Lipreading: Remembering Saartjie Baartman. *Australian Journal of Anthropology* 5 (1–2): 11–40.

Young, Jean. 1997. The re-objectification and re-commodification of Saartjie Baartman in Suzan-Lori Parks's Venus. *African-American Review* 31 (4): 699–708.

Zack, Naomi. 2005. *Inclusive feminism: A third wave theory of women's commonality*. Lanham, MD: Rowman and Littlefield.

Philosophy Uprising

The Feminist Afterword

CHELA SANDOVAL

⸙ Imagine there's no country, it's easy if you try.
—YOKO ONO AND JOHN LENNON

THE BOOK *Asian and Feminist Philosophies in Dialogue* travels alter-worlds of sense, an Anzaldúan journey—it bridges as it goes. Each chapter invokes a present-time-culture designed to transform that which came before . . . and that which will come after.[1] In this sense each chapter represents an important contribution to what has become a planetary twenty-first-century project. The unique intervention of this collection occurs through its integration of feminist theory with Japanese Zen articulations of nondual subjectivities, its comparison of Confucian care ethics with the consciousness-raising rites of feminist politics, and through its purposeful rehearsal of decolonizing third-space feminisms as examples of middle-way Buddhist *dharma*. Such connections link through an uprising of "the mind-body-emotion matrix" that in this book is guided by methodologies of feminist comparative philosophy. *Asian and Feminist Philosophies in Dialogue* does this and much more by making clear the methods and contours of a "wisdom politics" that rose alongside the same radical forces that produced early twentieth-century revolutionary continental philosophies, critical and cultural theories, and third world liberationist, pan-indigenous, East-West and decolonial philosophies.

Liberation philosophies such as these continue to function today as insurrectional knowledge systems insofar as each remains connected-in-resistance against the colonial exploits of capitalism's monopoly stage. Indeed, it is against such powers that nineteenth- and twentieth-century humanity developed alternative *planetary* modes of consciousness and action. Social and philosophical movements like third world liberation, Marxism, socialism, communism, and feminism were aimed at emancipating humanity from its own (historically self-made) fetters. In this volume the legacies of these movements are made visible as ideas, methods, compassions; and what is clearly identified here as a self-reflexive, decolonial, and differentially feminist methodology of liberation.

The effect of such movements has been the liberation of Western philosophies from their ancient Greek roots, the recognition of planetary stores of profoundly inspiring knowledges, and the release and circulation of the wisdoms of the dispossessed.[2] Valorized and traditional Euro-continental philosophies have been exceeded by proliferating visions of egalitarianism. These are tracked in this book by scholars capable of comparing and contrasting diverse Asian and feminist philosophies in relation to one another. Their research thus extends culturally diverse perceptions, understandings, and ethics across what were once historically severed ideoscapes. *Asian and Feminist Philosophies in Dialogue* is a book that links, valorizes, aligns, extends, and deepens inner and interexchanges across selves, genders, ethnicities, cultures, and nations—as well as across the academic and intellectual boundaries that divide the human, social, and natural sciences.

These same aims were forcefully advanced during the twentieth century by a distinctive feminist social movement. During the 1970s the political practices of U.S. third world feminism were similarly organized for the very purpose of hearing-speaking-and-exchanging across national, cultural, racial, class, sexual, and gendered divides. Like the current disciplinary aims of feminist comparative philosophy that are enacted in these chapters, this movement was aimed at developing a method of emancipation designed to pull diverse orders of meaning into alliance. The scholarship in this book extends the aims of this methodology of emancipation as it compares and discloses unexpected alliances within and between Asian and feminist philosophies. Their results advance a mode of *post*continental, twenty-first-century emancipation philosophy and method that, across disciplines, insists that humanity learns to move with, through, and beyond the "mind-body-emotion matrix."

The Middle Way and Third-Space Politics

In 1854 the great U.S. comparative philosopher Sojourner Truth de-livered a now famous lecture to a primarily U.S. Anglo audience. The lecture was designed to detail how conditioned perceptual apparati were incapable of distinguishing "women of color" as gendered "fe-male" beings. Truth's lesson was a demonstration of how conscious-ness is enslaved by its own cultural histories, by its own Euro-colonial gender, sex, race, and economic strictures. One hundred years later, Truth's lessons were delivered once again to similar allies, this time by collectives of U.S. "radical-feminists-of-color."[3] To understand and advance Truth's lessons, they argued, human beings must rec-ognize that there is an unrecognized location for consciousness that can liberate perception from hierarchically organized binary oppo-sitions. Their insistence was that, from this other space, individuals and groups become capable of undoing the damages of hierarchized binaries and their resultant colonizations, slaveries, and conquests.

In the post–World War II period, U.S. third world feminist philoso-phers defined and named this emancipatory space, along with its myr-iad possibilities-for-being, by developing a lexicon of mobile termi-nologies. In 1981 they described it as an embodied "bridge" between meanings—"this bridge called my back"—and as a hopeful location be-tween binaries the literature identified as a "third" realm or "world" of possibility (Mirikatani 1972; Moraga and Anzaldúa 1981; Sandoval 1991; Peréz 1999). So too, Amy Ling's 1990 book identifies the libera-tory space that occurs "between worlds," while in 1988 Lakota Paula Gunn Allen identifies it as "that other place" that we must now live—"an idea, because whiteman took all the rest" (Allen 1988, 148). For many feminists of color, this in-between space is where "some of us are brave" even if all the "women are white, and all the Blacks are men" (Hull, Scott, and Smith 1982). Lorde unravels the mysteries of what we might continue to call a third space in her description of a "house of difference" (Lorde 1981), while Anzaldúa and Keating identify it as the "bridge that we call home," writing that it functions in the same way as *nepantla*, the Mayan word for "the world-in-between-worlds" (Anzaldúa and Keating 2002). At this time Anzaldúa also calls for a new mode of "global tribalism" that can only be enacted by practitioners she names *nepantleras*. Much of the diverse scholarship in *Asian and Feminist Philosophies in Dialogue* represents forms of engagement with the terms of this realm. Yet all these engagements continue to raise the following questions: What are the individual and collective techniques necessary for recognizing and engaging this space? What methods are necessary to allow the forms of subjectivity and coalition to emerge that are its promise? What would feminist forms of "consciousness-raising" look like should they be organized inside its terms?

These questions and their provisions are not meant to create the (sometimes violent) binary oppositions that occurred between *and within* "third" and "first" world feminisms during the 1970s and 1980s. Rather, the aim of early third world feminist philosophy was to deepen and extend the possibilities for feminism itself and beyond: to create the conditions for dialectically activating *post*colonial terms for consciousness-raising, to unravel the destructive knots-that-divide Being and connections between peoples, and to advance humanity's understandings of what it means to be "emancipated."[4] These very aims have been taken up and extended by the scholarship in this collection. Diverse answers to the questions raised here are found within its pages.

Feminist Comparative Philosophy Is a Wisdom Politics

Entering this third space of *nepantla* requires the development of innovative truth-telling technologies. *Asian and Feminist Philosophies in Dialogue* advances the development of these technologies and the activism and modes of consciousness this kind of truth-telling requires. Feminist third-space philosophical terms have named and theorized these processes as *la facultad, situated subjectivities, differential perception and consciousness, intersectionality, la conciencia de la mestiza,* and *conocimiento.* They have identified organizational formations including consciousness-raising groups, *Nahual*-witness circles, and cyborg alliances as well as modes of politics that are engaged through *nepantlera* activism, the "feminist anarchism" of the Zapatistas, and the "methodology of the oppressed." In 1981 Anzaldúa wrote that all these processes are designed to link peoples who "do not share" the same cultures, languages, races, sexual orientations, genders, or ideologies and that within their rationality such differences "do not become opposed to each other" (Anzaldúa 1981, 209). Instead, that same year,

Audre Lorde understood that the profound differences must be gathered together and *re*-understood as "a fund of necessary polarities between which our creativities spark like a dialectic" (Lorde 1981, 58). It is "only within that interdependency," she emphasizes, when every difference becomes "acknowledged and equal," that "the power to seek new ways of being in the world generate," as well as "the courage and sustenance to act where there are no charters" (58). These statements call for the development of new modes of consciousness and coalition, and they mark what became the philosophical foundations of a third-space feminist mode of perception, knowledge, and action. Third-space feminist praxis represents the enactment of a consciousness and perceptual apparatus that is capable of handling psychic and social powers as though they are transformable pieces in an aesthetic-of-emancipation. Thus understood, third-space feminism is a wisdom politics, a mode of liberation philosophy that is also shared in the comparative philosophy that is being enacted here.

Third-space feminist comparative philosophies like these deploy what philosopher María Lugones describes as nomadic and determined travel across worlds-of-meaning (Lugones 1987). This is a mode of epistemological and affective travel that imbricates the scholarship in this book insofar as it moves among diverse cultural and philosophical positions while allying contending forms and contents. The philosophy encoded in this book draws from disparate ideological forms and contents while moving between distinct disciplines and philosophical framings. The chapters move variably between competing literatures, disciplinary frames, and diverse cultural traditions. Their movement summons the same third space of possibility out of which Gloria Anzaldúa imagined an intertribal and planetary wisdom politics (2002).

The Feminist Afterword: *Conocimiento*'s Other Mode of Consciousness

This book's afterworld shimmers with realities foreseen by such great third-space feminist philosophers as Gloria Anzaldúa, Amy Ling, Ruth Frankenberg, Lata Mani, Rosa Villafañe-Sisolak, Paula Gunn Allen, Maxine Hong Kingston, Laura Peréz, Cornel West, Jacqui Alexander,

Alice Young Chai, Russell Means, Donna Haraway, Audre Lorde, and Inés Hernandez-Avila. These writers deploy spiritual symbols and practices as part and parcel of building a revolutionary twenty-first-century, pan-indigenous approach to life. Their writing demechanizes disciplinized Western philosophy to reveal at its heart the love of wisdom.

These writers similarly invoke a mystical, progressive, feminist praxis that theorizes consciousness as that which includes but also lies outside the West's most familiar understandings of consciousness (for example, consciousness as mapped through a Freudian grid of id/ego/superego and unconscious/preconscious/consciousness, wherein we expect to discover who we are and to hold on to that self over time). Indeed, consciousness as apprehended under third-space feminist comparative philosophy cannot be understood only within the terms provided by cultural studies approaches to *ideology, culture,* and *consciousness.* Instead, third-space feminist liberation philosophers conceptualize consciousness as that which coalesces for each individual differently within her own matrix of mind-body-emotion. This kind of consciousness is processual, that is, its "matrixing" occurs through movement inside, through, and with each location of mind-body-emotion. Self-conscious awareness of this movement and its conjunctural points inside the matrix is understood as "meta-witnessing" work. Meta-witnessing work of this sort travels beyond the limitations of ideology. In this sense, it can be understood as a meta-Althusserian understanding of consciousness. This is the very meta-witnessing activity that Anzaldúa has identified as the work *conocimiento.*

The meta-witnessing consciousness allows its practitioners to become aware of the structural formations that give possibility to and yet limit what they have become. *Asian and Feminist Philosophies in Dialogue* itself performs this meta-witnessing work not simply through the accumulated learning, insights, realizations, and discoveries it provides, but through each scholar's different but nevertheless self-reflexive methodological approaches to analysis. The result is that these chapters document cross-cultural connections while simultaneously revealing new modes of individual/psychic and public/coalitional modes of consciousness. Wisdom politics like these are becoming an intensifying and escalating epistemological life force for all planetary beings. In *Asian and Feminist Philosophies in Dialogue*

these wisdom politics materialize in the form of a feminist comparative philosophy that is aimed toward connecting humanity through
the powers of an aesthetics of peace. This afterword is written to recognize and support this philosophy uprising. ·

Notes

1. See Anzaldúa (1981).
2. Such wisdoms are traced by decolonial philosophers such as Mao (1990),
Césaire (1951), Fanon (1963), Anzaldúa (1981), Wynter (2003), and Maldonado-
Torres (2004).
3. For examples, see Mirikatani (1972), Anzaldúa (1981, 1990), hooks (1982),
and Woo (2003).
4. See Chai (1985), Lorde (1981), Peréz (1999), and Sandoval (2000).

References

Allen, Paula Gunn. 1988. Some like Indians endure. In *Living the spirit: A gay American Indian anthology*, compiled by Gay American Indians, ed. Will Roscoe, 148.
New York: St. Martin's.
Anzaldúa, Gloria. 1981. La Prieta. In *This bridge called my back: Writings by radical
women of color*, ed. Cherrie Moraga and Gloria Anzaldúa, 198–209. Pittsburgh:
Persephone.
——, ed. 1990. Making face, making soul/Haciendo caras: Creative and critical
perspectives by women of color. San Francisco: Aunt Lute.
——. 2002. Now let us shift . . . The path of conocimiento . . . Inner work, public
acts. In *This bridge we call home*, ed. Gloria E. Anzaldúa and Analouise Keating,
540–78. New York: Routledge.
Anzaldúa, Gloria E., and Analouise Keating, eds. 2002. *This bridge we call home.*
New York: Routledge.
Césaire, Aimé. 1951. *Discours sur le colonialisme*. Paris: Présence Africaine.
Chai, Alice Yun. 1985. Toward a holistic paradigm for Asian American women's
studies: A synthesis of feminist scholarship and women of color's feminist
politics. *Women's Studies International Forum* 8:59–66.
Fanon, Frantz. 1963. *The wretched of the earth*. New York: Grove.
Frankenberg, Ruth. 2004. *Living spirit, living practice: Poetics, politics, epistemology.*
Durham, NC: Duke University Press.
hooks, bell. 1982. *Ain't I a woman? Black women and feminism*. Boston: South End.
Hull, Gloria T., Patricia Bell Scott, and Barbara Smith, eds. 1982. *All the women are
white, all the blacks are men, but some of us are brave*. New York: Feminist Press.

Ling, Amy. 1990. *Between worlds: Women writers of Chinese ancestry*. New York: Pergamon.

Lorde, Audre. 1981. Comments at Second Sex Conference, New York, September 1979. In *This bridge called my back*: Writings by radical women of color, ed. Cherrie Moraga and Gloria Anzaldúa, 98–102. Pittsburgh: Persephone.

Lugones, María. 1987. Playfulness, "world"-traveling and loving perception. *Hypatia* 2 (2): 3–19.

——. 2010. Toward a decolonial feminism. *Hypatia* 25 (4): 742–59.

Maldonado-Torres, Nelson. 2004. The topology of being and the geopolitics of knowledge: Modernity, empire, coloniality. *City* 8 (1): 29–56.

Mani, Lata. 2009. *SacredSecular: Contemplative cultural critique*. New York: Routledge.

Mao Tse-Tung. 1990. *Quotations from Chairman Mao Tse-Tung*. San Francisco: China Books and Periodicals.

Mirikitani, Janice. 1972. *Third world women*. San Francisco: Third World Communications.

Moraga, Cherrie, and Gloria Anzaldúa, eds. 1981. *This bridge called my back: Writings by radical women of color*. Pittsburgh: Persephone.

Peréz, Emma. 1999. The poetics of an (inter)nationalist revolution: El partido liberal Mexicano, third space feminism in the United States. In *The decolonial imaginary: Writing Chicanas into history*, 55–75. Bloomington: Indiana University Press.

Sandoval, Chela. 1991. U.S. third world feminism: The theory and method of oppositional consciousness in the postmodern world. *Genders* 10:1–23.

——. 2000. *Methodology of the oppressed*. Minneapolis: University of Minnesota Press.

——. 2006. Chela Sandoval: Interview. In *Spectator Journal: Chicana spectators and mediamakers: Imagining transcultural diversity*, ed. Osa Hidalgo de la Riva, 89–94. Los Angeles: University of Southern California Press.

Woo, Merle. 2003. *Three Asian American writers speak out on feminism*. Berkley: Red Letter.

Wynter, Sylvia. 2003. Unsettling the coloniality of being/power/truth/freedom: Towards the human, after man, its over-representation—an argument. *CR: The New Centennial Review* 3 (3): 257–337.

Feminist Comparative Philosophy and Associated Methodologies

A Bibliography

·

The purpose of this bibliography is to provide readers with a sense of what has already been published in the emerging field of feminist comparative philosophy and to serve as an invitation to further explore its literature, history, and methodologies. Consistent with our present desire to render visible those philosophical inquiries that emerge jointly from the insights of feminist and Asian traditions, we have limited our list of publications in feminist comparative philosophy to those that engage Asian philosophical texts. However, as explained in this book's introduction, we believe that many other pairings of cultural and social locations are consistent with feminist comparative practice and we hope that the future of this field will blossom with a diversity of fresh juxtapositions. In regard to this bibliography's sections on "Feminist Methodology" and "Comparative Methodology," we have sought to list only those resources that speak to these philosophical methodologies *in general* and have therefore not included publications on specialized methodologies like those used to address, for example, feminist ethics or Chinese-Greek comparisons. Moreover, our accounts of feminist methodology and comparative methodology respectively reflect those sources most relevant to the development and proliferation of feminist comparative practice, rather than to different or broader understandings of feminism and comparative studies.

Feminist Comparative Philosophy

Allen, Douglas. 1997. Social constructions of self: Some Asian, Marxist, and feminist critiques of dominant Western views of self. In *Culture and self*, ed. Douglas Allen, 3–26. Boulder: Westview.

Arisaka, Yoko. 2000. Asian women: Invisibility, locations, and claims to philosophy. In *Women of color in philosophy*, ed. Naomi Zack, 209–34. Malden, MA: Blackwell.

Aristarkhova, Irina. 2012. Thou shall not harm all living beings: Feminism, Jainism, and animals. *Hypatia* 27 (3): 636–50.

Bailey, Cathryn. 2009. Embracing the icon: The feminist potential of the trans Bodhisattva, Kuan Yin. *Hypatia* 24 (3): 178–96.

Barlow, Tani. 1994. Theorizing woman: *Funü, guojia, jiating* (Chinese women, Chinese state, Chinese family). In *Scattered hegemonies: Postmodernity and transnational feminist practices*, ed. Inderpal Grewal and Caren Kaplan, 173–96. Minneapolis: University of Minnesota Press.

Birdwhistell, Joanne D. 2007. *Mencius and masculinities: Dynamics of power, morality, and maternal thinking.* Albany: State University of New York Press.

Bose, Mandakranta. 2004. Confrontation, transgression, and submission: Ideals of womanhood in the *Manasāmaṇgala*. In *Playing for real: Hindu role models, religion, and gender*, ed. Jacqueline Suthren Hirst and Lynn Thomas, 102–16. New York: Oxford University Press.

Brandli, Mara. 2011. Radicalizing feminist theory with Marx and Buddha. *Dialogue: Journal of Phi Sigma Tau* 54 (1): 42–49.

Butnor, Ashby. 2001. Self and social engagement in Zen Buddhism and Western feminism. *East-West Connections* 1 (1): 29–47.

——. 2011. Cultivating self, transforming society: Embodied ethical practice in feminism and Zen Buddhism. In *Buddhism as a stronghold of free thinking? Social, ethical, and philosophical dimensions of Buddhism*, ed. Siegfried C. A. Fay and Ilse Maria Bruckner, 56–74. Nuestall, Germany: Ubuntu.

——, and Jen McWeeny. 2009. Why feminist comparative philosophy? *American Philosophical Association Newsletter on Asian and Asian American Philosophers and Philosophies* 9 (1): 4–5.

Chan, Sin Yee. 2008. Gender and relationship roles in the *Analects* and the *Mencius*. In *Confucian political ethics*, ed. D. Bell, 147–74. Princeton: Princeton University Press.

Chen, Ellen Marie. 1974. Tao as the great mother and the influence of motherly love in the shaping of Chinese philosophy. *History of Religions* 14 (1): 51–64.

Chen, Ya-chen. 2011. *The many dimensions of Chinese feminism.* New York: Palgrave Macmillan.

Dalmiya, Vrinda. 1993. Are old wives' tales justified? In *Feminist epistemologies*, ed. Linda Alcoff and Elizabeth Potter, 217–44. New York: Routledge.

——. 1998a. Not just "staying alive." *Journal of Indian Council of Philosophical Research* 15 (3): 97–116.

——. 1998b. The Indian subcontinent. In *A companion to feminist philosophy*, ed. Alison M. Jaggar and Iris Marion Young, 118–27. Malden, MA: Blackwell.

——. 2000. Loving paradoxes: A feminist reclamation of the goddess Kali. *Hypatia* 15 (1): 125–50.

——. 2001a. Dogged loyalties: A classical Indian intervention in care ethics. In *Ethics in the world religions*, ed. Joseph Runzo and Nancy M. Martin, 293–308. New York: Oxford University Press.

——. 2001b. Particularizing the moral self: A feminist-Buddhist exchange. *Sophia* 40 (1): 61–72.

——. 2002. Cows and others: Toward constructing ecofeminist selves. *Environmental Ethics* 24 (2): 149–68.

——. 2007. Unraveling leadership: "Relational humility" and the search for ignorance. In *Changing education: Leadership, innovation and development in a globalizing Asia-Pacific*, ed. Peter D. Hershock, Mark Mason, and John N. Hawkins, 297–322. Dordrecht: Springer.

——. 2009. Caring comparisons: Thoughts on comparative care ethics. *Journal of Chinese Philosophy* 36 (2): 192–209.

——. 2009. The metaphysics of ethical love: Comparing practical Vedanta and feminist ethics. *Sophia* 48 (3): 221–35.

Despeux, Catherine, and Livia Kohn. 2003. *Women in Daoism*. Cambridge: Three Pines.

Dhand, Arti. 2008. *Woman as fire, woman as sage: Sexual ideology in the Mahabharata*. Albany: State University of New York Press.

Foust, Matthew. 2008. Perplexities of filiality: Confucius and Jane Addams on the private/public distinction. *Asian Philosophy* 18 (2): 149–66.

Galia, Patt-Shamir. 2009. Learning and women: Confucianism revisited. *Journal of Chinese Philosophy* 36 (2): 243–60.

Goldin, Paul Rakita. 2000. The view of women in early Confucianism. In *The sage and the second sex: Confucianism, ethics, and gender*, ed. Chenyang Li, 133–62. Chicago: Open Court.

Goswami, Namita. 2008. Auto-phagia and queer trans-nationality: Compulsory hetero-imperial masculinity in Deepa Mehta's *Fire*. *Signs* 33 (2): 343–69.

Goswami, Namita, and Paul B. Courtright. 2001. Who was Roop Kanwar? *Sati*, law, religion, and postcolonial feminism. In *Religion and personal law in secular India: A call to judgment*, ed. Gerald James Larson, 200–25. Bloomington: Indiana University Press.

Gu, Linyu. 2000. Process and *shin no jiko* (true self): A critique of feminist interpretation of "self-emptying." *Journal of Chinese Philosophy* 27 (2): 201–13.

——. 2009a. Contemporary feminism vs. Chinese thought? A metaphysical inquiry. *American Philosophical Association Newsletter on Asian and Asian American Philosophers and Philosophies* 9 (1): 8–11.

——. 2009b. Preface: Contemporaneity and feminism. *Journal of Chinese Philosophy* 36 (2): 185–86.

——. 2009c. "Waiting for Godot"? Contemporaneity, feminism, creativity. *Journal of Chinese Philosophy* 36 (2): 313–33.

Hall, David L., and Roger T. Ames. 2000. Sexism, with Chinese characteristics. In *The sage and the second sex: Confucianism, ethics, and gender*, ed. Chenyang Li, 75–96. Chicago: Open Court.

282

Herr, Ranjoo Seodu. 1993a. Feminism and autonomy (in Korean). *Philosophy and Reality*: 227–42.

——. 1993b. A feminist challenge to L. Kohlberg's moral development theory (in Korean). *Major Issues in Social Philosophy* III, 328–52. Seoul: Mineum.

——. 1995. Is cultural diversity compatible with feminism: Confucianism and the women's cause. *Journal of American Studies* (Korean) 27: 153–70.

——. 1996. Overcoming "femininity" and "masculinity" (in Korean). In *Philosophy and Emotion*, 175–212. Seoul: Mineum.

—— trans. 1997. *Darun moksoriro* (Korean translation of *In a different voice* by Carol Gilligan). Seoul, South Korea: Dong-Nyuk.

——. 2003a. Is Confucianism compatible with care ethics? A critique. *Philosophy East and West* 53 (4): 471–89.

——. 2003b. The possibility of nationalist feminism. *Hypatia* 18 (3): 135–60.

——. 2004. A third world feminist defense of multiculturalism. *Social Theory and Practice*: 30 (1): 73–103.

——. 2008. Politics of difference and nationalism: On Iris Young's global vision. *Hypatia* 23 (3): 39–59.

——. 2010. Japan's national responsibility toward comfort women (translated into Korean). *Journal of Asiatic Studies* 53 (3): 7–40.

Hiltebeitel, Alf, and Kathleen M. Erndl. 2000. *Is the goddess a feminist? The politics of South Asian goddesses*. New York: New York University Press.

Hu, Hsiao-Lan. 2007. Rectification of the four teachings in Chinese culture. In *Violence against women in contemporary world religion: Roots and cures*, ed. Daniel C. Maguire and Sa'diyya Shaikh, 108–30. Cleveland: Pilgrim.

——. 2011. *This-worldly nibbāna: A Buddhist-feminist social ethic for peacemaking in the global community*. Albany: State University of New York Press.

Ivanhoe, Philip J. 2000. Menzi, Xunzi and modern feminist ethics. In *The sage and the second sex: Confucianism, ethics, and gender*, ed. Chenyang Li, 57–74. Chicago: Open Court.

——. 2009. Introductory remarks. *Journal of Chinese Philosophy* 36 (2): 187–91.

Iveković, Rada. 1990. *Orients: Critique de la raison postmoderne*. Paris: Noël Blandin.

——. 2000a. Introduction. Trans. Penelope Deutscher. *Hypatia* 15 (4): 221–23.

——. 2000b. Coincidences of comparison. Trans. Penelope Deutscher. *Hypatia* 15 (4): 224–35.

Jiang, Xinyan. 2000. The dilemma faced by Chinese feminists. *Hypatia* 15 (3): 140–60.

——. 2009. Confucianism, women, and social contexts. *Journal of Chinese Philosophy* 36 (2): 228–42.

Kalmanson, Leah. 2012. Buddhism and bell hooks. Liberatory aesthetics and the radical subjectivity of no-self. *Hypatia* 27 (4): 810–27.

Klein, Anne C. 1994. Presence with a difference: Buddhists and feminists on subjectivity. *Hypatia* 9 (4): 112–30.

——. 1995. *Meeting the great bliss queen: Buddhists, feminists, and the art of the self.* Boston: Beacon.

Ko, Dorothy, JaHyun Kim Haboush, and Joan R. Piggott. 2003. *Women and Confucian cultures in premodern China, Korea, and Japan.* Berkeley: University of California Press.

Kupperman, Joel. 2000. Feminism as radical Confucianism: Self and tradition. In *The sage and the second sex: Confucianism, ethics, and gender,* ed. Chenyang Li, 43–56. Chicago: Open Court.

Lai, Karyn. 2000a. The *Daodejing*: Resources for contemporary feminist thinking. *Journal of Chinese Philosophy* 27 (2): 131.

——. 2000b. Introduction: Feminism and Chinese philosophy. *Journal of Chinese Philosophy* 27 (2): 127–30.

——. 2006. *Learning from Chinese philosophies: Ethics of interdependent and contextualised self.* London: Ashgate.

Lal, Sanjay. 2008. Gandhi's universal ethic and feminism: Shared starting points but divergent ends. *Asian Philosophy* 18 (2): 185–95.

Lee, Pauline. 2000. Li Zhi and John Stuart Mill: A Confucian feminist critique of liberal feminism. In *The sage and the second sex: Confucianism, ethics, and gender,* ed. Chenyang Li, 113–32. Chicago: Open Court.

Li, Chengyang. 1994. The Confucian concept of jen and the feminist ethics of care: A comparative study. *Hypatia* 9 (1): 70–89.

——. 1999. Ethics: Confucian *jen* and feminist care. In *The Tao encounters the West: Explorations in comparative philosophy,* 89–114. Albany: State University of New York Press.

——. 2000a. Confucianism and feminist concerns: Overcoming the Confucian "gender complex." *Journal of Chinese Philosophy* 27 (2): 187–99.

——. 2000b. Introduction: Can Confucianism come to terms with feminism? In *The sage and the second sex: Confucianism, ethics, and gender,* ed. Chenyang Li, 1–22. Chicago: Open Court.

——, ed. 2000c. *The sage and the second sex: Confucianism, ethics, and gender.* Chicago: Open Court.

——. 2002. Revisiting Confucian *jen* ethics and feminist care ethics: A reply to Daniel Star and Lijun Yuan. *Hypatia* 17 (1): 130–40.

Liu, Lydia. 1994. The female body and nationalist discourse: *The field of life and death* revisited. In *Scattered hegemonies: Postmodernity and transnational feminist practices,* ed. Inderpal Grewal and Caren Kaplan, 37–62. Minneapolis: University of Minnesota Press.

Luo, Shirong. 2007. Relation, virtue, and relational virtue: Three concepts of caring. *Hypatia* 22 (3): 92–110.

Ma, Lin. 2009. Character of the feminine in Lévinas and the *Daodejing. Journal of Chinese Philosophy* 36 (2): 261–76.

Man, Eva Kit Wah. 2000. Contemporary feminist body theories and Mencius's ideas of body and mind. *Journal of Chinese Philosophy* 27 (2): 155–69.

284

FEMINIST COMPARATIVE PHILOSOPHY AND ASSOCIATED METHODOLOGIES

McCarthy, Erin. 2003. Ethics in the between. *Philosophy, Culture, and Traditions* 2:63–77.

———. 2008a. Towards peaceful bodies. In *Philosophieren über den Krieg: War in Eastern and Western philosophies*, ed. Hans-Georg Moeller and Günter Wohlfart, 147–64. Berlin: Parerga.

———. 2008b. Towards a transnational ethics of care. In *Frontiers of Japanese philosophy II: Neglected themes and hidden variations*, ed. James Heisig, Victor Hori, and Melissa Curley, 113–28. Nagoya: Nanzan Insitute for Religion and Culture.

———. 2009a. Relations entre-deux: Une étude feministe de Watsuji. In *Enjeux de la philosophie japonaise du XXe siècle*, ed. Jacynthe Tremblay. Montréal: Presses de l'Université de Montréal.

———. 2009b. Vers une ethique transnationale de la solicitude. In *La modernité philosophique en Asie*, ed. Veronique Alexandre Journeau, 153–74. Perros Guirec: Anagrammes.

———. 2010. Beyond the binary: Watsuji and Irigaray in dialogue. In *Japanese and continental philosophy: Conversations with the Kyoto school*, ed. Bret Davis, Brian Schroeder, and Jason Wirth, 212–28. Bloomington: Indiana University Press.

———. 2010. *Ethics embodied*. Lanham, MD: Lexington.

McWeeny, Jennifer. 2010. Liberating anger, embodying knowledge: A comparative study of María Lugones and Zen Master Hakuin. *Hypatia* 25 (2): 295–315.

Miller, Mara. 2002. Ethics in the female voice: Murasaki Shikibu and the framing of ethics for Japan. In *Varieties of ethical reflection: New directions for ethics in a global context*, ed. Michael Barnhart, 175–202. Lanham, MD: Lexington.

Nylan, Michael. 2000. Golden spindles and axes: Elite women in the Achaemenid and Han empires. In *The sage and the second sex: Confucianism, ethics, and gender*, ed. Chenyang Li, 199–222. Chicago: Open Court.

Pang-White, Ann A. 2009a. Chinese philosophy and woman: Is reconciliation possible? *American Philosophical Association Newsletter on Asian and Asian American Philosophers and Philosophies* 9 (1): 1–2.

———. 2009b. Reconstructing modern ethics: Confucian care ethics. *Journal of Chinese Philosophy* 36 (2): 210–227.

Pauwels, Heidi. 2004. Is love still stronger than *Dharma*? Whatever happened to Sita's choice and the *Gopis's* voice? In *Playing for real: Hindu role models, religion, and gender*, ed. Jacqueline Suthren Hirst and Lynn Thomas, 117–40. New York: Oxford University Press.

Peach, Lucinda Joy. 2002. Human rights law, religion, and the gendered moral order. In *Varieties of ethical reflection: New directions for ethics in a global context*, ed. Michael Barnhart, 203–34. Lanham, MD: Lexington.

Powers, John and Deane Curtin. 1994. Mothering: Moral cultivation in Buddhist and feminist ethics. *Philosophy East and West* 44 (1): 1–18.

Raphals, Lisa. 1998. *Sharing the light: Representations of women and virtue in early China*. Albany: State University of New York Press.

——. 2000. Gendered virtue reconsidered: Notes from the warring states and Han. In *The sage and the second sex: Confucianism, ethics, and gender,* ed. Chenyang Li, 223–48. Chicago: Open Court.

——. 2009. Feminism, Chinese philosophy, and history. *American Philosophical Association Newsletter on Asian and Asian American Philosophers and Philosophies* 9 (1): 4–5.

Rosemont, Henry. 1997. Classical Confucian and contemporary feminist perspectives on the self: Some parallels and their implications. In *Culture and self,* ed. Douglas Allen, 63–82. Boulder: Westview.

Rosenlee, Li-Hsiang Lisa. 2004. *Neiwai,* civility, and gender distinctions. *Asian Philosophy* 14 (1): 41–58.

——. 2006. *Confucianism and women: A philosophical interpretation.* Albany: State University of New York Press.

——. 2009. What is the use of philosophy in general and Asian philosophy in particular to feminism? *American Philosophical Association Newsletter on Asian and Asian American Philosophers and Philosophies* 9 (1): 3–4.

——. 2010. Confucian trajectories on environmental understanding. In *Confucianism in context: Classic philosophy and contemporary issues, East Asia and beyond,* ed. Wonsuk Chang and Leah Kalmanson, 191–210. Albany: State University of New York Press.

Saldanha, Arun. 2012. Against yin-yang: The dao of feminist universalism. *Angelaki* 17 (2): 145–68.

Schafer, Ingrid. 2000. From Confucius through ecofeminism to partnership ethics. In *The sage and the second sex: Confucianism, ethics, and gender,* ed. Chenyang Li, 97–112. Chicago: Open Court.

Son, Heung-Chul. 2005. Globalization, eco-feminism, and Im-Yunjidang's philosophy. *Prajña Vihara: Journal of Philosophy and Religion* 6 (1): 108–35.

Stepaniants, M. N. 1992. The image of woman in religious consciousness: Past, present, and future. *Philosophy East and West* 42 (2): 239–47.

Tao, Julia Po-Wah Lai. 2000. Two perspectives of care: Confucian *ren* and feminist care. *Journal of Chinese Philosophy* 27 (2): 215–40.

Tsomo, Karma Lekshe, ed. 1999. *Buddhist women across cultures: Realizations.* Albany: State University of New York Press.

Wang, Robin R. 2003. *Images of women in Chinese thought and culture: Writings from the pre-Qin period to the Song dynasty.* Indianapolis: Hackett.

——. 2005. Dong Zhongshu's transformation of yin/yang theory and contesting of gender identity. *Philosophy East and West* 55 (2): 209–232.

——. 2006. Virtue, talent, and beauty: Authoring a full-fledged womanhood in Lienuzhuan (biographies of women). In *Authority in the Confucian culture,* ed. Peter Hershock and Roger T. Ames, 93–115. Albany: State University of New York Press.

——. 2009. *Kundao:* A lived body in female Daoism. *Journal of Chinese Philosophy* 36 (2): 277–92.

Wawrytko, Sandra A. 1981. *The undercurrent of "feminine" philosophy in Eastern and Western thought.* Lanham, MD: Rowman and Littlefield.

——. 1989. Beyond liberation: Overcoming gender mythology from a Taoist perspective. In *Movements and issues in world religions: A sourcebook and an analysis of developments since 1945,* ed. Charles Wei-hsun Fu and Gerhard E. Spiegler, 105–122. Westport, CT: Greenwood.

——. 1991. The path to ultimate awakening: Women's liberation in the context of Taoism and Zen. In *Buddhist ethics and modern society: An international symposium,* ed. Charles Wei-hsün Fu and Sandra A. Wawrytko, 265–80. Westport, CT: Greenwood.

——. 1994. Sexism in the early *sangha*: Its social basis and philosophical dissolution. In *Buddhist behavioral codes (sila/vinaya) in the modern world,* ed. Charles Wei-hsün Fu and Sandra A. Wawrytko, 265–80. Westport, CT: Greenwood.

——. 1995. The "feminine" mode of mysticism. In *Mysticism and mystical experience: East and West,* ed. Donald H. Bishop, 195–229. Selingsgrove, PA: Susquehanna University Press.

——. 2000a. Kong Zi as feminist: Confucian self-cultivation in a contemporary context. *Journal of Chinese Philosophy* 27 (2): 171–86.

——. 2000b. Prudery and prurience: Historical roots of the Confucian conundrum concerning women, sexuality, and power. In *The sage and the second sex: Confucianism, ethics, and gender,* ed. Chenyang Li, 164–97. Chicago: Open Court.

——. 2009a. Buddhism: Philosophy beyond gender. *Journal of Chinese Philosophy* 36 (2): 293–312.

——. 2009b. Feminism and/in Asian philosophies. *American Philosophical Association Newsletter on Asian and Asian American Philosophers and Philosophies* 9 (1): 5–8.

Wei, Xiao. 2007. Caring: Confucianism, feminism, and Christian ethics. *Contemporary Chinese Thought* 39 (2): 32–48.

Woo, Terry Tak-ling. 2009. Emotions and self-cultivation in *nü lunyu* (*women's analects*). *Journal of Chinese Philosophy* 36 (2): 334–47.

Yuan, Lijun. 2002. Ethics of care and concept of *jen*: A reply to Chenyang Li. *Hypatia* 17 (1): 107–29.

Feminist Methodology

Addelson, Kathryn Pyne. 1994. Feminist philosophy and the women's movement. *Hypatia* 9 (3): 216–24.

Alcoff, Linda. 1988. Cultural feminism versus post-structuralism: The identity crisis in feminist theory. *Signs* 13 (3): 405–36.

——. 1997. Philosophy and racial identity. *Philosophy Today* 41 (1): 67–76.

——. 1998. What should white people do? *Hypatia* 13 (3): 6–26.

Al-Hibri, Azizah Y. 1999. Is Western patriarchal feminism good for third world/minority women? In *Is Multiculturalism bad for women?* ed. Joshua Cohen, Matthew Howard and Martha C. Nussbaum, 41–46. Princeton: Princeton University Press.

Allen, Paula Gunn. 1986. Kochinnenako in academe: Three approaches to interpreting a Keres Indian tale. In *The sacred hoop: Recovering the feminine in American Indian traditions*, 222–44. Boston: Beacon.

Alvarez, Sonia A., Elisabeth Jay Friedman, Ericka Beckman, Maylei Blackwell, Norma Chinchilla, Nathalie Lebon, Marysa Navarro, and Marcela Ríos. 2002. Encountering Latin American and Caribbean feminisms. *Signs* 28 (2): 537–80.

Amos, Valerie, and Pratibha Parmar. 1984. Challenging imperial feminism. *Feminist Review* 17:3–19.

Ang, Ien. 1995. I'm a feminist but . . . "Other" women and postnational feminism. In *Transitions: New Australian feminisms*, ed. Barbara Caine and Rosemary Pringle, 57–73. New York: St. Martin's.

Anzaldúa, Gloria. 1999. *Borderlands/La frontera: The new mestiza*. 2d ed. San Francisco: Aunt Lute.

———. 2002. Now let us shift . . . The path of conocimiento . . . Inner work, public acts. In *This bridge we call home*, ed. Gloria E. Anzaldúa and Analouise Keating, 540–78. New York: Routledge.

Bailey, Alison. 1998. Locating traitorous identities: Toward a view of privilege-cognizant white character. *Hypatia* 13 (3): 27–42.

Bartky, Sandra Lee. 1990. *Femininity and domination: Studies in the phenomenology of oppression*. New York: Routledge.

Benhabib, Seyla. 2002. "Nous" et les "autres": Is universalism ethnocentric? In *The claims of culture: Equality and diversity in the global era*, 24–48. Princeton: Princeton University Press.

Bordo, Susan. 1988. The feminist as Other. In *Philosophy in a feminist voice: Critiques and reconstructions*, ed. Janet A. Kourany, 298–312. Princeton: Princeton University Press.

———. 1992. Feminist skepticism and the "maleness" of philosophy. In *Women and reason*, ed. Elizabeth D. Harvey and Kathleen Okruhlik, 143–62. Ann Arbor: University of Michigan Press.

Braidotti, Rosi. 1991. Feminist discursive tactics in philosophy; or, I think therefore he is. In *Patterns of dissonance: A study of women in contemporary philosophy*, trans. Elizabeth Guild, 174–208. Oxford: Polity.

———. 1994. Ethics revisited: Women and/in philosophy. In *Nomadic subjects: Embodiment and sexual difference in contemporary feminist theory*, 213–31. New York: Columbia University Press.

Chai, Alice Yun. 1985. Toward a holistic paradigm for Asian American women's studies: A synthesis of feminist scholarship and women of color's feminist politics. *Women's Studies International Forum* 8: 26–41.

Christian, Barbara. 1994. Diminishing returns: Can black feminists survive the academy? In *Multiculturalism: A reader*, ed. David Theo Goldberg, 168–179. Cambridge: Blackwell.

Cixous, Hélène. 1976. The laugh of the medusa. Trans. Keith Cohen and Paula Cohen. *Signs* 1 (4): 875–93.

Code, Lorraine. 1993. Taking subjectivity into account. In *Feminist epistemologies*, ed. Linda Alcoff and Elizabeth Potter, 15–48. New York: Routledge.

———. 1995. Must a feminist be a relativist after all? In *Rhetorical spaces: Essays on gendered locations*, 185–207. New York: Routledge.

Collins, Patricia Hill. 2000. *Black feminist thought: Knowledge, consciousness, and the politics of empowerment.* New York: Routledge.

Crenshaw, Kimberlé Williams. 1994. Mapping the margins: Intersectionality, identity politics, and violence against women of color. In *The public nature of private violence: The discovery of domestic abuse*, ed. Martha Albertson and Roxanne Mykitiuk Fineman, 93–118. New York: Routledge.

Cordova, V. F. 2000. Exploring the sources of Western thought. In *Women of color and philosophy: A critical reader*, ed. Naomi Zack, 69–90. Malden, MA: Blackwell.

DuCille, Ann. 1994. The occult of true black womanhood: Critical demeanor and black feminist studies. *Signs* 19 (3): 591–629.

Ferguson, Ann. 1994. Twenty years of feminist philosophy. *Hypatia* 9 (3): 197–215.

Ferguson, Kathy E. 1991. Interpretation and genealogy in feminism. *Signs* 16 (2): 322–39.

———. 1993. *The man question: Visions of subjectivity in feminist theory.* Berkeley: University of California Press.

Fraser, Nancy, and Linda Nicholson. 1990. Social criticism without philosophy: An encounter between feminism and postmodernism. In *Feminism/postmodernism*, ed. Linda J. Nicholson, 19–38. New York: Routledge.

Friedman, Susan Stanford. 1995. Beyond white and other: Relationality and narratives of race in feminist discourse. *Signs* 21 (1): 1–49.

Frye, Marilyn. 1983. *The politics of reality.* Berkeley: Crossing.

Garry, Ann. 1995. A minimally decent philosophical method? Analytic philosophy and feminism. *Hypatia* 10 (3): 7–30.

Gines, Kathryn T. 2011. Being a black woman philosopher: Reflections on founding the collegium of black women philosophers. *Hypatia* 26 (2): 429–37.

Gould, Carol C. 1976. The woman question: Philosophy of liberation and the liberation of philosophy. In *Women and philosophy: Toward a theory of liberation*, ed. Carol C. Gould and Marx Wartofsky, 5–44. New York: Perigee.

Grewal, Inderpal, and Caren Kaplan. 1994. Introduction: Transnational feminist practices and questions of postmodernity. In *Scattered hegemonies: Postmodernity and transnational feminist practices*, ed. Inderpal Grewal and Caren Kaplan, 1–36. Minneapolis: University of Minnesota Press.

Grimshaw, Jean. 1986. *Philosophy and feminist thinking.* Minneapolis: University of Minnesota Press.

Haraway, Donna J. 1991. Situated knowledges: The science question in feminism and the privilege of partial perspective. In *Simians, cyborgs, and women: The reinvention of nature*, 183–202. New York: Routledge.

Harding, Sandra. 1987. Is there a feminist method? In *Feminism and methodology*, ed. Sandra Harding, 1–14. Bloomington: Indiana University Press.

Harding, Sandra, and Merrill B. Hintikka. 1983. Introduction. In *Discovering reality: Feminist perspectives on epistemology, metaphysics, methodology, and philosophy of science*, ed. Sandra Harding and Merrill B. Hintikka, ix–xix. Dordrecht, Holland: Reidel.

Hernandez, Adriana. 1989. A pedagogy of difference: Feminist theory, plurality of voices and cultural imperialism. *Philosophical Studies in Education* 13: 59–71.

Holland, Nancy. 1990. *Is women's philosophy possible?* Savage, MD: Rowman and Littlefield.

hooks, bell. 1984. *Feminist theory from margin to center*. Cambridge: South End.

——. 1994. *Teaching to transgress: Education as the practice of freedom*. New York: Routledge.

Hurtado, Aída. 1998. *Sitios y lenguas*: Chicanas theorize feminisms. *Hypatia* 13 (2): 134–61.

——. 1996. Strategic suspensions: Feminist of color theorize the production of knowledge. In *Knowledge, difference, and power*, ed. Nancy Rule Goldberger, Jill Mattuck Tarule, Blythe McVicker Clinchy, and Mary Field Belensky, 372–92. New York: HarperCollins.

Jaggar, Allison M., ed. 2008. *Just methods: An interdisciplinary feminist reader*. Boulder: Paradigm.

Kaplan, Caren. 1987. Deterritorializations: The rewriting of home and exile in Western feminist discourse. *Cultural Critique* 6:187–98.

——. 1994. The politics of location as transnational feminist critical practice. In *Scattered hegemonies: Postmodernity and transnational feminist practices*, ed. Inderpal Grewal and Caren Kaplan, 137–52. Minneapolis: University of Minnesota Press.

——. 1996. *Questions of travel: Postmodern discourses of displacement*. Durham: Duke University Press.

Kishwar, Madhu. 1990. Why I don't call myself a feminist. *Manushi* 61: 2–8.

Kourany, Janet. 1998. Philosophy in a feminist voice? In *Philosophy in a feminist voice: Critiques and reconstructions*, ed. Janet Kourany, 3–16. Princeton: Princeton University Press.

Lal, Jayati, Kristin McGuire, Abigail J. Steward, Magdalena Zaborowska, and Justine Pas. 2010. Recasting global feminism: Toward a comparative historical approach to women's activism and scholarship. *Feminist Studies* 36 (1): 13–39.

LeDeouff, Michelle. 2003. *The sex of knowing*. Trans. Kathryn Hamer and Lorraine Code. New York: Routledge.

Lindemann, Kate. 2001. Persons with adult-onset head injury: A crucial resource for feminist philosophers. *Hypatia* 16 (4): 105–23.

Lloyd, Genevieve. 1984. *Man of reason: "Male" and "female" in Western philosophy*. Minneapolis: University of Minnesota Press.

Lorde, Audre. 1984. *Sister outsider: Essays and speeches by Audre Lorde*. Berkeley: Crossing.

Lugones, María. 1987. Playfulness, "world"-traveling and loving perception. *Hypatia* 2 (2): 3–19.

———. 1991. On the logic of pluralist feminism. In *Feminist ethics*, ed. Claudia Card, 35–44. Lawrence: University Press of Kansas.

———. 2003. *Pilgrimages/peregrinajes: Theorizing coalition against multiple oppressions.* Lanham, MD: Rowman and Littlefield.

———. 2006. On complex communication. *Hypatia* 21 (3): 75–85.

———. 2007. Heterosexualism and the colonial/modern gender system. *Hypatia* 22 (1): 186–209.

———. 2010. Toward a decolonial feminism. *Hypatia* 25 (4): 742–59.

———, and Elizabeth V. Spelman. 1983. Have we got a theory for you! Feminist theory, cultural imperialism, and the demand for "the woman's voice." *Women's Studies International Forum* 6 (6): 573–81.

MacKinnon, Catherine A. 1982. Feminism, Marxism, method, and the state: An agenda for theory. *Signs* 7 (3): 515–44.

———. 1989. *Toward a feminist theory of the state.* Cambridge: Harvard University Press.

Martin, Biddy, and Chandra Talpade Mohanty. 1986. Feminist politics: What's home got to do with it? In *Feminist studies/Critical studies*, ed. Teresa de Lauretis, 191–212. Bloomington: Indiana University Press.

Maynard, Mary. 1994. Race, gender, and the concept of "difference." In *The dynamics of "race" and gender*, ed. Heleh Afshar and Mary Maynard, 9–25. New York: Taylor and Francis.

McAlister, Linda Lopez. 1994. On the possibility of feminist philosophy. *Hypatia* 9 (3): 188–96.

McDowell, Deborah E. 1992. Recycling: Race, gender and the practice of theory. In *Studies in historical change*, ed. Ralph Cohen, 246–63. Charlottesville: University Press of Virginia.

Mohanty, Chandra. 1984. Under Western eyes: Feminist scholarship and colonial discourses. *Boundary 2* 12(3)/13(1): 333–58.

———. 1991. Cartographies of struggle: Third world women and the politics of feminism. In *Third world women and the politics of feminism*, ed. Chandra Talpade Mohanty, Ann Russo, and Lourdes Torres, 1–50. Bloomington: Indiana University Press.

———. 2003. *Feminism without borders: Decolonizing theory, practicing solidarity.* Durham: Duke University Press.

Moulton, Janice. 1989. A paradigm of philosophy: The adversary method. In *Women, knowledge, and reality: Explorations in feminist philosophy*, ed. Ann Garry and Marilyn Pearsall, 5–20. Boston: Unwin Hyman.

Namaste, Viviane. 2009. Undoing theory: The "transgender question" and the epistemic violence of Anglo-American feminist theory. *Hypatia* 24 (3): 11–32.

Narayan, Uma. 1988. Working together across difference: Some considerations on emotions and political practice. *Hypatia* 3 (2): 31–48.

———. 1997. *Dislocating cultures: Identities, traditions, and third world feminism.* New York: Routledge.

———. 1998. Essence of culture and a sense of history: A feminist critique of cultural essentialism. *Hypatia* 13 (2): 86–106.

Nelson, James Lindemann. 2007. Philosophy in a dissonant key. *Hypatia* 22 (3): 223–33.

Nicholson, Linda. 1999. Bringing it all back home: Reason in the twilight of foundationalism. In *The play of reason: From the modern to the postmodern,* 117–28. Ithaca: Cornell University Press.

Ong, Aihwa. 1988. Colonialism and modernity: Feminist re-presentations of women in non-Western societies. *Inscriptions* 3, 4: 79–93.

Ortega, Mariana. 2006. Being lovingly, knowingly ignorant: White feminism and women of color. *Hypatia* 21 (3): 56–74.

Oyewumi, Oyeronke. 1997. Invention of women: Making an African sense of Western gender discourses. Minneapolis: University of Minnesota Press.

———. 2001. Multiculturalism or multibodism: On the impossible intersections of race and gender in American white feminist and black nationalist discourses. In *Black studies: Current issues, enduring questions,* ed. Claudine Michel and Jacqueline Bobo, 57–67. Dubuque, IA: Kendall/Hunt.

Ramazanoğlu, Caroline, with Janet Holland. 2002. *Feminist methodology: Challenges and choices.* London: Sage.

Sandoval, Chela. 1991. U.S. third world feminism: The theory and method of oppositional consciousness in the postmodern world. *Genders* 10: 1–23.

———. 1995. Feminist forms of agency and oppositional consciousness: U.S. third world feminist criticism. In *Provoking agents: Gender and agency in theory and practice,* ed. Judith Kegan Gardiner, 208–26. Urbana: University of Illinois Press.

———. 2000. *Methodology of the oppressed.* Minneapolis: University of Minnesota Press.

———. 2002. Dissident globalizations, emancipatory methods, social-erotics. In *Queer globalizations: Citizenship and the afterlife of colonialism,* ed. Arnaldo Cruz-Malave and Martin Manalansan, 20–32. New York: New York University Press.

———. 2006. Chela Sandoval: Interview. In *Chicana spectators and mediamakers: Imagining transcultural diversity,* ed. Osa Hidalgo de la Riva, 89–94. Los Angeles: University of Santa Cruz Press.

Schutte, Ofelia. 1998. Cultural alterity: Cross-cultural communication and feminist theory in North-South contexts. *Hypatia* 13 (2): 53–72.

Sherwin, Susan. 1988. Philosophical methodology and feminist methodology: Are they compatible? In *Feminist perspectives: Philosophical essays on methods and morals,* ed. Lorraine Code, Sheila Mullett, and Christine Overall, 13–28. Toronto: University of Toronto Press.

Sholock, Adale. 2012. Methodology of the privileged: White anti-racist feminism, systematic ignorance, and epistemic uncertainty. *Hypatia* 27 (4): 701–14.

Spelman, Elizabeth V. 1988. *Inessential woman: Problems of exclusion in feminist thought.* Boston: Beacon.

Springer, Kimberly. 2002. Third wave black feminism? *Signs* 27 (4): 1059–82.

Spivak, Gayatri. 1988. Can the subaltern speak? In *Marxism and the interpretation of culture*, ed. Cary Nelson and Lawrence Grossberg, 271–313. Urbana: University of Illinois Press.

———. 1996. Transnationality and multiculturalist ideology: Interview with Gayatri Spivak. In *Between the lines: South Asians and postcoloniality*, ed. Deepika Bahri and Mary Vasudeva, 64–92. Philadelphia: Temple University Press.

———. 1999. *The critique of postcolonial reason: Toward a history of the vanishing present*. Cambridge: Harvard University Press.

Stone-Mediatore, Shari. Chandra Mohanty and the revaluing of "experience." *Hypatia* 13 (2): 116–33.

Thompson, Becky. 2002. Multiracial feminism: Recasting the chronology of second wave feminism. *Feminist Studies* 28 (2): 337–55.

Townley, Cynthia. 2006. Toward a revaluation of ignorance. *Hypatia* 21 (3): 37–55.

Tuana, Nancy. 2001. Introduction to *Engendering rationalities*, ed. Nancy Tuana and Sandra Morgen, 1–22. Albany: State University of New York Press.

Witt, Charlotte. 1996. How feminism is re-writing the philosophical canon. The Alfred Stiernotte Memorial Lecture in Philosophy delivered at Quinnipiac College, Hamden, CT.

Zack, Naomi. 2000. Introduction. In *Women of color and philosophy: A critical reader*, ed. Naomi Zack, 1–22. Malden, MA: Blackwell.

———. 2005. Inclusive feminist social theory: Requirements and methodology. In *Inclusive feminism: A third wave theory of women's commonality*, 61–82. Lanham, MD: Rowman and Littlefield.

Zinn, Maxine Baca, Lynn Weber Cannon, Elizabeth Higginbotham, and Bonnie Thornton Dill. 1986. The costs of exclusionary practices in women's studies. *Signs* 11 (2): 290–303.

———, and Bonnie Thornton Dill. 1996. Theorizing difference from multiracial feminism. *Feminist Studies* 22 (2): 321–31.

Comparative Methodology

Allinson, Robert E. 1998. Complementarity as a model for East-West integrative philosophy. *Journal of Chinese Philosophy* 25 (4): 505–17.

———. 2001. The myth of comparative philosophy or the comparative philosophy malgré lui. In *Two roads to wisdom? Chinese and analytical philosophical traditions*, ed. Bo Mou, 269–91. Chicago: Open Court.

Ames, Roger T. 1988. Confucius and the ontology of knowing. In *Interpreting across boundaries: New essays in comparative philosophy*, ed. Gerald James Larson and Eliot Deutsch, 265–79. Princeton: Princeton University Press.

Angle, Stephen C. 2002. Pluralism in practice: Incommensurability and constraints on change in ethical discourses. In *Varieties of ethical reflection: New directions for ethics in a global context,* ed. Michael Barnhart, 119–37. Lanham, MD: Lexington.

Arisaka, Yoko. 1997. Beyond East and West: Nishida's universalism and a postcolonial critique. *Review of Politics* 59 (3): 541–60.

Bahm, Archie J. 1995. *Comparative philosophy: Western, Indian and Chinese philosophies compared.* Rev. ed. Albuquerque: World.

Benesch, Walter. 2002. Comparative philosophy as feedback loops and fractals of philosophical space: The butterfly effect meets the butterfly dream. *American Philosophical Association Newsletter on Asian and Asian American Philosophers and Philosophies* 2 (1): 32–35.

Berman, Michael. 2007. Merleau-Ponty's hermeneutics of comparative philosophy revisited. *Phenomenological Inquiry: A Review of Philosophical Ideas and Trends* 31:1–13.

Bernstein, Richard J. 1991. Incommensurability and otherness revisited. In *Culture and modernity: East-West philosophic perspectives,* ed. Eliot Deutsch, 85–103. Honolulu: University of Hawaii Press.

Bhattacharya, Sibajiban. 1975. Philosophy as self-realisation. In *Indian philosophy today,* ed. N. K. Devaraja, 54–81. Delhi: Macmillan.

Bilimoria, Purushottama. 2003. What is the "subaltern" of the comparative philosophy of religion? *Philosophy East and West* 53 (3): 340–66.

Botz-Bornstein, Thorsten. 2006. Ethnophilosophy, comparative philosophy, pragmatism: Toward a philosophy of ethnoscapes. *Philosophy East and West* 56 (1): 153–71.

Brightman, Edward Sheffield. 1952. Goals of philosophy and religion, East and West. *Philosophy East and West* 1 (4): 6–17.

Burik, Steve. 2009. *The end of comparative philosophy and the task of comparative thinking: Heidegger, Derrida, and Daoism.* Albany: State University of New York Press.

Burtt, E. A. 1951a. Basic problems of method in harmonizing Eastern and Western philosophy. In *Essays in East-West philosophy,* ed. Charles A. Moore, 103–23. Honolulu: University of Hawaii Press.

———. 1951b. The problem of world philosophy. In *Radhakrishnan: Comparative studies in philosophy presented in honour of his sixtieth birthday,* ed. W. R. Inge, L. P. Jacks, M. Hiriyanna, E. A. Burtt, P. T. Raju, 29–42. New York: Harper.

Chakrabarti, Arindam. 2002. Analytic versus comparative: A bogus dichotomy in philosophy. *American Philosophical Association Newsletter on Asian and Asian American Philosophers and Philosophies* 2 (1): 39–42.

Chan, W. T. 1951. The unity of East and West. In *Radhakrishnan: Comparative studies in philosophy presented in honour of his sixtieth birthday,* ed. W. R. Inge, L. P. Jacks, M. Hiriyanna, E. A. Burtt, P. T. Raju, 104–117. New York: Harper.

Chari, C. T. K. 1975. Culture, language, and the philosophical enterprise. In *Indian philosophy today,* ed. N. K. Devaraja, 82–99. Delhi: Macmillan.

Chatterjee, Margaret. 1975. Towards an anthropological view of philosophy. In *Indian philosophy today,* ed. N. K. Devaraja, 127–54. Delhi: Macmillan.

Chan, W. T. 1951. The unity of East and West. In *Radhakrishnan: Comparative studies in philosophy presented in honour of his sixtieth birthday*, ed. W. R. Inge, L. P. Jacks, M. Hiriyanna, E. A. Burtt, P. T. Raju, 104–17. New York: Harper.

Cheng, Chung-ying. 2001. Onto-hermeneutical vision and analytic discourse: Interpretation and reconstruction in Chinese philosophy. In *Two roads to wisdom? Chinese and analytical philosophical traditions*, ed. Bo Mou, 87–130. Chicago: Open Court.

Chinn, Ewing. 2007. The relativist challenge to comparative philosophy. *International Philosophical Quarterly* 47 (4): 451–66.

Dallmayr, Fred. 1996. *Beyond Orientalism: Essays on cross-cultural encounter*. Albany: State University of New York Press.

Daor, Dan. 1978. Modes of argument. In *Philosophy East/Philosophy West: A critical comparison of Indian, Chinese, Islamic, and European Philosophy*, ed. Ben-Ami Scharfstein, 162–95. New York: Oxford University Press.

Dasgupta, S. N. and A. C. Mukerji. 1952. On philosophical synthesis. *Philosophy East and West* 1 (4): 3–5.

Datta, Dhirendra Mohan. 1963. On philosophical synthesis. *Philosophy East and West* 13 (3): 195–200.

Deutsch, Eliot. 1967. Some remarks on contemporary Western approaches to Indian philosophy. *Proceedings of the Indian Philosophical Congress*, 12–15. Banares.

——. 1969. Preface. In *Advaita Vedānta: A philosophical reconstruction*. Honolulu: University of Hawaii Press.

——. 1988. Knowledge and the tradition text in Indian philosophy. In *Interpreting across boundaries: New essays in comparative philosophy*, ed. Gerald James and Eliot Deutsch, 165–73. Princeton: Princeton University Press.

——. 2002. Comparative philosophy as creative philosophy. *American Philosophical Association Newsletter on Asian and Asian-American Philosophers and Philosophies* 2 (1): 23–26.

Devaraja, N. K. 1967. Philosophy and comparative philosophy. *Philosophy East and West* 17 (1/4): 51–59.

——. 1975. Notes towards a definition of philosophy. In *Indian philosophy today*, ed. N. K. Devaraja, 127–54. Delhi: Macmillan.

Dewey, John, S. Radhakrishnan, and George Santayana. 1951. On philosophical synthesis. *Philosophy East and West* 1 (1): 3–5.

Dotson, Kristie. 2012. How is this paper philosophy? *Comparative Philosophy* 3 (1): 3–29.

——. 2012. Well, yes and no: A reply to Priest. *Comparative Philosophy* 3 (2): 10–15.

Fleischacker, Samuel. 2002. The moral interpretation of culture. In *Varieties of ethical reflection: New directions for ethics in a global context*, ed. Michael Barnhart, 139–72. Lanham, MD: Lexington.

Fleming, Jesse. 2003. Comparative philosophy: Its aims and methods. *Journal of Chinese Philosophy* 30 (2): 259–70.

Halbfass, Wilhelm. 1985. India and the comparative method. *Philosophy East and West* 35 (1): 3–15.

——. 1988. *India and Europe: An essay in understanding.* Albany: State University of New York Press.

Hall, David L. 2001. The import of analysis in classical China—a pragmatic appraisal. In *Two roads to wisdom? Chinese and analytical philosophical traditions,* ed. Bo Mou, 153–67. Chicago: Open Court.

Herrera, Maria L. 1991. On the interpretation of traditional cultures. In *Culture and modernity: East-West philosophic perspectives,* ed. Eliot Deutsch, 505–25. Honolulu: University of Hawaii Press.

Hocking, William Ernest. 1944. Value of the comparative study of philosophy. In *Philosophy—East and West,* ed. Charles A. Moore, 1–11. Princeton: Princeton University Press.

Jenko, Leigh K. 2012. How meaning moves: Tan Sitong on borrowing across cultures. *Philosophy East and West* 62 (1): 92–113.

Kaipayil, Joseph. 1995. *The epistemology of comparative philosophy: A critique with reference to P. T. Raju's views.* Rome: Centre for Indian and Inter-religious Studies.

Kamiat, Arnold H. 1952. On the synthesis of East and West. *Philosophy East and West* 1 (4): 41–44.

Kitarō, Nishida. 1998. The forms of culture of the classical periods of East and West seen from a metaphysical perspective. In *Sourcebook for modern Japanese philosophy,* trans. and ed. David A. Dilworth and Valdo H. Viglielmo with Agustin Jacinto Zavala, 21–36. Westport, CT: Greenwood.

Kresse, Kai. 2002. Towards an anthropology of philosophies: Four turns, with reference to the African context. In *Thought and practice in African philosophy,* ed. Gail M. Presbey, Daniel Smith, Pamela Abuya, and Oriare Nyarwath, 29–46. Nairobi: Konrad Adenauer.

Krishna, Daya. 1988. Comparative philosophy: What it is and what it ought to be. In *Interpreting across boundaries: New essays in comparative philosophy,* ed. Gerald James Larson and Eliot Deutsch, 71–83. Princeton: Princeton University Press.

Kupperman, Joel J. 2002. The purposes and functions of comparative philosophy. *American Philosophical Association Newsletter on Asian and Asian American Philosophers and Philosophies* 2 (1): 26–29.

——. 2003. Philosophies? Or philosophy? *American Philosophical Association Newsletter on Asian and Asian American Philosophers and Philosophies* 2 (2): 142–46.

Künstler, Mieczyslaw Jerzy. 1979. To compare or not to compare? *Dialectics and Humanism* 6: 137–40.

Larson, Gerald James. 1986. Interpreting across boundaries: Some preliminary reflections: Society for Asian and comparative philosophy presidential address. *Philosophy East and West* 36 (2): 131–42.

——. 1988. Introduction: The "age-old distinction between the same and the other." In *Interpreting across boundaries: New essays in comparative philosophy,* ed. Gerald James Larson and Eliot Deutsch, 3–18. Princeton: Princeton University Press.

Leibniz, Gottfried Wilhelm. 1994. *Writings on China.* Trans. Daniel J. Cook and Henry Rosemont Jr. Chicago: Open Court.

Li, You-zheng. 2001. Chinese philosophy and semiotics. In *Two roads to wisdom? Chinese and analytical philosophical traditions*, ed. Bo Mou, 169–94. Chicago: Open Court.

Liat, J. Kwee Swan. 1951. Methods of comparative philosophy. *Philosophy East and West* 1 (1): 10–15.

———. 1953. *Methods of comparative philosophy*. Leiden: Universitaire pers Leiden.

Liu, Shu-hsien. 2001. Philosophical analysis and hermeneutics: Reflections on methodology via an examination of the evolution of my understanding of Chinese philosophy. In *Two roads to wisdom? Chinese and analytical philosophical traditions*, ed. Bo Mou, 131–52. Chicago: Open Court.

Maitra, Keya. 2006. Comparing the *Bhagavad-Gita* and Kant: A lesson in comparative philosophy. *Philosophy in the Contemporary World* 13 (1): 63–67.

Maitra, S. K. 1953. On philosophical synthesis. *Philosophy East and West* 3 (3): 195–98.

Matilal, Bimal K. 1991. Pluralism, relativism, and interaction between cultures. In *Culture and modernity: East-West philosophic perspectives*, ed. Eliot Deutsch, 141–60. Honolulu: University of Hawaii Press.

Masson-Oursel, Paul. 1926. *Comparative philosophy*. New York: Harcourt, Brace.

———, and Harold E. McCarthy. 1951. True philosophy is comparative philosophy. *Philosophy East and West* 1 (1): 6–9.

McCarthy, Erin. 2008. Comparative philosophy and the liberal arts: Between and beyond—Educating to cultivate geocitizens. *Canadian Review of American Studies* 38 (2): 293–309.

McDermott, Robert A. 1970. Radhakrishnan's contribution to comparative philosophy. *International Philosophical Quarterly* 10:420–40.

McWeeny, Jennifer. 2007. The disadvantages of radical alterity for a comparative methodology. In *The proceedings of the twenty-first World Congress of Philosophy*, vol. 7: *Philosophy of culture(s)*, ed. Venant Cauchy, 125–30. Ankara: Philosophical Society of Turkey.

Merleau-Ponty. 1964. Everywhere and nowhere. In *Signs*, trans. Richard C. McCLeary, 126–58. Evanston, IL: Northwestern University Press.

Mohanty, J. N. 1975. Philosophy as reflection on experience. In *Indian philosophy today*, ed. N. K. Devaraja, 169–85. Delhi: Macmillan.

Moore, Charles A. 1944. Comparative philosophies of life. In *Philosophy East and West*, ed. Charles A. Moore, 248–320. Princeton: Princeton University Press.

———. 1949a. A preliminary report of the second East-West philosophers' conference 1949. In *The second East-West philosophers' conference: A preliminary report*, ed. Charles A. Moore, 3–10. Honolulu: University of Hawaii Press.

———. 1949b. The second East-West philosophers' conference: A preliminary report. Occasional Paper 52, December 1949. Honolulu: University of Hawaii Press.

———. 1951a. An attempt at world philosophical synthesis. In *Essays in East-West philosophy*, ed. Charles A. Moore, 1–16. Honolulu: University of Hawaii Press.

———. 1951b. Some problems of comparative philosophy. *Philosophy East and West* 1 (1): 67–70.

Montefiore, Alan. 1996. Philosophy in different cultural contexts. In *Philosophy and pluralism*, ed. David Archard, 7–18. New York: Cambridge University Press.

Moran, Dermot. 1996. A case for philosophical pluralism: The problem of intentionality. *Philosophy*. Supplement no. 40:19–32.

Mou, Bo. 2001. An analysis of the structure of philosophical methodology—in view of comparative philosophy. In *Two roads to wisdom? Chinese and analytical philosophical traditions*, ed. Bo Mou, 337–64. Chicago: Open Court.

———. 2002. Three orientations and four "sins" in comparative studies. *American Philosophical Association Newsletter on Asian and Asian American Philosophers and Philosophies* 2 (1): 42–45.

———. 2010. On constructive-engagement strategy of comparative philosophy: A journal theme introduction. *Comparative Philosophy* 1 (1): 1–32.

Nakamura, Hajime. 1964. *Ways of thinking of Eastern peoples: India-China-Tibet-Japan*. Trans. Philip P. Wiener. Honolulu: University of Hawaii Press.

———. 1975. *A comparative history of ideas*. London: KPI.

———. 1988. The meaning of the terms "philosophy" and "religion" in various traditions. In *Interpreting across boundaries: New essays in comparative philosophy*, ed. Gerald James Larson and Eliot Deutsch, 137–51. Princeton: Princeton University Press.

Nasr, Seyyed Hossein. 1972. Conditions for meaningful comparative philosophy. *Philosophy East and West* 22 (1): 53–61.

Neville, Robert Cummings. 2001a. Methodology, practices, and discipline in Chinese and Western philosophy. In *Two roads to wisdom? Chinese and analytical philosophical traditions*, ed. Bo Mou, 27–44. Chicago: Open Court.

———. 2001b. Two forms of comparative philosophy. *Dao: A Journal of Comparative Philosophy* 1 (1): 1–13.

———. 2002. Beyond comparative to integrative philosophy. *American Philosophical Association Newsletter on Asian and Asian American Philosophers and Philosophies* 2 (1): 20–23.

Northrop, F. S. C. 1951a. Methodology and epistemology, Oriental and Occidental. In *Essays in East-West philosophy*, ed. Charles A. Moore, 151–62. Honolulu: University of Hawaii Press.

———. 1951b. The relation between Eastern and Western philosophy. In *Radhakrishnan: Comparative studies in philosophy presented in honour of his sixtieth birthday*, ed. W. R. Inge, L. P. Jacks, M. Hiriyanna, E. A. Burtt, P. T. Raju, 362–78. New York: Harper.

Outlaw, Lucius. 1991. Lifeworlds, modernity, and philosophical praxis: Race, ethnicity, and critical social theory. In *Culture and modernity: East-West philosophic perspectives*, ed. Eliot Deutsch, 21–49. Honolulu: University of Hawaii Press.

Panikkar, Raimundo. 1980. Aporias in comparative philosophy of religion. *Man and World* 13:357–83.

——. 1988. What is comparative philosophy comparing? In *Interpreting across boundaries: New essays in comparative philosophy*, ed. Gerald James Larson and Eliot Deutsch, 116–36. Princeton: Princeton University Press.

Parkes, Graham. 1991. Between nationalism and nomadism: Wondering about the languages of philosophy. In *Culture and modernity: East-West philosophic perspectives*, ed. Eliot Deutsch, 455–67. Honolulu: University of Hawaii Press.

Prabhu, Joseph. 2001. Philosophy in an age of global encounter. *American Philosophical Association Newsletter on Asian and Asian American Philosophers and Philosophies* 1 (1): 29–31.

Priest, Graham. 2012. In the same way that this one is: Some comments on Dotson. *Comparative Philosophy* 3 (2): 3–9.

Radhakrishnan, S., and P. T. Raju, eds. 1966. Introduction. In *The concept of man: A study in comparative philosophy*. Delhi: Motilal Banarsidass.

Raju. P. T. 1970. *Lectures on comparative philosophy*. Ganeshkhind: University of Poona.

Raman, N. S. S. 1975. Is comparative philosophy possible? In *Indian philosophy today*, ed. N. K. Devaraja, 201–17. Delhi: Macmillan.

Rosán, Laurence J. 1952. A key to comparative philosophy. *Philosophy East and West* 2 (1): 56–65.

——. 1962. Are comparisons between East and the West fruitful for comparative philosophy? *Philosophy East and West* 11 (4): 239–43.

Rosemont, Henry Jr. 1988. Against relativism. In *Interpreting across boundaries: New essays in comparative philosophy*, ed. Gerald James Larson and Eliot Deutsch, 36–70. Princeton: Princeton University Press.

Said, Edward W. 1978. *Orientalism*. New York: Vintage.

Scharfstein, Ben-Ami. 1978. Cultures, contexts, and comparisons. *Philosophy East/ Philosophy West: A critical comparison of Indian, Chinese, Islamic, and European Philosophy*, ed. Ben-Ami Scharfstein, Illai Alon, Shlomo Biderman, Dan Daor, and Yoel Hoffman, 9–47. New York: Oxford University Press.

——. 1988. The contextual fallacy. In *Interpreting across boundaries: New essays in comparative philosophy*, ed. Gerald James Larson and Eliot Deutsch, 84–97. Princeton: Princeton University Press.

——. 1998. The three philosophical traditions. In *A comparative history of world philosophy: From the Upanishads to Kant*, 1–54. Albany: State University of New York Press.

Schreiner, Peter. 1978. The Indianness of modern philosophy as a historical and philosophical problem. *Philosophy East and West* 28: 21–37.

Sengupta, Santosh. 1975. Philosophy—theory and practice. In *Indian philosophy today*, ed. N. K. Devaraja, 218–34. Delhi: Macmillan.

Sheldon, Wilmon H. 1956. What can Western philosophy contribute to Eastern? *Philosophy East and West* 5 (4): 291–304.

Sheldon, Wilmon H., and Daisetz Teitaro Suzuki. 1951. On philosophical synthesis. *Philosophy East and West* 1 (3): 3–7.

Singh, Shakuntala A. 1988. The creative and the comparative. *Indian Philosophical Quarterly* 15: 189–208.

Smart, Ninian. 1988. The analogy of meaning and the tasks of comparative philosophy. In *Interpreting across boundaries: New essays in comparative philosophy*, ed. Gerald James Larson and Eliot Deutsch, 174–83. Princeton: Princeton University Press.

Smid, Robert W. 2009. *Methodologies of comparative philosophy: The pragmatist and process traditions*. Albany: State University of New York Press.

Solomon, Robert C. 2001. What is philosophy? The status of non-Western philosophy in the profession. *American Philosophical Association Newsletter on Asian and Asian American Philosophers and Philosophies* 1 (1): 27–29.

Staal, Frits. 1988. Is there philosophy in Asia? In *Interpreting across boundaries: New essays in comparative philosophy*, ed. Gerald James Larson and Eliot Deutsch, 203–29. Princeton: Princeton University Press.

Sze-Kwang, Lao (Lao Yng-Wei). 1989. On understanding Chinese philosophy: An inquiry and a proposal. In *Understanding the Chinese mind: The philosophical roots*, ed. Robert E. Allinson, 265–93. New York: Oxford University Press.

Tong, Lik Kuen. 2001. The art of appropriation: Towards a field-being conception of philosophy. In *Two roads to wisdom? Chinese and analytical philosophical traditions*, ed. Bo Mou, 57–83. Chicago: Open Court.

Tuck, Andrew P. 1990. *Comparative philosophy and the philosophy of scholarship: On the Western interpretation of Nāgārjuna*. New York: Oxford University Press.

Wadia, A. R. 1951. The philosophical outlook in India and Europe. In *Radhakrishnan: Comparative studies in philosophy presented in honour of his sixtieth birthday*, ed. W. R. Inge, L. P. Jacks, M. Hiriyanna, E. A. Burtt, P. T. Raju, 87–103. New York: Harper.

Willman, Marshall D. 2009. Illocutionary force and its relation to mood: Comparative methodology reconsidered. *Dao: A Journal of Comparative Philosophy* 8 (4): 439–55.

Yasuo, Yuasa. 1987. Method and attitude in studying Eastern thought. In *The body: Toward an Eastern mind-body theory*, ed. T. P. Kasulis, trans. Nagatomo Shigenori and T. P. Kasulis, 75–80. Albany: State University of New York Press.

Yijie, Tang. 1987. The significance of comparative philosophy and comparative religion: A view from the introduction of Indian Buddhism into China. *Chinese Studies in Philosophy* 18: 3–63.

Yu, Ji-yuan, and Nicholas Bunnin. 2001. Saving the phenomena: An Aristotelian method in comparative philosophy. In *Two roads to wisdom? Chinese and analytical philosophical traditions*, ed. Bo Mou, 293–312. Chicago: Open Court.

Yung-Tung, Tang. 1951. On "ko-yi," the earliest method by which Indian Buddhism and Chinese thought were synthesized. In *Radhakrishnan: Comparative studies in philosophy presented in honour of his sixtieth birthday*, ed. W. R. Inge, L. P. Jacks, M. Hiriyanna, E. A. Burtt, P. T. Raju, 276–86. New York: Harper.

Zhang, Wei. 2006. *Heidegger, Rorty, and Eastern thinkers: A hermeneutics of cross-cultural understanding.* Albany: State University of New York Press.

Zhang, Xianglong. 2010. Comparison paradox, comparative situation and inter-paradigmaticy: A methodological reflection on cross-cultural philosophical comparison. *Comparative Philosophy* 1 (1): 90–105.

Contributors

ASHBY BUTNOR received her Ph.D. from the University of Hawaii, Manoa in 2009 under the direction of Graham Parkes and Vrinda Dalmiya. Her recent scholarship focuses on embodied ethical skill and the cultivation of moral perception and action through bodily training. She has published a number of articles and book chapters on the intersection of feminist and Buddhist ethics as well as on philosophical pedagogy. She is now the lead lecturer and faculty coordinator for Learning Communities and First Year Success at Metropolitan State University of Denver. For her work with first-year students, she is the recent recipient of the Outstanding Faculty Leadership Award.

VRINDA DALMIYA is associate professor of philosophy at the University of Hawaii, Manoa. She received her Ph.D. from Brown University and has taught at Montana State University and the Indian Institute of Technology, Delhi. She has been a Fellow at the Indian Institute of Advanced Study in Shimla, India from 2011–2013. Her research interests include comparative philosophy, feminist epistemology, care ethics, environmental ethics, and disability studies. Her work in comparative feminist philosophy uses resources from classical Indian philosophy and contemporary feminist theory; it has appeared in journals such as *Hypatia, Sophia, Journal of Chinese Philosophy,* and *Environmental Ethics.* She is currently working on developing a feminist virtue epistemology centered on the notion of care.

ELIOT DEUTSCH is professor emeritus of philosophy at the University of Hawaii, Manoa. He is a past editor (1967–1987) of the international journal *Philosophy East and West,* director of the Sixth East-West Philosophers' Conference, and a past president of the Society for Asian and Comparative Philosophy. Deutsch received his Ph.D. from Columbia University and has been a visiting professor at the University of Chicago and Harvard University, and a visiting fellow and life member at the University of Cambridge. He is the author of sixteen books, including *Advaita Vedānta: A Philosophical Reconstruction* (1969), *Studies in Comparative Aesthetics* (1975), *On Truth: An Ontological Theory* (1979), *Creative Being: The Crafting of Person and World* (1992), *Religion and Spirituality* (1995), *Essays on the Nature of Art* (1996), and *Persons and Valuable Worlds: A Global Philosophy* (2001), and approximately 115 articles and reviews in professional journals. His work has been translated into French, Italian, Russian, Spanish, Korean, Chinese, and Japanese.

NAMITA GOSWAMI is associate professor of philosophy at Indiana State University. Her work combines continental philosophy and postcolonial, critical race, and feminist theories. She has published in a wide range of journals including *Signs*, *Angelaki*, *Contemporary Aesthetics*, and *South Asian Review,* as well as in anthologies such as *Rethinking Facticity* and *Constructing the Nation: A Race and Nationalism Reader*. She is currently finishing revisions on a book manuscript on philosophy, feminism, and postcolonial theory with State University of New York Press.

RANJOO SEODU HERR is associate professor of philosophy at Bentley University. She received her B.L. and B.A. from Seoul National University and her Ph.D. from the State University of New York, Buffalo. Her current research interests are democracy, human rights, nationalism, multiculturalism, third world feminism, and comparative philosophy involving East Asia and the West. Her articles have been published in journals such as *Political Theory*, *Philosophical Forum*, *Social Theory and Practice*, *Hypatia*, *Philosophy East and West*, and *Asian Philosophy*. She is currently working on a book tentatively titled *Nonliberal Democracy and Equal Respect for Democratic Peoples*.

HSIAO-LAN HU is associate professor of religious studies and women's and gender studies at the University of Detroit Mercy. She received her M.A. and Ph.D. in religion from Temple University. She is the author of *This Worldly Nibbāna: A Buddhist-Feminist Social Ethic for Peacemaking in the Global Community* (2011) and *Taoism* (2005). The former is an interdisciplinary study that combines the philosophy and sociology of early Buddhism, engaged Buddhism, poststructuralist feminist theory, liberation theology, socioeconomic studies on globalization, and peace studies. She has recently published a number of book chapters addressing the intersection of religion and culture.

XINYAN JIANG is professor of philosophy at the University of Redlands. She received her B.A and M.A. from Peking University and her Ph.D. from the University of Cincinnati. Before leaving China, she was a faculty member of the Department of Philosophy at Peking University. Her interests are primarily in Chinese philosophy, comparative philosophy, and ethics. She has published in journals such as *History of Philosophy and Logic*, *Philosophy East and West*, *Journal of Chinese Philosophy*, *Philosophical Inquiry*, and *Hypatia*, as well as in several anthologies. She is also the author of *John Stuart Mill: For the Well-*

being of Mankind (2013), and the editor of *Chinese Philosophy in the English World* (2009) and *The Examined Life: Chinese Perspectives* (2002). She was the founding chair of the Committee on the Status of Asian/Asian American Philosophers and Philosophies of the American Philosophical Association and held leadership positions for the Association of Chinese Philosophers in North America and the International Society for Chinese Philosophy.

KYOO LEE is associate professor of philosophy at John Jay College, CUNY, where she is also affiliated faculty for the gender studies, justice studies, and honors programs. Additionally, she teaches comparative literature, feminist theory, and critical theory at CUNY Graduate Center. Dually trained in European philosophy and literary theory, Lee works widely in the intersecting fields of the theoretical humanities such as aesthetics, Asian American studies, comparative literature/philosophy, continental philosophy, critical race theory, cultural studies, deconstruction, feminist philosophy, gender studies, poetics, postphenomenology, and translation. Her first book, published with Fordham University Press, is titled *Reading Descartes Otherwise: Blind, Mad, Dreamy, and Bad* (2012).

KEYA MAITRA is associate professor and chair of the Department of Philosophy at University of North Carolina, Asheville. Her current research interests include philosophy of mind, third world feminism, and feminist philosophy of mind. She has published articles in *Asian Philosophy*, *Philosophy in the Contemporary World*, *Southwest Philosophy Review*, *Hypatia*, and *International Journal of Philosophical Studies*. She contributed *On Putnam* (2002) to the Wadsworth Philosophers series. Maitra's fresh translation of the Hindu text *Bhagavad Gītā* is forthcoming with Edwin Mellen Press (2014). Her current book project focuses on the topics of consciousness, self-consciousness, and mindfulness from classical Indian and contemporary Western perspectives.

ERIN MCCARTHY is professor of philosophy and Asian studies at St. Lawrence University. Her research areas are in Japanese philosophy, ethics, and feminist and continental philosophy. She is the author of *Ethics Embodied: Rethinking Selfhood Through Continental, Japanese, and Feminist Philosophies* (2010), as well as several articles that have appeared in both French and English in journals and anthologies. McCarthy has served as chair of the board of directors of ASIANetwork. Currently, she is working on a comparative feminist project titled *(Re)imagining Maternity*, which involves a philosophical rethinking of the norms of maternity and an examination of the ways in which contemplative education can be enriched by incorporating feminist philosophies.

JENNIFER MCWEENY is associate professor of philosophy at Worcester Polytechnic Institute. She received her Ph.D. in philosophy from the University of Oregon and her M.A. in philosophy from the University of Hawaii, Manoa. She also holds degrees in women's and gender studies and french literature from the University of Oregon. Her research and teaching interests are in the areas of feminist philosophy, phenomenology, philosophy of mind, epistemology, comparative methodology, decolonial theory, and Buddhism. Her articles have appeared in *Continental Philosophy Review, Hypatia, Journal for Critical Animal Studies,* and *Simone de Beauvoir Studies,* among other venues. McWeeny is a past executive secretary for the Society for Women in Philosophy and is currently writing a book on phenomenological approaches to embodied cognition.

LI-HSIANG LISA ROSENLEE is professor of philosophy at the University of Hawaii, West Oahu. She received her Ph.D. in philosophy from the University of Hawaii, Manoa where she also received an M.A. in philosophy and a B.A. in political science. She is the author of *Confucianism and Women: A Philosophical Interpretation* (2006). Rosenlee's work has appeared in journals such as *Hypatia, Philosophy East and West, Philosophical Quarterly, International Studies in Philosophy, Journal of Chinese Religions, Dao: A Journal of Comparative Philosophy, China Review International,* and *Asian Philosophy,* as well as in a number of anthologies. Her research interests include Confucianism, Chinese philosophy, and feminist philosophy.

CHELA SANDOVAL is associate professor and chair emerita of the Department of Chicana/o Studies at the University of California, Santa Barbara. Her award-winning book, *Methodology of the Oppressed* (2000), is one of the most influential contemporary theoretical texts worldwide. She has also published a variety of articles and chapters on social movement, third-space feminism, and critical media theory. Sandoval regularly teaches courses on decolonial feminism, power and truth, liberation philosophy, and radical semiotics. She received a Ph.D. in the history of consciousness from the University of California, Santa Cruz. Her current book project is on story-wor(l)d-art-performance as activism (SWAPA) and the shaman-nahual/witness ceremony. Her most recent coedited book, *Performing the U.S. Latina/o Borderlands,* is published by Indiana University Press (2013).

Index

Actions: in individual construction, 41–45; of Dao, 67; of past, 39–40, 43; ritual action extended to, 38; self and, 53–54; of social embeddedness, 235; speech as, 46–47

Adultery, 96n8

African American feminism, 25–26, 261–65, 266n1; *see also* Black female body

Agency, 126; angry perceptions and, 137–38; body related to, 248–49; causal agent, 53; choices and, 119–20; in Confucian self, 84; embodied agency, 261–62; in feminist consciousness, 104, 107–8; first-order anger and, 125; in language, 46–47; no-self and, 43–44; self and, 44–45; *see also* Free will

Agnatic principle, 80–83

Akriyāvāda, 43

Alcoff, Linda, 108–9, 111–12, 120n2

Alienation, 15, 182

Allen, Paula Gunn, 273

Ames, Roger, 75n2

Analects, 80, 84–89, 91, 93–94, 96n12, 192, 194–96

Anātman, 116, 233; agency and, 43–44; anger and, 130, 136, 139; in enlightenment, 131–32; *kamma* and, 37–38

Anger, 21; first-order, 124–26; as knowing experience, 123–24, 134–37, 140; limen and, 136–38; operative intentionality in, 124, 134; operative view of, 124, 134–38; oppression and, 135–39; reality and, 135–37; self-less anger, 132; *see also* Second-order anger

Anger and enlightenment: habits and, 129–30, 139; *kōan* study related to, 132–33; self-less anger in, 132–34

Angry perceptions: agency and, 137–38; intentionality and, 135–36; reality and, 135–36; as realizations, 136–37

Aṅguttara Nikāya, 54n8, 114

Animals, 151, 165n6; bodies of, 258–59; without free will, 258–59; rebirth

Animals (*continued*)
related to, 38; *see also* Dark female animal
Anthropology, 29*n*14, 68–69, 257, 267*n*16
Anzaldúa, Gloria, 6, 127–28, 271, 273–74
Arisaka, Yoko: on comparative philosophy, 7; on double-alienation, 15
Ātman, 102; *see also* Self
Attachment, 118, 132–33, 159–60, 163, 211–12, 230, 233; to body, 213–14; empathy related to, 230–31; habits of, 230
Attention: to body, 231; inattention, 229–30, 237; *see also* Mindfulness meditation
Autonomy, 119; *see also* Agency; Free will; Volition

Baartman, Saartjie, 261, 264–65; abolitionists for, 251–52; background of, 251–52; case on, 252, 257, 266*n*7, 267*n*14; death of, 251, 253; enacted ethnography of, 267*n*16; free will of, 257–59; as Hottentot Venus, 248, 257, 259, 267*n*15; objectification of, 258; remains of, 251; as scientific curiosity, 253, 258–59, 267*n*15; *see also* Black female body
Barad, Karen, 2
Bar On, Bat-Ami, 237–39
Bartky, Sandra, 21, 101–8, 110–11, 119, 236
Battersby, Christine, 72
Beauvoir, Simone de, 60, 189
Bentinck, William, 248
Betweenness, 138–39; *ki* as, 211; for nondual subjectivity, 216–19; in self as *ningen,* 207, 209, 211; *see also* Limen
Black female body, 247; gender of, 260–61; Hindu female body compared to, 259–64; sexuality of, 261; visibility of, 260–61
Blainville, Henri de, 259, 267*n*15
Bodhi, Bhikkhu, 42
the Body, 40, 128, 135–37; as agency, 248–49; of animals, 258–59; attachment to, 213–14; attention to, 231; in embodied know-how, 229, 232; ethics and, 237–39; ethics-as-practice and, 226–27; in Japanese philosophy, 206; mind related to, 115–16, 213–14; Plato on, 212–13; polygyny, 81–82, 96*n*7; postcolonial female body, 247; in self as *ningen,* 206–9; subjectivity related to, 215; violence related to, 237–39; *see also* Black female body; Female bodies; Hindu female body
Bodymind, 231; casting off of, 232; cultivation of, 209–11; intercorporeality in, 233–34; *ki* for, 210–11; oneness of, 209–10; in self as *ningen,* 206, 208–11, 220
Boers, 251–52
Book of Changes, 82
Book of Rituals, 195
Boucher, Sandy, 118
Brennan, Samantha, 196
"Bridge Through My Windows" (Lorde), 247
Buddha, 37–38; against determinism, 40; doing and nondoing of, 41; on *kamma,* 39–41, 48, 51; Kassapa with, 48; *kriyāvāda* from, 43; on mindfulness, 114; past actions and, 39–40, 43; for positive changes, 40–41; on self, 50, 102; on suffering, 48–50
Buddhadhamma, 43, 49
Buddhism, 19–21, 25, 119–20, 240–41; causal agent in, 53; classical, 37, 45, 54*n*2; individual construction in, 45–50; Mahāyāna, 49, 54*n*3, 130–31; Rinzai Zen, 124, 129–32, 139, 141*n*2,

141n8; *rūpa* in, 45–46; sense bases in, 45–46, 54n11; Sōtō Zen, 224; wisdom in, 211; *see also Kamma*; Mindfulness

Buddhist mindfulness, 101, 103; Buddhism in, 119–20; clarity capacity in, 114; feminist self-consciousness and, 113–14, 119–20; self-centering in, 113–14

Butalia, Urvashi, 250

Butler, Judith, 1, 19, 49; on agency, 44–45; on gender, 2–3; on no-self and *kamma*, 37–38; on performativity, 2–3, 19, 38, 44, 50; on speech, 46

Butnor, Ashby, 25

Care ethics, 1, 23–25, 187–88, 190–91, 197; hybridization of, 198–201; justice and, 193

Carter, Robert, 217–18, 229–30

Cezar, Hendrik, 251–52

Cezar, Peter, 251

Chakrabarti, Arindam, 5–6

Chan, Joseph, 97n25

Chinese characters, 57, 59–61, 64, 66–70, 74–75, 96n3

Chinese philosophy, 58–74, 149; *see also* Confucianism; Confucius; Daoism; Laozi; Mencius; Zhuangzi

Chosŏn Confucians, 80–82, 96n7

Chosŏn Dynasty, 20, 79–83

Christian, Barbara, 248

Class, 164

Coalitions, 15–16, 274–75

Collins, Patricia Hill, 117, 121n4

Colonialism, 9–11, 29n14, 188, 247–48, 254–55

Colonization, 25–26, 188; culture and, 17, 189; logic of, 170–72

Communitarian, 196–98

Comparative philosophy, 8–9, 28n6, 29n14, 138–40; feminist philosophy compared to, 4–7, 10–11, 29n10,

29n16; *see also* Feminist comparative philosophy

Confucian ethics of *ren*: appropriateness in context and, 197–98; compatibility with feminism, 187–93; filial care in, 189–90, 192–95, 200–1; gender parity from, 198; Great Society and, 195, 200; hierarchy and, 191, 196–97; imperialism and, 189, 199; patriarchy and, 192–93, 196; politics within, 193–98, 200–201; reciprocity in, 191, 195–96, 200; ritual property related to, 195–96, 198, 200

Confucian family, 92, 189, 191–97; family-state in, 93–94; father and son relationship in, 80, 87, 197; parent and child in, 87–89, 95–96; patrilineage within, 80–82, 87–88; *see also* Marriage; Parent and child

Confucianism, 15, 20, 24, 188–93; contemporary, 92–93, 95–96, 96n2, 97n19, 97n25; Daoism and, 58, 63; democracy and, 95–96, 97n25; patriarchy in, 78–84, 189–91, 193; people-centeredness in, 93–94; politics in, 95–96, 97n25; public realm participation, 82, 91–92, 96n10; self in, 84–86; *see also* Chosŏn Confucians; Korean Confucianism

Confucius, 79–80, 84, 86, 192; on extension of *ren*, 194, 196

Conocimiento, 274, 276

Consciousness, 15–16, 115–18; coalition of, 274–75; consciousness-raising, 20–21, 101–2, 105, 107, 109–10, 120n1; meta-witnessing, 276–77; planetary, 272; self-consciousness and, 113–14, 119–20; third-space feminists on, 275–76; voice, 254; *see also* Feminist consciousness; Feminist self-consciousness

Creativity, 70–73, 170–71, 275

Culture, 46, 169, 180, 272; colonization and, 17, 189; female bodies and, 263–64; in feminist comparative philosophy, 7–8, 15; nature as, 261–62; of rural life, 173–74

Cuvier, Frédéric, 259

Cuvier, Georges, 253, 258–59, 267n15

Dalmiya, Vrinda, 23

Dao, 57, 164n3, 195; creativity of, 70–71; death and, 70–71, 73; fluidity of, 67–68; without gender, 59; perspectives of, 159–60, 165n9; reality and, 162; sex of, 58, 62–63, 65–66

Daodejing, 19, 57; birth mother in, 71–72; maternal norm in, 59, 63; valley in, 57–58, 71, 75n4; valley spirit in, 57–58, 69, 72–73, 75n4; yin and yang in, 59, 63–65

Daoism, 19–20, 73–74, 164n3; birthing and, 67–70; complementarity within, 63–65, 67; Confucianism and, 58, 63; female fertility cult and, 68–69; five images of women in, 63–64; universality in, 64–65; valley in, 57–58, 75n4; yin and yang in, 59, 64

Dark female animal (Xuanpin): complementarity of, 63–65; creativity and, 72–73; femininity of, 65–66; fertile metaphorics of, 66–70, 73–74; genealogy of, 61–62; generalization of, 61–66; interpretations of, 61–63, 65–70; male compared to, 66–68; Moeller on, 58, 65–66; as mother of all, 66–67; multiple signatures of, 70–74; power of, 60, 63, 67–68; questions for, 59–61; subjectivity of, 60–61; triangle related to, 68–69; valley spirit in, 57, 69

Death: of Baartman, 251, 253; Dao and, 70–71, 73

Democracy, 95–96, 97n25, 169

DesAutels, Peggy, 241

Descartes, René, 212

Determinism, 37, 40–44, 46–53; bodies and, 249, 259–60, 263

Deutsch, Eliot, 12

Dewey, John, 225

Dhagamwar, Vasudha, 250, 256

Dhamma, U Rewata, 42

Dhamma/Dharma, 54n3, 271

Dharmaśāstra, 254

Differential consciousness, 15–16, 274

Distinction, 89–91

Disvalues, 224, 234–37

Dockett, Kathleen H., 52

Dōgen, 224, 232–33

Dong Zhongshu, 82–84

Double-alienation, 15; see also Alienation

Dreyfus, Hubert, 225–26

Dreyfus, Stuart, 225–26

Dualism, 203–5, 209; feminist criticisms of, 110; logic of, 170; mind-body dualism, 208–9, 212; between nirvāṇa and saṃsāra, 131; of philosophers, 214–15; reality and, 138–39; self and, 138–39; of subjectivity, 214–15

DuCille, Ann, 247–48, 258

Dukkha (duḥkha), 43, 52–54

Dunlop, Alexander, 251

Earth First!, 168, 181

Ecospirituality, 167–69, 181–82

Egge, James R., 39

Eisai, Zen Master, 209

Embodied know-how: body in, 229, 232; care in, 228–29; context in, 226–27; expertise in, 225–26; intersubjectivity and, 226; primary intersubjectivity and, 226–28

Embodiment, 140, 224; embodied agency, 261–62; embodied beings, 207–8; embodied disvalues, 235–36; embodied moral practice, 240–41;

postcolonial female body, 247; *see also* black female body; female bodies; Hindu female body

Emotion, 141*n*11, 213; empathy, 227–28, 230–31; hope, 129; *see also* Anger

Empowerment, 51–52

Enlightenment, 129, 232; *nirvāṇa* in, 130–31; nondualism of, 131, 133; no-place and, 131–32, 141*n*9; no-self in, 131–32; post-*satori* practice of, 131–32; as spontaneous, 131; *see also* Anger and enlightenment

Environmentalism, 167, 170–71

Epistemic multiculturalism, 169, 180

Epistemology, 5, 123–25, 131–32, 149, 176–81, 233, 275; of anger, 133–34, 136–38; externalism, 140; of prakriti, 169, 174–75, 182; reliabilism, 140; universalist, 5, 22–23, 149; virtue epistemology, 140; *see also* Feminist epistemology; Standpoint epistemology

Essentialism, 111

Ethics, 24–25, 223; body and, 237–39; of embodied moral practice, 240–41; feminist, 191–92; know-how and, 224–29; from primary intersubjectivity, 227; from self as *ningen*, 207; *see also* Care ethics; Confucian ethics of *ren*; Feminist ethics

Ethics-as-practice, 226–27

Ethnoscience, 175–76

Externalism, 140

External sense bases, 45–46, 54*n*11

Family-state, 93–94

Father and son relationship, 80, 87, 197

Fausto-Sterling, Anne, 259

Felt inter-resonance, 234–35

Female bodies, 247; culture and, 263–64; history and, 262–64; nature and, 263–64; restoration of, 264; *see also* Black female body; Body; Hindu female body

Feminism, 120, 220; African American feminism, 25–26, 261–65, 266*n*1; care ethics as, 190–91; Chicana feminism, 9–10, 14, 124, 127–28, 274–76; criticisms of dualism, 110; decolonial feminism, 6, 17, 271–72; first world feminism, 274; global feminism, 27–28, 120; Latina feminism, 9–10, 14, 124–29; pluralist feminism, 2, 6, 9–10, 12–13, 272–74; postcolonial feminism, 13, 22, 25–26, 247–50, 261–64; purist version of, 198–99; social embeddedness of care and, 235–40; third world feminism, 272–74; U.S. third world feminism, 6, 9, 272–73

Feminist comparative philosophy, 2–6, 271; coalitions in, 15–16; culture in, 7–8, 15; demographics and, 13–14, 29*nn*15–16; expansion from, 27–28; future of, 26–28; gender in, 7–8; interdisciplinary approach of, 16; as liberatory praxis, 13–18; methodologies for, 138–39; politics of, 17–18; reorientation in, 13; subjectivity in, 12–13; theorizing in, 14; as wisdom politics, 274–77; world-traveling and, 11–13

Feminist consciousness, 114, 119–20; agency in, 104, 107–8; community in, 107; contradictions in, 104–5; description of, 103–4, 120*n*1; divided consciousness in, 106–7; essentialism and, 111; feminist self-consciousness compared to, 108–10, 113; generality of, 105–8; personal as political in, 106; as raised consciousness, 105, 109–10; social reality and, 101–2; subjectivity and, 108; victimization in, 105–6, 110–11

Feminist epistemology, 148, 157–58, 164n1; *see also* Standpoint epistemology

Feminist ethics, 191–92; *see also* Care ethics; Confucian ethics of *ren*

Feminist philosophy: comparative philosophy compared to, 4–7, 10–11, 29n10, 29n16; diversity for, 199–200; as reorientation, 199–200; world-traveling and, 9–10

Feminists: African American, 25–26, 261–65, 266n1; Chicana, 9–10, 14, 124, 127–28, 274–76; class of, 157–58; of color, 273–74; Latina, 9–10, 14, 124–29; postcolonial, 13, 22, 25–26, 247–50, 261–64; third-space, 271, 274–76; U.S. third world, 6, 9, 272–73

Feminist self-consciousness: articulation of, 102; authenticity and, 120; Buddhist mindfulness and, 113–14, 119–20; descriptions of, 108; feminist consciousness compared to, 108–10, 113; habits and, 112; positionality and, 109, 111–12, 120; self-centering in, 112; self in, 110–12; subjectivity in, 109

Ferguson, Kathy E., 8

Filial care, 189–90, 192–95, 200–201

Filial piety, 88–89; Confucius on, 192

First-order anger, 124–26

Five aggregates, 42, 45–51

Five human relations, 96n5

Fraire, Manuela, 108

Free will, 48–49; animals without, 258–59; of Baartman, 257–59; ideology and, 248–49; manipulations for, 258; *sati* and, 250, 253–56; *see also* Agency; Autonomy; Volition

Freud, Sigmund, 71–72

Fricker, Miranda, 178

Friedman, Marilyn, 191–93, 196, 198

Fruits of action (*karmaphala*), 43

Frye, Marilyn, 125

Fukanzazengi (Dōgen), 233

Fung, Yu-lan, 160

Gakudō Yōjin-shū (Dōgen), 232

Gallagher, Shaun, 227

Gender, 2–3, 259–60; of black female body, 260–61; and class, 157; Dao without, 59; of female Hindu body, 259–60; five images of women and, 63–64; identity and, 44; knowledge and, 164n1; and language, 47; norms and, 164; parity of, 198; of philosophers, 13–14, 29nn15–16; potentiality and, 18–20; race related to, 273; standpoint and, 156–58; stereotypes, 52; third world feminism and, 272; traveling and, 10; universalist epistemologies and, 149; universality compared to, 64–65; violence and, 238; volition and, 52–53; Zhuangzi and, 149

Genjō kōan (Dōgen), 233

Gier, Nicholas F., 43

Gilligan, Carol, 187

Globalization, 11, 15–16, 27, 170, 181–82

Global tribalism, 273–74

Goddesses, 169–83; Kanwar as, 250–51; nature, 167–68; *see also* Prakriti

Gómez, Luis O., 43

Goswami, Namita, 6, 25–26

Greek philosophy, 272

Grosz, Elizabeth, 204–5, 213–16, 221

Gu, see Valley

Gudō Toshōku, 130, 132–33, 141n8

Guenther, Herbert, 53

Gunaratana, Bhante, 115–16

Gushen, see Valley spirit

Habits, 25–26; anger and enlightenment and, 129–30, 139; of attachment, 230; embodied habits, 14, 18, 25, 234–35, 237–39; feminist self-consciousness and, 112; retraining of, 239; sedimentation of, 45–51; of violence, 237–39

Hakuin Ekaku, 21, 130, 141*n*2, 141*n*8; see also Anger and enlightenment

Hall, David L., 75*n*2

Hamington, Maurice, 228

Hansen, Chad, 151, 165*n*5

Harding, Sandra, 22, 147, 152; criticism of, 149–51, 153–60, 163; see also Standpoint epistemology

Held, Virginia, 24, 187–88, 190, 192–93, 199

Herr, Ranjoo Seodu, 20

Hershock, Peter D., 51

Hindu female body: black female body compared to, 259–64; gender of, 259–60; visibility of, 260

Hinduism, 23, 54*n*3; prakriti-spirituality and, 180–83; see also Kanwar, Roop; Sati

Hindutva (neoconservative Hindu fundamentalism), 168, 181–82

Hine, Darlene Clark, 261

Hirschmann, Nancy J., 108, 119–20

Hobson, Janell, 261

Holism, 218–19

Holland, Nancy, 28*n*5

Hope, 129

Hottentot, 266*n*6

Hottentot Venus, 248, 257, 259, 267*n*15

Hu, Hsiao-Lan, 19

Husband-wife relationship: in marriage, 80–84, 89–91; open system for, 91–92; public realm participation and, 82, 91–92, 96*n*10

Husserl, Edmund, 209

Identity, 1, 63; gender and, 44; inner sphere as, 82–83

Ideology, 248–49

Imperialism, 11, 13, 189, 199, 255

In a Different Voice (Gilligan), 187

Inattention, 237; mindfulness related to, 229–30

Indian philosophy, 168–69, 171–75; classical Buddhism, 37, 45, 54*n*2; globalization and, 170; Indian-ness, 181–82; Mahāyāna Buddhism, 49, 54*n*3, 130–31; see also Buddha; Hindu female body; Hinduism; Jainism; Meera Nanda; Nāgārjunr; Prakriti-spirituality; Sati; Vandana Shiva

Intellectual property rights (IPRs), 171, 178

Intentionality, 124; angry perceptions and, 135–36; description of, 134; objects and, 134–35; operative, 21, 124, 134; perception in, 134–35

Intercorporeality, 233–34

Internal sense bases, 45–46, 54*n*11

Intersubjectivity, primary, 226–28

Irigaray, Luce, 71, 204–5, 214–17, 219–21, 221*n*2

Iveković, Rada, 14, 16–17, 27–28, 30*n*18

Jainism: akriyāvāda of, 43; kamma in, 38–40, 54*n*10; Mahāvīra in, 54*n*6; restraint in, 41

Japanese philosophy, 126–33, 206–11, 217–21; Japanese tradition, 24–25; see also Hakuin; Dōgen; Nagatomo; Rinzai zen; Sōtō Zen; Watsuji; Yuasa

Jeong Do-Jeon, 93–95, 97*n*23

Jīva, 38

Justice: and care ethics, 193; testimonial injustice, 178–79

Kaipayil, Joseph, 28*n*1

Kalupahana, David J., 43, 49

Kamma/karma: bodily features from, 40; Buddha on, 39–41, 48, 51; consolidation of, 51; dukkha and, 43, 52–54; empowerment in, 51–52; in

Kamma/karma (*continued*)
  individual construction, 41–45; in
  Jainism, 38–40, 54*n*10; justifications
  and, 40–41; no-self and, 37–38; past
  and, 39–40; present and, 39–40;
  relevance of, 39–40; *rūpa* and, 48;
  social dimension of, 46–50; speech
  as, 46–47; term use of, 37–40; as
  volition, 41–43, 48–49, 51–54
Kanwar, Roop, 248; background on,
  249–50; as goddess, 250–51; *see also*
  Hindu female body; Sati
Karmaphala, 43
Kasulis, Thomas, 218
Keating, Ana Louise, 273
Kenshō, 131, 139
Khoikhoi, 251–52, 266*n*6
Ki, 210–11, 220
Kishwar, Madhu, 167
Kjellberg, Paul, 43
Klein, Anne, 113–14, 116–17, 119
Know-how: ethics and, 224–29; failure
  in, 223–24; *see also* Embodied
  know-how
Knowing experience, 123–24, 134–37,
  140
Knowledge: distortions in, 148–49;
  gender and, 164*n*1; location of,
  158, 175; partial, 148–49; percep-
  tion and, 8–9, 11–13, 16, 21, 25–26,
  45–46; reductionism of, 170–71;
  for traveling, 12; *see also* Feminist
  epistemology; Standpoint episte-
  mology; Zhuangzi
Kōan study, 132–33
Korean Confucianism, 20, 68, 79–83,
  96, 96*n*7; *see also* Chosŏn Confucians; Chosŏn Dynasty
Krishna, Daya, 29*n*14
Kriyāvāda, 43
Kumar, Radha, 256

Lai, Whalen, 89
Lai Tao, Julia Po-Wah, 194–95

Language: agency in, 46–47; gender
  and, 47; speech, 46–47; volition
  in, 47
Laozi, 70; *see also Daodejing*
Larson, Gerald James, 8–9, 17–18
Lauretis, Teresa de, 106, 108–9, 112
Lee, Kyoo, 19–20
Lee-Lampshire, Wendy, 110
Lennon, John, 271
Li, 20, 84; Confucian ethics of *ren* re-
  lated to, 195–96, 198, 200; *ren* and,
  86, 91; Zhuxi on, 80, 83
Li, Chenyang, 187, 189–90
Liat, J. Kwee Swan, 11
Liberation from suffering; *see Nirvana*
Liberation philosophies, 1, 3, 8, 13–18,
  271–72
Liberatory praxis, 26–27; differential
  consciousness in, 15–16; feminist
  comparative philosophy as, 13–18;
  legitimacy in, 16–17
Limen, 139; anger and, 136–38; of
  second-order anger, 127, 129; *see
  also* Betweenness
Lindfors, Bernth, 257
Ling, Amy, 273
Linji, 129, 131–32; *see also* Rinzai Zen
Location: bridge as, 273; of knowledge,
  158, 175; places of knowing, 22–23;
  race and, 273–74; self-reflexivity of,
  182–83; in standpoint epistemology,
  148, 151–52, 158; between worlds,
  127, 129, 136–39, 209, 211, 273; in
  Zhuangzi, 158–60
Logic: of colonization, 170–72; of
  dualism, 170; either/or logic, 24;
  excluded middle, 6; of noncontradiction, 22
Lorde, Audre, 138, 247, 273–75
Love: with distinction, 89; *ren* as, 86,
  89; *see also* Emotion
Loy, David, 49
Lugones, María, 21, 124–26, 275; on
  methodology, 12–13; pluralist

feminism, 125–27; world-traveling of, 9–10, 12, 125–27; *see also* limen; Second-order anger

Maffie, James, 180
Mahāvīra, 54n6
Mahāyāna Buddhism, 49, 54n3, 130–31
Maitra, Keya, 20–21
Majjhima Nikāya, 39–41, 49, 54n7
Marriage: adultery in, 96n8; in Chosŏn Dynasty, 79–83; cosmology related to, 82–83; distinction in, 90–91; husband-wife relationship in, 80–84, 89–91; inevitability of, 96n9; polygyny, 81–82, 96n7; *see also* Sati
Marx, Karl, 151, 157
Maternal care: demands of, 238; help with, 92, 97n21; Mr. Mom, 53; norms of, 59, 63; patriarchy and, 196–97
Matus, Jill, 258
McCarthy, Erin, 24–25
McLeod, Ken, 231
McWeeny, Jennifer, 20–21
Mencius, 79–80, 89, 94–95; on extension of *ren*, 194; family-state and, 93; on moral mind, 84
Merleau-Ponty, Maurice, 21, 134–36, 140, 205
Metanarrative, 154–55
Meta-witnessing consciousness, 276–77
Methodologies, 5–6; for feminist comparative philosophy, 1–18, 138–40, 259–65; Lugones on, 12–13; Sandoval on, 8; world-traveling as, 8–13
Meyers, Diana, 236
Mind, 40–42, 45–47, 84–85, 102, 110, 131, 134–36; body related to, 115–16, 213–14
Mindfulness, 101, 103, 115, 241; attention and, 231; Buddha on, 114; and feminist self-consciousness,

101–20; inattention related to, 229; self-centeredness and, 230–31; *see also* Buddhist mindfulness
Mindfulness meditation: autonomy in, 119; characteristics of, 115–16; continuity in, 116; description of, 114–15; detachment and, 118; equanimity in, 118–19; exercises in, 115; feminist activism and, 118–19; freedom in, 118; objects for, 115; self-acceptance from, 118–19; self-cultivation from, 117–18; sense of self in, 117–19; social dimension of, 118–19; *see also* Buddhist mindfulness
Moeller, Hans-Georg, 58, 65–66
Mohanty, Chandra Talpade, 5, 17–18
Monism: nondual subjectivity and, 216; of prakriti, 172–73
Moral mind, 84
Mother, 91–92; of all, 66–67; in *Daodejing*, 71–72; *see also* Maternal care
Moulton, Janice, 5

Naess, Arne, 167
Nāgārjuna, 49; *see also* Indian philosophy; Mahāyāna Buddhism
Nagatomo, Shigenori, 210, 232–34; *see also* Japanese philosophy
Nanda, Meera, 168–69, 173, 175–76, 180–81
Narayan, Uma, 137–38, 189
Nature, 57, 71–73; as culture, 261–62; female bodies and, 263–64; Nature goddesses, 167–68; in Zhuangzi's philosophy, 150–51, 161–62
Navdanya, 179–80
Nepantla: bridge of, 273–74; truth for, 274–75
Nikāya texts, 40, 48–49, 54n2, 54nn7–9
Ningen, 24–25; *see also* Self as *ningen*
Nirvāṇa: identity with *saṃsāra*, 130–31; *saṃsāra* and, 130–33; *see also* Enlightenment

Noddings, Nel, 187, 195

Nondualism: cultivation of, 209–11; description of, 204; of enlightenment, 131, 133; framework of, 206; *ki* and, 210–11; of self as *ningen*, 208–9

Nondual subjectivity: betweenness for, 216–19; dialectical unity and, 217; encounter in, 217; Grosz and, 215–16; holism in, 218–19; individuality and, 217–18; monism and, 216; movement in, 218–19; patriarchy related to, 219–20; reciprocity in, 217; Zen Buddhism and, 218

Norsworthy, Kathryn L., 118–19

No-self, *see* Anātman

Objectification, 258, 262

Objectivity, 22; prakriti-spirituality and, 176–80; of science, 176; in standpoint epistemology, 152, 155, 165*n*8; trust and, 176–78; and Zhuangzi's philosophy, 155–56

Objects: intentionality and, 134–35; for mindfulness meditation, 115; six sense organs and, 45–46, 48–50, 54*n*11

Ono, Yoko, 271

Oppression, 1, 39, 79, 235–37, 241; anger and, 123–27, 135–39; awareness of, 104–7, 153, 156–57, 172; patriarchy and, 83, 149, 197, 199; from rulers, 95; standpoint epistemology and, 125, 157–58, 163

Orategama (Hakuin), 130

Orategama Zokushō (Hakuin), 130

Origin (*yuan*), 60–61

Ortega, Mariana, 11, 141*n*4

Panikkar, Raimundo, 5, 27; on dangers of comparative studies, 11

Parent and child, 189–90, 192–97; in Confucian family, 87–89, 95–96;

reciprocity related to, 88–89; *see also* Mother

Patriarchy: agnatic principle as, 80–83; Confucian ethics of *ren* and, 192–93, 196; in Confucianism, 78–84; generalization and, 107; and maternal care, 196–97; nondual subjectivity related to, 219–20; *sati* and, 250–51, 255–56; traditions related to, 197; *see also* Marriage

Pels, Dick, 158–59

Perception, 141*n*11; borderland, 135; felt inter-resonance and, 234; and intentionality, 134–35; in social embeddedness of care, 236–37; *see also* Angry perceptions

Performativity, 2–3, 13–14, 19, 38, 44, 46, 50, 63

Perspectives: of Dao, 159–60, 165*n*9; in second-order anger, 128–29; standpoint compared to, 157; in standpoint epistemology, 151–52, 157, 163–64, 165*n*8; on truth, 155–56, 163–64; for world-traveling, 12; in Zhuangzi's philosophy, 149–51, 153–54, 158–64, 165*n*5

Philosophers, 2–3; gender of, 13–14, 29*nn*15–16; race of, 13–14, 29*n*15; traditions of, 16–17

Planetary consciousness, 272

Plato, 70–71; on body, 212–13; on women's inferiority, 212–14

Politics: within Confucian ethics of *ren*, 193–98, 200–201; in Confucianism, 95–96, 97*n*25; of feminist comparative philosophy, 17–18; of Indianness, 181–82; for *nepantla*, 274–75; personal as political, 106, 259–64; *ren* and, 93–95, 97*n*24, 193–98; third-space, 273–74; of third world feminism, 272; wisdom, 271, 274–77; Zhuangzi's philosophy without, 160–61, 165*n*12

Postcolonial theory, 247–48

Post-*satori* practice, 131–32

Power: of dark female animal, 60, 63, 67–68; empowerment, 51–52; traveling and, 10–11

Prakriti, 23; definition of, 171–72; as epistemic multiculturalism, 169, 180; as first principle, 172–73; monism of, 172–73; rural life and, 173–74

Prakriti-spirituality: as ethnoscience, 175–76; functions of, 169–70, 172–76; globalization and, 181–82; harm from, 180–81; Hinduism and, 180–83; inclusiveness in, 177–80; objectivity and, 176–80; self-reflexivity of, 182–83; testimonial injustice and, 178–79; trust and, 176–79

Praxis, 13; *see also* Liberatory praxis

Primary intersubjectivity, 226; ethics from, 227; interest in, 228

Race: gender related to, 273; location and, 273–74; of philosophers, 13–14, 29n15

Racism, 235–37

Raising consciousness, 20–21

Rationalism, 203–4

Reality, 101–2; anger and, 135–37; angry perceptions and, 135–36; Dao and, 162; dualism and, 138–39; *koan* study and, 132–33

Rebirth, 38–39

Reciprocity (*shu*): in Confucian ethics of *ren*, 191, 195–96, 200; in nondual subjectivity, 217; parent and child related to, 88–89; of *ren*, 87–88, 90–92

Reductionism, 174, 178; in forestry, 170–71; by Hindutva, 181–82; of knowledge, 170–71; logic of colonization and, 170–72

Ren, 24, 78; as affection, 88–89; centrality of, 85, 96n12; Confucian self

related to, 85–86; as conscientiousness, 86–87; description of, 85; distinction compared to, 90–91; ethics of, 188, 191; *li* and, 195–96, 198, 200; as love, 86, 89; politics and, 93–95, 97n24, 193–98; precept of, 79; realization of, 85; reciprocity of, 87–88, 90–92; ritual propriety and, 86, 91; sociality of, 86; *yi* and, 197–98; *see also* Confucian ethics of *ren*

Republic (Plato), 212–14

Rich, Adrienne, 111

Rinzai Zen Buddhism, 124, 129–32, 141n8

Ritual action, 38

Root of heaven and earth (*tiandigen*), 57, 63, 70

Rosenlee, Li-Hsiang Lisa, 24

Ruddick, Sara, 187

Rūpa, 45–46, 54n11; *kamma* and, 48; suffering and, 48–50

Salleh, Ariel, 169

Sambongjip (Jeong), 97n23

Saṃsāra: anger and enlightenment beyond, 133; description of, 130; *nirvāṇa* and, 130–33

Saṃyutta Nikāya, 48–50, 54n9

Sandoval, Chela: on apartheid of theoretical domains, 15; on differential consciousness, 15–16; on feminist activism, 6; against homogenization, 6; on methodologies, 8

Sangari, KumKum, 250, 253

Saṇkhāra/saṃskāra: meanings of, 42; *rūpa* and, 45–46; volition as, 47–48

Sarkar, Tanika, 250

Sati, 266n4; ambivalence about, 250–51; colonialism related to, 254–55; as crime, 254–56; displacement of, 256; exceptionalism in, 254–56; free will and, 250, 253–56; imperialism and, 255; nationalism in, 256;

Sati (*continued*)
  patriarchy and, 250–51, 255–56;
  voice consciousness in, 254; *see also*
  Kanwar, Roop
Satori, 129, 232–33
Satt, 250, 253
Scharfstein, Ben-Ami, 2
Scheman, Naomi, 176, 178
Schrire, Carmel, 257–58
Science, 170–71; curiosity in, 253,
  258–59, 267*n*15; ethnoscience,
  175–76; inclusiveness for, 179–80;
  objectivity of, 176–78; testimonial
  injustice and, 178–79; trust in,
  176–79, 182
Second-order anger: description of,
  125–26; first-order anger compared
  to, 124–26; hope and, 129; intimate
  terrorisms and, 127–28; limen of,
  127, 129; perspective in, 128–29;
  spatiality of, 127–29; traveling in,
  125, 127–29, 134; worlds of sense
  in, 124–29
The Second Sex (Beauvoir), 60, 189
Self, 97*n*18; actions and, 53–54; agency
  and, 44–45; as body, 138, 211;
  Buddha on, 50, 102; Buddhism
  without, 102–3; in Confucianism, 84–86; dualism and, 138–39;
  elements of, 203; embodiment of,
  140; in feminist self-consciousness,
  110–12; five aggregates as, 42,
  45–51; gender stereotypes and, 52;
  as multiple, 125–26; as orientation
  system, 139–40, 142*n*12; others'
  feelings and thoughts with, 50;
  pluralism of, 125–26, 139–40; *see
  also* Ātman; anātman
Self as *ningen*, 24–25, 205; betweenness in, 207, 209, 211; body in,
  206–9; bodymind in, 206, 208–11,
  220; concept of, 206–7; embodied
  beings from, 207–8; ethics from,
  207; Husserl and, 209; intercon-

nectivity of, 206–11; nondualism
  of, 208–9; vocabulary for, 208; Zen
  Buddhism and, 218; *see also* Non-
  dual subjectivity
Self-centeredness, 230–31
Self-centering, 113–14
Self-consciousness, 21; conscious-
  ness and, 113; *see also* Feminist
  self-consciousness
Self-examination, 241
Self-identity, 1
Self-reflexivity, 182–83
Senses, 124–29; *see also Rūpa*
Sex, 215, 261; of Dao, 58, 62–63, 65–66;
  Dao of, 58, 65; Hottentot Venus,
  248, 257, 259, 267*n*15
Sharpley-Whiting, T. Denean, 251
Sherwin, Susan, 5–6
Shinjin Gakudō (Dōgen), 232
Shiva, Vandana, 23, 167–68, 170; *see
  also* Prakriti
Shu, see Reciprocity
Siddhāttha Gotama (Siddhārtha), 37
Six sense organs and their objects, *see
  Rūpa*
Smid, Robert, 28*n*6
Social embeddedness of care: embod-
  ied disvalues and, 235–36; femi-
  nism and, 235–40; perception in,
  236–37; racism related to, 235–37;
  strategies for, 240–41; violence
  and, 237–38
Sōtō Zen, 224; *see also* Dōgen; Japanese
  philosophy; Zen Buddhism
Spatiality, 127–29
Speech, 46–47
Spelman, Elizabeth V., 125, 212
Spirituality: ecospirituality, 167–69,
  181–82; victimization or, 250–51;
  see also Prakriti-spirituality
Spivak, Gayatri, 249–50, 252–56
Standpoint epistemology, 147; goal of,
  163; location in, 148, 151–52, 158;
  metanarrative and, 154–55; objec-

tivity in, 152, 155, 165n8; oppression and, 125, 157–58, 163; perspectives in, 151–52, 157, 163–64, 165n8; rural life and, 175; standards and, 154–55; standpoint in, 157; truth and, 154, 162–64; women's lives in, 152–54, 156–57; see also Zhuangzi

Star, Daniel, 190–91, 196–98

Strother, Z. S., 258, 267n15

Structure, 126–27

Subjectivity: body related to, 128, 136, 138, 215; of dark female animal, 60–61; dualism of, 214–15; in feminist comparative philosophy, 12–13; feminist consciousness and, 108; in feminist self-consciousness, 109; nondualism of, 215–16; primary intersubjectivity, 226–28; see also Nondual subjectivity; Self

Suffering (dukkha; duḥkha), 237–38; attention related to, 231; Buddha on, 48–50; dukkha as, 43, 52–54; individual and, 48–50; liberation from, 130–33; Middle Way on, 48–49; perception of, 228; rūpa and, 48–50; society and, 49–50; see also Attachment; Oppression; Victimization; Violence

Sunder Rajan, Rajeswari, 250, 253, 256

Swachhnarayani (Goddess of Cleanliness), 167

Taylor, Bron, 167–168, 181

Taylor, Harriet, 159

Teaching that deeds are fruitless, see Akriyāvāda

Terrorisms, intimate, 127–28

Testimonial injustice, 178–79

Thera, Soma, 101

Third world feminism: first world feminism or, 274; location for, 273–74; politics of, 272; third-space feminists, 271, 274–76; third-space politics, 273–74; see also Feminism

Tiandigen, 57, 63, 70

Timaeus (Plato), 71

Traditions: liberation of, 1; origin in, 61; patriarchy related to, 197; personal as political in, 259–64; of philosophers, 16–17; term philosophic usage of, 2, 28n1

Transforming discourse, 25–26

Triangle, 68–69

Trust: objectivity and, 176–78; prakriti-spirituality and, 176–79; in science, 176–79, 182

Truth: for nepantla, 274–75; perspective on, 155–56, 163–64; satt as, 250, 253; standpoint epistemology and, 154, 162–64; in Zhuangzi, 160–63, 165n10

Truth, Sojourner, 273

Tu, Wei-ming, 88, 97n24

Tuana, Nancy, 2, 28n1

Universalist epistemologies, 5, 22–23, 149

Upaniṣads, 38, 54n5

Vaid, Sudesh, 250, 253

Valley (gu), 57–58, 71, 75n4

Valley spirit (gushen), 57–58, 69, 72–73, 75n4

Values, 147–48; disvalues, 224, 234–37

Vedas, 38, 54n4, 254

Vetlesen, Arne Johan, 228, 237

Victimization, 40; divided consciousness and, 106–7; in feminist consciousness, 105–6, 110–11; solidarity in, 106; spirituality or, 250–51

Violence, 127–28, 132; body related to, 237–39; in ecospirituality, 167–68; embodied habits of, 237–39; gender and, 238

Visvanathan, Shiv, 168–69

Voice consciousness, 254

Volition: gender and, 52–53; kamma as, 41–43, 48–49, 51–54; in language,

Volition (*continued*)
47; *see also* Agency; Autonomy;
Free will

Walker, Alice, 72
Wang, Keping, 73–74
Wang, Robin, 63
Wang Bi, 60–62, 66
Watsuji Tetsurō, 24, 204–6, 208–11,
216–20
*The Way of Mindfulness: The Satipat-
thana Suta and Its Commentary*
(Thera), 101, 115
Wedderburn, Robert, 252
West, 220, 276
Western philosophy: Greek philoso-
phy and, 272; methods of, 5–6
Widow burning, *see* Sati
Wisdom, 211
Wisdom politics, 271, 274–77
Wiss, Rosemary, 252, 257–59
Wolff, Janet, 10
Woo, Terry, 189
World-in-between-worlds, *see*
Nepantla
Worlds-of-meaning, 275
Worlds of sense, 129; for intimate
terrorism, 128; official, 124–25;
permeability of, 126; structure
related to, 126–27; and world-
traveling, 10
World-traveling: authenticity of, 11;
in comparative philosophy, 8–9;
discomfort in, 13; experience of,
11–12; in feminist comparative
philosophy, 11–13; in feminist
philosophy, 9–10; gender and, 10;
knowledge for, 12; for Lugones,
9–10; as methodology, 8–13; and
multiple selves, 125; of oppressed
individuals, 125; perspective for,

12; power and, 10–11; in second-
order anger, 125, 127–29, 134; and
structure, 127, 134, 138; across
worlds-of-meaning, 275

Xiao, Bing, 68–69, 73–74
Xuanpin, *see* Dark female animal

Yi (appropriateness), 197–98
Yin and *yang*, 19–20; in Confucianism,
82–83; in *Daodejing*, 59, 63–65; in
Daoism, 59, 64
Yoga, 113, 220–21, 221n2
Young, Iris Marion, 236
Young, Jean, 258
Yōzan Rōshi, 130
Yuan, 60–61
Yuan, Lijun, 190–91, 196
Yuasa, Yasuo, 24, 205–6, 209–11, 216,
219–20

Zack, Naomi, 266n1
Zen Buddhism, 139, 141n2, 218, 224;
see also Dōgen; Hakuin; Linji; Rinzai
Buddhism; Sōtō Zen
Zen meditation, 129–33
Zhuangzi, 22; without absolutes,
153–54; contemporary value of,
147; convention and, 160–61; criticism of, 161–62; Daoist perspective,
159–60; gender and, 149; location in, 158–60; nature in, 150–51,
161–62; objectivity and, 155–56; as
partial, 150–51, 153–54; perspectives in, 149–51, 153–54, 158–64,
165n5; without politics, 160–61,
165n12; sage, 159–60; standard for,
155; truth in, 160–63, 165n10
Zhuxi, 80, 83–84
Zhu Xi, 196
Zimmerman, Michael, 168